Hitler's Panzer Armies on the Eastern Front

I rode a tank,
Held a generals' rank,
When the blitzkrieg raged
and the bodies stank.

Hitler's Panzer Armies on the Eastern Front

Robert Kirchubel

Pen & Sword
MILITARY

First published in Great Britain in 2009 by
Pen & Sword Military
an imprint of
Pen & Sword Books Ltd
47 Church Street
Barnsley
South Yorkshire
S70 2AS

ISBN 978-1-84415-928-4

A CIP catalogue record for this book is
available from the British Library.

Typeset in 11/13 Ehrhardt by Concept, Huddersfield, West Yorkshire
Printed and bound in England by the MPG Books Group

Pen & Sword Books Ltd incorporates the Imprints of Pen & Sword Aviation,
Pen & Sword Maritime, Pen & Sword Military, Wharncliffe Local History,
Pen & Sword Select, Pen & Sword Military Classics, Leo Cooper, Remember
When, Seaforth Publishing and Frontline Publishing.

For a complete list of Pen & Sword titles please contact
PEN & SWORD BOOKS LIMITED
47 Church Street, Barnsley, South Yorkshire, S70 2AS, England
E-mail: enquiries@pen-and-sword.co.uk
Website: www.pen-and-sword.co.uk

Contents

Preface

This book is written to the glory of God. I wish to extend my heartfelt thanks to my wife Linda, and sons Mason and Marc for their forbearance and patience. During hundreds of hours stretched over dozens of weeks, I literally ignored them (in the highest tradition of the historian/author) while sequestered in the War Room doing research and writing. I also want to acknowledge the 'editing team' that has supported me since the earliest days of my Osprey *Operation Barbarossa* trilogy: fact-checker Gary Komar, and grammarian Joe Wilson – the Henry Higgins of the group. Gary, a fine military historian in his own right, provided the basic research for the sidebars on commanders, weapons, training, etc. Thanks also to my map-maker, Chris Mankey. Kudos as well to the Inter-Library Loan Department at Purdue University's HSSE Library.

I also want to show appreciation to the editing staff at Pen & Sword Books. Based on my earlier works, Rupert Harding contacted me with an offer to write for them on almost any military history topic I wanted. For about twenty years I had been mulling over the idea of a history of the German panzer armies. I pitched the idea to Rupert and he immediately agreed. The only downside to the whole preparation process was a stillborn visit to the great Russian battle-fields described herein, cancelled in 2007 by an emergency just a fortnight before realization. That trip was meant to be a bookend to my fantastic visit to the Ukraine in 2005.

Hitler's Panzer Armies on the Eastern Front is a work of synthesis. Its writing involved no archival research, nor did I discover a treasure trove of never-before-seen documents. I have taken existing materials, mainly secondary source books, and have mined them for insights on the operations of the four panzer armies that fought in the Nazi-Soviet War from Barbarossatag (22 June 1941) until VE Day (8 May 1945). I used both old and 'new' classics – Erickson, Ziemke, Glantz, as well as recent scholarship and German unit histories (often of uneven quality) from Haupt to Scheibert. Where practical, I have tried to look at First, Second, Third and Fourth Panzer Armies through the lens of the operational level of war. Sometimes this was practical – usually during the major offensive operations – other times it was not – when the panzer armies were just another slab of human flesh Hitler threw into the giant meat-grinder that represented the so-called 'Eastern Front'. A final caveat: the fact that the main characters here are German is in no way meant to detract from the heroism and skill of the Workers and Peasants Red Army and the Soviet people. As a retired US Army officer, I have absolutely no qualms about giving the USSR the lions' share of the credit for destroying Hitler's Third Reich.

Some notes on naming units and other technicalities: the Germans reorganized panzer groups into panzer armies 5 October 1941 (First and Second) and 1 January 1942 (Third and Fourth). However, for the sake of consistency and simplicity, beginning with Operation Barbarossa, I will only use the term 'panzer army'. Also, through much of Barbarossa, panzer corps were technically named 'Corps (Motorized)', but again, I will use 'panzer corps' throughout. I will follow the German convention for numbering their formations: Arabic ordinals for divisions, Roman numerals for corps, and spelled-out ordinals for armies. Consistent with the official *History of the Great Patriotic War of the Soviet Union, 1941–1945*, Red Army units will be described by Arabic ordinals in all cases except for named 'fronts'. Further, mainly due to the massive and confusing nature of the Nazi-Soviet War, even the most-respected and well-intentioned secondary sources often disagree on dates, orders of battle and other details. Therefore, for ranks and dates on which various German generals took or relinquished command, I referred to Wolf Keileg, *Das deutsche Heer, 1939–1945*. For dates when a certain city changed hands, etc., if secondary sources conflicted, I used H-A Jacobsen, A Hilgruber, W Hubatsch, PE Schramm (eds), *Kriegstagebuch des Oberkommandos der Wehrmacht*. For all German orders of battle, in the text and appendices, I used the official Federal German *Bundesarchiv-Militarchiv* Internet site (unless otherwise noted). While these sources may not be one-hundred per cent accurate themselves, they do provide a uniform standard.

List of Maps

Key to Maps

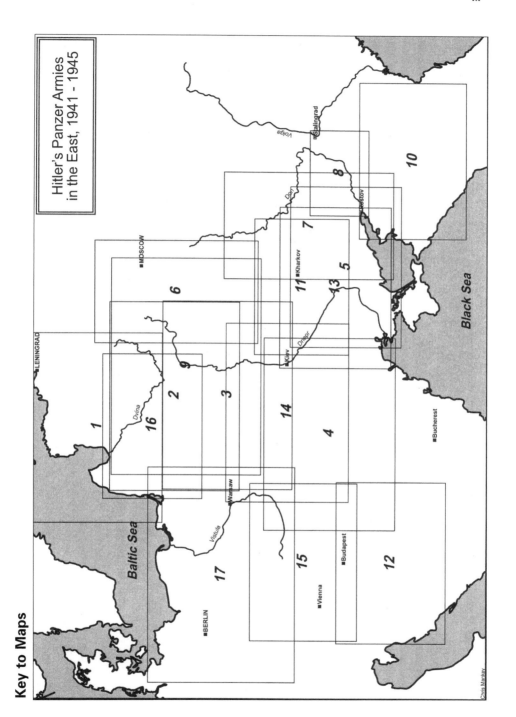

Hitler's Panzer Armies
in the East, 1941 - 1945

Map 1

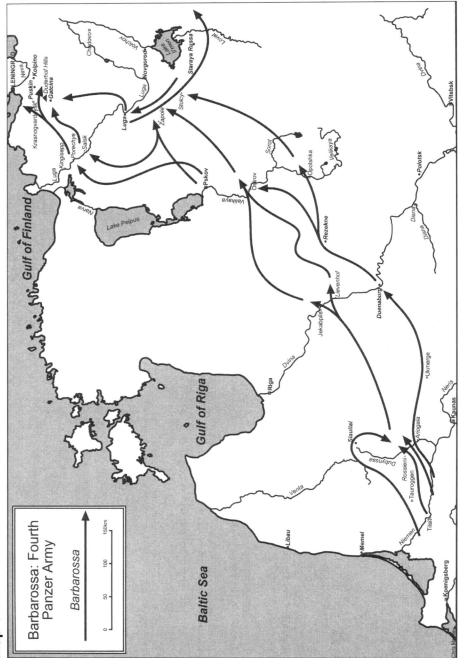

Barbarossa: Fourth
Panzer Army

Barbarossa

0   50   100   150km

Map 2

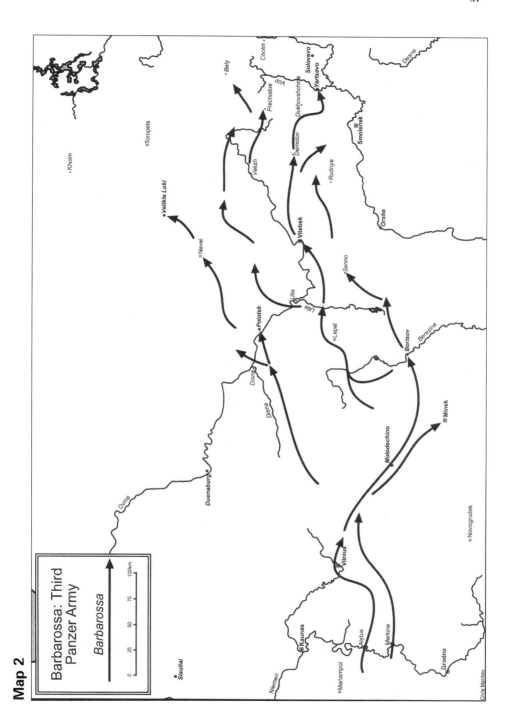

Barbarossa: Third Panzer Army

Barbarossa

0   25   50   75   100km

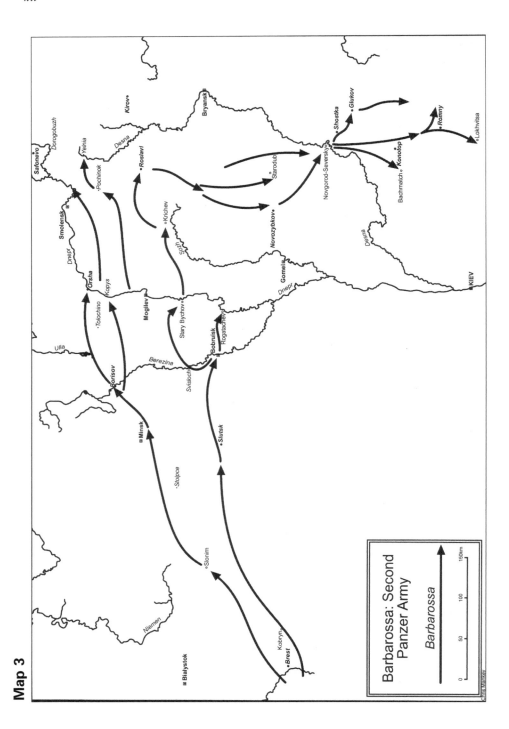

Map 3

xii

Barbarossa: Second Panzer Army

Barbarossa

0   50   100   150km

Map 4

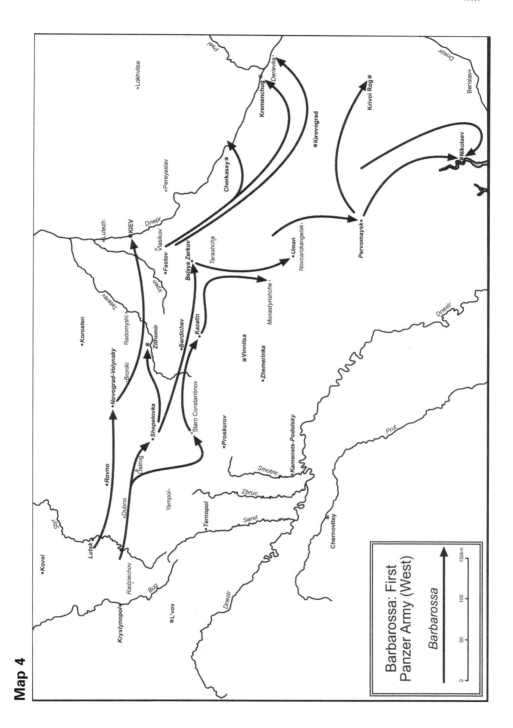

Barbarossa: First
Panzer Army (West)

Barbarossa

Map 5

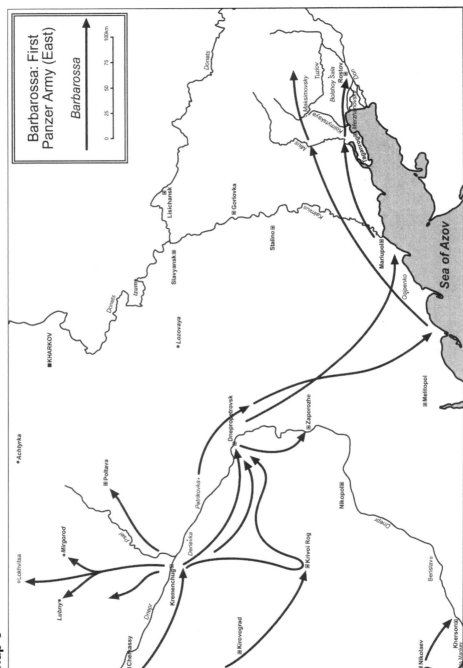

Barbarossa: First Panzer Army (East)

Barbarossa

0   25   50   75   100km

Map 6

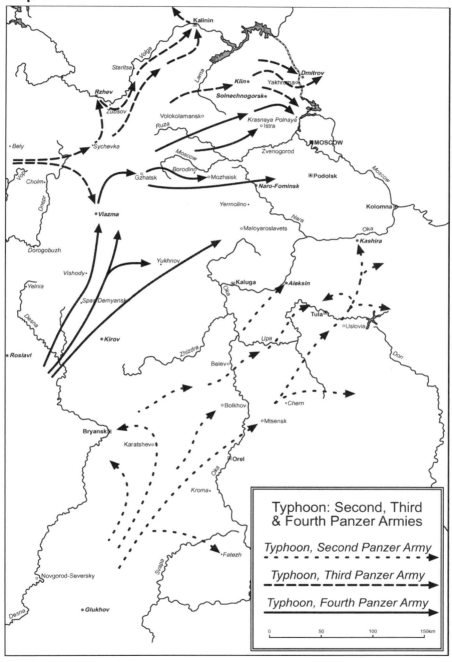

Map 7

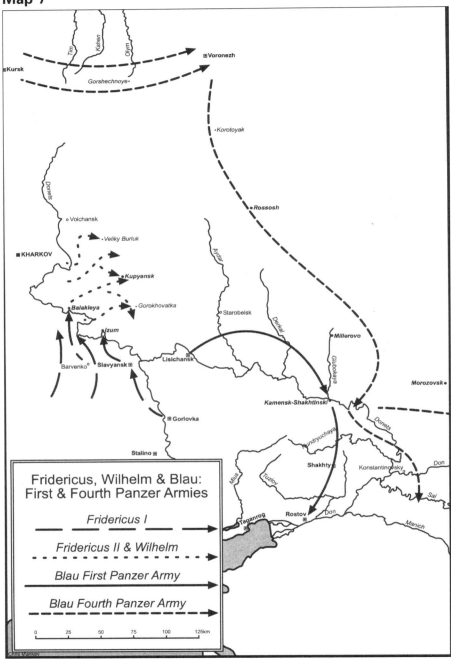

Map 8

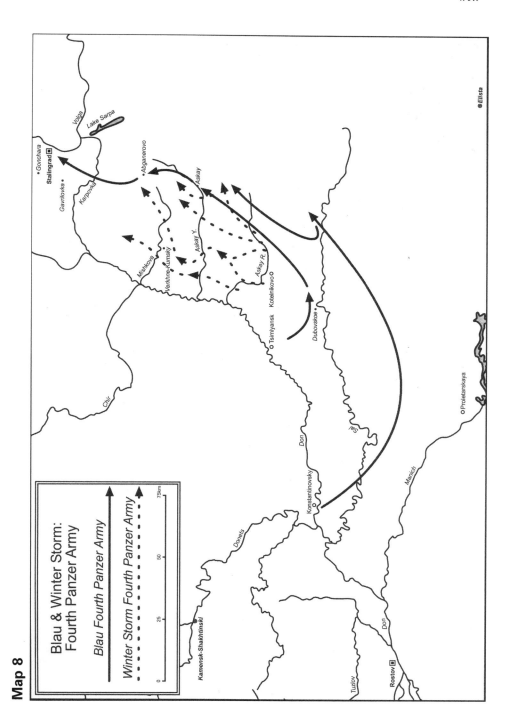

Blau & Winter Storm:
Fourth Panzer Army

Blau Fourth Panzer Army

Winter Storm Fourth Panzer Army

Map 9

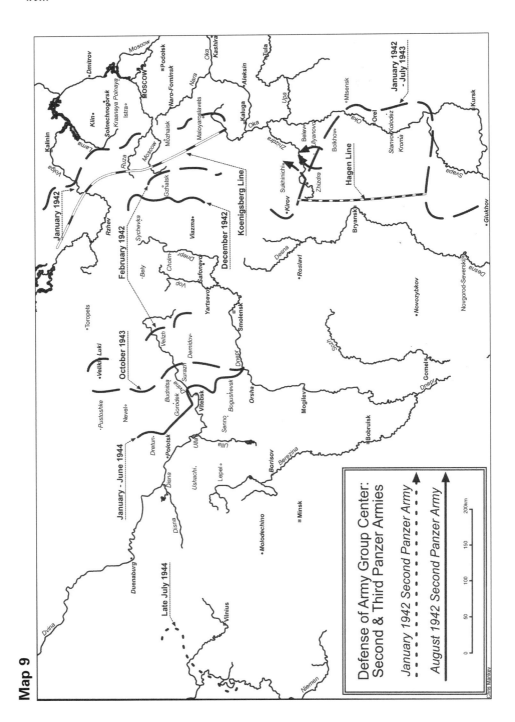

Map 10

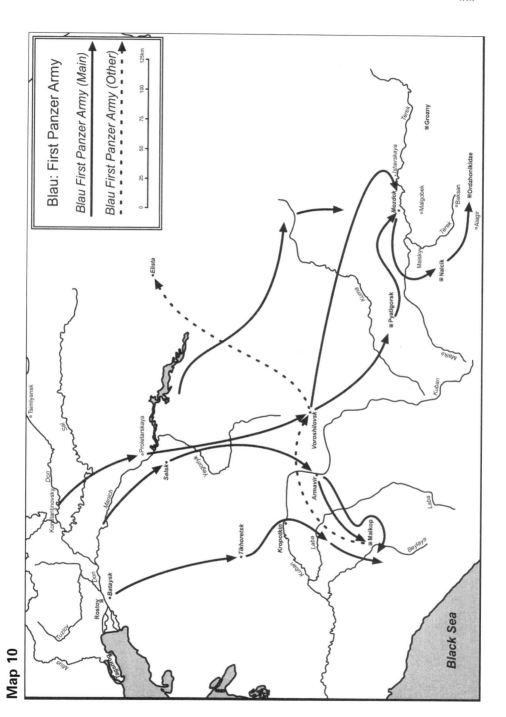

Blau: First Panzer Army

Blau First Panzer Army (Main)

Blau First Panzer Army (Other)

Map 11

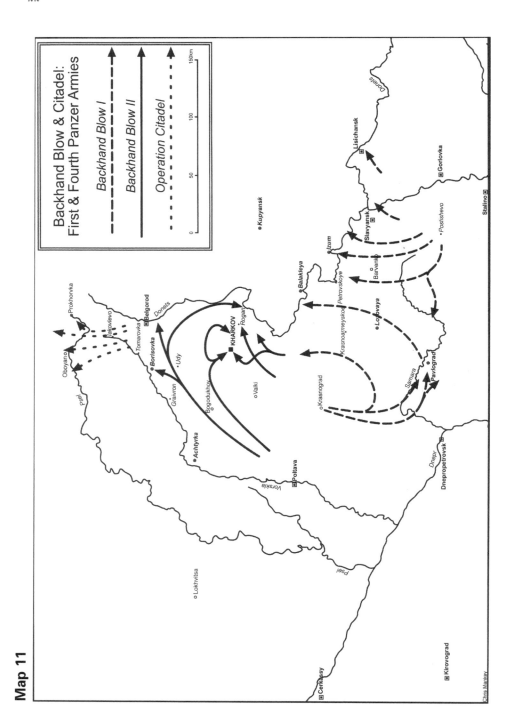

Map 12

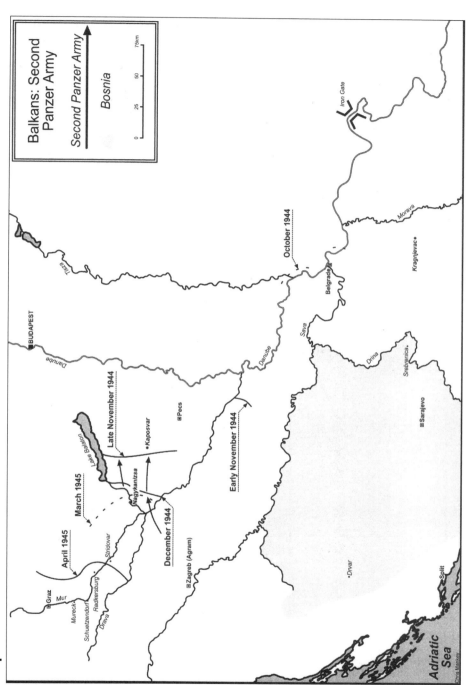

Balkans: Second Panzer Army

Second Panzer Army

Bosnia

0   25   50   75km

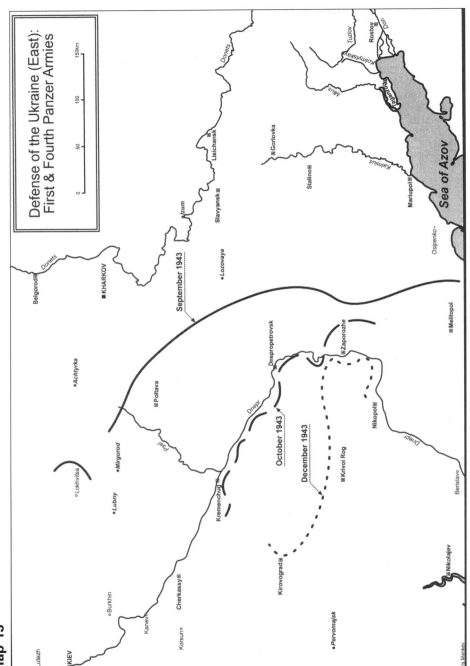

Map 13

xxii

Defense of the Ukraine (East):
First & Fourth Panzer Armies

Map 14

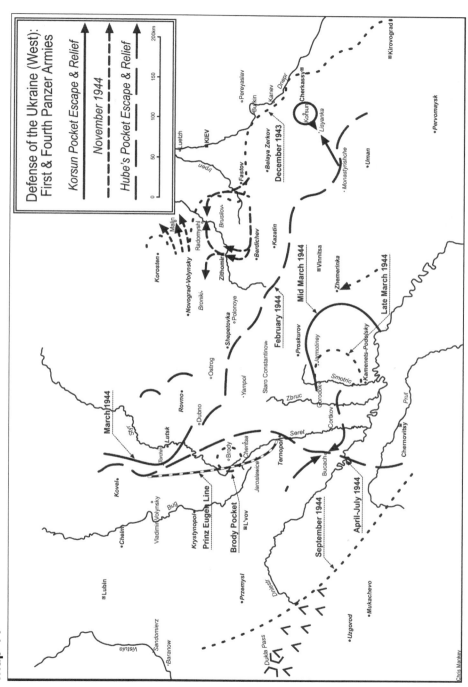

Defense of the Ukraine (West):
First & Fourth Panzer Armies

Korsun Pocket Escape & Relief
November 1944

Hube's Pocket Escape & Relief

0   50   100   150   200km

Map 15

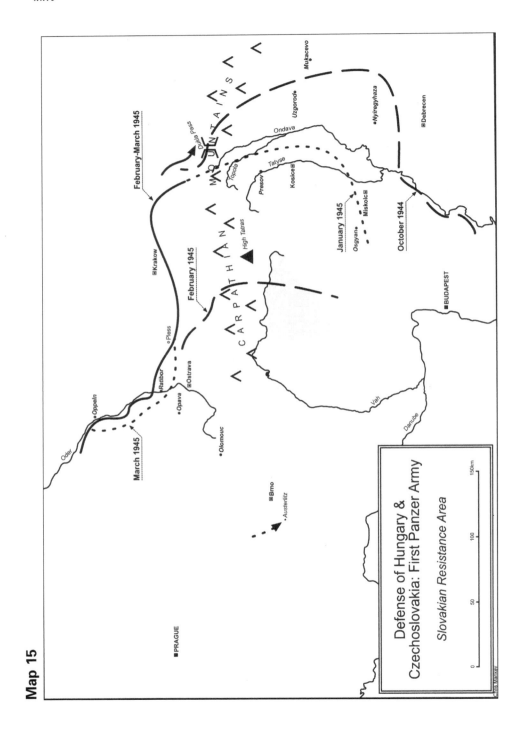

Defense of Hungary &
Czechoslovakia: First Panzer Army

Slovakian Resistance Area

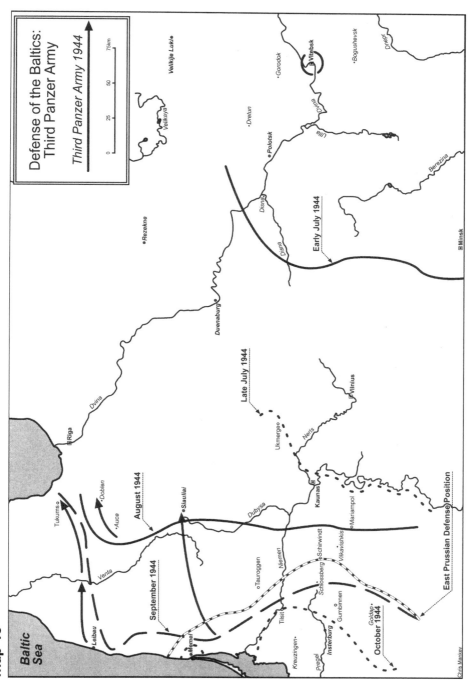

Map 16

Defense of the Baltics:
Third Panzer Army

Third Panzer Army 1944

Map 17

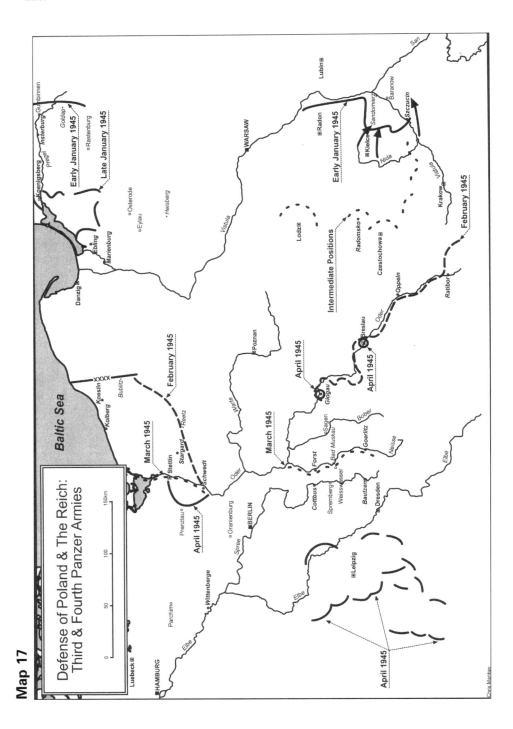

Defense of Poland & The Reich:
Third & Fourth Panzer Armies

Introduction

This book tells the story of Germany's panzer armies in action during the Nazi-Soviet War from 1941–45. To a large extent the Wehrmacht's successes through 1942, and frequently beyond, rested on the shoulders of a new weapon, the Panzerwaffe (armor branch) and a new technique, the blitzkrieg (the name later given to mechanized maneuver air-ground warfare) employed to achieve tactical, operational and often strategic goals. Especially during the first years of the war, large panzer formations represented the highest development of the military arts on all three levels.

In the First World War, tanks did not achieve their intended decisive effect mainly due to the small number and unreliability of the machines. More importantly, military leadership lacked a suitable doctrine for their employment: the ideas that came to be called the blitzkrieg were always more critical than the actual vehicles. During the interwar period, the militaries of major nations attempted to develop tanks and accompanying techniques in order to prevent a repetition of disastrous trench warfare of the First World War. British, French, Italian and American armies could do neither, although British theorists did give much thought to the matter. The Red Army invented some excellent tanks and periodically developed advanced doctrine, but internal politics prevented the creation of a workable, stable principle for their employment. Only Germany managed to develop both viable equipment AND methods, in other words, the correct combination of hardware and software. During the Second World War, this mechanized combined-arms warfare became known as the blitzkrieg, and dominated the European theater as aircraft carrier task forces did in the Pacific.

Although made up of German root words, the term blitzkrieg was not used by them; Hitler claims to have hated the word, saying it was an Italian concoction. The new form of warfare introduced in Poland and perfected in France was actually a combination of traditional Prussian/German, Auftragstaktik (mission-type orders), Bewegungskrieg (maneuver warfare), Vernichtungskrieg (war of annihilation) and other concepts. The term blitzkrieg was a post-facto attempt by military observers to describe what was happening on the battlefields of Europe from 1939–41. Since then, blitzkrieg has become shorthand for maneuver warfare that wedded a flexible command structure to combined-arms tactics, the internal-combustion engine, radios[1] and aircraft. The word will be used in that sense in this book.

The blitzkrieg was a good choice for a mid-sized country of limited means such as Nazi Germany. Since the days of Frederick the Great, Prussia/Germany sought to fight outnumbered and win, while avoiding wars of attrition against larger enemies such as France, Austria or Russia. Accordingly, Führer Adolf Hitler aimed to isolate strategically his enemies and defeat them episodically by concentrating his entire military potential at a single point for a brief time. Surprise and violent action played critical roles.[2] So long as Germany fought relatively smaller or weaker states such as Poland, France or Yugoslavia this method worked; against the USSR, which was neither small nor weak, it would fail. The Soviet Union's almost limitless space dissipated the blitzkrieg's shock value, while the ruthless Stalinist state survived the most massive defeats suffered by any nation in history.

The blitzkrieg's decentralized command model is perhaps best exemplified by the Auftragstaktik and the flexible Schwerpunkt (main effort), which could constantly shift in order to adapt to changing situations. The elder von Moltke's admonition that 'omission and inactivity are worse than resorting to the wrong expedient' suited the German psyche and stimulated blitzkrieg leaders. They idolized past iconic leaders like Frederick, von Blücher, von Moltke, von Hindenburg/Ludendorff, von Seeckt and memorialized 'mythical' or legendary exploits of yore – the more hopeless the situation the better. But fatally, this kind of thinking eventually led to accepting excessive risk and substituted 'taking action' for solid staff work and preparation. Thinking and acting faster than one's enemy was also critical; the terms 'decision loop', 'OODA Loop' or 'Boyd Loop' will be used here. The ground-breaking work of US Air Force Colonel John Boyd in explaining the success of fighter aces applies equally to most military situations. Its four components are: Orientation – for example, does the subject come from a culture of free-thinking initiative or top-down conformity; Observation – speed and accuracy of his situational awareness; Decision – speed and correctness of his choices; Action – once decision is made, how well do subordinates carry them out.[3]

Likewise, the Bewegungskrieg had long been Prussia/Germany's preferred substitute for attritional warfare. For example, in the von Schlieffen plan of the First World War, German soldiers had been called upon to perform unparalleled feats of marching in order to put the French in a position of fatal disadvantage – something they did not accomplish.[4] Military motorization, which came of age late in the war, promised to breathe new life into future wars of maneuver. However, Germany's modest size and lack of resources betrayed this hope as well. The Wehrmacht never reached the level of modernization necessary to make the blitzkrieg truly work on a global scale, and in particular, its lack of sufficient oil was a constant limitation. Throughout the Second World War, and even at the height of Hitler's successes, the great mass of the German Army marched on foot at the pace of a Roman legion. Its leg infantry plus horse-drawn artillery and logistics did most of the fighting and dying, despite pride of place being given to panzers, Stukas and other 'elites'. In fact, the infantry branch was further hamstrung because it lost many of its best divisions when the Army needed foundations for new mechanized units.

The concept of the Vernichtungskrieg rounds out the blitzkrieg's historical legacies.[5] Prussia/Germany long operated under an enemy oriented, instead of a terrain-oriented, system. Destruction of enemy forces in the field became the main objective, with Hannibal's victory at Cannae serving as the classic example. The Germans considered huge encirclement battles such as Sedan in 1870 and Dunkirk in 1940 models of the penultimate victory. Blitzkrieg forces were the perfect weapon to achieve the prerequisite breakthroughs and envelopments, plus the concluding exploitation necessary to create the desired Kessels (cauldrons). However, there was a steep price to pay: the Germans accepted risk taking and high casualties as an unfortunate part of the bargain.

Current United States Army doctrine acknowledges three levels of warfare: strategic, operational and tactical. Unfortunately, all three words are used inaccurately and interchangeably in both popular literature and military history, so clarifying their use in the present work is appropriate. At the top of the spectrum is strategy, where nations establish policies and goals and in extreme cases, fight wars. At the low end of the spectrum is tactics; here units approximately up to the size of divisions fight engagements and battles. In between, and often most difficult to understand, is the operational level, called grand tactics during the Napoleonic period. Here corps, armies or army groups fight campaigns. Good operational-level commanders put battles together to win campaigns. Successful national-level leaders string together campaigns to win wars.

During the wars of German unification in the largely dynastic nineteenth century, strategy lay in the hands of Prussian Chancellor Otto von Bismarck, which allowed the Army to concentrate on the operational and tactical levels. In the twentieth century, this method fell apart under the less-capable and more-erratic dilettantes Wilhelm II and Hitler. With them, strategy was integrated, 'if at all',[6] mainly in the minds of the supreme leaders. As is so often the case in military history, success, such as Bismarck's nation building from 1864–71, did not engender much serious analysis. Therefore, the German military never really questioned the prominence of operations and tactics over strategy. As a result of this lopsided emphasis, in 1914–18 and 1939–45, Germany demonstrated an amazing ability to win battles and campaigns, but thankfully, not the capacity to win the wars themselves.

The history of the genesis of the Panzerwaffe should be well known to the reader and need not be repeated here. The Germans conceived of panzer divisions as early as 1931–32, as the tool to execute the blitzkrieg. Initially there were two types of mechanized formations: heavy panzer divisions to attack and create breakthroughs, and light divisions for deep maneuver, encirclements and exploitation. In Poland, however, the light units proved inadequate so were transformed into regular panzer divisions.[7]

With the creation of the first panzer corps in 1935, the Panzerwaffe ceased to be merely a tactical or infantry support weapon. It had finally become an independent combat arm. The Germans turned to concentrating panzers into increasingly larger formations. The panzers' ability to function independently on the operational level continued with the establishment of four panzer groups in early 1941 and again with the short-lived Fourth Panzer Army (combining two panzer groups) later that summer.

Panzer armies were where the blitzkrieg and operational-level warfare came together. During the Polish campaign, panzers represented simply another tactical weapon, although a unique one. In the West, the Wehrmacht first experimented with the Panzerwaffe at the operational level; Group von Kleist broke through the Ardennes Forest and trapped the Anglo–French armies against the Channel coast. This was the decisive maneuver of the 1940 campaign.[8] Early in 1941, Group von Kleist deployed to Bulgaria in anticipation of action against Greece, was ultimately reoriented against Yugoslavia, but did not play such a critical role in the Balkans as it had in France.

German planners sought to capitalize on their 1940 success by pinning their hopes for Operation Barbarossa on four massive panzer groups. Further, between 26 June and 28 July 1941, Panzer Groups Two and Three were consolidated into an even larger formation, Fourth Panzer Army, along the Minsk–Smolensk axis. The reasoning behind this restructuring was sound, but the wrong selection for commander condemned the concept.[9] However, the seeds had been sown and in the autumn and winter of 1941 the panzer groups were renamed panzer armies and reorganized to include artillery, engineer, signal, logistical and other support common to numbered armies.

For several reasons, Barbarossa failed to destroy the USSR and a war of attrition developed in the east. The transition to war of attrition meant both disaster for Nazi Germany and, according to many histories, the end of the blitzkrieg era. (However, I will continue to use the 'shorthand' term blitzkrieg as described earlier.) Only two panzer armies played critical roles in Operation Blau, the assault on Stalingrad and the Caucasus Mountains in 1942, and only one participated in Operation Citadel against the Kursk bulge in 1943. In a dangerous trend, the Second and Third Panzer Armies remained holding defensive positions on the Moscow sector. By 1944 the structure of the German Army was breaking down.[10] The Red Army had always outnumbered the Germans, but now in terms of skill it had caught up to, and arguably surpassed, the invaders. Initiative passed to the Soviets and, despite retaining their fearsome-sounding names, panzer armies often ceased to be operational maneuver weapons and instead merely occupied ground. They lost most unique qualities and, in numerous cases, did not even have any panzer or mechanized formations under their command.

Three months prior to launching Operation Barbarossa, German Army Commander Field Marshal Walther von Brauchitsch told a group of officers to rely on the 'ruthless spirit of attack, boldness and resolute action inspired by confidence in the superiority of the German soldier over any opponent and by unshakable faith in final victory'.[11] This one comment proved to be a harbinger of both the panzer army's success and decline.

Chapter 1

Group von Kleist as Precursor

The Panzerwaffe's baptism of fire came in Poland. With a greater than four-to-one superiority in tanks and numerous other German advantages, it is no wonder that the blitzkrieg through Poland was successful. However, the Wehrmacht did not employ its panzer divisions in an operational mass there. Rather, these formations were divided, as were the light and motorized infantry divisions, among numerous armies. Clearly, the Germans would need to make many adjustments in order to be successful when they faced more evenly matched enemies in the future.

Events leading up the Nazi's western campaign in 1940 are among the best known in military history. When Hitler first ordered the attack for the late autumn of 1939, the Wehrmacht could do no better than plan an unimaginative repetition of the 1914 von Schlieffen Plan. At that time, the Führer had suggested a plan somewhat close to what the Germans would actually employ, but his generals resisted.[1] For a number of reasons, including opposition by Army Commander Colonel General Walther von Brauchitsch, weather and the compromise of German plans as the result of the crash of a liaison airplane in Belgium, Hitler pushed back the invasion date.

In the meantime, Colonel General Gerd von Rundstedt's chief of staff at Army Group A Headquarters, Lieutenant General Erich von Manstein, developed and submitted alternative plans up the chain of command. His novel plan called for a true Vernichtungsschlacht (battle of annihilation) not just an 'ordinary victory' called for by existing plans. Army Chief of Staff, General of Artillery Franz Halder, however, repeatedly squashed the plan. Thanks only to a chance luncheon between Hitler and von Manstein just months before the invasion, did the general's unconventional option come to the Führer's attention. Hitler ordered adaption of the 'sickle cut' operation the next day. Furious, Halder banished von Manstein to the relative obscurity of corps command shortly thereafter.

As conceived by von Manstein, the Wehrmacht first moved against the Netherlands and Belgium, replicating their opening gambit of the First World War. This maneuver, designed to divert the Allies, produced the desired effect and drew them northeast. Airborne landings in this area, coupled with apparent passivity opposite Luxemburg and the Maginot Line, confirmed Wehrmacht intentions to Allied intelligence. After a brief delay, the Germans revealed their Schwerpunkt through the Ardennes Forest. Only when the Allies were fully committed and it was too late, did they notice the danger. Slashing across the French and British rear, the largest armored grouping the world had seen trapped the enemy against the Channel coast. Figuratively, Napoleon must have been spinning in his grave.

Another familiar feature of the western campaign is that the Allies outnumbered the Germans both in divisions and in tanks deployed on the battlefield. Many marks of Allied tanks had thicker armor and bigger guns, but they suffered in the areas of communications and the arrangement of their fighting compartments. The French in particular misused their armor; according to General of Panzer Troops Walther Nehring, thirty-three of sixty-one French tank battalions served in the infantry support role.[2] During the 1940 campaign, they never mounted an operation involving more that two armored divisions. Not that it mattered; essentially their morale was broken before the first shot was fired. Strategically the French were hiding behind the Maginot Line. Meanwhile, the British Army, basically a glorified constabulatory designed to guard the empire, fielded a force also unequal to the upcoming ordeal.

As early as 1938, French peacetime maneuvers betrayed their weaknesses in the Ardennes region. Nevertheless, they defended the area with weak 'B'-quality divisions. German intelligence also noted the vulnerable boundary between the French 2nd and 9th Armies near Dinant and Sedan. Accordingly, German planners knew they would surprise the French at precisely this point with the unexpected arrival of massed panzers along the Meuse River.[3]

The Germans made the following assumptions: 1. That the sizeable French Army was dispirited and had learned nothing from Poland; 2. The Allies would go northward into the Low Countries; and 3. One critical hit would demolish the French and, indeed, the entire Allied cause. The intended breakthrough near Sedan would in turn give the Wehrmacht three options: 1. Go west to the coast; 2. Turn south to Paris; or 3. Go southeast and roll up the Maginot Line. Any of these courses of action would have been disastrous for the Allies. However, the operational objective of both Hitler and von Manstein was the Channel coast and the utter destruction of French and British forces which only the first solution would provide.[4] With Allied armies in the field defeated, Paris and Maginot fortresses would fall with comparative ease.

Von Manstein's earlier plans of mid-December did not include the accumulation of panzers the Wehrmacht would historically employ. This decisive concentration took form during the second half of February. The panzer formation's official name was 'Gruppe von Kleist', named after its commander,

General of Cavalry Ewald von Kleist, and subordinated to the Twelfth Army under Colonel General Wilhelm List. Historians speculate that von Kleist was given the job as a cautious counterweight to the impetuous General of Panzer Troops, Heinz Guderian. His headquarters had once been that of the XXII Corps. The Group's XIV, XIX and XLI Corps included 1,254 panzers, nearly half of the German total. Guderian's XIX Panzer Corps held nearly two-thirds of that number (818), while Lieutenant General Georg-Hans Reinhardt's XLI Panzer Corps had the remainder (436). General of Infantry Gustav von Wietersheim's XIV Corps consisted of motorized infantry, and would mainly secure the group's southern flank. Covering von Kleist's northern flank, and often acting in coordination with him, stood General of Infantry Hermann Hoth's XV Panzer Corps (542 panzers), part of the Fourth Army.[5]

All told, von Kleist commanded 41,000 vehicles that would eventually have to negotiate only four routes through the Ardennes. Echeloned under Army Group A, by noon on the first day of operations, 10 May, Guderian had passed through Luxemburg into Belgium, Reinhardt's formation reached back to the Rhine, while von Wietersheim's corps still occupied their assembly areas near Giessen. Von Kleist's huge force went undetected by Allied air reconnaissance largely because of concentrated flak and Luftwaffe air superiority.[6]

Von Kleist's tactical objective was to achieve crossings over the Meuse in the vicinity of Sedan and Givet, while his operational goal was to get into the Allies' rear before the enemy suspected such a potentially catastrophic maneuver. His strategic goal was to win the war quickly so there would be no repetition of the First World War stalemate. Orders read 'thrust through Luxemburg and southern Belgium [to] gain the west bank of the Meuse River in a surprise attack'. Guderian commanded the Schwerpunkt, aiming for Sedan, while Reinhardt's much smaller corps headed for Monthme, at the confluence of the Semois and Meuse Rivers. They were to strike at the boundary of two armies, the 2nd and 9th, a perfect target for any attack. Reinhardt had to negotiate more difficult terrain than did Guderian and would not face weak, 'B'-quality divisions. Wisely, the panzer group's chief of staff considered logistics critical to mission accomplishment. Therefore he created three motorized detachments totaling 4,800 tons of carrying capacity that would insure necessary supplies all the way to Calais.[7] As the rest of this book will repeatedly make clear, not all German generals showed the requisite high opinion for logistical matters. By any measure, Gruppe von Kleist was definitely set up for success.

Luxemburg essentially gave Guderian free passage through the country. Assisted by Brandenburger commandos, XIX Panzer Corps entered Belgium on the afternoon of 10 May. While French cavalry and Belgian Chasseurs Ardennais quickly gave way before the 10th Panzer Division, stalwart Belgian defenders halted the 1st Panzer. The remainder of the panzer group wound its way through the Ardennes – even moving during the night with headlights blazing – demonstrating their contempt for Allied reconnaissance. By the end of the invasion's second day, Guderian had brushed aside the French 5th Light Division, his last serious opposition until he reached the Meuse.[8]

A day later, he was almost to the Meuse, whereas Reinhardt remained jammed up in the Ardennes. The XLI Panzer's task got a little easier when the 3rd Spahi (North African) Brigade turned over the frontier defense to cavalry units which proved too light to stand up to the panzers. The Germans took heart that the French made no effort to adjust their defenses, giving no indication that they had located the Schwerpunkt. French intelligence did not identify von Kleist's panzer divisions until late on the 12th. Strategically, German intelligence observed French railroad traffic patterns indicating they expected a German assault against the Maginot Line. German deception, essential at all times if the blitzkrieg was to succeed, worked as well as could be expected.[9]

Colonel General Georg-Hans Reinhardt

Reinhardt was born in Saxony in 1887. He became a lieutenant in Infantry Regiment 107 in 1908. During the 1930s he commanded 1st Rifle Brigade and 4th Panzer Division. In this latter position he led the attack on Warsaw, for which he received promotion to lieutenant general and the Knight's Cross. He led the XLI Panzer Corps across France, and as a newly promoted general of panzer troops would have been one of the principal panzer commanders during Operation Sealion.

During Barbarossa's first week, Reinhardt initially surrendered the limelight to von Manstein while the XLI Panzer fought the bulk of the Northwestern Front's defenses. Afterwards, he raced toward Leningrad, capturing Luga River bridges barely three weeks into the campaign. The drive on Leningrad failed to yield the desired results, and XLI Panzer moved to the central theater for Operation Typhoon. Days into that offensive, Reinhardt replaced Hoth at Third Panzer Army, a position he would hold until August 1944. Reinhardt's men came close to the Soviet capital, only to relinquish their gains to fresh units from Siberia. While his former superior, Colonel General Erich Hoepner, was cashiered during the defensive fighting that winter, Reinhardt earned the Oak Leaves.

Third Panzer remained on the northern edge of Army Group Center, beating back Soviet attacks, combating partisan raids and trying to maintain a solid connection with Army Group North. Enemy pressure slowly pushed the panzer army back, and from the autumn of 1943 through the winter of 1944, its main objective was holding the important rail junction of Vitebsk. Reinhardt's defensive efforts earned him the Swords to his Knight's Cross, but greatly weakened his forces. With the Soviet's Operation Bagration in June 1944, Vitebsk became encircled and Hitler was anxious that the town be held. The Führer ordered Army Group Center commander Field Marshal Ernst Busch to instruct Reinhardt to parachute in a staff officer to stiffen the garrison commander's resolve. Reinhardt replied, 'Field marshal, please inform the Führer that only one officer in the Third Panzer Army can be considered for this jump and that is the army commander. I am ready to carry out his order.' That ridiculous answer was the only possible response to such a ridiculous plan.

With Busch's utter failure at the head of the army group, Reinhardt took over on 16 August. Shortly afterwards, the Soviet offensive shot its bolt and an uneasy stalemate settled over East Prussia and northern Poland. The Soviets maintained local pressure until their winter 1944–45 offensive destroyed Reinhardt's command. Fed up, Hitler relieved him on 25 January. Samuel Mitcham believes Reinhardt would have left soon in any event: he had sustained serious head wounds a short time earlier. Reinhardt was tried for numerous war crimes after the war, was convicted and sentenced to fifteen years in prison. His captors released him in 1952 and he died in 1963. The great promise as a panzer leader with which he began the war did not survive much past Typhoon.

Late on 11 May, von Kleist issued orders for the Meuse crossing. The 12th would be a big day for the Panzer Group as it made up for time lost in the Ardennes and closed on the river. Meanwhile, harsh words passed between von Kleist and Guderian and their chiefs of staff, Kurt Zeitzler and Walther Nehring all day long. Consequently, everyone's nerves were on edge that night during the conference at Panzer Group headquarters as details of the final plan for the cross-river assault operation were hammered out. Guderian wanted to delay twenty-four hours in order to bring the 2nd Panzer forward alongside the 1st and 10th. Von Kleist wanted to keep up the pressure on the French and told him 'No', the assault would go off the next day as planned and further, the corps commander needed to obey orders. It seems that Halder's choice of the soft-spoken but firm leader von Kleist had been a wise one. As was his nature, Guderian always pushed to the point of disobedience but in the end did as instructed.[10]

Across the lines, French 2nd Army commander General Charles Huntziger wishfully continued to believe that the Wehrmacht moved at no more than at the pace of the French Army. He assumed that the Germans would need five days to close on Sedan en masse and another week to launch a deliberate river crossing operation. In his thinking, the French had almost a fortnight to improve the Class 'B' 55th Division's defenses. He was confident in their ability to hold the Meuse Line.[11]

Von Kleist allowed no such breathing space. If his artillery stood strung out to the rear, he would shore up the assault with tank guns, 88mm flak and most importantly, close air support (CAS). French artillery outnumbered German guns 350:150, but assuming a two-week-long engagement, they sought to ration their ammunition against this 'feint'. If Guderian's combat engineers were trailing behind and not available, his Landsers would have to man the assault boats themselves. Starting late in the morning of the 13th, the Stukas came in force. The approximately 1,400 aircraft that Bruno Loerzer and Wolfram von Richthofen (VIII Fliegerkorps) provided to von Kleist that Sunday (and most of these were thrown at Sedan) practically equaled the total number of Allied planes in the entire theater. The Luftwaffe silenced the French artillery and initiated a general panic among the defenders.[12] Therefore, in terms of pace, location of attack and morale, von Kleist's men held every advantage.

In the northern sector, Reinhardt managed to get two companies across the Meuse on the morning of 13 May. The 102nd Fortress Division counter-attacked, regained the river and managed to stall the 6th Panzer there for three days. At the Germans' main point of assault, in one of the war's best-known episodes, Colonel Herman Balck's 1st Rifle Regiment stormed over the Meuse at Sedan, capturing the heights above the west bank. Despite the fact he had no artillery or anti-tank weapons, he managed to expand his bridgehead through-out the 13th. By midnight the Germans had built three tactical bridges over the Meuse River. Allied air forces made repeated weak, ineffective bombing raids against the bridges, but either missed their targets or caused insignificant damage.[13] Huntziger did not realize it at the time, but his entire defensive structure was about to collapse.

On the morning of the 14th, a French tank brigade counterattacked against Balck, whose men held out by using newly arrived anti-tank guns against the uncoordinated enemy. Balck thereby demonstrated the inestimable value of combined-arms Kampfgruppen. For the next five years the Germans would employ these ad hoc formations in the most imaginative ways. Altogether 570 panzers crossed the Meuse that day to push the German advantage as far as the Ardennes Canal. The Allies continued their fruitless aerial assault, launching twenty-seven attacks, each with a meager ten to twenty planes. The Luftwaffe and Guderian's 300 flak guns accounted for 100 of the 400 attacking aircraft. The French planned a counterattack near Flavigny by the 3rd Armored, 3rd Motorized Infantry and 5th Cavalry Divisions, but never pulled the trigger. They proved singularly incapable of functioning in the blitzkrieg milieu.

Guderian's Schwerpunkt, the 1st Panzer stood poised to break into the French rear, with the 2nd Panzer finally ready to enter the action as back-up.[14]

While Guderian was generally free of the Ardennes by the time he reached the Meuse, Reinhardt still had to contend with poor terrain and a dearth of Luftwaffe CAS. However, by the morning of the 15th, he had finally overcome the resistance of the 41st Corps. Thanks to the initiative of the 6th Panzer's commander, the XLI Corps crossed the river at Montherme. Simultaneously, the 8th Panzer crossed at Nouzonville, rendering useless further French resistance at the major rail junction of Chareville. A large traffic jam developed at Moncoronet on the small Serre River, 50km west, where the 1st, 2nd and 6th Panzer Divisions all tried to pass. Commanders on the scene ironed out this problem, freeing von Kleist to exploit into the Allied hinterland.[15]

The French high command continued to have no clue about developments along the Meuse. On the same day von Kleist's men achieved true freedom of action west of the river, General Joseph Georges blithely told Maurice Gamelin, 'the breach at Sedan has been contained and a counterattack with strong formations was carried out at 0430'.[16] Of course, none of this was true. The 10th Panzer and Infantry Regiment Grossdeutschland on Guderian's left shoulder hit prepared French defenses near Artaise and remained stuck there for three days. This did not delay von Kleist, who adroitly shifted his Schwerpunkt. Covered by Rommel's 7th Panzer on his right (part of Hoth's corps), Reinhardt took advantage of the French concentration against Guderian to press on. The perceived threat to von Kleist's southern flank soon grabbed the attention of von Rundstedt's headquarters. The Army High Command (OKH) was also getting nervous over von Kleist's continued westward movement.[17] Events even began to out-pace the Wehrmacht's ability to manage.

The Germans definitely moved too fast for the Allies. The French needed time but the blitzkrieg gave them none. So far, the panzers had not played a critical role; marching infantry could have almost moved as fast through the Ardennes and across the Meuse. But now, free of the narrow confines of the forest and river valley, von Kleist's panzers began to move faster than even their own high command could tolerate. With events on the ground happening at a tempo within the Boyd Loop of their own plans, the Germans became apprehensive of their own success and put the brakes on von Kleist's panzers.

At his Second Army headquarters, Huntziger assumed von Kleist would now wheel left and roll up the Maginot Line from the north. But von Kleist had no such conservative plan in mind. Instead, prodded by Guderian and Reinhardt, he convinced higher headquarters to allow him to turn his back on Huntziger and head west. The race to the Channel was on. Alert to potential dangers on the Panzer Group's southern flank, the initiative passed to Reinhardt, covered by Guderian on his left with Hoth guarding his right. French 'B' divisions uniformly gave way as XLI Panzer Corps destroyed the weak flank of the 'interim line' of General Andre Corap's 9th Army. The 6th Panzer discovered an intact bridge at Montcy, hit the newly arriving French 2nd Armored and over 15/16 May, defeated the French formation in detail. Reinhardt pushed west and soon created a 60km-wide gap in the French line. Meanwhile, at Stonne, Guderian's 10th Panzer and Grossdeutschland fought a tough defensive battle dominated by anti-tank guns (PAKs).[18]

Far too late – by the 15th, the French finally awakened to the danger of the Ardennes maneuver. That evening President Paul Reynaud telephoned British Prime Minister Churchill to say 'We have been defeated . . . we are beaten'. At approximately the same point, the German high command began to doubt its own success. It turned out that the French threat at Stonne was more anecdotal than real. Therefore, during the night of 15/16 May, von Rundstedt ordered von Kleist not to cross the Oise River, instructions he duly passed down to his panzer corps. Guderian, nevertheless, kept moving west. During the 16th, he crossed the First World War battlefields near St Quentin on the Somme (significantly west of the Oise!), while Sixteenth Army infantry assumed the 10th Panzer and Grossdeutschland's defensive duties along the Panzer group's southern flank.[19] The concentrated panzer formations were having a decisive effect as an operational weapon.

Successes aside, von Kleist could not abide Guderian's refusal to obey the halt order. At 0700 on the 17th he flew to XIX Panzer's headquarters and after a heated argument accepted Guderian's resignation. The corps commander immediately contacted von Rundstedt (visited by Hitler that day), who in turn told all parties to wait until List arrived to sort things out. Only when the Twelfth Army commander explained to Guderian that the halt order came from the OKH, and not from von Kleist, did the panzer corps commander relent. List and Guderian, without informing either von Rundstedt or von Kleist, made an under-the-table deal to continue west with a 'reconnaissance in force'. Army group headquarters later endorsed the move and by the end of the day Guderian stood over 100km beyond Sedan. Meanwhile, on von Kleist's right, newly arrived Hoepner repulsed a weak counterattack near Gembloux.[20] Fortunately for them, nervousness at the strategic level and willfulness at the operational level had not robbed the Germans of momentum.

By the 18th Hitler backed off and the panzers were heading west again. De Gaulle used the pause to rebuild his tank strength back up to 155 vehicles, and at 0400 hours on the 19th launched another counterattack near Loan and Crecy. His 4th Armored Division, acting alone, could not halt four panzer corps. Stukas meted out a severe beating and by the end of the day, the French lost over half of the attacking force. By now every panzer division except the 9th was within 75 km of the English Channel. In fact, von Kleist's men started arriving at the coast on the 20th, the 2nd Panzer covering the last gap along the Somme between Abbeville and the mouth of the river at Noyelles in one day.[21]

The final threat to von Manstein's dazzling plan came on the 21st in the form of an attack against Hoth near Arras by two battalions of seventy-four British tanks (north flank), plus about seventy French tanks (south flank). Allied forces under overall command of the British 50th Infantry Division, Major General Harold Franklyn, made a slight penetration into Hoth's flank and inflicted some casualties on Rommel's 7th Panzer. This caused a little anxiety among the Germans, including another overreaction by von Rundstedt, but, as before, the Allied response was too little, too late.[22] Every Allied counterattack and been limited to the tactical realm with corresponding little effect, and so are relegated to the status of footnotes in the history of the campaign.

This non-threat neutralized, the panzers now headed north with complete disregard to their rear security. By the 22nd, the bulk of von Kleist's men were closer to Dunkirk than the Allied armies. But one day later (with half of the group's panzers out of action mainly as a result of mechanical problems), Hitler, still insecure in his new position of warlord, again overestimated the remaining French strength and the corresponding danger to his southern flank. No sooner had von Kleist captured 30,000 POWs at Boulogne and Calais, taken Arras and turned north over the Aa Canal at St Omer on 24 May, then that evening Hitler issued another 'halt' order and pulled the panzers back. Along with von Rundstedt, the Führer decided to leave reduction of the pocket to the Luftwaffe and infantry. Soon it became obvious that the British and French were evacuating Dunkirk and the infantry was too slow in closing in. Therefore, two days after holding back von Kleist, Hitler relented and told the panzers to advance up to the point where the bridgehead could be taken under artillery fire.[23]

With his panzer group reconsolidated, von Kleist pushed forward. Within a day his men were within artillery range of Dunkirk, but the massive panzer attack never materialized. In little more than a day the golden opportunity had passed. Von Kleist considered the entire Dunkirk operation a 'patchwork'.[24] There are many theories why Hitler did not press for the Vernichtungsschlacht on the Channel coast that was clearly within his grasp. Dunkirk, the most bungled encirclement battle on French territory until that at Falaise over four years later, meant that von Manstein's operationally brilliant plan ended as a strategic blunder of the first order. The long-term impact of allowing a third of a million Allied soldiers to escape and the boost to British morale is as huge as unimaginable.

On 28 May, OKH divided the massive panzer group into two smaller ones and redeployed them south against the 'Weygand Line'. Henceforth, Panzer Group von Kleist included XIV and XVI Panzer Corps, while Panzer Group Guderian consisted of XXXIX and XLI Panzer Corps, so it is appropriate to speak of both. The final phase of the Battle for France, Operation Red, began on 9 June, with the panzers moving out the following day. While von Kleist's men struggled initially against strong French defenses south of St Quintin, Guderian, having assembled in the battlefields southwest of Sedan over which he had just fought, preferred to have his panzers follow infantry breakthrough forces. Eventually both panzer groups broke into open country but the ensuing pursuit had none of the spectacular allure of the dash through the Ardennes. Guderian picked up the Marne and followed the river valley almost to the Swiss border. His men reached the frontier southeast of Besancon in force on the 17th. There his panzer group transferred to Army Group C and, taking the Maginot Line from the rear, completed what the Germans call the Battle of Alsace-Lorraine, collecting POWs in 10,000 multiples.[25]

Von Kleist and his reorganized panzer group had a more interesting hussar's ride through central and southern France during Operation Red. He attacked over the First World War battlefield of Château-Thierry, and once free of the initial defenses, began to eat up the French landscape in huge bites. The panzer group crossed the Marne on 12 June and the Seine two days later. Coming between Fontainebleau and Romilly, he cut a clockwise swath around Paris. By the 17th, he closed on the middle Loire, rounding up two French divisions and another 30,000 POWs in the process. On 20 June, he detached a Kampfgruppe under Hoepner via Lyon toward the Italian border, while the bulk of the panzer group followed the lower Loire toward the Atlantic coast. He passed through Tours and Cognac on his way to the Bay of Biscay and the Spanish border, which he reached on 30 June, over a week after the armistice had been signed.[26]

During the western campaign Panzer Group von Kleist had proven that concentrated armored formations functioning at the operational level could achieve strategic goals. Panzers, aggressively led from the front, acting in concert with other arms, including CAS and aided by the element of surprise, had been an unbeatable combination. The Germans had staked all on the risky maneuver over the Meuse and behind the bulk of the Allied armies and had won big. Every army in the world immediately took notice and began to reevaluate their own armored arsenals and theories.

Hitler had further plans for his new weapon. Von Kleist's panzer men had one more warm up before the penultimate test. Not to be outdone by German successes during the western campaign, during the autumn of 1940, Mussolini (against Hitler's advice) attacked Greece from Albania. The Italian Army immediately ran into trouble against the Greeks and their British supporters. To shore up Barbarossa's southeastern flank Hitler had already been putting diplomatic pressure on numerous Balkan states, and now redoubled his efforts. During the winter of 1940–41 he concluded treaties to occupy Romania and Bulgaria. The recently renamed First Panzer Group deployed through the first country and into the second. Its mission was to attack through the Metaxas Line into eastern Greece in order to deny the British any opportunity to build air-bases from which they could threaten Romania's oilfields (Operation Marita).

In the meantime, Hitler concluded a treaty with Yugoslavia on 25 April, which was in turn invalidated by a *coup d'état* a day later. In a rage the following day, Hitler demanded the destruction of the Yugoslav state. In Vienna on the 29th, von Kleist attended a planning conference for the upcoming operation. Subsequently, von Kleist turned his panzers 90 degrees from south to west and prepared to invade Yugoslavia on 8 April (they would attack two days early). He would assault along the Nis–Kragujevac axis, aiming to take the capital Belgrade from Morava River valley to the southeast. Under his command, von Kleist had the XIV Panzer and XI Army Corps, for a total of two panzer divisions, one motorized, one infantry and one mountain division, a much smaller force than the year before. The difficult terrain favored the Yugoslavs, who were expected to fight hard to defend their capital.[27]

With Luftwaffe CAS flying overhead, the 11th Panzer led von Kleist's group through the main defensive line on the first day, 6 April. The Yugoslav 5th Army commander quickly pulled his men behind the Morava (four divisions and two brigades, with an additional three divisions on the border with Greece), but von Kleist pushed his men without regard to flank security. By the 9th his panzers had already rolled into Nis. Two days later, the Yugoslavs failed to hold at Kragujevac, losing 5,000 POWs there to the 11th Panzer. North of Nis, two Yugoslav regiments attacked that division's exposed lines of communication, a situation rectified that same day by elements of 5th Panzer (the mass of the 5th took Pristina, also on the 11th). Von Kleist was not going to allow such a small diversion, no matter how well intentioned, to keep the panzer group from achieving its mission. By 12 April, closing in on Belgrade, XIV Panzer Corps slammed into the right flank of the Yugoslav 6th Army (facing Romania with two divisions and two brigades, reinforced by the 2nd Cavalry Division), rolling it up from south to north. In just a few days, von Kleist had advanced some 200km through rough terrain, overcome all resistance and stood 60km from Belgrade. The following morning, with the panzer group commander at its head, the 11th Panzer entered the city.[28] Mission complete, the First Panzer Group did not continue on toward Greece, but turned its attention to the upcoming war with the Soviet Union.

Against a much smaller enemy, the Germans employed almost as many panzers in the Balkan campaign as they had against the western Allies, so there could be but one outcome to the spring campaign. Von Kleist's role in 1941 had not been nearly as significant as the year before – against Yugoslavia he basically acted as a normal army headquarters versus a totally outclassed enemy. A legitimate question regarding both campaigns is: 'Were the Germans that good or were the Allies and Yugoslavs that bad?' The answer is 'Yes'. In both cases their opponents stuck to a fixed plan and tried to fight a set-piece battle, so proved unable to improvise. The defenders thought in terms of cumulative destruction of forces and outmoded concepts of attritional warfare. Von Kleist used a doctrine of relational maneuver warfare wherein the destruction of the defensive **system** was paramount. The tactical battles near the front were not an end in themselves as in the attritional model, but merely a pre-condition for the next, decisive phase of the operation. Therefore, with the example of France, the tactical action along the Meuse River did not matter nearly as much as the deep penetration that followed.[29] The fact that the French Army failed to perform in either phase doomed its nation.

In both 1940 and 1941, von Kleist proceeded opportunistically, while the defenders did not think operationally, but simply plugged holes in their lines. In the ensuing chaos, Allied and Yugoslav commanders read the battle wrong, made poor choices and became dispirited when 'doing the right thing' according to military tradition only brought more defeats. The same thing happened on the battlefield, so crippling demoralization spread both up and down the chain of command. Halting the panzers at one point might represent a tactical victory for the defenders, but since the blitzkrieg sought the line of least resistance, such a temporary success usually led to ultimate operational failure. Intangibles such as command skill and momentum dominated objective measures like numbers of men or caliber of artillery.[30] However, the panzers moving too fast for even the German high command (unable to keep pace with developments) did periodically cause similar command paralysis on their side of the front. This fact condemned Dunkirk to be an ordinary victory instead of the crushing Vernichtungsschlacht it could, and should, have been.

Von Kleist, the commanders and men of his panzer group had mastered the various challenges. Panzer corps commanders from the French campaign,

Guderian, Hoepner and Hoth, would all lead huge panzer armies of their own in the supreme test of the blitzkrieg, the German Army and the Nazi Reich: Operation Barbarossa. Staff planners for this campaign gave the panzer groups significant operational objectives and large, self-contained orders of battle. The whole world indeed would await the outcome of this massive contest.

Chapter 2
First Panzer Army

First Panzer Army, the legacy of Gruppe von Kleist, spent the entire war in the southern part of the front. It probably travelled a greater distance than the other panzer armies, or perhaps any other formation in the German Army. During Operation Barbarossa it belonged to Army Group South, and participated in the encirclement battles of Uman, Kiev and the Sea of Azov. It ended the campaign in temporary possession of Rostov. During 1942 it contributed to the recapture of Rostov and led the drive to the Caucasus oil region.

In early 1943, von Manstein extracted First Panzer back through Rostov, then employed it in his defensive battles following the Soviet's successful campaign to retake Stalingrad. During that summer and fall, the panzer army fought defensive battles in the Ukraine, often retracing its steps taken during Barbarossa. It narrowly avoided total destruction at Korsun, and then withdrew over the Carpathian Mountains. During the last year of the war, First Panzer retreated through Hungary and Slovakia, before finally it came to rest near Prague. It remained in constant and decisive combat with the Red Army during the nearly four-year-long Nazi-Soviet War.

Campaign	Battles and Engagements
Barbarossa, **22 June–21 November 1941**	Galicia, Bug, Styr, Stalin Line, Tarnopol, Berdichev, Kiev, Uman, Dnepr bend, Cherkassy, Dnepropetrovsk, Kiev encirclement, Sea of Azov, Donbas, Rostov
Donbas Defense, **22 November 1941–8 July 1942**	Donets, Mius
1942 Offensive, **9 July–30 December 1942**	Donbas, lower Don, Maikop, Terek
Retreat and Defensive Battles, **31 December 1942–27 July 1944**	Middle Donets, Mius, Izyum, Dnepropetrovsk, Krivoi Rog, Kirovograd, Nikopol, Vinnitsa, Podolsk, Brody, Bug
Hungary and Czechoslovakia, **28 July 1944–8 May 1945**	Carpathian passes, Slovakia, Beskides, Moravian Basin, Altvater Mountains

Von Rundstedt's Army Group South, of which First Panzer was a major component, had extremely difficult missions: attack the Soviet's main defensive effort; attack with only one panzer army; eliminate Red Army forces south of the Rotkino marshes, capture Kiev, occupy the wealthy (in terms or raw materials) Ukraine and reach Rostov on the Don River, approximately 2,100km from its starting point in occupied Poland. Von Kleist commanded three panzer (III, XIV, XLVIII) and one infantry corps (XXIX), including 9th, 11th, 13th, 14th and 16th Panzer, 16th, 25th, SS Leibstandarte Adolf Hitler and SS Viking Motorized and 44th, 57th, 75th, 111th, 298th and 299th Infantry Divisions plus the Luftwaffe's II Flak Corps.[1] German doctrine at the time subordinated a panzer army under an infantry army for the purpose of creating the initial breakthrough; accordingly, First Panzer fell under Sixth Army. According to Barbarossa's plan, taking Kiev by *coup de main* represented von Kleist's first operational objective. The operations order issued to Panzer Regiment 15 of the 11th Panzer Division on the day before the invasion read thus:

> As soon as the infantry has broken open a hole, attacks as the lead panzer division of the corps along the central Panzerstrasse ... as soon as the Styr River crossing is accomplished at Szczuroice, push without looking back or stopping ('ruchsichtlos und unaufhaltsam') over Dubno, Ostrog, Polonne, Berdichev to the Dnepr. Thereafter quickly overcome all enemy resistance with rash assaults, when possible break into individual battle groups, quickly overcome every difficulty along the way via action of all arms. Enemy attacks will be dispatched quickly with our antitank weapons in immediate counterattacks.[2]

Opposite von Kleist stood the Southwest Front under Colonel General MP Kirponos, consisting of 5th, 6th, 12th and 26th Armies backed up by eight mechanized corps. However, the mechanized corps, while larger than a panzer corps, were also unwieldy for the inexperienced Red Army commanders and many had significant problems: the 9th and 19th had only one combat-ready tank division each (the 35th and 43rd, respectively), the 15th had no trucks for its 212th Motorized Rifle Division and the 8th was especially scattered across the Ukrainian countryside. Kirponos did not suffer from the fearfulness and passivity of many Soviet leaders. On 10 June, he alerted his forces and sent them toward the front, only to be discovered by the NKVD and have Zhukov order him back in accordance with Stalin's 'no provocations' guidance. By the 13–14 June, he again had his units inch toward the frontier. Two such units were the 87th Rifle Division paired up with the 1st Antitank Brigade in the

Vladomir–Volynsky area. Their insubordinate preparedness gave 14th Panzer, leading von Kleist's left, a nasty welcome to the USSR.[3]

Kirponos' men made many other similar moves that put them in a better position than their comrades to the north, but even these measures could not blunt the fury that struck the Soviet Union on Barbarossatag. The 44th and 298th Infantry Divisions blasted openings for 13th and 14th Panzer Divisions in the north (III Panzer); 57th and 75th Infantry did the same for 11th Panzer in the center (XLVIII Panzer); XIV Panzer Corps followed some distance to the rear. Almost immediately Kirponos ordered his mechanized corps to the point of rupture in a much more realistic counterattack than the one Stavka ordered. The 41st Tank Division of 22nd Mechanized Corps was already stationed on the border, and the 9th (Major General KK Rokossovsky) and 19th Mechanized followed close behind. Two great rivers of armored vehicles moved toward each other. The 14th Panzer hit the combined 87th Rifle and 1st Antitank bulwark; the defenders conducted a fighting withdrawal only when outflanked by Landsers, but maintained their cohesion. However, there would be only a few bright spots such as this for the Southwest Front. On the first day of the invasion, at Alexandrovka – almost within sight of the border, III Panzer Corps destroyed 267 tanks. Near Radziechov, a see-saw battle raged between Panzer Regiment 15 (11th Panzer Division), reinforced with 88mm flak guns and a Soviet tank division. By 1600 hours on the 23rd, 46 KV 1s and 2s littered the battlefield. Fierce Luftwaffe interdiction, spread-out deployments, poor roads, untried leaders and units resulted in uneven combat. Soviet counterattack forces arrived and attacked in small groups of twenty to thirty tanks which the Germans defeated in detail. Entire regiments became mired in swamps.[4] Nearly everywhere in those first days von Kleist's men came out on top.

After two days, the 87th Rifle had lost two regiments and when that division could no longer maintain itself on the battlefield the position of the 1st Antitank Brigade also became untenable. On 24 June, the 13th and 14th Panzer Divisions advanced abreast down the Lutsk road. North of the town around noon, 215th Motorized and 19th Tank Divisions counterattacked against the 14th Panzer with disastrous results. Thus the maneuvers by the 22nd and 15th Mechanized Corps ended in failure. The next day, the III Panzer Corps made for Rovno, where the 9th Mechanized awaited them. Slightly south, the 11th Panzer neared Dubno, with the 16th Panzer in tow close behind. Attempting to intercept this force came the 8th Mechanized, which had just marched 500km perpendicular across the German axis of advance from its peacetime bases southwest of the Dniester River. Its 34th Tank Division in particular took massive amounts of abuse from panzers, artillery and the Luftwaffe. By the 25th, it seems the Soviets had conceded the border battle and began to escape east. Some units, such as the 8th Mechanized, had plenty of fight left in them, however, and continued to resist. The German infantry halted to round up groups of Red Army stragglers and therefore could not assist the panzer spearheads. In many cases, the mechanized corps had ceased to exist as cohesive formations so Soviet commanders simply threw random collections of tank and motorized infantry against von Kleist's thrusts.[5] Predictably, these counterattacks ended poorly for the defenders. Nevertheless, von Kleist did not enjoy the spectacular initial success of the other three panzer armies.

Already, just two days into Barbarossa, some Army Group South generals attempted to dilute the effects of massed panzers. Worried about Seventeenth Army's relatively slower progress around L'vov in the south, von Rundstedt received a recommendation to send XIV Panzer Corps in that direction. The corps commander, General of Infantry Gustav von Wietersheim, prevailed and the army group ordered that von Kleist's concentrated armored fist remained intact.[6] First Panzer would need all of its strength for the upcoming battle. Unfortunately, however, a dangerous precedent had been suggested: that when the going got tough somewhere else, it was permissible to split up panzer formations and deny their massed essence.

By 27 June, First Panzer had breakthroughs almost to Ostrog and Rovno, over 200km deep into Soviet territory. Kirponos assembled all the motorized forces he could and a day later had the remnants of four mechanized corps on either of von Kleist's flanks, while the 36th Rifle Corps attempted to limit any further German advance. When 13th Panzer hit these well-prepared defenses it took serious losses, especially from the massed Red artillery. The 12th and 34th Tank Divisions cut 11th Panzer's rearward communications, which were only restored by the 16th Panzer. In four days' combat, 16th Panzer destroyed 261 tanks and 11th Panzer knocked out another 150. By this time, German infantry marched onto the scene, adding a new level of complexity. Lieutenant General Robert Ritter von Greim's V Fliegerkorps provided excellent CAS, despite Red Army Air Force air superiority and the fact it had no Stukas. Barely 10km separated Kirponos' northern and southern pincers, but Soviet command and control was so poor the general did not know he stood on the brink of a noteworthy achievement. Blind to actual conditions on the battlefield, he called off the assault. Writing after the war, Zhukov described the fighting around Dubno as the worst in the Ukraine.

Thanks to Hitler's exclusion of Hungary from Barbarossa's planning and delays in Romania, during the campaign's first fortnight, Kirponos could concentrate his entire front against three German armies. First Panzer also had to compensate for the handicap of being tied to Field Marshal Walther von Reichenau, the commander of the Sixth Army, who did not perform as well as many of his contemporaries. Some historians credit Kirponos' counterattack with causing a significant delay to both von Kleist and von Rundstedt.[7] Not to deny Kirponos his due, and while chronologically true enough, this interpretation is overly simplistic, however. The interruption in First Panzer's march was temporary, while Red Army losses, especially in armored fighting vehicles (AFVs), could not be replaced during Barbarossa, and would be sorely missed days and weeks later as combat moved into the Ukrainian interior. Despite the relative skill of Kirponos when compared to the bulk of Soviet generals across the entire front, the clashes around Dubno represent a battle of annihilation of the Southwest Front's best. Von Kleist accomplished this through old-fashioned toe-to-toe combat, not encirclement. While Red Army forces in other sectors periodically halted the Germans throughout the summer and fall, the Soviets' southern theater did not regain its balance until Rostov.

Kirponos ordered one more counterattack for the last day of the month but it was too weak. Nevertheless, he believed that the Southwest Front's armored attacks had dealt von Kleist a severe blow and that he could pull away from the L'vov salient. Stavka authorized a withdrawal generally to the pre-1939 frontier, shortening the front lines in the south from 1,400 to 900km. Days earlier, von Rundstedt had considered the breakthrough phase complete, so gave First Panzer its operational freedom, thereby releasing von Kleist from Sixth Army control. His Order #2 instructed the panzer army to rush the old Soviet defenses before Kirponos could properly man them. Midway between Rovno and Novgorod-Volynskiy and just east of Ostrog, the Ostheer left Soviet-occupied Poland and crossed into the USSR. This second-named town marked the Germans' first experience with the Soviet inter-war fortifications they called the Stalin Line. Starting around 4 July, units of III Panzer took some losses here, however von Kleist's men began a small but noticeable detour toward the southeast. Another reason to avoid moving directly east was the presence of remnants from the 9th and 22nd Mechanized Corps, and most importantly, the 5th Army, lurking untouched to the northeast.[8]

Facing the Stalin Line fieldworks during the first week of July, the Panzertruppen in the lead spearheads had to make a decision: break on through or wait for the marching infantry? Logistic support had already become problematic to the point where Ju-52 aircraft had to fly fuel and ammunition to forward units. Von Kleist opted to go it alone, assaulted through the defenses and pushed east. Some units overcame the obstacles quickly, while others, such as the 14th Panzer required five days. Once they were through, Kirponos had little in the way of mobile reserves with which to dispute the panzer army's advance: the strength of his mechanized corps stood as follows: 4th – 40 percent; 9th and 19th – 30 percent; 8th and 15th – 15 percent and 22nd – 10 percent.

First Panzer Army slipped south and made for Berdichev and Zithomir without concern for its flanks. But casualties were heavy once the town came under attack: 11th Panzer suffered 2,000 dead and wounded in fighting around Berdichev, which fell on 7 July. That same day, Zhukov ordered Kirponos to send the fresh 16th Mechanized Corps (plus scraps of the 4th and 15th Mechanized) to counterattack and regain the town. Von Kleist's men were ready for them and the human-wave attacks launched by the Red Army infantry. Three days later, Zithomir fell as well.[9]

As it had at Dubno weeks earlier, the Soviets' determination to counter-attack whenever and wherever possible took its toll on the German advance. In the case of Berdichev, the defensive battle there meant von Kleist's two panzer corps in that area could not link up with the Seventeenth Army and create an encirclement battle at Vinnitsa. Only a small portion of the panzer army made it to this city and the disappointing number of Red Army assets neutralized there angered Hitler. Meanwhile, III Panzer Corps had made a straight line toward Kiev. Its orders on 9 July read: 'Occupy Kiev as a deep bridgehead east of the Dnepr as the basis of continued operations east of the river.' On the following day, 13th Panzer reached and crossed the Irpen River (to the city's west) and hung on to a small bridgehead while it waited for the rest of General of Cavalry Eberhard von Mackensen's corps (14th Panzer and 25th Motorized). The suddenness of the panzers' arrival surprised the unprepared defenders, led by Marshal SM Budenny's Commissar, NS Khrushchev. At this point, the Soviet 5th Army, basically between the Rokitno Marshes and III Panzer Corps, received orders from Kirponos to attack southward into the panzer corps' rear, near Broniki and Cheritsa. Von Mackensen's Irpen position stood at the end of a 120km-long gap between it and the Sixth Army's infantry, doing all they could to close the distance. Both of the Army group's motorized SS divisions pulled duty keeping the lengthy supply line open for nearly a week.[10]

The 25th Motorized arrived at the Irpen bridgehead on 19 July, while the Sixth Army fought its way forward to fend off 5th Army attacks along the Zithomir corridor and relieve III Panzer. The commander of the Sixth, von Reichenau, wanted to keep III Panzer in order to deal with the 5th Army more thoroughly. Both Hitler and von Rundstedt turned down this bad idea; they had bigger plans for First Panzer Army. Despite Kirponos' repeated attempts to destroy, halt or simply blunt von Kleist's advance, the panzer army would not be denied and now planned to wheel south to create Army Group South's first major encirclement. Zhukov later wrote that by being involved in so many costly frontal attacks, von Rundstedt's panzers had not been used to their full potential as operational breakthrough weapons. But on the other hand, by mid-July the Southwest Front no longer possessed any motorized forces, and henceforth relied purely on artillery and the Dnepr to defend the Ukraine.[11]

Between 5–7 July, Hitler and Halder decided to execute an encirclement battle west of the Dnepr River. Two days later, von Rundstedt received orders to create a Kessel using his panzer forces in conjunction with Seventeenth Army infantry marching generally along the southern Bug River from Vinnitsa. When III Panzer Corps halted in front of Kiev yet did not attack, Kirponos thought he had been successful. He did not understand the significance of the fact that von Kleist's men turned south once they reached their pivot point of Belaya Zerkov. By 13 July, the Southwest Front's intelligence officer, Colonel Bondarev, noticed the maneuver, but Kirponos still did not see the battle of annihilation developing. Toward the third week of July, XLVIII Panzer headed southeast directly on Uman, while XIV Panzer had extricated itself from the fighting near Fastov and covered the panzer army's left flank along the Dnepr. Von Mackensen turned the investment of Kiev over to Sixth Army and followed the other two panzer corps.[12] The earlier missed opportunity at Vinnitsa only meant another, larger one, at Uman.

First Panzer Army plunged south, leaving Kiev behind with the corps-sized Group Schwedler maintaining its rearward communications. Von Kleist had effectively split the 6th and 26th Armies: the latter drifted east and eventually over the Dnepr, while the former joined the 12th Army in a chaotic retreat from Vinnitsa (although they left behind much of their heavy equipment). Of course the panzers moved faster than the Red infantry, but the Landsers of Seventeenth Army also performed prodigious feats of marching, which put the defenders in serious jeopardy. At hill 251 just north of Uman, Soviet resistance stopped Captain Pricken's 1st Battalion, Panzer Regiment 15. Regimental commander Lieutenant Colonel Riebel pulled his panzer next to Pricken's and yelled, 'Shoot, shoot!' The captain answered, 'I only have a toy gun (Gummikanone)!' Riebel replied, 'That doesn't mean shit (Scheissegal), shoot!' The entire regiment then took hill 251, destroying thirty tanks in the process, as the commanding general, Major General Ludwig Crüwell, looked on. Kirponos ordered a counterattack by units outside the developing pocket. Accordingly, elements of the 26th Army still on the west bank of the Dnepr moved against XIV Panzer Corps near Vasilkov and Tarashcha. To meet the threat, the Germans changed facing 90 degrees from south to east. Additionally, on 21 July, 13th Panzer had to come to their rescue from the north. On the same day, the 11th Panzer Division reached the town of Uman, while 16th Panzer occupied Monastyrishche, which only 24 hours earlier had been the headquarters of Budenny's Southwestern Direction.[13]

Very heavy rain fell from 22–29 July, just when von Rundstedt's men tried to close the trap. Only tracked vehicles and native panje wagons could move: bridges were essential for crossing rivers, fording them were out of the question. The Soviets made frantic attempts to escape, predictably to the northeast through the XLVIII Panzer Corps. Until 27 July, the 16th Panzer and 16th Motorized fought for their lives near Monastyrishche against the last vestiges of the 4th Mechanized Corps and elsewhere on the XLVIII sector, the town of Novo Arckangelsk changed hands many times. On the 25th, corps commander von Wietersheim inserted the Leibstandarte between 11th and 16th Panzer Divisions, stabilizing the situation. Despite the downpours, Seventeenth Army infantry marched to the rendezvous point, now established at Pervomaisk. On 3 August, 16th Panzer crossed the 100m wooden bridge over the Bug there, linking up with the Hungarian Fast Corps, assigned to the Seventeenth Army. At Uman, Army Group South captured 103,000 POWs (including commanding generals of 6th and 12th Armies and 13th Rifle Corps) belonging to twenty-five divisions, plus 317 tanks, 858 artillery pieces and 242 anti-tank and anti-aircraft guns. But not much of the First Panzer would be there to clean up the mess. Two days later, the bulk of von Kleist's army headed east to his next objective, the great bend of the Dnepr.[14]

With only one panzer army, von Rundstedt had difficulty creating the encirclements required of the Vernichtungssclacht philosophy. In fact, as originally conceived, von Kleist would have cast his net much wider and attempted a much larger Kessel in the area of Kirovograd. However, von Brauchitsch preferred a smaller, 'safer' pocket at Uman. In view of the facts that one arm of the encirclement consisted solely of marching infantry and that the Soviets resisted so hard, this compromise solution was perhaps the best the Germans could have hoped for. Now the panzer army headed for the Ukrainian resource areas that were among Barbarossa's main objectives, plus the Dnepr crossings essential for the continuance of operations to the east. This coincided with Stavka's decision on 10 August to abandon the west bank of the mighty river. At Uman, von Rundstedt had split the Southwestern from the Southern Front, so there was not much else the Soviets could do. That same day, Army Group South issued Order #5, which laid out German plans to capture the very same ground Stalin was giving up. One bright spot in the First Panzer Army's logistic picture was the fact that German rail traffic now reached almost as far as Pervomaisk. At the end of July, von Kleist's operational rate stood at 70 to 80 percent for the 9th, 13th and 14th Panzer Divisions, but only 40 percent for the 11th and 16th Panzer. Ideally he would have taken a pause to refresh and repair his panzers, but there was no slack in Barbarossa's timetable for such a luxury.[15]

Panzerwaffe *Ethos and Attitudes*

The Third Reich excelled in psychological warfare, even against its own people. The black uniform and insignia of the fabled 5th Hussar Regiment only represented the beginning. Propaganda Minister Josef Goebbels' publicity machine furthered the ideal by prominently featuring the panzers at Nazi Party rallies and in his newsreels. Even before Poland and despite its small size, the Panzerwaffe took its place at the top of the army. As a new branch of service, it did not have the traditions of say, the infantry or even the cavalry, from which came 40 per cent of the first panzer officers. Leaders like Guderian could invent 'new' traditions, creating a 'weapon of opportunism' that would win Hitler's upcoming war.

In the blitzkrieg the old military concept of the elite, no different from that of Napoleon's Old Guard, was wedded to the internal combustion engine, the radio and airplane. Following leaders not easily scared and trained to resist fear, the panzer troopers fought inside their armored boxes, with a new-found unity of a tank crew, a variation on that basic military building block, the small group who will share any fate. This comradeship was a two-way street: from the men up and from their commanders down. The Panzerwaffe had a special code of communication based on intellect, training and language that made, in Kenneth Macksey's words, 'something apart from the rest of the German Armed Forces and superior to most opponents . . . that remains to this day almost irresistible'.

Defeating Britain and France in western Europe signaled the arrival of the military era sometimes known as the age of velocity. Panzer leaders operated within the Boyd Loop in a fraction of the time required by their enemies. Their objective was not 'command paralysis' touted by interwar British theorists: it was nothing less than the enemy's total destruction. So it was during Barbarossa; the early victories in the USSR, spearheaded by the panzer armies, have no equal in military history. By December 1941, the panzer troops had been betrayed when Germany's small size and dysfunctional strategic leadership collided with a titanic enemy under even more ruthless national rulers. Velocity became less important, and once the world-wide war turned from one based on maneuver to one based on attrition, the Third Reich could not win. Even without the benefit of hindsight, by the end of Stalingrad, most German soldiers must have seen that the war could have but one ending, not favorable for Germany. The panzer troops, like most of the Wehrmacht, somehow continued to resist like the good soldiers they were. Their loyalty to the small group – their crew – and a mystical faith in their Führer kept them fighting.

Following Uman, First Panzer spread out across the entire lower Dnepr, losing all cohesion and mass; there were simply too many assigned tasks for its relatively small size. Reinforcement by the Hungarians (three brigades totaling 24,000 men supported by 81 indigenous 'Toldi' tanks) and the Italian

Expeditionary Corps in Russia (CISR: 62,000 men in three divisions with one battalion of L6/40 light tanks), hardly compensated for its expansive area of responsibility. Luftflotte Four commander, General Alexander Lohr, divided his force into two groups, with 'Close Combat Leader South' supporting von Kleist with I/StG 77, II/JG 3 and III/JG 52. III Panzer reached Kremenchug during the first week of August (13th and 14th Panzer), and Dnepropetrovsk the next week (SS Viking). Von Mackensen was to gain bridgeheads across the Dnepr and hold them until Seventeenth Army units arrived. Close to the end of the month, 9th Panzer Division captured an intact bridge at Zaporozhe. XIV Panzer's objective was the resource-rich area near Krivoi Rog, which it captured on 14 August with most of its industrial capacity intact. After freeing itself from Uman, XLVIII Panzer's 16th Panzer Division (only 23 of 140 panzers operational) headed for the port city of Nikolaev. Once it arrived to take possession of the empty city on the 18th, the position of Red Army units facing the Eleventh Army and the Romanians became untenable. At the far southeastern extent of the panzer army, SS Leibstandarte reached Kherson at the mouth of the Dnepr on 20 August. One might assume that denying the Soviets any opportunity to cross the massive river would lead directly to another battle of annihilation, but von Rundstedt could not make the necessary blocking positions. Despite Fliegerkorps V achieving forty-two hits on Dnepr bridges, the Soviets repaired the damage quickly and continued their retreat eastward. Combined with a rare example of Stalin permitting a common-sense withdrawal, Hitler's insistence on occupying locales such as Nikolaev (instead of clearing the Dnepr bend) meant that many enemy formations escaped destruction. These Ukranian cities were going to fall to the Germans anyway, so eschewing maneuvers that would lead to annihilation can only be explained for reasons of short-sighted prestige, not long-term military logic. Additionally, von Kleist's dispersal, plus his low fuel and ammunition stocks, all conspired to deprive First Panzer Army's post-Uman pursuit of much of its effect. In any event, as Field Marshal Friedrich Paulus later wrote, securing Kiev and the Dnepr crossings 'proved to be very prolonged and costly'.[16]

By the end of August, Army Group South had closed up the Dnepr along its entire length, except for the Irpen position occupied by Sixth Army west of Kiev. Although many Red Army forces had escaped, the Battle of the Dnepr bend netted another 90,000 POWs, 481 guns and 206 tanks – a smaller version of Uman. Believing a fighting withdrawal through the western Ukraine had only resulted in disaster at Uman, Stalin resolved to hold on to eastern Ukraine. On 5 August, he replaced Zhukov as Red Army Chief of Staff for pointing out the inherent weakness of the Kiev position. Sensing which way the wind blew, three days later Kirponos told the generalissimo he could hold the city. Now the Battle of the Dnepr bridgeheads began.[17]

The first German bridgehead did not last long. On 19 August, 9th Panzer won a foothold across the river at Zaporozhe, only to lose it to a Soviet counter-attack. Then it was the turn of 13th Panzer. Early in August, it had attempted to capture bridges between Kremenchug and Krujkow, only to find them in ruins. The next crossing downstream was Dnepropetrovsk, an industrial city of half a million, defended by three rifle divisions. After three days of fighting through three successive defensive lines, the division entered the city on the morning of 25 August, and it was in German hands by nightfall. Retreating Soviets had destroyed two of the city's bridges, but the 13th Panzer managed to cross the third, artillery damaged, 1,400m-long floating bridge and establish a presence on the east bank. A day later, 60th Motorized joined it there, and within a week SS Viking and 198th Infantry Divisions also occupied the bridgehead. Red artillery and CAS pounded von Mackensen's men from three sides. The Luftwaffe saved the day and the situation stabilized, although life in the exposed salient remained very dangerous.[18] German bridgeheads over the Dnepr were essential for the next phase of Barbarossa.

While the army group chief of staff anticipated an upcoming battle at Poltava, the German high command had bigger plans. By the end of August, Hitler had finally prevailed over his generals and committed the Ostheer to a massive battle of annihilation around Kiev. Guderian's Second Panzer Army would be coming south following the successful completion of the Battle of Smolensk. Von Kleist would keep up Army Group South's end of the bargain by attacking northward from the Dnepr. Von Rundstedt preferred to launch his assault from somewhere closer to Kiev than Dnepropetrovsk. With that in mind he ordered Seventeenth Army to create bridgeheads near Kremenchug. The Seventeenth actually created two, one at the city proper (31 August–2 September) and another nearby at Derievka (29 August–4 September) and either repaired or built bridges at each. Immediately, the Germans reinforced, and the Soviets attacked them. The skies above all the bridgeheads were full of aircraft of both sides. Responsible for the defense of the Dnepr was the 38th Army, guarding 200km with 7 rifle divisions made up of 40,000 men. To take heat off the Dnepropetrovsk and Kremenchug sites, von Rundstedt ordered a decoy attack upstream at Cherkassy. This move alarmed Budenny, who began to organize a counterattack. While he was doing this, von Kleist turned over significant portions of the Dnepropetrovsk defense to infantry, and by 10 September had quickly shifted much of First Panzer up to Kremenchug. On the 12th, von Kleist's panzers came flying out of Kremenchug.[19] The Battle of Kiev had begun in earnest.

Budenny saw these developments right in front of his eyes. He argued with the Red Army's new Chief of Staff, Marshal BM Shaposhnikov and requested permission to withdraw to the Psel River. To this, Stalin had the following reactions on 11 September: order Kirponos to stand fast and relieve Budenny. Marshal SM Timoshenko took the old cavalryman's place with only a couple of hours before the assault to prepare. Rain fell hard those days, and von Kleist only had 331 panzers (53 percent of what he had on Barbarossatag) in Kremenchug with which to attack, but it would not be a fair fight. The 297th Rifle Division took the worst of it on the 11th, and since all Soviet reserves were arrayed against Guderian, very few faced von Kleist. After crossing the Dnepr at night and following preparatory fire by artillery and Nebelewerfer, the XLVIII Panzer Corps took the lead. On 12 September, with 16th Panzer on the left, 9th on the right and 14th right behind, they covered 70km. The 2nd Battalion, Panzer Regiment 2, captured the 38th Army headquarters and commander Major General NV Feklenko escaped only by jumping out of a window. The Luftwaffe contributed with its Fliegerkorps V and the II Flak Corps. On 14 September, Shaposhnikov instructed Kirponos, 'You must fulfill comrade Stalin's order of 11 September', in other words, the Southwest Front must stand and die. Fanatical resistance in Lubny by NKVD troops did their part to slow XLVIII Panzer Corps. On the next day, 15 September, with 16th Panzer leading the way as it often did, First Panzer Army fought its way into Lokhvitsa and a rendezvous with Guderian coming down from the north. Only on the 18th, 72 hours after it was too late, did Stalin's written permission to retreat from Kiev arrive. With his staff, trying to escape history's greatest encirclement battle, Kirponos died a hero's death southwest of Lokhvitsa.[20] With the invaluable assistance of the Second, Sixth and Seventeenth Armies, von Kleist and Guderian had encircled two-thirds of a million Red Army soldiers and killed and wounded hundreds of thousands more in a trap the size of Belgium. For the first and only time in the Nazi-Soviet War the Ostheer outnumbered the Soviets on the battlefield.

The final attack on Moscow, which the Soviets had been expecting for nearly two months after the Battle of Smolensk, and which most German generals had been anticipating for nearly a year, began with Operation Typhoon. Von Kleist promptly lost XLVIII Panzer Corps to Guderian. Von Rundstedt considered First Panzer Army to be so broken that he requested OKH limit its movement to no farther than the Don River. Halder replied in the negative, that future operations required bridgeheads east of the river. The field marshal asked OKH to clarify its priorities: either the Crimea or the Don River crossings? Hitler's answer was typical: he wanted both. Von Kleist received his new mission,

Rostov. The Soviets had not been idle after Kiev either, and their defenses south of Dnepropetrovsk demanded significant German efforts to overcome.[21]

With his panzer army weakened by the loss of the panzer corps and concentrated on a narrow breakthrough front, von Rundstedt's infantry armies, Sixth, Eleventh and Seventeenth, assumed ever lengthier portions of the front line. While von Kleist was otherwise occupied executing the Kiev Kessel, the 9th and 18th Armies combined to attack Eleventh Army between its Berislav bridgehead and Melitopol. Von Manstein, Eleventh's new commanding general, managed the immediate crisis about the time First Panzer had reassembled in the Dnepropetrovsk bridgehead preparatory to continuing eastward. Von Rundstedt saw an opportunity to entrap more Soviet armies so redirected von Kleist to the southeast. He sent XIV Panzer out of the Petrikovka bridgehead held by the CSIR while III Panzer broke out of Dnepropetrovsk proper. Coming down the Dnepr, First Panzer took Zaporozhe from the east on 1 October, by which time the danger to the rear of 9th and 18th Armies became apparent to the Soviet high command. On the next day therefore, they tried to disengage from von Manstein's men but it was too late. The SS Leibstandarte had already penetrated between the two Soviet armies and was racing toward a rendezvous with von Kleist. With XIV Panzer on the right, III Panzer in the center and CSIR covering the left flank, First Panzer had all the advantages. Two fighter and one Stuka Gruppe flew CAS overhead. On 7 October, near Osipenko, his forces linked up with the Leibstandarte, ending the Battle of the Sea of Azov and closing the trap on 106,000 more POWs, 766 guns and 212 tanks. Lieutenant General AK Smirnov, commanding 18th Army, fell in combat and the Germans buried him with honors.[22] To von Rundstedt, it seemed that the way to the Donbas and Rostov lay wide open.

At this point, weather and logistics conspired to slow the panzer army and give the defenders a much-needed breather. Between 6–11 October, heavy rains and cold delayed the Germans. Then, even before the Sea of Azov battle had concluded, logistics began to hamstring Barbarossa again. The closest railhead remained at Pervomaisk, but many Dnepr bridges were down and various river ferries were not an adequate substitute for a functioning railroad. Foraging parties of the 125th Infantry Division called themselves 'Rindvieh Abteilung 125' (Cattle Detachment 125). In order to keep von Kleist advancing, army group consolidated what trucks it had and dedicated them to First Panzer. All other units came to a stop and lived off the land. Red Army forces were 'fighting without any enthusiasm and running away', yet the Germans could not exploit this situation. The fuel shortage grounded the Luftwaffe as well, so only single-engine aircraft could fly. By 11 October, III Panzer had made it as far as Taganrog on the Mius River. Two days later, even the panzer army ground to a halt. On the 17th, as 13th and 14th Panzer Divisions reached the Sambek River, north of Rostov, the panzer army described the supply situation as 'catastrophic.' Finally, three days later, III Panzer received some fuel and could begin to inch eastward. By 22 October, 13th Panzer reached the Tuzlov River, north of Rostov. But the damage had been done, First Panzer and the rest of Army Group South were too spread out and the Soviets had used the pause to improve their defenses.[23] The weaknesses of the Wehrmacht's serendipitous logistics planning had come home to roost: foraging and 'living off the land' will only take a modern army so far.

During the fuel crisis, the marching and horse-drawn elements of First Panzer moved as fast as the motorized. In many cases, 'pursuit detachments' consisted of Landsers using panje carts. Von Kleist had received the CSIR as partial compensation for the loss of XLVIII Panzer, and the latter was assigned the twin missions of maintaining contact with Seventeenth Army to the north and of capturing Stalino. Divisions Celere and Pasubio led the way, with Torino bringing up the rear as usual. Alongside marched XLIX Mountain Corps, one of the fastest leg-infantry outfits in the Ostheer. On 18 October, von Kleist ordered the assault on Stalino for the 20th. The attack went off after some delays and the city fell by the end of the month. Months' supplies of diesel fuel were captured. However, keeping communications with Seventeenth Army proved to be a much more difficult matter. The Italians attacked northeast and took Gorlovka on 2 November, but the Seventeenth remained dozens of kilometers away. Simultaneously, on the panzer army's southern flank wet weather and resistance by the 9th Army slowed III and XIV Panzer Corps after some initial gains a few days earlier. Von Kleist lost most of his air support on 12 November, when Kampfgeschwader (KG) 54 and most of KG 55 left the Russian theater for Belgium.[24]

On 3 November, von Brauchitsch visited Army Group South headquarters in order to 'knock the lead out of' von Rundstedt's command. The logistic situation was extremely dire, the first rail traffic over the Dnepr was still days in the future. Von Kleist's men did receive some aerial resupply into the airfields of Mariupol and Taganrog. In the words of a III Panzer Corps soldier, German troops simply wanted some food and to hear their own artillery for a change. The Army Commander in Chief told his astonished audience that the high command still expected First Panzer to take the Maikop oil region 'at all costs this winter'. By the 13th, the first frost hit the southern theater, making the roads useable but at a cost of hard-to-start engines and cold men (temperatures were −22° C). Von Kleist planned his assault on Rostov for 17 November. Using a 'grand tour' maneuver, he would swing in a wide counter-clockwise arc and take the city from the north and northeast. The III Panzer Corps

(13th and 14th Panzer, 60th Motorized, Leibstandarte) would play the role of Schwerpunkt on the inside track, while XIV Panzer (16th Panzer, SS Viking, Slovakian Motorized Division) covered von Mackensen's left on the outside track.[25]

First Panzer's last attack of Barbarossa began with the usual spectacular success. Under CAS offered by KG 27 and Stukageschwader (StG) 77, it broke through the 56th Independent Army with minimal delay. Prepared defenses and 100 tanks at Bolshoy Sala could not hold the 14th Panzer, von Mackensen's vanguard. As he had also long planned, Timoshenko coincidentally began his own counterattack on the 17th, mainly hitting SS Viking. His 37th Army had only mass in his favor: thousands of drunken frontovicki (front-line soldiers) without training or heavy weapons and no CAS of their own. The Soviet attack petered out by the 19th. Not so with First Panzer, which kept advancing on the 'gateway to the Caucasus'. The final lunge by III Panzer began at 0600 hours, 20 November, when it crossed the Sultan Saly River, just northeast of Rostov. With 14th Panzer and Leibstandarte in the lead, the Germans captured the airport by 1230 hours and the city center by that afternoon. By Barbarossa's standards, men and booty captured represented a paltry amount. However, the entire German chain of command, from Hitler to von Mackensen was excited to have cut Soviet communications with the south. On that same day, the OKH issued another nonsensical order to von Kleist: move on Maikop immediately.[26]

Literally and figuratively, the First Panzer Army dangled at the end of a long tether. Its dangerously exposed spearhead in Rostov anticipated that at Stalingrad, almost to the day a year into the future, complete with shaky Hungarians and Italians guarding its flank. Timoshenko had been planning to resume his counteroffensive and on 22 November, Stalin told him that the German occupation of Rostov had altered nothing: the attack would go off as scheduled. Von Kleist's advance into the city had exaggerated German vulnerabilities present the last time Timoshenko attacked, just days earlier. Now, however, the panzer army was even more dispersed and the gap to Seventeenth Army even larger. Sensing his vulnerability, on the same day Stalin told his marshal to attack, von Kleist planned to evacuate Rostov in favor of the better defensive terrain in the Mius River valley. Prodded by von Brauchitsch, on the 23rd, von Rundstedt countermanded that idea. On 25 November, the first Soviet attacks hit Leibstandarte.[27]

The deluge came two days later when Timoshenko struck the Rostov salient with 21 divisions. His 56th Army led the way, soon followed by the 9th, 37th and 18th Armies. Perhaps hardest hit was 1st SS, holding both ends of the Don River bridge. Linked arm-in-arm and screaming 'Urrah!', they crossed the frozen river. The SS lines were so depleted, 'even the heaviest of Soviet bombardments were negligible ... so thin were the troops on the ground'. Dozens of T-34s accompanied the Red infantry, disregarding the anti-tank mines the Germans had laid on the ice. Initially, von Kleist believed his men could hold their positions, and Hitler concurred. But after one day, 56th and 9th Army units plus members of the Rostov militia cleared the city of the invader. Von Kleist ordered a retreat to the Kolmytskaya River. A day later, 30 November, he had given up even that half measure and ordered First Panzer back to the Mius as he had anticipated over a week earlier. At 2000 hours that night, when informed of the decision, Hitler countermanded that order and told von Kleist to remain at his present positions along the Maksimovsky–Merzhanovsky line 'for the time being'. Keitel explained, in any event it was essential to retain the good airfields in and around Taganrog. Three hours later, OKH instructed Army Group South to reinforce the panzer army. 'With what?' von Rundstedt asked, explaining that no 'intermediate position' existed between Rostov and the Mius. Hitler merely assumed the field marshal refused to obey orders. Having received no satisfaction, therefore 'the grumbling, growling bear of a Junker from Courland' asked to be relieved. Shortly after midnight, the Führer accepted, and by 0550 hours assigned von Reichenau the new duty of army group commander in addition to his current job at the head of Sixth Army. Hitler reiterated his demand that First Panzer stop and fight along the Maksimovsky–Merzhanovsky Line. Von Reichenau said that was out of the question and Hitler relented. Luftwaffe attacks kept the Red Army from pursuing too closely. On 2 December, Hitler took the highly unusual step and flew to First Panzer Army headquarters to meet with von Reichenau, von Kleist, the chief of staff of Luftflotte Four and his old Nazi crony, Leibstandarte commander Sepp Dietrich. It was the last named whose testimony affected the Führer most. Although he owed his position to Nazi Party politics, Dietrich stood up for von Rundstedt, von Kleist and von Mackensen, saying that the three old-style generals had done everything humanly possible given the un-workable situation at Rostov. The dictator finally got the clue. On his way back to Rastenburg the next day, he stopped at Poltava and gave von Rundstedt the closest thing to an apology any German general would receive during the war.[28]

First Panzer Army had performed as a true operational weapon during Barbarossa. Initially hamstrung by the fact it was not paired with another panzer army, von Rundstedt compensated by using the fast-moving Seventeenth Army. During a two-week period in the middle of September it both unhinged the Red Army's main Dnepr defensive line and closed off the southern half of the Kiev pocket. By adroitly wheeling to the Sea of Azov, it kept the Soviets' entire southern defensive structure on its heels. Von Kleist had little option other than to follow unrealistic orders and keep driving on to Rostov. Barbarossa culminated for Army Group South at that point, and along with it, so did First Panzer Army's operational maneuvering.

The Mius River valley served as a dividing line numerous times during the sea-saw battles that raged across the eastern Ukraine from 1941 to 1943. During the winter of 1941–42, it was a good enough position for the two exhausted armies and they shared little of the aggressive excitement common with the rest of the theater. Both sides settled down to defenses anchored by strongpoints in small villages, and harassed each other with patrols and artillery fire. Small groups of soldiers took turns going to the old tsarist palace at Taganrog for a few days of rest and relaxation in the land of electricity and plumbing. A 125th Infantry Division soldier remembered Christmas Eve as experienced by troops in the field:

> Suddenly the door [to their shelter] was thrown open and a runner stuck his head in and yelled, 'Two men from every group to the field kitchen now to pick up mail!' You can bet that any one of us would carry that little bit of mail for us all. But about ten men went. And when they returned each dragged in a sack, an entire sack full of mail! Man oh man, we'd never received such mail before! After it was distributed, each of us had a small pile. Now it was really Christmas! A few furtive tears ran down the hollow, unshaven cheeks.[29]

On Christmas Day, officers and first sergeants (Spiess) pulled guard duty on the front-line outposts so their men could celebrate a bit. The Soviets remained quiet that day. At this relatively early point in the war, the Wehrmacht had evidently begun to scour all of occupied Europe for manpower replacements: in the 100th Light Division's area alone, Croatian and Wallonian battalions helped man the line.[30]

Further north, in mid-January, Timoshenko concluded he could threaten the lines of communication for both First Panzer and Seventeenth Armies by attacking southwest from the Izyum bridgehead over the Don River. For about ten days the Soviets threatened the stability of Army Group South. Claiming Hoth's staff suffered from overwork during the crisis, new army group commander von Bock placed 'the very enterprising' von Kleist in charge of both formations. Presumably his thinking was that in this case, First Panzer would ride to the rescue of the Landsers all the more quickly. This is indeed what happened as Group von Mackensen (14th Panzer, 113th and 298th Infantry, 100th Light and 1st Romanian Divisions plus the 60th Panzer Battalion, all under control of Headquarters, III Panzer Corps) moved out on

2 February in the direction of Barvenko. A number of ad hoc combat groups, generally of regimental size, also participated in the counterattack. Progress was measured in a few kilometers, and a single Sturmgeschutz, or self-propelled PAK, made the difference between success and failure. Heavy fighting developed around Barvenko and Slavyansk until the second half of the month. Von Bock threw in additional units, including an Italian division. Only in early March, when the 1st and 5th Cavalry Corps had been separated from its tank support did the Soviets' pressure on the German lines subside.[31]

The spring rasputitsa brought further offensive maneuver on both sides to a temporary halt. Hitler continued thinking about natural resources in the southern USSR as he had the year before with Operation Barbarossa. In 1942, he would continue the drive toward the Caucasus and Baku on the Caspian Sea, at that time, location of some of the world's largest known oil fields. As outlined in Führer Directive 41, dated 5 April, the first step would be encirclement and destruction of Red Army forces defending the southern theater, in what became known as Operations Blau I and II. He envisioned a Vernichtungsschlacht 'similar to the double envelopment at Viazma and Bryansk'. Afterwards, Blau III would secure Stalingrad and Don River crossings, with the final objective, the Caucasus, belonging to Blau IV. Across the front, Stalin labored under the false impression that the Ostheer would once again try to capture Moscow, so arranged his defenses accordingly. A German deception plan, Operation Kremlin, reinforced this notion (see p. 85). A major difference in the methods the Soviets would use in 1942 compared to 1941, was the Red Army would not 'die in place' as it had during Barbarossa. Their planned withdrawal wreaked havoc with the Vernichtungsgeschlacht doctrine and added another layer of tension to the later campaign.[32]

Fighting was not over in the Izyum bulge, however. As von Bock began to assemble troops for Blau, on 12 May, Timoshenko burst out of Izyum and into the Sixth Army in what is often called the Second Battle of Kharkov. The Sixth lost sixteen battalions in 17 hours. Timoshenko had pre-empted an Army Group South attack, planned to start in just six days. Unfortunately for the Soviets, the location of von Bock's troops was tailormade for a counterattack, as Hitler, von Bock and von Kleist all agreed. For his part, the panzer leader, still commanding the Seventeenth Army as part of Armeegruppe von Kleist, contributed the III Panzer and XLIV Corps. First Panzer attacked at 0315 hours on 17 May, under heavy Luftflotte Four CAS. It tore into the 9th Army on the Timoshenko's southern flank and soon created a 60km gap. The Soviet spearhead had been separated from its base and in vain the Red Army Chief of Staff asked Stalin for permission to abandon the offensive. Within a week, von Kleist's men had reconquered the familiar ground on either side of Barvenko, and by 22 May continued to Balakleya, where 14th Panzer made a rendezvous with Sixth Army units. Attacking into the teeth of German forces preparing for Blau could have hardly been any worse for the Soviets, who in 10 days lost about 27 divisions and 14 tank brigades destroyed and 240,000 men, 1,200 tanks and 2,600 artillery pieces captured. The Red Army nevertheless maintained a large salient east of Kharkov, and Hitler saw a chance to kill off some more of the enemy and tidy up the Operation Blau start line all at the same time.[33]

The Führer had to wait for von Manstein to capture the Crimea anyway, so in mid-June he launched two assaults. The common feature of both was the leading role played by III Panzer Corps, at times 14th, 16th and 22nd Panzer plus 60th Motorized Divisions. From 10–15 June, as Sixth Army eliminated the northern bulge southeast of Volchansk, it participated in Operation Wilhelm. A week later, now as part of First Panzer, von Mackensen's men had turned 90 degrees from east to south and attacked toward Kupyansk. Von Kleist's objective was trapping the 9th and 38th Armies between III Panzer (with the temporary addition of 44th Infantry) and XLIV Corps. After numerous delays due to bad weather, Operation Fridericus II began on the first anniversary of Barbarossa. By the evening, the 16th Panzer had almost reached Kupyansk, while 22nd Panzer, followed by 14th Panzer and 60th Motorized, turned south toward XLIV Corps. At the same time, against tough Soviet defense, the infantry corps levered a bridgehead over the Donets, east of Izyum. Soon the LI and XI Corps joined the action, creating a crescent of Germans pressing the salient from three sides. After two days the 101st Jäger Division coming up from the north met 22nd Panzer near Gorokhovatka. Inside the trap were a further 22,800 POWs and about 100 tanks and 250 guns. In his diary, von Bock wrote about a troubling trend, quite unlike 1941: for the last two months the Soviets retreated instead of allowing themselves to be encircled in great numbers. This would bode ill for Operation Blau.[34]

Only in the most limited sense of the term can one say First Panzer Army functioned as an operational weapon during that winter and spring. Von Kleist improvised defense and counterattack as part of Army Group South's overall defensive scheme. A greater test for operational maneuver lay ahead that summer.

Blau I began on 28 June when Hoth's Fourth Panzer attacked toward Voronezh. As planned, after Hoth turned south to roll up the Soviet defenses, Blau II, including First Panzer, would start. Along with Sixth Army, the two panzer armies were to inaugurate the 1942 campaign with a massive Barbarossa-style Vernichtungsschlacht. But as just mentioned, the Soviets had demonstrated during the spring that they had no intention of repeating the mistakes of 1941.

When, during Blau I, Red Army forces pulled back almost as soon as the Germans attacked, Hitler decided to pull the trigger on Blau II two weeks early.[35] Ready or not, von Kleist had to move out if the Germans hoped to annihilate the enemy's main armies, considered to be an essential prerequisite of a successful campaign against Stalingrad and the Caucasus oil region.

What can be called Blau II (because barely a week after its start, the Germans were having a terrible time adjusting to the realities of the campaign) began on 9 July when the newly activated Army Group A initiated its offensive with First Panzer Army. Strangely, von Kleist led off with his infantry since his panzers, still recuperating from Fridericus, had not left their assembly areas 50–60km behind the fighting. He would launch a right hook through Lisichansk and Starobelsk to Vysochanovka, where he was to meet Hoth and complete the giant Kessel. It took less than 24 hours for the first change of plans: the new rendezvous point with Fourth Panzer would be Milerovo. On von Kleist's right, Seventeenth Army also advanced, with the Soviets also withdrawing.[36]

Again, 'Group von Mackensen' represented First Panzer's main striking force, made up of III Panzer (14th, 16th and 22nd Panzer plus 60th Motorized Divisions) and LI Corps (44th, 62nd, 71st, 297th and 384th Infantry). By the 10th, they had closed on the Donets River, only to find that the retreating Soviets had demolished all the bridges. The 1st Mountain (XI Corps) managed a crossing, however, and on that same day 76th Infantry occupied Lisichansk, while the two panzer divisions forced their own bridgeheads. Two days into the campaign the Germans had crossed the Aydar River and their movement resembled a pursuit. The 14th and 22nd Panzer outpaced the marching 1st Mountain to the extent that the latter became the panzer army reserve. Unfortunately for the Germans, the Ostheer's Achilles heel flared up again: by 13 July the high command could neither agree on strategic objectives nor on how to achieve goals it did have. Adding greatly to the complications, on that day Hitler relieved von Bock and reorganized his southern flank again.[37]

Evidently, in the nine months since Viazma and Bryansk, the Wehrmacht had forgotten how to conduct a Vernichtungsschalcht. Of course, Stalin no longer cooperated, either. On 15 July, von Kleist's 14th Panzer met Hoth's 3rd Panzer near Millerovo, thereby trapping elements of the 9th and 38th Armies. In view of the high expectations for Blau, however, this was a weak performance. By mid-July, the area around Millerovo became home to one of the world's largest concentrations of armor, belonging to First and Fourth Panzer and Sixth Armies. It had no enemy to attack and no where to go. Von Kleist was at a serious disadvantage, due to casualties and wear and tear caused by action in Operations Wilhelm and Fridericus. Unable to complete refitting after these offensives due to the rushed start, First Panzer began Blau II with a 40 percent operational rate, but had lost a quarter of that value in the ensuing week of maneuver. The German propensity for logistics on a shoestring, a fatal weakness of Barbarossa, would soon cripple Blau as well. New orders also flowed from Führer Headquarters, in the form of instructions issued late on the night of 13 July to Field Marshal Wilhelm List's massively reinforced Army Group A to attack Rostov. While Sixth Army stood guard along the middle Don, Fourth Panzer joined First Panzer and Seventeenth Armies on a drive due south. Army Groups A and B had come up empty-handed when the Millerovo option failed. Now, based on more faulty military intelligence from Fremde Herre Ost (FHO – Foreign Armies East), Hitler looked to Rostov for another huge enemy concentration to annihilate.[38] He was to be severely disappointed, with fatal consequences for Blau.

Von Kleist's men had not been idle during these high-level machinations, they merely changed azimuth with each succeeding order. With 14th and 22nd Panzer Divisions leading across the steppe like two great racehorses, III Panzer described a 180 degree clockwise arc, heading northeast on 9 July and southwest two weeks later. Covering the left wing was XL Panzer. Considering the arid terrain, von Mackensen's men had to cross a surprising number of rivers. Retreating Soviets had been very diligent in demolishing most bridges. Naturally, in view of the need to keep combat power well forward and with the severe fuel shortage (German logistic woes did not improve with distance), bulky bridging equipment often seemed to be at the back of the column. In quick succession, the III Panzer crossed the Derkal (12 July), the Glubokaya (14th), the Donets – again (15th), the Kundryuchya (19–20th) and the Tuzlov (21st). Right until the gates of Rostov the fighting was light. After a time-wasting reorganization, and against non-existent resistance, Seventeenth Army approached the city via the direct route, over the same ground used by von Kleist the previous November. These Landsers, along with von Kleist's 22nd Panzer, entered the outskirts of Rostov on 23 July. The XLIX Mountain Corps joined the fight on the 24th, but despite the efforts of determined NKVD units, again the Red Army eschewed a serious defense of a hopeless location. Portions of the 12th and 18th Armies had been trapped north of Rostov, but this was certainly not the Kessel on a Barbarossa scale that the Germans hoped for. First Panzer's POW haul for the first four weeks was negligible: 83,000 after a 300km tour of the steppe. As happened at Millerovo ten days earlier, Rostov also witnessed a massive concentration of fuel-starved panzers, waiting for orders.[39]

Hitler issued Directive 45 on the same day Rostov fell. Blau was long forgotten and the directive introduced Operation Braunschweig. As it applied to von Kleist, the typically unclear directive ordered an assault on Maikop. Army

Group A translated Directive 45 into its own Operation Edelweiss. List's order saw a three-phase operation: first, an encirclement of Red Army forces south and southeast of Rostov, to be closed by First Panzer and Seventeenth Armies near Tikhoretsk, 120km from the city; second, an advance on Maikop and Armavir, and; third, occupying the mountain passes of the Caucasus and oil-rich Baku. At least Army Group A had better logistical arrangements than B did. On 27 July, while consulting with von Kleist and Hoth at the latter's command post, List began to tweak his own plan and that of Hitler as well. He had huge distances to cover over daunting terrain, only 400 panzers, little air support, too few mountain divisions and other problems. All indications pointed to continued Soviet retreats so the three generals decided among themselves to ignore the intermediate objective of Tikhoretsk (to the southwest), and instead move south-southeast.[40]

For Edelweiss, von Kleist commanded the following: XLIV Corps (97th and 101st Jäger Divisions), III Panzer (13th Panzer and 16th Motorized), LII Corps (370th and 111th Infantry) and LVII Panzer (SS Viking and the Slovakian Motorized), and after 30 July, XL Panzer (3rd and 23rd Panzer). They moved out on a 150km-wide front on 26 July. On the 27th, lead elements crossed the Manich River, considered by many to be the boundary between Europe and Asia. Upstream, the Soviets demolished dams that held back large reservoirs, flooding the valley and increasing the width of the river a hundredfold, from 40m to 4km. It would be three days until the 60th Motorized crossed the river to reinforce the small bridgehead. The terrain, the 40° C weather and ever-present logistic problems were all that held First Panzer back; the Red Army offered virtually no resistance. With von Kleist halfway to the Kuban River, List officially asked OKH to cancel the planned maneuver to Tikhoretsk. The idea of a Kessel had been overcome by events, but von Kleist continued to veer southwest – to help trap Budenny's North Caucasus Front along the Black Sea coast, rather than toward the oil to the southeast. As had been the case prior to the capture of Rostov, von Mackensen conducted a series of almost unopposed river crossings: Yegorlyk (1 August), Kuban (5th), Laba (8th) and finally Byelaya (10th). General of Panzer Troops Friedrich von Kirchner's LVII Panzer took a parallel course, some 50km to the west, but also converging on Maikop. The XLIV Corps stood between III and XL Panzer corps, eventually moving up the upper Kuban valley. The XL Panzer aimed for Pyatigorsk, while LII Corps covered First Panzer's far eastern flank, reaching Elitsa and beyond. Once across the Byelaya River, 13th Panzer stormed Maikop on 13 August, aided by Stukas and Brandenburgers. But the heavily wooded foothills of the Caucasus beyond the city were no place for a panzer army and therefore Seventeenth Army infantry began relieving the panzers. Von Kleist turned east once again.[41]

Although First Panzer had scattered the 18th, 12th, 37th, 51st and 56th Armies before it, von Kleist could not create the desired Vernichtungsschlacht. He had lost the relatively light Grossdeutschland (an asset in the steppe) because of Hitler's concern over an Allied invasion in the west (the Dieppe raid was only days in the future). By early August, German overconfidence told them the battle for the Caucasus was over and so the Schwerpunkt switched to Army Group B, now approaching Stalingrad. As of 18 August, the Seventeenth Army had responsibility for the Black Sea coast, while First Panzer aimed for Baku, via Grozny. The 1,300km distance from Rostov to Baku was equivalent to that from the German–Soviet frontier to Rostov, and von Kleist was down to two corps: III and XL Panzer. As had been the case for nearly two years, German staffers did not allow such reality to intrude on their planning. Meanwhile, across the front lines, on 28 July, Stalin issued his famous Order #227, with its well-known injunction, 'Ni shagu nazad!' ('Not one step back!'). Therefore, near the Kuban River, Soviet forces had finally stopped retreating and faced about to offer resistance for the first time during the summer. A week later, Tyulenov announced to the Red Army chief of staff that his Trans-Caucasus Front would defend along the Terek River, with which Stavka concurred.[42]

By 16 August, von Kleist reoriented his forces on Voroshilovsk and began heading southeast toward the Kuma River. Two days later, despite the ever-present fuel shortages, they had levered Maslennnikov's Northern Group out of those positions. From then on, movement came in lunges as fuel shipments arrived. Around the 24th, what was left of III Panzer reached the Terek at Isherskaya, while XL Panzer did the same at Mozdok, 40km west. Tyulenev rushed to reinforce the already formidable river, 300m of white-water rapids, well covered by defensive fire. Except for distance, itself a considerable obstacle to von Kleist, the Terek represented Tyulenev's last natural barrier west of Grozny. Help for the defenders came from an unexpected source: the German high command. By mid-August First Panzer lost the 22nd Panzer, the three divisions of the Italian Alpine Corps, Flak and Nebelwerfer units, and perhaps most importantly, almost all support from Luftflotte Four. On 22 August, it additionally lost the 16th Motorized, sent by Hitler on a fool's errand to Elitsa.[43]

Despite being desperately short on fuel, III Panzer moved nearly 100km west to the vicinity of Maisky, near the confluence of the Terek and Malka Rivers. With the addition of the Romanian 2nd Mountain Division, reinforced by some German Jägers, and weakened elements of the 23rd Panzer, von

Mackensen anchored his line on the Caucasus foothills to the southwest. With his right flank thus secure, on 2 September, 3rd Panzer Division and some Brandenburger commandos of XL Panzer finally had a bridgehead over the Terek at Mozdok on the panzer army's left. On the 18th, LII Corps, relieved of guard duty at Elitsa and now manning the center, gave a nudge against the Soviet lines only to have them cave in completely; for over a week von Kleist's men pursued the retreating defenders. The trusty 13th Panzer, the newly arrived SS Viking and even the 111th Infantry Division gobbled up ground like the glory days of July. Unfortunately for von Kleist, Viking could get no further than Malgobek by 26 September, while 13th Panzer stalled at Elkhotovo on 3 October.[44]

On 25 October, First Panzer began one last push, one assumed to carry it past Ordzhonikidze and on to Grozny. As before, the Romanian 2nd Mountain Division (again reinforced by 1st Battalion, Mountain Jäger Regiment 99) initiated the attack, coming from the direction of Baksan. Heavily supported by the Luftwaffe, they managed to destroy the command post of the 37th Army, leaving the defenders figuratively headless. The main attack began the next day, with 13th Panzer to the right and 23rd Panzer to the left. The Romanians captured Nalchik the day after that and the two panzer divisions swung left toward Ordzhonikidze. On 1 November, 23rd Panzer took Alagir, the northern terminus of the Ossetian Military Road, while its sister division pushed on against the still disorganized defenders. The 13th Panzer took Gizel, less than 10km from Ordzhonikidze, the capital of the Caucasus region and more importantly from a strategic standpoint, where the Grusinian Military Road exited the mountains. If the Germans blocked both military roads, over which much of the logistic support for the entire Soviet southern theater flowed, the impact would be tremendous. At this point the heavily reinforced defenses stiffened. Under massive Luftwaffe CAS, von Mackensen shifted his Schwerpunkt left, right, left to find a weak spot upon which to capitalize. There was none. By 5 November, the Red Army had seized the initiative to the extent that 13th Panzer was temporarily encircled. When that storied formation, the keystone of Von Kleist's operations since Barbarossatag, had to break out to the west in order to avoid destruction, First Panzer Army knew its 'massive expedition' had reached the limits of its endurance.[45]

The SS Division Viking took over for the bruised 13th Panzer at the First Panzer's easternmost point. For a few more weeks it remained close enough to Ordzhonikidze to keep the military road under sporadic artillery fire, but not close enough seriously to interdict the traffic. On 1 November, Hitler left Vinnitsa and returned his headquarters to East Prussia. He simultaneously relinquished command of Army Group A to von Kleist, while von Mackensen rose to command First Panzer Army.[46]

Because they are relatively confined in time and space, Operations Blau, Braunschweig and Edelweiss make interesting study. However, as military undertakings they failed in every one of their objectives: the Red Army's southern tier of forces were not annihilated, Stalingrad resisted capture and hardly a drop of oil was taken out of the ground in the Caucasus. Changing missions and priorities plus logistics woes deprived von Kleist of much operational impact. Perhaps allowing Seventeenth Army to deal with Maikop while First Panzer raced to seal off the Caucasus military roads would have brought more success in capturing the oil fields at the eastern end of the mountain range. Soon First Panzer Army, and indeed the entire Ostheer, would be fighting for its very existence.

Hitler did not stay long at Rastenburg, but within a week was in Munich, congratulating himself over the 1942 campaign in a speech marking the anniversary of his Beer Hall Putsch nineteen years earlier before taking a much-deserved vacation in Berchtesgaden. News, first of the Allied invasion of North Africa, and then of the Soviet counteroffensive on either side of Stalingrad, Operation Uranus, dampened his festivities. However, Stalin had more ambitious objectives than simply destroying the Axis armies assaulting his namesake city. The follow-on Operation Saturn aimed at Rostov and the destruction of First Panzer and Seventeenth Armies fighting hundreds of kilometers to the south in the Caucasus.[47] The German high command was lethargic: slow to awaken to the threat to Stalingrad, slow to arrange a rescue effort for the entrapped garrison and slow to recognize the danger to Army Group A. For much of the remainder of the war, the Soviets would operate within the Boyd Loop of the Germans.

The attention of both armies concentrated on the main front around Stalingrad. Unsurprisingly, the Soviets made little effort in the far south, correctly believing that if they succeeded at Stalingrad and Rostov, the problem of Germans in the Caucasus would solve itself. Toward the end of 1942, panzer army rear echelon troops began an orderly withdrawal to the north. At the time, it consisted of the following subordinate units: LII Corps (Ott, 50th, 111th and 370th Infantry Divisions), III Panzer (Lieutenant General Hermann Breith, 13th Panzer and Romanian 2nd Mountain), XL Panzer (3rd Panzer, Cossack Regiment von Jungschulz) and various Cossack squadrons and volunteer units of Caucasus Mountain peoples (but not SS Viking, which Hitler sent to von Manstein's new Army Group Don). First Panzer had reached the Kuma River before Tyulenov began actively pursuing on about 7 January 1943. Stavka knew that in order to destroy Army Group A, the Southern (at Stalingrad) and Trans-Caucasus Fronts would have to work together, but they were too slow. By mid-January, with 16th Motorized between them, First and Fourth Panzer Armies had made contact and enjoyed a measure of 'operational cooperation'. The danger area for them, and Seventeenth Army, was the narrow German bottleneck around Rostov, which von Manstein knew he had to keep open. Less that 40km separated General AI Eremenko's men at Bataysk and mouth of the Don on the Sea of Azov. The field marshal pleaded with Hitler to allow First Panzer to escape. By 27 January, the Führer had made a decision. He would break up Army Group A, have Seventeenth Army retreat to the Kuban Peninsula opposite the Crimea, while First Panzer became part of Army Group Don. Further, he allowed the panzer army headquarters, two corps headquarters, one panzer division, one infantry division and two security divisions to escape, the rest would fall in on the Seventeenth Army. On the same day, von Mackensen's troops evacuated Armavir, which they had first occupied six months earlier. A week later, Hitler decided to pull First Panzer across the Don completely, while Fourth Panzer held open the door at Rostov. Panzers and heavy vehicles went through the city, while infantry and Cossacks escaped over the frozen Don River delta. By the end of the month, the panzer army passed through the 'gateway to the Caucasus' one last time. It had retreated 550km in one month.[48]

By the second week of February, First Panzer was back on the middle Donets near Slavyansk. With 100,000 men and 40 serviceable panzers, it took control of the front to the left of Armeeabteilung Fretter-Pico, and absorbed this corps-sized collection of mostly broken units trying to avoid being ridden down by Operation Gallup, the Soviets' post-Stalingrad offensive. Von Mackensen's main panzer striking force, 3rd and 11th Panzer Divisions, remained stuck in the deep snow around Rostov so were of no help at that time. On 12 February, Hitler ordered First Panzer to firm up the Donets River Line and regain contact with Armeeabteilung Lanz in order to protect the approaches to Zaporozhe. Von Richthofen's Luftflotte Four maintained a large airbase at Stalino from which to provide CAS. However, Mobile Group Popov and significant Red Army forces had already broken through the German lines and were making for the Dnepr. A gap of nearly 200km already existed between First Panzer and Lanz (on the 20th renamed 'Kempf'), so von Mackensen attempted to stretch northward a bit to narrow the distance. At the time, the following units made up First Panzer: III Panzer Corps, (3rd and 17th Panzer Divisions), Group Schmidt (19th Panzer plus one regiment from 7th Panzer) and XL Panzer (7th (–) and 11th Panzer, 333rd Infantry). Given its small size this proved impractical, and besides, von Manstein had conceived, and equally important, had sold Hitler on the idea of an operational counter-stroke using the rapidly growing Fourth Panzer Army. Hoth would cover the northern edge of the penetration, while von Mackensen would deal with Popov on the southern edge.[49]

Popov's three tank corps counted only twenty-five operational tanks between them on 22 February, and when First Panzer struck it achieved complete surprise. Von Mackensen had freed up 7th Panzer from Slavyansk, and with the return of SS Viking to his command, XL Panzer Corps packed a powerful punch. By the second day of the counterattack, Popov requested permission to abandon his salient only to have front commander Vatutin tell him such a move was 'counter to the assignments given the mobile group'. Von Mackensen dispatched Viking (five panzers in running order) directly west with 7th and 11th Panzer Divisions (Group Balck, thirty-five and sixteen panzers, respectively) on a sweeping maneuver initially southwest toward the railway station at Krasnoarmeyskoye. After reaching that point, they would head back northeast, link up with Viking and encircle Popov. With Soviet forces over extended, isolated and out of supply, plus with the ground frozen solid, First Panzer enjoyed weeks of good fortune. On 18–19 February, heavy fighting took place between the panzers (with 333rd Infantry) against the 4th Guards Tank Corps at Krasnoarmeyskoye. The Soviets mistook this generally westward movement for a retreat. Popov knew better, realized by the 23rd that he was in real danger and began to maneuver northward toward Barvenko. By 24 February, Popov's command was hardly mobile – its tanks could not move due to lack of fuel and maintenance, and it was hardly a group – it had broken into many small pockets. The XL Panzer pinched off the small Kessels, but the cordons were fairly porous and many Soviets escaped to fight another day.[50] First Panzer's contributions to von Manstein's gutsy Backhand Blow maneuver are less well known that those of Fourth Panzer, but following the twin debacles of Stalingrad and flight from the Caucasus, the Ostheer welcomed any good news.

Panzerwaffe Selection, Training and Organization

It is well known that older, traditional leaders of the German Army initially opposed mechanization and the Panzerwaffe. By the late 1930s, this resistance collapsed in the face of Hitler's support and the tremendous expansion of the Third Reich which brought in masses of middle-class officers in place of the 'aristocrats'. In his classic *Misbrauchete Infantrie*, General of Infantry Maximillian von Fretter-Pico may have lamented that the panzer troops got the best men, best equipment, high-calorie food and countless other benefits over his long-suffering infantry, fighting and dying for the Fatherland. However, from the start, with their black uniforms and Death's Head emblems for example, the Panzerwaffe was made to feel special. The rebellious 'us versus them' attitude of early panzer leaders like Guderian seeped 'into the souls of the first panzer soldiers' and later into the entire armor branch.

Training resources were lavished on the panzers. The army created new and expanded panzer schools at Wünsdorf, Bergen, Potsdam, Erlangen and Paderborn and elsewhere, teaching new mechanics, tactics and command and control techniques. With his professional background in training, Guderian took an intense interest in this area. Therefore a highly trained and experienced cadre of panzer leaders carried the Wehrmacht through spectacular early victories, especially in the West and during Barbarossa. Unfortunately for Germany, as happened elsewhere (e.g., Japanese naval aviators in the Pacific), once this core of experts had been attrited and once the enemy recovered from its initial shock and losses, the odds first evened, then turned against it. As history and this book show, by 1943 the Soviets caught up with the invader. A year later we can see that the tide had turned against Germany. Its shrinking manpower pool, now ever more diluted with foreign soldiers less enamored with Nazism, training time in increasing short supply, panzers desperately needed at the front plus fuel and ammunition for training considered a luxury, the relative advantage disappeared.

Operation Barbarossa almost de-mechanized the Wehrmacht, its losses in that campaign were so great. After 1941, the Panzerwaffe lurched from campaign to campaign, rebuilding its strength then losing disastrously, only to repeat the cycle. Tactically, by the middle of the struggle, German and Soviet used many of the same tactics. Here, Red Army numerical superiority and approaching equity in training and quality made themselves felt. During 1943–44, a formulaic dance of action, reaction and counteraction developed, with the usual result being the Germans were pushed back. By 1945, there was no semblance of evenness.

From the very beginnings of Panzerwaffe, divisions were organized as combined arms teams. With the general de-mechanization and dilution of the panzer branch over its ten-year existence, the proportion of actual panzers declined relative to other arms. By the time of Barbarossa, a panzer division had a headquarters, one panzer regiment of two battalions, two motorized infantry/panzergrenadier regiments (sometimes organized into a brigade) each of two battalions, an artillery regiment plus one battalion each of engineers, reconnaissance, anti-tank, Flak, signal and support troops. Ad hoc Kampfgruppen (battle groups) were common throughout the war, and came in two principal varieties: a combined arms task force created for a particular mission, and as a way to describe a division so reduced that it could not be legitimately counted as a division any longer. In the first case, it was probably named after the senior commander or the commander of the largest sub-unit, e.g., KG Rothenberg, and in the second case it took the name of its former division, e.g., KG 297.

As is the case with most of the world's armies, formations above division did not have a permanent establishment. Most panzer corps had a headquarters, an artillery command (Arko) to coordinate attached artillery units, signal and support troops. In addition, it might have any combination of anti-tank, engineer, Flak, machine-gun and replacement detachments. Panzer army orders of battle also changed with mission or situation on the ground. The only constant units would be the headquarters, a higher artillery command (Harko – again only to coordinate, with no units of its own) and a signal regiment. Temporary attachments would be artillery, construction, support and training assets.

No sooner had Popov's threat to Zaporozhe been neutralized and Kharkov recaptured, than the spring rasputitsa brought operations to a halt. The front lines stood where attack and counterattack during the winter left them, and included many salients and jagged edges. The high commands of both sides cast about for plans for the upcoming summer. Hitler had grown accustomed to taking the initiative during good campaigning weather and had no reason not to do the same in 1943. Stalin, on the other hand, was beginning to feel strong enough to not simply take a passive wait-and-see attitude. Both had big plans for the summer of 1943. In First Panzer's sector, the Soviets still occupied a dangerous bulge near Izyum on the Donets. On 22 March, the Führer issued orders for Operation Hawk (Habicht) only to supersede it two days later with a larger scaled assault, Operation Panther. Both would be joint endeavors of First Panzer and Armeeabteilung Kempf and in the case of Panther, include Hoth's panzer army as well. In both cases, von Mackensen's objective was the area around Kupyansk. Hitler tied Panther to the summer's major offensive, Operation Citadel (Zitadelle) against the Kursk bulge. Therefore, all the formations intended for Hawk and the other operations stood at the ready for days and weeks (and in the case of Kursk, eventually months), waiting for Hitler to give the green light. Bearing in mind all the intangible factors involved with large military undertakings, plus Germany's numerous weaknesses, the Führer cancelled both Hawk and Panther in favor of Citadel.[51] As can be said about Blau the year before, and many other German operations, Hitler figuratively waited for the planets to align with the perfect combination of weather, developments on either side, the correlation of forces, new weapons systems and numerous other variables. Of course this alignment never occurred, while Stalin went ahead with his own counter moves that inevitably complicated Hitler's calculations.

Except for a small attack launched by III Panzer toward the Izyum bend in early April, the spring was quiet in expectation of the anticipated showdown at

Kursk. Stavka had come to the conclusion that the Red Army could deflect whatever Hitler threw at it that summer, then promptly take the initiative from him. Accordingly, German intelligence noticed that the Soviets began to build up forces across the Donets from First Panzer Army. Von Mackensen's men did not have a role to play in Citadel, but from a safe distance watched the entire operation unravel from the beginning. After barely a dozen days, the offensive was over. Two days after Hitler pulled II SS Panzer Corps out of the line, on 17 July, the Southwest and South Fronts counterattacked. The First Panzer's exposed positions near Izyum were obvious targets of opportunity. As a precaution, three days earlier, Hitler ordered XXIV Panzer Corps (23rd Panzer and SS Viking) behind von Mackensen's front as a reserve. The Red Army's main blows hit Fourth Panzer and Eighth Armies, but First Panzer fought a vicious 10-day defensive battle that cost the attackers over 500 combat vehicles lost. The main danger to von Mackensen came from the southern flank, however. The Soviets attacked across the Mius against the (resurrected) Sixth Army. Contrary to their earlier fears, von Manstein did not withdraw, he instead sent in III Panzer and II SS Panzer Corps. Of course a force this massive stabilized the situation, but only temporarily. Elsewhere along the eastern front, and indeed in the entire European theater, conditions rapidly deteriorated so these assets had to be transferred away.[52]

During the various Stalingrad battles the Soviets outperformed the Germans both in terms of operational skill and functioning within a faster decision cycle. Except for a skillful retreat, First Panzer Army cannot be said to have performed in an operational manner. Its participation in the Backhand Blow maneuver was significant but tactical and its role during Citadel, even more limited. The First Panzer's days as an operational actor were over, and it would spend the remainder of the war largely reacting to Red Army initiatives.

To defend its 155km front, First Panzer Army had 8 infantry and 3 mechanized divisions with a total of 220 AFVs. Von Manstein estimated that his real combat value in divisions stood at five-and-a-half infantry and one-and-a-half panzer and panzergrenadier. Between 13 and 18 August, the South Front renewed its attacks around Izyum and against Sixth Army. As in July, First Panzer held on despite receiving tremendous artillery fire. Unfortunately the Sixth Army, as in July, allowed penetrations, but in this case, von Manstein no longer had two panzer corps to send to the breach. Within a week, von Mackensen's exposed Izyum positions were becoming untenable. On the last day of August, the field marshal allowed his two southern armies to withdraw to the Kalmius River, a decision seconded 'in principle' by Hitler that night. First Panzer occupied that new river line on 4 September, only to have Southwest Front attack and overwhelm these defenses two days later. On 6 September, the 1st Guards Mechanized Corps split the junction with Sixth Army and on the following day, without looking back, 23rd Tank Corps joined them. With two mobile formations rampaging in his rear areas, von Mackensen had no option but to pull back himself. A major problem was that the enemy was much closer to the Dnepr and the critical Dnepropetrovsk and Zaporozhe crossings than the Germans. On 8 September, Hitler again flew to von Manstein's command post at Zaporozhe, scene of their famous meeting six months earlier; Soviet spearheads were again just as close. This time the field marshal had no Backhand Blow trick up his sleeve. The Ostheer had squandered its last mobile reserves at the poorly conceived and executed disaster at Kursk, it had been losing a battle of attrition during the ensuing two months and a confident Red Army was bearing down, fast. First Panzer would be allowed to retreat to the Dnepr – if it could get there before the enemy.[53]

The panzer army had already begun to withdraw before Hitler gave *de jure* approval. On 12 September, it made contact with the Sixth Army for the first time in over two weeks and by the 16th it began to close on the Dnepr bridgeheads. Meanwhile, the damage done, Southwest Front ordered its two mobile corps to turn around and seek safety with their own kind. Von Mackensen tried for two days to hunt them down, only to have them escape, battered but unbowed, through loopholes in the Sixth Army Front which had no panzers or anti-tank guns. First Panzer generally fell behind the Dnepr, believing in the illusory safety of the great river. Hitler stressed the importance of Zaporozhe and the manganese mines at Nikopol. Von Mackensen maintained a bridgehead on the east bank at Zaporozhe, which the Southwest Front attacked but failed to capture on 1 October. On 10 October, two Guards Armies, 3rd and 8th, attacked again. The XL Panzer Corps had improved its positions in the interim, including a half-dozen Ferdinand self-propelled 88mm gun platforms, but the Soviets had brought forward their new artillery divisions and prodigious amounts of ammunition. First Panzer units faltered but held on the second day. By the third day they reported massive losses and numerous breakthroughs in their lines. Hitler, von Manstein and von Kleist debated the wisdom and practicality of holding the bridgehead. On the night of 13 October, 1st Guards Mechanized and 23rd Tank Corps surprised von Mackensen's defenders and drove them back to the city, first to the Heinrich positions and then to the Friedrich. The Germans gave up the city on the 14th, but not before demolishing the bridges and dam consistent with Hitler's scorched earth policies.[54]

There would be no rest for the Germans, because on the next day, General IS Konev's 2nd Ukrainian Front (four infantry and one tank army) broke out of its bridgeheads downstream from Kremenchug and along the seam dividing First Panzer and Eighth Armies. For days it poured units across the river, while von Manstein and von Mackensen were powerless to do more than watch and wait for the Soviets to reach their objectives. Within three days, the 2nd Ukrainian had cut the rail line to Dnepropetrovsk and was half way to Krivoi Rog. First Panzer had vague promises of reinforcements, at least four panzer divisions inbound from various places. But von Mackensen could not wait to create the ideal counterattack force, he had to defend the city, a major resource and transportation center, the site of a huge German supply dump and the pivot point of the entire Dnepr bend. By 21 October, he had received 11th Panzer and SS Totenkkopf from Eighth Army, but the situation at the front had become so tense that these had to man front-line positions and could not be consolidated into even a tactical counterattack force. Two days later, the panzer army's outpost at Dnepropetrovsk became problematic when the 46th (north) and 8th Guards Armies broke out of their own bridgeheads and threatened to cut off the city. Von Mackensen withdrew his forces by the 23rd, and was left with contact along the Dnepr on either side of Zaporozhe and a dangerously narrow front stretching west past Krivoi Rog. That was enough for von Manstein, who transferred XL Panzer Corps (14th and 24th Panzer Divisions plus SS Totenkopf) back to the panzer army with orders to execute an immediate counterattack against Konev's 5th Guards Tank Army, now very close to Krivoi Rog; he could not wait for other reinforcements which might not arrive. Red Army troops began to probe the city's defenses on the 25th, prompting XL Panzer to attack a day earlier than planned. The panzers launched on the 27th, destroying much of two mechanized corps and nine rifle divisions, giving Krivoi Rog a 30km buffer by the end of the month. That would be von Mackensen's last feat as panzer army commander; on 29 October, General of Panzer Troops Hans Hube, a veteran of panzer battles in the southern theater since Barbarossatag, took over.[55]

Most of the excitement within Army Group South at the end of 1943 took place in Fourth Panzer Army's area; First Panzer was locked in a battle of attrition that it would doubtless lose. On New Year's Day 1944, von Manstein reorganized his forces and moved First Panzer north adjacent to Fourth Panzer: only in this case 'adjacent' meant separated by a gaping 70km hole. Hube took over Fourth Army's VII and XLII Corps. Higher headquarters promised him III Panzer as a mobile striking force of two panzer divisions, one panzer-grenadier division and one Jäger division. Additionally, Hube had the misfortune of taking over the Germans' last positions on the Dnepr, what the Landsers near Cherkassy called the 'Wacht am Dnepr'. A couple of days later, Marshal Vatutin's 1st Ukrainian Front, which had been working over Fourth Panzer's right, turned its attention of Hube's left. By 4 January, the gap between the two panzer armies exceeded 100km. The VII Corps gave up Belaya Zerkov. At about the same time, 2nd Ukrainian attacked First Panzer in the direction of Krivoi Rog and Kirovograd. Any semblance of a cohesive front between First and Fourth Panzer Armies vanished. By 10 January, 1st Guards Tank Army pushed on toward Zhmerinka (as three days earlier von Manstein had predicted it would), nearly 250km southwest of the Dnepr. The III Panzer only managed to contain this threat after two days of heavy fighting. Farther south, 40th Army opened another gap, this time between VII Corps and III Panzer, almost reaching the huge German logistics base at Uman.[56] With this, First Panzer lost contact with both neighbors, Fourth Panzer and Eighth Armies.

Von Manstein judged the breakthrough at Zhmerinka as the most dangerous, so assembled a counterattack force under Breith's III Panzer (17th and most of 16th Panzer). This assault began on 15 January, and within 48 hours had covered most of the 40km separating it from VII Corps. For two days near Vinnitsa, Hube had been putting together another counterattack force based on the XLVI Panzer Corps (under Lieutenant General Hans Gollnick, mainly the 18th Panzer). A thaw in the weather slowed both sides, allowing von Manstein further to reinforce Gollnick with the Leibstandarte plus the new and unique 18th Artillery Division. By the 24th, both panzer corps were ready. The XLVI Panzer led off, but quickly ran into trouble that not even the 1st SS Panzer could overcome. The next day, III Panzer attacked but halted almost immediately. It seemed 1st Guards Tank and the rest of the Soviet thrust would survive with minimal damage. However, by the last days of January, the two panzer corps eventually succeeded in chopping off the penetration, destroying over 700 AFVs in the process.[57] Elsewhere on the front, however, things had gone from bad to worse.

With the VII Corps ingloriously shoved aside to the north and Eighth Army giving way at Kirovograd to the south, a small German promontory at Korsun stood strong as the 1st and 2nd Ukrainian Fronts swirled past it and to the east. On 28 January, 5th Guards Tank and 6th Tank Armies linked up, surrounding the Eighth Army's XI and XLII Corps there, just west of Cherkassy. The 57th, 72nd, 88th, 389th, plus elements of 112th, 255th and 332nd Infantry Divisions, SS Viking and the SS Wallonien Brigade, totaling 54,000 men, had been encircled. Fortunately for them, the hilly terrain favored the defense, and until the weather really turned bad on the 15th, the Luftwaffe managed to fly in up to 185 tons of supplies per day. The XI Corps commander, General of Artillery Wilhelm Stemmermann, took control as the senior man in the pocket. He insured a lively and effective defense along an amazing 250km front. Against them Konev was in the process of amassing a force of 27 rifle divisions, 4 mechanized and 1 tank corps, supported by approximately 4,000 guns.[58]

Hitler could not make up his mind what to do, but von Manstein lost no time creating two relief forces. By 1 February he decided that First Panzer Army would employ III Panzer Corps (1st, 16th, 17th Panzer and Leibstandarte) coming from the southwest, while Eighth Army would utilize XLVII Panzer Corps (Lieutenant General Nikolas von Vormann, 3rd, 11th, 14th and 24th Panzer) moving from the south. The rescue effort began on 4 February, 24 hours later than planned, and made good progress despite the conditions. Panzer crewmen carried fuel in buckets, while Landsers went barefoot rather than pull their boots out of the mud every few steps. Meanwhile, the pocket itself crept southwest toward its would-be saviors. The III Panzer only had to go the final 30km, but even this seemed problematic. On 10 February, von Kleist told Breith go 'no matter what' on the 11th. With its panthers in the lead, the 1st Panzer Division indeed pushed forward, but not fast enough and by the 12th had stalled on the Gniloy Tikich stream. Its Panthers had run into an 'armored wasp nest' of T-34s supported by 85mm anti-tank guns. There were renewed efforts on 13 February, with 16th Panzer and Heavy Panzer Regiment Bäke coming up to the left of 1st Panzer. Bäke possessed 11 Tigers and 14 Panthers which had destroyed over 400 tanks in the previous 3 weeks. On the night of the 14th, led by Viking, the healthiest of the emaciated formations inside the pocket, Stemmermann began the final lunge toward III Panzer. But even the most desperate and determined efforts by men inside and outside the pocket could not close the final few kilometers. On the 15th, von Manstein personally sent the following teletext message to Lieutenant Colonel Dr Bäke:

> Bravo, despite mud and Russians already much accomplished. There only remains to take the last step. Bite down and onward. That too will be successful.[59]

With the pocket now measuring 20km by 45km and the Soviets crushing in on every side, there was no option for the 16th except a breakout in three columns. The escape, especially negotiating the Gniloy Tikish, reads just like Napoleon's disastrous crossing of the Berezina at the end of November 1812. Ziemke and Haupt claim between 20–30,000 Germans escaped, while the rest died (including Stemmermann) or were captured. Glantz and House, using 'far more credible' Soviet numbers, write that virtually none escaped, that over 70,000 perished or became POWs. In either case, First Panzer and Eighth Army's defenses had been ripped apart.[60]

The Soviets only gave the panzer army a fortnight's pause before renewing their offensive. Hube, who upon taking command confidently told the men of the 125th Infantry Division, 'Don't weaken before the Russian Scheiss-Infantrie', would soon have more trouble than he could handle. Ukrainian separatists ambushed Vatutin on 29 February, just before the offensive's start date. After a long battle he died of his wounds, so Zhukov personally took command of the 1st Ukrainian Front. His goal was to attack down the Seret and Zubruch River valleys to Chernovtsy, practically in the foothills of the Carpathians. The objective of Konev's neighboring 2nd Ukrainian Front was to aim past Uman and Yampol, also in the general direction of Chernovtsy beyond the Dniester. First Panzer would be caught between a rock and a hard place. Both fronts fielded thirty-six rifle divisions and three tank armies. After the smaller 3rd and 4th Ukrainian Fronts entered the fray, von Manstein's men (and those in the Sixth Army of von Kleist's Army Group A) were fighting for their lives along a 1,100km front.[61]

By 4 March, von Manstein had reorganized his Dnepr defense, and reinforced by the Fourth Panzer's far-right corps. Hube received the mission of defending Shepetovka and Proskurov (Chemel'nicki). German intelligence had it right this time, for on that same day, Zhukov ripped the seam between First and Fourth Panzer Armies and pushed LIX Corps off to the south, away from Sheptovka. The 3rd Guards Tank Army stormed through the gap and down the rail line towards Chernovtsy. Fourth Panzer could offer little assistance, but von Manstein ordered III Panzer (four panzer divisions) to rail up from the Eighth Army area. Hube maintained a cohesive defense by pulling LIX Corps back even with the Soviet advance, first to Staro Constantinov. By the 6th, III Panzer elements began to arrive around Proskurov, and Breith's corps got steadily stronger from arriving reinforcements until it managed to halt the Red tank armies on the 7th. Fourth Panzer held the northeastern shoulder of the penetration with the two divisions of XLVIII Panzer. Together, the two panzer armies delayed Zhukov for nearly two weeks, preventing the liberation of Ternopol, an important rail junction and, after Hitler's Order 11 of 8 March, a Fester Platz (fortified place). Other fortified places in Hube's area included Proskurov and Vinnitsa, each of which was to be held until the last man in what amounted to a personal contract between Hitler and the senior commander on the scene. Reinforcements arrived to stabilize the panzer army's center. However, on either of Hube's flanks, the Soviets managed significant penetrations. The weak position of Fourth Panzer has already been mentioned, and Eighth Army's lines were compromised by the loss of Uman with its massive German supply dumps.[62]

Zhukov's 1st and 4th Tank and 3rd Guards Tank Armies finally unhinged Hube's positions on 21 March when 200 tanks scattered Kampfgruppen of the Leibstandarte, 7th Panzer and 68th Infantry Divisions.[63] They crossed the

Dniester in numerous locations by the 24th, as other Kampfgruppen of the 1st and 6th Panzer Divisions tried to keep the trap from slamming shut. Despite these efforts, three days later the 38th and 4th Tank Armies linked up and Zhukov and Konev created a loose cordon around First Panzer, twenty-one weakened divisions stretching all way from Kamenets-Podolsky to the Proskurov Fester Platz. Von Manstein saw the danger developing and on 24 March ordered First Panzer to begin to 'breakout to the west to cut off the enemy'. Phrasing a retreat as an attack into the enemy flank was a good way to get the Führer's approval. Simultaneously, 4th Tank occupied Kamenets-Podolsky, forcing Hube to displace his headquarters to Dunajevcy to the south. The next day the field marshal flew to Hitler's Berchtesgaden retreat and argued until he received post facto permission to do what he had already ordered. Accordingly, also on the 25th, Panzer Group Waldenfels (elements of 6th, 11th and 19th Panzer Divisions under commanding general of the 6th, Major General Rudolf Freiherr von Waldenfels) attacked early in the morning from the area near Jarmolincy toward Gorodok with the intention of joining up with 1st Panzer, fighting alone at the time, and together creating a bridgehead over the Smotrich. From there the entire panzer group would continue west on the way to freedom.[64]

Hitler relented and provided an additional force with which to break into the pocket, II SS Panzer Corps (SS 9th Hohenstaufen and 10th Frundsberg Panzer Divisions) plus the 100th Jäger and 367th Infantry Divisions assembling in the Fourth Panzer Army sector. Hube wanted to escape to Romania to the south, which is where Zhukov expected him to go. But von Manstein had three reasons why he wanted Hube to go west: 1. Fourth Panzer could assist in the rescue; 2. the Germans could cut the lines of communication of the 1st and 4th Tank Armies; and 3. the two panzer armies could cooperate to keep the army group's northern flank more 'solid'. At 0400 hours on the 26th, the field marshal radioed Hube, 'Solution west. Orders to follow. Manstein'. By the next day the entire panzer army was creeping westward, with armor units facing that direction, rear services troops making up the rear guard with infantry in between. Hube issued the following Order of the Day:

> Any soldier who fails to obey or fight any longer, so long as he has a weapon, is an enemy identical to every Russian and must be handled exactly the same by commanders and subordinate leaders ... The fate of one of the most glorious armies of the Führer hangs in the balance.[65]

Hube divided his army into northern and southern halves that would negotiate the Zbruch River crossings one at a time. They could escape through a 15km gap that the sixty tanks of 4th Tank Army could not keep closed. The north group first crossed the Zbruch, then the Seret, while the southern group followed perhaps two days behind. Together, von Manstein and Hube had achieved operational and tactical surprise.[66]

Zhukov soon realized his mistake and started shifting forces to the threatened area. First, he ordered the pocket crushed by 31 March. When his troops could not accomplish that, on 2 April he called on First Panzer to surrender. At the time, the panzer army had only 24 operational panzers (1st, 17th, 19th, 20th Panzer Divisions and the SS Das Reich had none!), 86 anemic battalions of infantry, 106 PAKs and 75 light and 35 heavy artillery batteries. In the meantime, a massive blizzard hit the area that actually helped the Germans. While Luftwaffe Ju-52 pilots braved the weather, Red Army Air Force CAS and reconnaissance aircraft were grounded. Zhukov renewed his attacks when weather improved on the 3rd. German defenders of the north group at Chortkhov rejected assaults by two tank corps the next day. The gravest danger to First Panzer passed on 4 April, despite its being almost completely surrounded. With Corps Groups Chevallerie and Breith protecting the army's north and south flanks and with a robust rearguard, Hube's command made its way west. On the 6th, it linked up with II SS Panzer Corps lead elements at Buchach. The escape was a qualified success, but there was no way that Hitler would consider a retreat of 100–150km a victory. For example, the 5 divisions of III Panzer could muster only 7,227 men in total. Frustrated with von Manstein's personality and techniques, he sacked the field marshal and renamed Army Group South, Army Group North Ukraine. A grateful Führer flew Hube to Berchtesgaden on 20 April to promote him to colonel general and add diamonds to his Knights Cross. Regrettably, the panzer general died the next day on his way back to the front when his plane crashed into the Alps.[67]

Framing defensive operations in terms of operational level warfare is difficult. During this period, First Panzer (along with the rest of Army Group South, lost all of the Ukraine and conducted offensive maneuvers with formations no larger than a corps. Von Mackensen and Hube and their men expended great energy in escaping from two deadly traps and merely remaining on the battlefield. At no point during the second half of 1943 nor the first quarter of 1944 did they have the luxury of time and resources to act in the operational realm as a real panzer army.

Advanced elements of 1st Tank Army reached the Carpathian foothills by 17 April, but fighting died down that spring, and both sides resorted to loud-speaker duels and other harassment. German soldiers received a new anti-tank weapon, the Panzerfaust, while Soviet raids became so bold the Germans had to chain down their machine-guns in their fighting positions to prevent them from being 'stolen'. In front of L'vov, the First Panzer Army laid 160,000 anti-personnel and 200,000 anti-tank mines in an intricate and well-coordinated defense. World attention increasingly turned to Italy, northwestern France and the crushing of Army Group Center. However, neither D-Day nor the botched assassination attempt against Hitler made much of an impression on the Landsers. The USSR was now strong enough to execute consecutive and cascading offensives along the entire front. Marshal Konev's 1st Ukrainian Front, the largest combat organization in the Red Army, launched an assault against First and Fourth Panzer Armies that would take the Soviets through L'vov to the Vistula River in Sandomirez, Poland. He had approximately 1 million men in 80 divisions organized into 10 armies supported by over 1,600 AFVs, 14,000 guns and mortars plus 2,800 aircraft. They faced 900,000 Germans, 900 AFVs, 6,000 guns and 700 aircraft arrayed in 3 defensive lines. So far as First Panzer was concerned, Konev planned to cut it off from its sister panzer army and drive it into the Carpathian Mountains.[68]

Colonel General Erhard Raus commanded First Panzer when Konev's 38th and 60th Armies assaulted on 14 July. Raus, his chief of staff and operations officer (Ia in German notation) believed they had deciphered the secrets to Soviet success:

- Annihilation of forward German troops along the main battle line by concentrated artillery fire;
- Neutralization or destruction of German artillery via heavy counterbattery fire and continuous air attacks;
- Elimination of German command and staff by air attack and surprise artillery fire on command posts up to army level;
- Harassing of reserves in their assembly areas by artillery and air attacks;
- Disruption of communication routes to the front which delayed the movement of reserves and cut off the flow of supplies;
- All of these preconditions led directly to massed armored thrusts in depth which enabled the Soviets to obtain freedom of maneuver.

Raus and his staff created the following solutions:

- Withdraw from front lines immediately prior to artillery preparation (a technique learned during the First World War);
- An elastic defense, deeply echeloned;
- Temporary retirement followed by an immediate counterattack on carefully chosen battlefields;
- Protected communications and reserve assembly areas and routes;[69]
- All of these measures pointed to a new respect for the Soviets.

The tricky parts were discerning the timing of the Soviet attack and ordering corresponding German withdrawals and reserve movement. The commanding general and his chief of staff paid particular attention to reconnaissance and radio intercepts (the latter provided 70 percent of German intelligence). Konev hit where Raus expected, but, by German calculations, two days late. Red artillery hit fairly harmlessly on evacuated front-line positions, while both command posts and reserve forces avoided serious damage. Therefore, initial counterattacks by Breith's 1st and 8th Panzer Divisions plus the SS 14th Division Galacian blunted the 38th Army, while the 60th enjoyed modest success. Red Army Air Force CAS, including 2,000 sorties against the 8th Panzer on 15 July alone, gave the frontovicki renewed freedom of maneuver. The fighting surged across recent battlefields of 1914 (history's last great cavalry charge at Jaroslawice), 1916 (the Bruislov Offensive) and 1941 (Barbarossa). By the 17th, Konev threw 3rd Guards Tank Army into the fray to exploit 60th Army's success, forcing the Germans back to the 'Prinz Eugen' intermediate position. The withdrawal of most of First Panzer caused the encirclement of the bulk of eight German divisions under XIII Corps that remained on the original line centered on the town of Brody. That same day, army group ordered XIII Corps to escape, but the commander, General of Infantry Arthur Hauffe, had not made adequate preparations to get away and so lost valuable time. Around the same time, the only mechanized formation capable of truly liberating the garrison, the II SS Panzer Corps, departed for the D-Day fighting in France. Led by his 'best unit', Korpsabteilung C (remnants of 183rd, 217th and 339th Infantry Divisions plus five captured Soviet tanks), the breakout finally began at 0330 hours on 20 July. Of 30,000 Germans originally encircled, only about 5,000 eventually made it to XLVIII Panzer Corps outposts by the 23rd. Hauffe was not among the survivors.[70]

Konev hoped to take L'vov from the march, but Raus managed to rush three divisions into the city. By 24 July, the city was surrounded except for one open segment to the southwest. By this time the 38th and 60th Armies had arrived and took much of the burden off the tankers. By evening of the 26th, the Germans had had enough street-to-street fighting and began to withdraw. The Soviets occupied the city on the next day, by which time advanced mechanized forces had also taken Przemysl on the panzer army's main supply route, almost another 100km west. One divisional history records that on 3 August 'all hell broke loose'. By now Konev's massive front was too spread out on too many divergent axes, so Stavka split the group in two and gave the new 4th Ukrainian Front the mission of dealing with First Panzer Army. Raus remembered the defensive value of the upper Dniester and the Carpathians from his experiences during the First World War. He petitioned Hitler to withdraw from the tenuous foothill line to the mountain ridges, only to be refused. Raus' entire southern flank became jeopardized when the Hungarian First Army unilaterally retreated from the Pruth River valley. Only when it was almost too late, the Führer relented and the First Panzer plus the Hungarian 1st Army pulled back to the relative safety of the Beskides and Carpathian Mountains.[71]

On 17 August, with one hour's notice, Raus flew off to take over Third Panzer, so two days later First Panzer got yet another commander, Colonel General Gotthard Heinrici. An infantry division commander during the Polish campaign, Heinrici had risen to positions of increasing responsibility, making a reputation as a 'defensive specialist' along the way. His combined German-Hungarian command, Armeegruppe Heinrici, was 'relatively unmolested' along most of its 350km length during August and September of 1944. Fighting and surviving at altitude had its costs: maintaining logistics was difficult, radios did not work well in the peaks and valleys, telephone lines were long and vulnerable and howitzers (able to elevate their guns to 45 degrees) were at a premium. The main danger came from the army group's deep rear, where the Soviets had made conquering the Balkans look easy against the German Sixth and Eighth Armies. They were poorly served by a motley collection of allied armies that increasingly chose to defect to the Soviet Union rather than die for Hitler. The stand-off between First Panzer and 4th Ukrainian Front along the mountain passes seemed quiet by comparison. The main excitement came from elements of the Slovak army plotting with Stalin to abandon the Axis, join up with partisans and attack Heinrici's rear areas. One Slovak division eventually did change sides, the SS disarmed the rest and by October the uncoordinated coup had run its course. The Dukla Pass, on the Slovak–Polish border was a prize coveted by both sides. Starting on 7 September, the 1st Guards Army attacked and gained 80km on that day, but Heinrici's men absorbed the shock, for a while even encircling the Soviets. They likewise trapped the 1st Guards Cavalry Corps (38th Army) for ten days during the second half of September. The trusty 1st and 8th Panzer Divisions, some Tiger tanks and other units fought spirited battles there over the summer. Heinrici held the pass until Hitler removed a panzer division overwatching the position, allowing the Soviets and their new Czech allies to take the corridor on 6 October. However, simple possession of that terrain feature did not mean the 4th Ukrainian would have the mountains' defenses handed to them without a fight.[72]

Winter set in to make already miserable conditions worse. The 'Free Slovakia' movement died from the internal strife that beset similar associations whenever Western- and Communist-backed personalities and ideas jockeyed for power. Casualties inflicted by First Panzer on Colonel General IE Petrov's 4th Ukrainian Front amounted to 80,000 men (one-quarter of those deaths) and

442 tanks destroyed. The Soviets slogged and fought up the northeastern slopes of the two mountain ranges and gained 20km in three weeks. In September, the correlation of forces was: First Panzer – 11 infantry divisions, 2 Jäger divisions and 1 panzer division assisted by 2 Sturmgeschütze brigades; Red Army – 30 rifle divisions, 3 tank corps, 1 guards cavalry corps and 1 Czech corps plus 1 tank brigade. The Soviet superiority was 4–5:1 in men and matériel. The 4th Ukrainian Front did enjoy some success on its eastern flank, taking Mukachevo on 27 October and Uzhorod on the 28th. On 1 November, First Panzer passed down Hitler's latest orders to its troop units: defend Slovakia 'to the last man'. With Petrov's recent victories, the Soviets put much of the Carpathians at their backs and had the Hungarian plain to their front. By the second half of November, the Führer's demands became even more unrealistic. With that, his right falling back, Heinrici gave up any pretenses of holding the mountain line. His vulnerable 'balcony' jutted dangerously far to the east of the rest of the German lines. Hitler realized this and on 25 November approved withdrawal to the 'Gisela' winter positions. At the time a battle of Stalingrad-like ferocity engulfed Budapest, and Petrov's mission was to push First Panzer into Czechoslovakia and away from Hungary where it might contribute to the German effort to hold the Magyar capital. Heinrici's men gave up ground but slowly, and by the beginning of 1945 still held the 'Karola' positions along the Ondava and Topola Rivers.[73]

During the first weeks of January, First Panzer fell back to the Tatyse River, but by the 18th and 20th had lost Kosice and Presov respectively so continued west down the Vah River valley. As the Battle of Budapest wound down and the battle for Germany began in earnest, Heinrici occupied an area of little interest to either side. Another exposed 'balcony' developed as huge armies passed to his north and south. By the end of the month First Panzer retreated to the High Tatra, the latest of Heinrici's mountain strongholds. On 6 February, the panzer army boundary shifted left to include the LIX Corps as far north as Pless (near Auschwitz). Throughout the month, Heinrici pulled back to keep generally even with armies to either flank. At the same time, Petrov submitted plans to rush the remaining 300km to Prague, with his initial objectives being the industrial region stretching from Ostrava in Czechoslovakia to Ratibor in eastern Poland. This represented the First Panzer's furthest extent, a well-prepared defense in very favorable terrain. Petrov attacked and between 10–17 March, 4th Ukrainian Front averaged at best 2km per day. Near Ratibor, LIX Corps held for one day before being overwhelmed, while the weakened 8th and 16th Panzer Divisions also managed a brief defense. Petrov's assault lines could create no opening through which to push his exploitation force, 5th Guards Mechanized Corps. In frustration, Stavka replaced Petrov with the more-experienced Eremenko. Under the new commander the Soviets tried again beginning on 24 March. However, the unwritten laws about combat in built-up areas still applied: it most generally favors the defender. In a dozen days the 'new and improved' 4th Ukrainian gained about 30km, not much better than it had earlier in March under Petrov.[74]

In early April, Eremenko planned a new offensive, this time in conjunction with the 2nd Ukrainian Front. The last commander of First Panzer Army, General of Panzer Troops Walther Nehring, had 20 badly depleted divisions manning nearly 200km, and 300 panzers supported by 280 aircraft (both respectable numbers for the last month of the war). Against him Eremenko fielded 40 rifle divisions (also weakened), a similar number of AFVs, but 6,000 guns and 435 aircraft. The assault began on 15 April, but again First Panzer defenses, many housed in pre-war Czech fortifications that had worried Hitler in 1938, remained steadfast. Nehring's men held on to Opava on the Czech–Polish border until 24 April. When the 60th Army took that town the road was open to the center of the Moravian industrial basin around Ostrava. With the 2nd Ukrainian Front coming up from the direction of Brno (Stavka had planned a sizeable encirclement battle involving the two fronts near Olomouc), First Panzer had to escape to the west. But Nehring had one last ace up his sleeve: near the Napoleonic battlefield of Austerlitz, the 8th and 16th Panzer Divisions and 6th Guards Tank Army fought one of the last armored battles of the war. First Panzer Army was caught between Soviet and American forces racing to see which would liberate Prague, one of the opening moves of the superpower conflict that would soon develop between the two nations. Squeezed on all sides, the panzer army continued to fight near Prague until 9 May, after the Second World War was technically over.[75]

General of Panzer Troops Walther Nehring

Nehring was born in East Prussia in 1892 and joined Infantry Regiment 152 in 1915. As a major in 1931, he was deputy to Colonel Guderian, chief of staff of General Lutz's Inspectorate of Motorized Troops. By 1937, he commanded Panzer Regiment 5, and then served as chief of staff of Guderian's XIX Corps in Poland and France. Between France and Barbarossa, Nehring was one of the few panzer generals to support the doubling of number of panzer divisions by halving the number of panzers in each: he believed in their original size, the divisions were too large and unwieldy. For Barbarossa Nehring received command of one of those new divisions, 18th Panzer, under Guderian as before.

Nehring stayed with Second Panzer Army through the battles of Minsk, Smolensk all the way to Moscow. After some defensive fighting near Sukhinichi in the winter, Nehring transferred to North Africa in March 1942. He took command of the Africa Corps (15th and 21st Panzer Divisions and the 90th Light Division) under Rommel's Panzer Army Africa. There he helped win the magnificent cauldron battle at Gazala and contributed to the capture of Tobruk. He was wounded during an Allied air attack that August while driving towards Alam Halfa and medically evacuated back to Germany. Nehring returned to Africa in November, and commanded the ad hoc XC Corps defending Tunis. Believing the Germans could not defend Tunisia, he soon fell foul of both his political and military masters (Goebbels' representative and Kesselring, respectively). He remained in North Africa less than one month.

Nehring was back on the Eastern Front by February 1943, to take command of the XXIV Panzer Corps under Hoth's Fourth Panzer Army. His corps was designated as a reserve of Operation Citadel's southern pincer. It later participated in the defense of the Ukraine, including the critical battle against the Soviet bridgehead over the Dnepr at Burkin and Kanev in September. The XXIV Panzer played key roles in the defensive battles of both First and Fourth Panzer Armies during the winter of 1943–44. He evidently returned to the good graces of his superiors, receiving the Oak Leaves in February 1944. A month later, Nehring's XXIV Panzer was part of the First Panzer's pocket that 'wandered' from Cherkassy–Korsun to relative freedom. During the summer of that year, Nehring served a month-long tour of duty as acting commander of the Fourth Panzer Army.

Back at XXIV Panzer in late summer, Nehring guided that formation westward through Poland as part of Army Group Vistula. By early 1945, his corps drifted toward Silesia, where it avoided destruction and joined up with Panzer Corps Grossdeutschland. Nehring ended the war commanding the First Panzer Army near Prague for six weeks. One would have to judge Nehring as a good tactical-level panzer general, but whose main claim to fame was his career-long association with Guderian. He died in 1983.

Chapter 3
Second Panzer Army

Ironically, the panzer army with the greatest promise at the beginning of Operation Barbarossa ended the war with the most meager history of the four. The Second went from being first among equals in 1941 to barely identifiable on a map in 1945. During Barbarossa, with panzer legend Guderian at its head, Second Panzer raced past Minsk and Smolensk to the Yelnia bridgehead, barely 300km from Moscow. It then swung south to help create the Kiev Kessel and then returned north for the final, failed assault on Stalin's capital.

In early December 1941, Second Panzer went over to the defensive, Field Marshal Günther von Kluge cashiered Guderian and the army settled down to a year and a half of essentially static defensive and anti-partisan operations. It would no longer be a weapon of operational significance to the Ostheer. From early 1942 on, it would be a panzer army in name only. As a final insult to its former glory, Schnelle Heinz's old outfit sat out Operation Citadel in favor of the Ninth Army. Its headquarters deployed to the Balkans during the summer of 1943 to lead more anti-partisan duty there. By spring 1945, it defended the Third Reich's last major natural oil fields in Hungary and ended the war fighting near Vienna.

As part of Army Group Center, Second and Third Panzer Armies were paired to create Barbarossa's main effort. Their mission was to drive from south and north of the Bialystok salient and destroy the dangerously exposed Western Front and any follow-on Soviet defenders trying to hold the relatively high

Campaign	Battles and Engagements
Barbarossa, 22 June–5 December 1941	Bialystok, Brest, Slonim, Minsk, Dnepr, Stalin Line, Smolensk, Roslavl, Yelnia, Kritchev, Gomel, Kiev, Bryansk, Tula
Defense of Army Group Center, 6 December 1941–15 August 1943	Yefremov, Tula, Orel, Suckhinichi, anti-partisan action, Bolkhov, Orel bulge, Bryansk
Yugoslavia, 22 August 1943–18 October 1944	Occupy Croatia, Serbia, Albania, disarm Italians, combat Tito's partisans
Danube, 19 October 1944–8 May 1945	Danube, Drau, Lake Balaton, Nagykanizsa, Carinthia, Steiermark

ground along the 'traditional' Warsaw–Minsk–Smolensk–Moscow invasion route. The Luftwaffe's premier CAS formation, von Richthofen's VIII Flieger-korps, flew overhead. Field Marshal von Bock intended for them to act in concert with the Fourth and Ninth (and later, Second) Armies to create massive encirclement battles along the way. Once Smolensk had fallen, the German high command would decide where the two panzer armies would go during Barbarossa's next phase. Capturing Moscow itself was not an explicit goal of the Barbarossa campaign, except in the minds of a few generals. For Hitler and consistent with centuries of German military thought, Moscow was merely a reason for enemy armies to concentrate, thence to be destroyed in a panzer-led Vernichtungsschlacht.

For Guderian's men the campaign began at 0315 hours on Sunday, 22 June, after a half hour of artillery preparation. There was little finesse in their opening moves, they simply plunged into the center of Major General AA Korobkov's 4th Army. Except for the fortress Brest, Red Army units on the frontier did not put up much of a fight. Second Panzer men used existing bridges as well as inflatable rafts, assault boats and eighty 'submarine' tanks of 1st Battalion, Panzer Regiment 18 of the 18th Panzer Division to swarm across the Bug River. German construction engineers built additional bridges by 0500 hours. The dearth of defensive fire caused the Germans to have a false impression of their own strengths and of enemy weaknesses. By 1500 hours, first the 3rd, then the 4th Panzer Division had slashed through the Soviet defenses and were heading east unhindered along the Panzerstrasse toward Bobruisk. By the second day of the campaign a dangerous trend developed as Guderian had already outrun his logistics and already required aerial resupply.[1]

Along much of the defensive line, commander of the Soviet Western Front, Colonel General DG Pavlov issued nonsense orders to imaginary units in accordance with unrealistic pre-war 'Red Folder' orders. His mission was to first halt Guderian then counterattack into the Reich. But he did manage to launch a counterattack against Guderian that first day with the 478 tanks of the 14th Mechanized Corps. Within 48 hours this formation lost nearly 50 percent of its tanks and by the 26th, its operational rate stood below one-tenth of that. Guderian's panzers brushed aside the threat and plunged ever eastward. With the help of Polish peasants guiding the way, the 3rd Panzer bypassed Red Army defenses near Kobryn and on the 23rd captured the 4th Army headquarters. Because of the sand and marshland to either side of Second Panzer's axis of advance, German vehicles had largely to remain on the road. The division had advanced 150km by 24 June, but the tail end of its rear services still had not left occupied Poland. Division commander and future field marshal, Walther

Model, escaped death that day when Soviet artillery destroyed his eight-wheeled armored car (killing its crew) moments after Model had dismounted.[2]

Soviet pioneers did a good job of demolishing bridges along the Panzer-strasse, but this did not significantly slow Guderian. While XXIV Panzer Corps continued east, XLVII Panzer angled northeast as part of Second Panzer's encircling force. At one point, the 17th Panzer Division stood so far in front of the bulk of his forces, it became encircled near Slonim on Guderian's left and needed to be rescued by its sister formation, 18th Panzer. In turn, the 29th Motorized had to keep the road open between both divisions and the panzer army's rear echelons. Four days into Barbarossa, XXIV Panzer Corps was through the flaming town of Slutsk, 300km deep in the USSR. On that same day, in order to appease Hitler, OKH ordered von Bock to close the proposed Kessel with inner (infantry armies at Bialystok) and outer pincers around Minsk (panzer armies). The army group commander disagreed since he wanted to continue toward Moscow, but nevertheless passed these orders down the chain of command. To the north, for the next two days, Hoth duly maneuvered his panzer army toward the Belorussian capital, entering it on the 28th. With Guderian racing east according to his own whims, not enough Second Panzer units came up to meet Hoth. For more than 24 hours, Soviet units escaped the trap until the 18th Panzer finally closed on Minsk from the south on the 29th.[3] As he had on more than on occasion during the French campaign, Guderian allowed his personal desires to override his professional duty. Nevertheless, the Ostheer had reason to be satisfied after the blitzkrieg had completely dismantled the Western Front's defensive structure in a matter of days.

At the beginning of Barbarossa, as had been the case during the western campaign, panzer armies had been tied to specific infantry armies, supposedly to ease command and control and logistics matters during an operation's break-through stage. This was not meant to be a permanent arrangement. So on the 28th, von Bock considered that Guderian had achieved 'operational freedom' and cut Second Panzer loose from von Kluge's Fourth Army. Guderian, who had been chafing under the plodding infantry army commander, must have breathed a sigh of relief. However, almost simultaneously, after a headlong rush, the 3rd Panzer Division slowed down when it encountered a destroyed bridge over the Beresina River. The Soviets had hoped to recreate a coherent defense along that line. Model had to wait for heavy artillery to come forward and assist the assault pioneers. At this point, he fought a two-day set-piece battle against the 20th Army at Bobruisk in which leader losses were especially high: the general was almost wounded again, as was a major standing right next to him. Aided by aerial reconnaissance, on the last day of June, 4th Panzer, on the right flank of General of Panzer Troops Leo Geyr von Schweppenburg's corps, took an important railroad bridge at Svisloch by coup, opening the way for Guderian once again.[4]

Von Bock had given Hoth 'operational freedom' on the second day of Barbarossa, already releasing him from Ninth Army control. Now that Guderian had the same privileges, he flew to Hoth's headquarters on 30 June. The ostensible reason for their meeting was to coordinate how they would negotiate the Berezina River obstacle. However, the meeting took on the aspect of a conspiracy when, on their own initiative, the two agreed to renew eastward movement and to not brook any delays in their advance imposed by higher headquarters. The next day, fighting in the various Minsk pockets officially ended. Army Group Center, behind the two panzer armies, had bagged 342,000 POWs, killed an estimated 200,000 men, eliminated 32 Soviet divisions and 6 brigades, destroyed 3,332 tanks and 1,809 guns at a cost of about 5,000 German dead and 18,000 wounded. After barely two weeks, the Ostheer had won its first great victory and the Red Army defense of the critical Moscow axis lay in shambles. The panzer armies had done the heavy lifting.[5] They had proved their value in the first major panzer operation since France the year before.

Nothing in the Nazi-Soviet War came easy, however. Despite the mass surrender, the Red Army contested every step. A Grossdeutschland soldier recalled an engagement near Stolpce, on 5 July:

> Rollbahn: enemy in the woods to the left. Sturmgeschütze are under Lieutenant Franz, with whom we coordinate and make plans to destroy the enemy. As they are still 400 meters in front of the grain field, the company advances across a broad front. When we get to the edge of the woods a platoon goes in. Then: 'Urrah!' the Russians attack with total surprise. Wild explosions, ricochets, panic. A few men run back to the road embankment. We build a new holding line here – that was quite a shock. One half hour later, accompanied by a 50mm PAK, the company pushes into the woods again to save our wounded comrades. There were 5–6 men ... Finally we reach them. There they lay, wickedly mutilated, bestially disfigured – all dead! That was quite a shock that all the men carried with them: everyone knew what it meant to fall into Russian hands.[6]

At this critical juncture, Army Group Center did something in common with many organizations (military and otherwise) that often pays minimum dividends at a steep cost: it reorganized. On 3 July, the German high command converted the Fourth Army into the Fourth Panzer Army with von Kluge at its head. Ostensibly, the reason behind this peculiar move so short into the campaign, was to make von Bock's job easier and both to coordinate better and somewhat rein in Hoth and Guderian by placing them under an intermediate headquarters. In reality the action may have been a salve to Hitler's nervousness that the two panzer armies were behaving completely unrestrained. Von Kluge turned over most of his infantry units to Headquarters Second Army, coming up from the rear. As conceived, he would lead the two panzer formations while the Second and Ninth Armies brought up the rear. Henceforth, von Bock would figuratively command two separate armies, one fast and one slow, each with radically different missions and neither in close contact with the other.[7] Even von Bock's choice of commander, von Kluge, was a curious one: at no time since the invasion of Poland nearly two years earlier had he shown the flair assumed to be required for the job of the senior panzer commander in the east. He had nothing to recommend him for the position, except that as a field marshal he outranked the two colonel generals. Within three days of assuming command first von Brauchitsch and then von Bock admonished him to get his new panzer army moving. By then Army Group Center's two field marshals were not even talking to one another. With von Kluge, equally as poor a subordinate as a superior (plus not at all comfortable with the blitzkrieg), this arrangement did not last beyond the 27th of the month. In the end this completely unsatisfactory command relationship served no useful purpose, and may have even been counterproductive.

The mighty Dnepr River represented both a strategic objective for the Germans and a key to the Soviet defense. A major characteristic of the blitzkrieg was quick and decisive action, thus preventing the enemy from catching his balance. Guderian would have to overcome the obstacle in short order, but for his men, getting over the river was not the difficult part, staying across was. Even at high flood because of the heavy and late rains that spring, advance elements of the 3rd Panzer Division crossed the 800m-wide river near Rogatachev, also on 3 July. Three 'submarine' panzers tackled the river but only two made it to the far bank. With no reinforcements to speak of, this tiny bridgehead held out until the 6th, as casualties mounted while ammunition and food dwindled. Similarly, the 4th Panzer crossed 75km upstream at Stary Bychov the next day, but was thrown back over the river by Red Army troops who then destroyed the bridge. In spite of contemporary military intelligence (and subsequent military history) to the contrary, from what the Germans on the scene could tell, the so-called Stalin Line was very real. The well-defended garrison town of Stary Bychow, with its stout anti-tank ditch, created definite challenges. With the help of the 210mm guns of Mortar Battalion 604, 4th Panzer Division blasted free of the Dnepr on the 7th. It curled around to attack the 117th Rifle Division that had successfully barred the way of 3rd Panzer. Two days later,

Guderian visited the command post of the 29th Motorized to stress the importance of its crossing operation 100km further north beginning on 10 July. Guderian tried to overload the Soviet's Dnepr Line by constantly switching his Schwerpunkt from one site to another. The Soviet defense there was likewise too tough, and the 29th could not reach the near bank to even attempt a crossing. Finally, by 1400 hours on the 11th, the division was across with help from Sturmgeschutz Battalion 203, a flak battery firing over open sights, a PAK battalion plus corps pioneer units.[8] At last Second Panzer Army could put the Stalin Line behind it.

Guderian's headquarters occupied the same building in Tolochino that Napoleon had used in 1812. Thus inspired, by 11 July, Second Panzer split the junction between the 13th and 20th Armies and presently had a string of Dnepr bridgeheads (and therefore equally important, a string of breaches in the Stalin Line) at Orsha, Kopys, Bychov and Rogatachev. The Soviet line had been fatally compromised. Only Mogilev stood unbowed, but Guderian would not waste any more time or effort than absolutely necessary reducing it; Colonel General Maximilian Freiherr von Weichs' Second Army could do that. The 13th Army had spent weeks making Mogilev into a fortress. Initially two rifle divisions defended the town, joined in the third week of July by two more. But as then-Lieutenant General AI Eremenko complained after the war, 'There were no troops ... to prevent the enemy from crossing the Dnepr and then advancing in any direction he pleased'.[9] Red Army front headquarters were underdeveloped and in no way qualified to master these simultaneous crises. The Soviets could only react to German moves. Stalin demanded action, but Stavka could give him none. Fortunately for the Soviets, the situation was not as dire as Eremenko made it sound. Anchored by 'Gallant Mogilev' (which held out for 17 days until the 27th), Guderian struggled to get past the Dnepr Line through 16 July. Guderian's next objective, the open country south of Smolensk.

This hard-won freedom of maneuver allowed von Bock to close his next great Kessel, at Smolensk. Hoth sent his 7th Panzer down from the north. Guderian dispatched the 29th Motorized up to meet it. Only 40km separated the two units, representing tips of opposing pincers. By 14 July, the 29th reached Lenino, opening the road to the famous city. Defenders of the 16th Army put up a stiff resistance leading to high casualties on both sides. By the next evening, the 29th Motorized entered the southern suburbs of Smolensk and linked up with Hoth's men on 16 July.[10] But Guderian, still looking east, had only allocated one division to the task of closing the southern portion of the trap. Inside the pocket, 16th Army commander Lieutenant General MF Lukin, NKVD commanders and Communist Party officials organized a viable defense and even a workable escape plan. House-to-house fighting in the city was costly to both sides. While Stalin demanded a defense to the last man, von Bock lamented that his Kessel 'has a hole'. Since Guderian paid scant attention to the encirclement and stubbornly headed east with the bulk of his panzer army, tens of thousands of Soviets soldiers escaped. Indeed, even though the rest of Second Panzer wreaked havoc with Marshal Timoshenko's defensive structure, in so doing it made the victory at Smolensk incomplete.

The men of XXIV Panzer Corps took their place at Guderian's right, a virtual outpost surrounded on three sides by Red Army khaki. A Kampfgruppe of 4th Panzer reached Krichev on the morning of 17 July and secured a bridge over the River Sozh. A couple of days later it reported its combat vehicle status: 44 panzers operational, 49 in repair, 40 awaiting parts and 42 total write-offs. With the division spread out in a long thin line, maintenance suffered as rear services struggled to keep up. In the 3rd Panzer, some companies had lost all their officers in less than a month of fighting. On 19 July, the Soviets attacked XXIV Panzer Corps command post, forcing von Schweppenburg to defend himself with a machine pistol.[11]

These attacks acted as harbingers of renewed Soviet efforts to dispute Smolensk. In early July, Stavka told Timoshenko to 'deliver a series of counter-strokes along the . . . Borisov and Bobruisk axes:'[12] – direct threats to Guderian. The speed and violence of the blitzkrieg still confounded the Soviets, however, so that by the time Timoshenko was ready to attack, Guderian had advanced far beyond Bobruisk. Orders were orders, especially when they came from Stalin, so the marshal created an attack force with units on hand and launched the assault as soon as he was ready. As would be the case throughout the Nazi-Soviet war, German strategic intelligence (Fremde Heere Ost) completely underestimated Soviet forces available. On 8 July, it told Hitler that Timoshenko had only eleven divisions with which to counter Army Group Center. In reality sixty-six divisions defended the Moscow axis, twenty-four of those in the first echelon alone. Frustrated by Timoshenko's slowness, Stavka (read: Zhukov) instructed him 'Immediately organize a powerful and coordinated counterstroke by all available forces from Smolensk [and] Orsha [and] conduct active operations along the Gomel and Bobruisk axis to exert pressure on the rear of the enemy's Bobruisk grouping.'[13] The Soviet leadership hoped that every tiny effort would cause Guderian to pause and the blitzkrieg to stumble.

As originally intended, Stavka launched the 'Timoshenko Offensive' in order to threaten German pincers encircling Smolensk, thereby saving the city and its defenders. By the time Timoshenko's units were finally ready, the Germans had Smolensk encircled, so his new mission was amended to break into the city and relieve the siege. Timoshenko directed most of his attention against Hoth, considered the most dangerous threat to Moscow. Only Group Kachalov (the 28th Army, from left to right, 145th and 149th Rifle and 104th Tank Divisions supported by the 209th Assault and 239th Fighter Aviation Regiments) attacked Guderian. NKVD Lieutenant General VI Kachalov began his assault on 23 July, from near Roslavl and toward Pochep. He blindsided 10th Panzer and Grossdeutschland, even threatening to encircle elements of the two units with the 145th Rifle and 104th Tank Divisions. Von Bock instructed Guderian to take stock of the situation.[14]

The two forces faced off between Roslavl and Smolensk. Guderian's solution was to counterattack toward the base of Kachalov's attack at Roslavl, an important Soviet communications node. On 27 July, he briefed his plan to von Brauchitsch and von Bock and received a green light. On the last day of July, Guderian pulled XXIV Panzer and VII Corps (23rd, 78th, 197th Infantry Divisions) out of the line near Krichev to counterattack toward the east and into Kacahalov's rear. The next day, he sent IX Corps (263rd and 292nd Infantry Divisions) from the opposite direction (southeast) to finish off the Soviet threat. Roslavl fell on 3 August, with 38,000 POWs taken and 250 tanks and 713 guns destroyed. Kachalov, personally commanding a tank, died trying to escape the trap. A week later the battle was over, as was the entire 'Timoshenko Offensive'.[15] From the German's perspective, the threat to Smolensk was past, and although German memoirs refer to Timoshenko's attack, little respect is shown for the Soviet effort. On the other side of the front, Stalin proved that he would grasp at the initiative whenever he could, although Red Army forces lost in July and August would be sorely needed two months later when von Bock threatened Moscow for real.

While Guderian devoted nearly half of his panzer army to holding back Kachalov, he still had the other half with which to accomplish his other two missions: contribute to reducing the Smolensk pocket and keeping the east-ward pressure on the Soviet defenders. Guderian's absorption with the second of these objectives and his inattention to the first, meant that many members of the 16th and 20th Armies escaped the Smolensk Kessel in the direction of Dorogobuzh. Eventually the cordon firmed up and the escapes ended. On 5 August, von Bock could announce that his army group had bagged another 302,000 POWs plus destroyed 3,205 tanks, 3,120 guns and 1,098 aircraft.[16]

Army Group Center's haul at Smolensk, coupled with that at Minsk and the numerous smaller encirclements Guderian and Hoth created along the way, give the impression of a flawless campaign. Problems with panzer army employment in fact plagued both the strategic and operational levels. The debates at Germany's highest level during late July and early August need not detain us here. Suffice it to say, that when Barbarossa hit this critical 'what next?' stage,

Führer Headquarters, Armed Forces High Command (OKW) and OKH could not operate with the necessary unity of effort. Nevertheless, at a conference of army chiefs of staff on 25 July, Army Commander in Chief von Brauchitsch criticized both von Bock's inability to mass his panzers and what he sensed as a lack of a unifying Schwerpunkt: such weaknesses would hamstring the successful conduct of any campaign. The army group's chief of staff, Colonel Hans von Greiffenberg came to his commander's defense: how could there be a Schwerpunkt when von Bock had to operate in three directions?[17] A similar problem existed with the Second Panzer Army, which also lacked a clear focus and had been pulled in three directions. The expedient of creating a unitary panzer army headquarters like the Fourth might have worked if there had been some forethought given to the matter and if it had had a suitable commander. Although the Germans proved again and again throughout the Second World War that they were masters of improvisation, the main effort of their most massive invasion was probably not the best place to experiment on the fly. As for von Kluge, his greatest failure, the inability to pull the trigger decisively on the main German assault against Moscow, still lay ahead of him months down the road.

With both the 'Timoshenko Offensive' and Smolensk behind them, Second Panzer Army now had two goals. The push east, always toward Moscow, was uppermost in Guderian's mind. However, the move south on Roslavl would also lead him in a new direction: to the Ukraine. Any delay at this point would allow the Soviets to recover their balance, anathema to the blitzkrieg. Sudden moves, such as Second Panzer's 90 degree turn, would surely compound Stavka's confusion. Von Bock would have to pick up the pace now that Guderian had turned south, where the terrain was less well suited to the defense, and better for the Panzerwaffe.

While strategic-level decisions may have been slow in coming out of Rastenburg and Zossen at this point, Guderian did not tarry. Until explicitly ordered south, he pushed his men onward in the direction of Stalin's capital. Before either the Smolensk or Roslavl battles had run their courses, on 20 July, XLVI Panzer Corps units occupied Yelnia midway between the two main east–west roads to Moscow. The town had three features that both sides coveted: high ground, a bridge over the Desna and a rail station on a main east–west line. Initially, 10th Panzer and SS Reich Divisions occupied the position and had to defend it until marching infantry arrived. Surrounded by Red Army forces to the north, east and south, meant that the salient also suffered from a shortage of infantry and CAS. At the end of July, Stalin ordered Zhukov to eliminate the threat at Yelnia. Therefore, four days after the Germans arrived, Timoshenko began to pound the town.[18]

The original and the senior panzer army commander: Field Marshal Evald von Kleist. A hussar lieutenant present at Tannenberg in 1914, von Kleist led First Panzer Army for over two years and was the only German field marshal to die in Soviet captivity after the war. (*US National Archives and Records Administration*)

Colonel General Hermann 'Papa' Hoth commanded the XV Panzer Corps and the Third and Fourth Panzer Armies from Poland through the end of 1943. Fighting in the Soviet Union between 1941 and 1943, he demonstrated mastery of both offense and defense on the twentieth-century battlefield. (*US Army Military History Institute*)

Once and future panzer army commanders. During Barbarossa, Fourth Panzer Army commander Colonel General Erich Hoepner talks on a field phone as XLI Panzer Corps commander, General of Panzer Troops Georg-Hans Reinhardt looks on. Hoepner was executed in connection with the July 1944 Attentat, while Reinhardt went on to command Third Panzer from October 1941 to August 1944. (*Podzun Verlag, Friedberg Germany*)

During the Second World War, Colonel General Erhard Raus commanded armored formations ranging from panzer brigades to panzer armies, the latter of which he led the First, Third and Fourth. (*Podzun Verlag, Friedberg Germany*)

Luftwaffe General Wolfram von Richthofen, a real friend of the Panzertruppen, surrounded by four army officers. He initially commanded Germany's premier CAS outfit, VIII Fliegerkorps, and later, Luftflotte Four in the southern theater. (*Podzun Verlag, Friedberg Germany*)

A collection of PzKw IIIs in a field of sunflowers in the Ukraine during Operation Barbarossa. These belong to 14th Panzer Division, III Panzer Corps in von Kleist's First Panzer Army. (*US National Archives and Records Administration*)

An excellent example of the cooperation of all branches. During Operation Barbarossa, 9th Panzer Division engineers span a demolished bridge used by tracked (a SdKfz 251/6 command half-track) and wheeled vehicles, while a Luftwaffe liaison Storch aircraft flies above. (*Podzun Verlag, Friedberg Germany*)

A K18, 105mm SP artillery piece passes a PzKw III during Operation Barbarossa. Only two of these K18s were made by Krupp for the assault on Gibraltar. They enjoyed considerable success against Soviet armor while serving with the 3rd Panzer Division in the summer of 1941. (*Ian Baxter*)

Fourth Panzer Army during Barbarossa: a PzKw III of Reinhardt's XLI Panzer Corps overlooking the Velikaya River south of Lake Pskov in July 1941. (*Ian Baxter*)

A mechanized column halted near Ostrov in July 1941, therefore probably 8th Panzer Division elements of von Manstein's LVI Panzer Corps. On the right are PzKW III Ausf E or F, and on the left are anti-tank and artillery prime movers, the closest being a light SdKfz 10. (*Ian Baxter*)

German panzers, infantry and a half-track advance over a freshly harvested field during Operation Barbarossa. (*Ian Baxter*)

A PzKw IV Ausf D/E/F heading one way as a truck convoy goes the other. Spare lengths of track hang on the hull as additional armor, while either the radio operator or loader enjoys the scenery for a change. (*Ian Baxter*)

A hastily whitewashed PzKw III Ausf F/G/H overwatching a Russian village in winter. (*Ian Baxter*)

A LVI Panzer Corps PzKw III traverses a temporary bridge near Stolcy during Operation Barbarossa. This photograph provides a good idea of the marshy terrain that panzer units of Army Group North had to deal with. (*Ian Baxter*)

Action front! Two SdKfz 250 half-tracks and two PzKw IIIs. In the middle ground lies a smoking Soviet BT-5 tank. *(Ian Baxter)*

Soviet partisans did not only attack German rear services. Here a 2nd Panzer Division PzKw III sits in the rubble of a demolished bridge. *(Podzun Verlag, Friedberg Germany)*

A 9th Panzer Division Igel (defensive perimeter) on the road to Stalingrad in 1942. Panzers on the horizon overwatch half-tracks and other vehicles. In the foreground, from left to right, are a SdKfz 250, three SdKfz 251s and a PzKw Ausf G. (*Podzun Verlag, Friedberg Germany*)

Three Tiger Is ford a stream in a village seemingly barely touched by combat. With little modification, the Tiger could ford water 4m deep. (*Ian Baxter*)

Two PzKw IV Ausf Ds, probably occupying defensive positions in a Russian village. Judging by the relaxed posture of troops, there is a lull in the fighting. *(Ian Baxter)*

Tiger I and a half-track working in tandem. In the foreground is MG42 mounted behind an armored shield on the armored personnel carrier. Many models of the SdKfz 251 carried this weapons mount. *(Ian Baxter)*

Panzergrenadiers hitch a ride aboard a Panther. The weathered whitewash camouflage paint does little good. Once it overcame initial teething problems, the Panther surmounted the T-34 as the best tank of the Second World War. (*Ian Baxter*)

Red Army POWs walk past an SS Sturmgeschütz III Ausf F and motorcycle with side car. The F model assault gun was the first up-gunned (75mm) second-generation version. Sturmgeschütze increasingly replaced actual panzers as the most numerous AFVs throughout the German Army. (*Nik Cornish at Stavka*)

A Tiger I on a muddy street in a Russian city. This vehicle uses spare track blocks to augment its frontal armor. The oil drum only hints at the Tiger's debilitating fuel consumption, a real problem for a petroleum-poor country like Germany. *(Ian Baxter)*

Panthers with panzergrenadiers on board and Tiger I panzers operating on a featureless Russian landscape. Soldiers cannot always choose the ground on which they fight, and this terrain offers no cover or concealment. *(Ian Baxter)*

A column of Tiger I panzers with infantry on board. The fortunes of the panzer armies generally improved when Tigers were present. (*Ian Baxter*)

A PzKw IV Ausf D and an Ausf G/H loaded on a railcar. During the second part of the war, coal-rich Germany made excellent use of railroads for strategic and operational movement of reserves despite Allied air superiority over most of Europe. (*Ian Baxter*)

Panzergrenadiers lead a Tiger I across a winter landscape. In order to succeed, infantry and armor had to cooperate with each other plus artillery and engineers and often the Luftwaffe. The man in front carries an MG42 tripod. *(Ian Baxter)*

In another Russian winter scene, a section of three StuG III assault guns and a Russian village under a light dusting of fresh snow. *(Ian Baxter)*

Tiger I and infantry share a road. The panzers may receive most of the glory but on both sides of the Nazi-Soviet War, the infantry did most of the fighting and dying. (*Ian Baxter*)

Two successful German armored fighting vehicle designs: in the background is the magnificent Panther, passing in front of is a Jagdpanzer 38 (t), a Czech-built chassis mounting a 75mm gun. (*Ian Baxter*)

Combined arms cooperation was central to the success of blitzkreig tactics. Here an 88mm Flak gun and a Panzer III Ausf E/F operate together in an open field. Judging by the early model weapons and paint schemes, this photo could be from Operation Barbarossa. (*Nik Cornish at Stavka*)

The Germans adapted the obsolete PzKw II to the late war battlefield by mounting a 105mm leFH18 artillery piece to the panzer chassis. The new weapon was named Wespe (Wasp) and matched the panzer's mobility. *(Taylor Library)*

The Hornisse (Hornet) married the new L43 version of the 88mm gun to a PzKw III or IV chassis (in this case a IV). They debuted with the 655th Heavy Tank Hunting Detachment during Citadel. Also called the Nashorn (Rhinoceros), it served with anti-tank units at the corps and army level. *(Taylor Library)*

In a successful effort to provide panzers with mobile artillery, the Germans joined a 150mm sFH18 howitzer to a PzKw III/IV chassis and named it Hummel (Bumblebee, in this photograph a IV). It fired a 95lb shell over 14km. (*Taylor Library*)

Crewman loads main-gun ammunition aboard a PzKw IV Ausf D. Supplemental armor can be seen on the turret and 30mm armor plate is bolted to the front of the hull. (*Ian Baxter*)

The following testimony to the severity of the fighting around Yelnia was written by a member of the 1st Battalion of Grossdeutschland on 23 July:

From 0100–0300 the artillery fire weakens. Then, near the rail crossing it beats like a drum. Early on my old Feldwebel Herald is brought back – he has lost his hearing and his great eyes stare into the emptiness. Lieutenant Hänert's foxhole is between his two machine guns. From here communications is very difficult. Radio interference is bad, dispatch runners cannot get through and he can hardly move. Ammunition and food gets forward in pitiable amounts.

Since morning twilight the lieutenant looks through his scissors binoculars. Back and forth one sees tracers into the woods. One slight movement is enough to recognize – They're coming! Great heaps of men advance near the stream. Everything in front of us is Russian brown. Here and there heads pop up from our foxholes.

The bulk of them are near the stream. The Russian artillery fire begins. Our ears ring. Only two of our infantry guns fire. Detonations churn up the ground but are way too few. A couple of mortars now help. The brown mass is in front of us. Despite our fire in the stream they do not weaken. They're coming! Always new attacks. It is oppressive. Lieutenant Hänert, commander of the machine gun company, can do nothing. Through the glasses one can see every man, every head is recognized. Now we see their faces. They're coming! From twelve barrels the machine guns shoot continuously. It begins and ends abruptly. For sure there is a drain on all weapons.

One cannot write here the astonished screams. In seconds the heaps of men are in front of us. Pause, ammo belts rattle, here and there a machine gun bolt rips back and forth ...

The Russians come closer and closer. Their fire sings, explodes and whistles everywhere ...[19]

By early August, Guderian threw his last reserve into the fight: the guard company of his own panzer army headquarters. With the Smolensk pocket finally cleaned up, German infantry began marching into Yelnia. These were soon joined by batteries from another Second Panzer Army asset: the Luftwaffe's I Flak Corps. After weathering many determined assaults, by 8 August, Guderian withdrew his mobile units from defending the exposed positions. With his attention now directed toward Kiev, he turned over responsibility for the salient to Ninth Army.[20] For them, Barbarossa became an old-fashioned battle of attrition, not the blitzkrieg war or maneuver.

By the second half of August, Hitler had finally prevailed over his unruly generals. As he had originally decided in the autumn of 1940, the Ostheer would take care of its flanks before turning on Moscow. Therefore much of Hoth's Third Panzer would turn north, while Guderian moved in the opposite direction. With its counterattack at Roslavl, the Second Panzer somewhat unintentionally began the southern trajectory that would lead to history's greatest encirclement battle. For Hitler, maneuvering against Gomel was the next logical step toward the Ukraine. In terms of blitzkrieg thinking, it was completely consistent with the 'line of least resistance' aim. To Stavka this move likewise made sense: the Soviet high command assumed von Bock merely sought to firm up his flanks in preparation for the anticipated assault on Moscow. Von Weichs' Second Army received the mission of taking Gomel, but due to a dearth of artillery ammunition, muddy roads and other factors, its attack developed slowly. Only on 12 August were his men ready. In order to prevent any defenders from escaping, Guderian sent his far right element, XXIV Panzer Corps, hooking around the city to the east. By the 17 August, the 21st Army defenders began to evacuate, but could not move faster than the panzers. Second Army and Second Panzer captured another 50,000 POWs between them, and at the twin battles of Rogatachev and Gomel, basically demolished the brand new Central Front.[21] But had Stalin bought an additional ten days to solidify his position?

The drama within the German high command over, Barbarossa's next move had not yet played out completely and Guderian himself would play a major part in the next scene. On 21 August, Hitler wrote a Denkschrift (thought paper) on the Moscow–Kiev debate, having the last word, so he believed, on the campaign's subsequent direction. After a month's wrangling back and forth with his senior generals, he now had good reason to believe that the matter was closed. The next day, OKH ordered Second Panzer to continue south. But Halder believed he had one last scam in his bag of tricks: the word of the Führer's favorite panzer general. On 24 August, he flew to Army Group Center headquarters and got agreement from von Bock, Guderian and others that Moscow should be the next objective. Guderian came back to Rastenburg and that same evening, had a conference with Hitler (Field Marshal Wilhelm Keitel and Colonel General Alfred Jodl were there, significantly, von Brauchitsch and Halder were not). That night, in exchange for Hitler's promise that Second Panzer Army would remain intact, Guderian recanted everything he had told Halder earlier in the day. Tasks that had been unachievable during the conference at army group headquarters all of a sudden were possible. When the Chief of Staff found out about this on the 25th, he was furious with Guderian.[22]

The Soviets only slowly alerted to the danger posed by the Second Panzer's southward movement. Stalin believed Guderian was attempting an end run toward Moscow, and could not fathom a 90 degree turn on Kiev. Stavka hastily threw the new Bryansk Front (Eremenko) and specifically, its 40th Army (Podlas) in Guderian's way. The Second Panzer advanced with XXIV Panzer (3rd and 4th Panzer, 10th Motorized Divisions) in the lead and XLVII Panzer (17th and 18th Panzer, 29th Motorized) covering the panzer army's left (outer) flank against Eremenko. As Guderian picked up speed and left the Second Army further behind, he also had to dedicate increasing scant resources, in this case XLVI Panzer (SS Reich and Grossdeutschland), to flank security. His movement south split the 40th Army, which drifted east toward Bryansk from the 21st Army, which slid toward Kiev. Stavka noted Guderian's increasingly lengthy and vulnerable flank, and ordered Eremenko to attack. The headquarters insisted Bryansk Front assault, not at one place but at two – Roslavl and Novozybkov. Eremenko lacked the requisite skill and mass and so failed as a result.[23] Likewise, the Germans had gained confidence and would not allow a flank attack to distract them. There would be no repeat of the nervousness that bedeviled Guderian at Stonne in May 1940.

As usual, Model's 3rd Panzer took its place at Guderian's front during the move south. His objective: the 800m-long bridge over the Desna River at Novgorod Seversky. The river was the last major obstacle before the Second Panzer broke into the relatively open Ukrainian countryside. As Model said at the time, 'That bridge is as good as a whole division'. Paul Carell relates the well-known story of its capture. One of Model's lieutenants noticed the bridge was still intact:

'It's still there!' Buchterkirch called out. Driver, radio operator and gunner all beamed. 'Antitank gun by the bridge! Straight at it!' the lieutenant commanded. The Russians fled. Lieutenant Störck and his men leaped from their armored carriers. They raced up to the bridge. They overcame the Russian guard. There, along the railings, ran the wires of the detonation charges. They tore them out. Over there were the charges themselves. They pushed them into the water. Drums of petrol were dangling from the rafters on both sides. They slashed the ropes. With a splash the drums hit the water. They ran on – Störck always in front . . .

Suddenly Störck pulled himself up . . . In the middle of the bridge lay a heavy Soviet aerial bomb, primed with a time fuse. Calmly, Störck unscrewed the detonator. It was a race to the death. Would he make it? He made it. The five men combined to throw the now harmless bomb out of the way.

They ran on. Only now did they realize what 800 meters meant. There did not seem to be an end to the bridge. At last they reached the far side and fired the prearranged flare signal for the armored spearhead.

Buchterkirch in his tank had meanwhile driven cautiously down the bank and moved under the bridge. Vopel with the rest of the tanks provided cover from the top of the bank. That was just as well. For the moment the Russians realized that the Germans were in possession of the bridge they sent in demolition squads – large parties of thirty or forty men, carrying drums of petrol, explosive charges and Molotov cocktails.[24]

The Germans prevailed and averted any further danger to the bridge. An hour later Guderian's units streamed across the Desna on their way south to their planned junction with von Kleist's First Panzer Army.

Both sides raced to occupy and then hold the Novgorod-Seversky bridge; Model won in each case. Not that the Soviets were giving up. In late August, the Red Army Air Force created Reserve Aviation Groups with their newest CAS aircraft, the Sturmovik, and threw most of these against Guderian. The Second Panzer kept coming. Model ordered a Kampfgruppe to Shostka to cut the direct rail connection between Moscow and Kiev. By early September, the Second Panzer, Second and Sixth Armies threatened the Soviet 5th Army from east, north and west. This elusive army that had been causing so much heartburn to von Rundstedt, was now in mortal danger. Over 300km to the south, von Kleist broke out of the Kremenchug bridgehead and the two panzer spearheads angled for a rendezvous. Marshal Budenny, coordinating the defensive efforts of the Southern and Southwestern Fronts sensed the danger to his flanks. On 4 September, he requested reinforcements. By the 6th, even Stavka knew that days were numbered for 21st Army, trying to maintain a connection between Budenny and the Bryansk Front. A day later Guderian's vanguard raced through Konotop and on towards Romny, deep in the marshal's rear.[25] The hopelessness of the Soviet's situation was becoming obvious to all. Faltering enemy morale was always a good omen to the blitzkrieg.

Stalin and the rest of the Soviet high command over-emphasized Romny's importance. The town represented Guderian's objective, here his men would link up with the First Panzer. But did Stavka really think holding on to yet another town would save two-thirds of a million men? Initially, only about ten tanks from the 10th Tank Division stood in Model's way. Soviet activity became frantic as the northern and southern jaws of the German encirclement got closer. On 8 September, Zhukov (relieved as Red Army Chief of Staff, but still a member of the Military Soviet) called for Timoshenko to replace Budenny at the helm of the Southwest Direction. On the next day, Stavka finally told the Southwest Front to reorient the 5th and 37th Armies away from the direct threat posed by Army Group South and against Guderian's oblique menace. On the 10th, Stalin fired his old crony Budenny for insubordination and Timoshenko arrived two days later to take over the ill-fated Southwest Direction. But half measures such as these amounted to the military equivalent of 'rearranging deck chairs on the *Titanic*'. On the same day, Stalin ordered 90 percent of the air assets in the Kiev sector against Romny. So tough was the Soviet defense that Model required two days to capture the town, which his men did on the 11th.[26]

Panzers

Panzers, German tanks, symbolize the Wehrmacht and the blitzkrieg to many. As is the case with the Luftwaffe and Kriegsmarine, Hitler began the war a few years too early for the Panzerwaffe. Training models, PzKw I and II, plus inadequate foreign types, such as the Czech 35(t), predominated in the force. Together with command panzers (no actual main gun at all) these 4 vehicle types made up 1,492 of the 3,512 panzers available to the 17 panzer divisions present on Barbarossatag, or 42 percent. Of course the Germans had other AFVs in their arsenal that day, armored cars, half-tracks and Sturmgeschütze. But of all these, panzers made up the main currency. It is a well-known fact that the Germans did not have the best or most numerous tanks during the war. But those they did have were adaptable, generally had three-man turrets and in the hands of trained crews, could generally prevail in a fair fight.

Prior to the invasion of Poland, like most armies of the world, the Panzerwaffe had not yet developed the main battle tank, a single version that could both support infantry and fight other tanks. Therefore two types were necessary, and the principal pairing in the early blitzkrieg days was the PzKw III and IV. The Wehrmacht intended that the III, with its 37mm main gun, and the IV, with its low-velocity 75mm gun, would fulfill the two respective roles. The Germans anticipated the weaknesses of the PzKw I, II and 35(t), but during Barbarossa, early marks of the III (Ausf – Ausführung or model – A through F) were also revealed to be inadequate. Fortunately for them, the vehicles' size and turret ring were big enough that it could be reengineered to mount larger 50mm guns (Ausf G-M). Even these upgunned models were insufficient for combat against superior Soviet types and production discontinued around February 1943.

The PzKw IV went on to become the mainstay of the Panzerwaffe. The stubby 75mm L24 main gun, familiar to most students of the war, gave way to a real anti-tank weapon (the L43) as early as Ausf F. Later models (Ausf G-J) mounted thicker armor and the higher velocity L48 main gun, making its firepower equal to the Panther and T-34. Its box-like construction made manufacture easy and the vehicle was roomy and reliable. During the war, engine horsepower increased from 250 to 300, and armor was augmented by Schürzen (skirts) bolted to the turret and hull. Over 9,000 PzKw IVs of all models were produced during the war, the last example coming off the assembly line only in March 1945.

The Red Army did have a main battle tank on 22 June 1941, and this T-34 came as a nasty surprise to the mass of the Ostheer (although the Germans had known of its existence for about six months). The Wehrmacht needed a response, and by January 1942 contracts were placed for a prototype panzer to match the T-34. The PzKw V Panther was the result. Initial marks (Ausf D) were sent to the battlefield before all 'teething troubles' had been solved, causing a bad first impression. Later Ausf A and especially Ausf G models, with more robust power plants, hull and coaxial machine-guns and other improvements, made the Panther one of the war's best tank designs. Armor was thick and sloped, the tracks wide and the 75mm L48 gun deadly. Panthers were employed in panzer divisions plus a bewildering number of independent brigades and battalions. Nearly 6,000 Panthers were produced by the end of the war.

Another German answer to massive Soviet tanks encountered in the east was the PzKw VI Tiger. Its main assets were the 88mm main gun and 100mm thick frontal armor; its main weaknesses were its 55-ton weight and ⅓-mile per gallon fuel consumption. These Achilles heels meant that many Tigers, immobilized for trivial reasons, were too heavy to tow or recover from the battlefield and had to be abandoned. The Ausf E was the most common variant, and made up the heavy panzer battalions and detachments in Grossdeutschland plus SS Leibstandarte, Das Reich and Totenkopf divisions and many independent formations. The larger Ausf B (King Tiger) had no equal on the battlefield but was made in numbers too small to have much impact on German fortunes. A total of 1,350 PzKw VI Ausf E were delivered.

In accordance with plans conceived months earlier and now completely overcome by events, Soviet reinforcements from Kharkov continued to pour into the developing trap. But von Kleist's panzers were nowhere near Romny. Fighting across the Dnepr, through the mud and against the Red Army was just too hard, and his First Panzer Army was behind schedule. Therefore, OKH ordered a new rendezvous 50km southward, closer to Lokhvitsa. On 15 September, an advance party of 3rd Panzer Division men led by Lieutenant Warthmann broke into the village and met soldiers from Hube's 16th Panzer coming up from the south. Now complete, the Kiev encirclement described a triangle 500km on a side, with an area of 135,000sq km. German forces around Lokhvitsa lined up back-to-back in order to face both into and out of the Kessel as Soviet escape and relief attempts began immediately.[27] Second Panzer Army represented the keystone dropped into an arc surrounding two-thirds of a million POWs. The annihilation of a serious threat to Army Group Center's right flank at Kiev, an essential precondition for the final offensive against Moscow, was complete.

The Ostheer's move south to the Ukraine and Guderian's participation in the Kiev Kessel is one of the most debated decisions of the Second World War. Many observers agree with Halder, that the Wehrmacht should have maintained its drive on Moscow. They accuse Hitler of grasping for low-hanging fruit in the form of a non-strategic victory at Kiev. But they do not see the danger posed by over a million Red Army men lurking to the east of the Ukrainian capital and the Rokitno Marshes. Beyond merely representing a massive force in being, these resources could have threatened either the southern flank of Army Group Center or the northern flank of Army Group South (or both) as they made their way east. Apparently these critics do not see Soviet forces arrayed along the Moscow axis weakened by losses incurred by the Timoshenko offensives of July and August. Many of these same critics likewise see the alternative capture of Moscow as a certainty. They see neither German weaknesses, nor Soviet strengths coupled with the determination of the Stalinist state to fight to the bitter end. The moves north and south by von Bock's two panzer armies that summer were correct in terms of the traditional German Vernichtungsgedanke, the original Barbarossa plan and necessities on the ground at the time.

In the third week of September, Guderian wheeled his forces (now reinforced by the XLVIII Panzer Corps from von Kleist) northeast for Barbarossa's upcoming showdown over Moscow. In fact, thanks to the panzer armies' rapid redeployment, Army Group Center rewrote its plans for Operation Typhoon, and added the Second Panzer to the offensive's order of battle, making the assault into a triple encirclement of the city's western-most defenses. Anxious about the possibility that the notorious Russian weather would turn bad at any moment, Guderian asked for and received permission to attack on 30 September, before the rest of von Bock's command. Although Second Panzer's operational rate for combat vehicles stood only at 50 percent, he commanded a sizeable force: XXIV Panzer Corps (3rd and 4th Panzer plus 10th Motorized Divisions); XLVII Panzer (17th and 18th Panzer, 29th Motorized Divisions); XLVIII Panzer (9th and 16th Panzer, 25th Motorized Divisions); XXXIV Corps (95th and 134th Infantry Divisions); XXXV Corps

(95th, 262nd, 293rd and 296th Infantry plus the 1st Cavalry Divisions) with Grossdeutschland in reserve. Opposing them was their familiar nemesis, Eremenko's Bryansk Front (3rd, 13th and 50th Armies plus Group Ermakov) guarding nearly 250km of front. The Germans felt comfortable about the manner with which they had addressed the flank issues at Leningrad and Kiev so had great confidence as well about Moscow.[28]

When Guderian struck on that cold and rainy morning, he hit Ermakov's five vulnerable divisions, just as the latter was about to launch his own attack toward Glukhov. This maneuver opened a 30km gap in the Soviet line, split the seam between two army sized units and exposed the flank of the unlucky but resilient 13th Army. But to Ermakov, the Second Panzer assault registered 'as only a diversion'. The next day, Eremenko remarkably dismissed the developing attack as 'not critical', and ordered Ermakov to continue with his planned maneuver, now becoming a very low-odds proposition. With the Luftwaffe pounding his headquarters, it is no wonder that the usually astute general missed the warning signs. The rest of Army Group Center began their Typhoon offensive on the second day of October, so now everyone in the Soviet high command knew that Guderian's move was no feint. But Stavka could not discern his objective: was it Kharkov, Kursk or Orel? In its confusion, the headquarters began to rail reserves back and forth across the Moscow defense line, but was always just a bit too slow. (Meanwhile, the rump of the Southwestern Front, smashed at Kiev, regrouped but posed no threat to Guderian's growing outer (eastern) flank.) Possibly on the strength of his reputation, Stavka focused on Guderian, making the job for the rest of von Bock's men all that easier. By 3 October, XXIV Panzer Corps captured Orel (Guderian's first objective) and stood nearly 200km deep inside the Soviet lines.[29] Seemingly beguiled by Guderian, Stalin fell for another blitzkrieg staple, the misdirection play wherein von Bock led with a supporting attack on his right (Second Panzer), caused Stavka to react, but then three days later launched his main effort with the center and left (Third and Fourth Panzer).

Logistics, especially fuel shortages, began to hamstring Guderian immediately. Seven Red tanks broke into the 4th Panzer Division's rear area near Orel and destroyed a dozen fuel and ammunition trucks. Fortunately for the Germans, depots captured in Orel had enough supplies to keep most of the Second Panzer Army advancing for nearly a week. For a while thereafter, the panzers had to run on low-grade Soviet fuel as other motorized units stood immobile with dry gas tanks for days.[30] Despite considerable logistics problems of their own, von Bock's armies executing the Viazma portion of Typhoon enjoyed better success. There were a number of reasons for this: both Second and Second Panzer Armies were relatively exhausted following the Kiev battle, and;

Guderian had two missions – close the Bryansk pocket and drive toward Moscow – and he clearly personally favored the second. Thus, in October Guderian earned the same bad rap as during Minsk and Smolensk: terminal inattention to sealing off encirclements satisfactorily. Evidently he did not subscribe to the Vernichtungsgedanke as did most of the German army.

Guderian received further direction at a conference at Army Group Center's headquarters on 7 October between von Bock's staff and von Brauchitsch and Heusinger: with the right wing of von Weichs' Second Army in tow, Second Panzer's next objective would be Tula. This did not bode well for German units still trying to seal and reduce the Bryansk Kessel. Apparently sublimating his personal obsession for Moscow, later that same day, Guderian ordered the XLVII Panzer to curl around counter-clockwise back toward the city of Bryansk and Second Army units advancing near there. The 17th Panzer Division entered the city and captured the Bryansk Front headquarters to the south (although most of the staff escaped). On 8 October, 18th Panzer finally linked up with elements of Second Army, officially closing the Bryansk half of Typhoon's triple envelopment. As before, largely because Guderian did not put the required emphasis on closing the pocket, 13,000 men from 3rd Army, 10,000 men from 13th Army and nearly 10 percent of the 50th Army escaped captivity. Nonetheless, together von Bock's forces had rent a 450km gash in the Soviet lines, while capturing another two-thirds of a million POWs. Zhukov, now in total command of Moscow's defenses, but with no apparent reserves to fill up the massive hole, decided he would establish the main line of resistance for the capital at Mozhaisk, and that in the south he would try to halt Guderian near Mtsensk. That mission fell on the 1st Guards Rifle Corps.[31] The weather offered the defenders a helping hand.

Rain and mud were nothing new to any German soldiers in the Ostheer. Unit war diaries, often starting well before Barbarossatag in occupied Poland, are full of examples of days when just a few hours of rain would turn roads into quicksand. Just as quickly, one hot day would dry up any traces of rain and turn the same road into choking dust. These anecdotal experiences did not prepare the invaders for the seasonal rasputitsa, literally, the time without roads. In the Second Panzer Army sector, serious rains began around the 7 October, and for the next month mobility improved only when temperatures sank below freezing. In the meantime rain and mud exhausted both men and beast, multiplied maintenance and fuel-consumption problems and generally helped to wreck German hopes.

Now it was the turn of OKH to issue nonsense orders, like those directing Guderian to capture Gorky, over 400km east of Moscow. Halder and the remainder of the German high command had no idea what its own men were capable of nor what resources the Red Army had available. Meanwhile, Guderian's spearhead, the XXIV Panzer Corps, made for Tula, 'Little Moscow', with its ultimate objective as Kolomna and Kashira. With 3rd Panzer on the left and 4th Panzer on the right, it headed north. A week after leaving Orel, they were nowhere close to Tula, but had run into a hornets' nest of T-34 tanks at Mtsensk. Only 88s, 105mm artillery pieces and Stukas had any effect against these monsters. By mid-October the entire panzer army counted only 271 panzers. With Guderian stalled far south of Tula, German hopes and Schwerpunkt shifted to the efforts of Third and Fourth Panzer Armies assaulting north of Moscow.[32]

Guderian was not about to allow his men to give up, however. He mustered elements of seven panzer, three motorized, five infantry divisions plus Grossdeutschland against Lieutenant General IV Boldin's 50th Army. But the Soviet general, who as Pavlov's deputy had launched one of the first Soviet counterattacks back in June and had escaped from both Minsk and Viazma pockets, would ruin the Second Panzer's chances. The 50th's defense would be crucial to the defense of Moscow's southern flank. On 25 October, XXIV Panzer renewed its attacks with the support of Grossdeutschland. A day later, the combination of Red infantry, T-34 and KV tanks, mud, Soviet CAS, half-completed anti-tank ditches and low fuel halted the Germans. That roadblock overcome, Guderian continued his northeast trek. Just to keep the drive alive, a few Ju-52 aircraft flew supplies to the muddy airfield at Tschern, south of Tula. A 3rd Panzer Division historian calls the battle against the 1st Guards Rifle Corps a 'labor of Sisyphus'. All of the corps' panzers were consolidated under Colonel Heinrich Eberbach, who earned the Oak Leaves to his Knight's Cross during these struggles. Toward the end of the month, Guderian measured progress in 5km per 48 hour increments. On 28 October, he visited the remnants of XXIV Panzer to exhort them to fight on the final 25km to Tula. The Red Army Air Force ruled the skies with the Luftwaffe nowhere to be seen. By the 29th, the Germans found that they had barely advanced 10km.[33]

On 30 October, the first Germans, a company of sixty men under a 19-year-old lieutenant, entered Tula's suburbs. Some Ju-52s managed to drop supply canisters from a height of 15m: many canisters broke into pieces upon impact with the frozen rock-hard ground. Fighting raged around Count Leo Tolstoy's estate, which the Germans tried not to damage. Dead Landsers were buried right next to the author's grave. On the same day, Hitler gave approval to the plan for the final push to surround Moscow. Seemingly divorced from reality on the ground, he ordered Guderian to attack over Kashira, swing around in a counter-clockwise direction east of Moscow, in order to meet up with Third Panzer Army coming from the opposite bearing. But, Second Panzer still had not solved the riddle of Tula; the city blocked the road to Moscow and could not be taken frontally. Fairly large (pre-war population: 300,000), it had many factories, elevations that offered good observation and fields of fire plus other features that favored the defense. On 8 November, near Uslovia, Boldin launched a preemptive attack against the master himself. Guderian's men occupied a great arc east, south and west of Tula: left to right, XLVII Panzer (General of Panzer Troops Joachim Lemelsen, 18th Panzer, 10th, 25th and 29th Motorized Divisions), LIII Corps (General of Infantry Karl Weisenberger, 167th and 112th Infantry), XXIV Panzer (General of Panzer Troops Leo Geyr von Schweppenburg, 3rd, 4th, 17th Panzer, Grossdeutschland) and XLIII Corps (General of Infantry Gotthard Heinrici, 31st and 131st Infantry). Panzer strength of the three assaulting divisions was pitiable: 3rd Panzer Division – 52 operational machines, 4th Panzer – 35, 17th Panzer – 15.[34]

Guderian launched his last attack at 0500 hours on 18 November. Aiming at Kolomna, and with Stukas flying overhead, he split the Western and Southwestern Fronts. Some 3rd Panzer troops captured an 80m bridge near Kamenka. However, four days into his last offensive, Guderian wanted to quit due to an extended eastern flank, debilitating weather and mounting casualties. The next day, the 23rd, von Bock even flew to his headquarters to urge the panzer general on to Kolomna. Everywhere the Germans made analogies to the Marne in 1914, and warned about the dangers of a premature halt to their attacks. The 17th Panzer somehow staggered into Kashira on the Oka River (last natural obstacle before Moscow), opening the road to Stalin's capital and established a feeble defense of scattered outposts. Boldin's 50th Army was at the end of its endurance, which alarmed Zhukov. Stavka sent in the 2nd Cavalry Corps (renamed the 1st Guards Cavalry Corps on the 26th), which counterattacked under heavy Red Army Air Force CAS on the 26th. This shock stunned the 17th Panzer and marked the beginning of the end for Guderian's thrust. After over five months of campaigning, by the end of November, 4th Panzer strength had sunk to 21 operational panzers, 18 artillery pieces and 4 infantry battalions with an average bayonet strength of 600 each. The XXIV Panzer tried to complete the encirclement of Tula, but only managed to cut rail and road connections to Moscow by 3 December. Guderian personally marched with the Landsers of XLIII Corps in order to share the hardships of his troops. The enemy only got stronger. At 0140 hours on 3 December, Army Group Center ordered its units to assume the defensive. The next day, OKH joined Second and Second Panzer Armies together as Armeegruppe Guderian.[35]

The end date of Operation Barbarossa is usually given as 5 December, the day the Soviet general counteroffensive began. In reality, the campaign culminated days or even perhaps weeks earlier as Zhukov mastered successive and sequential threats with successive and sequential reactions. With Moscow in sight, the German generals could not perform successfully in the climactic and 'war winning' battle they had always wanted. That November, von Kluge especially made a complete hash of Typhoon's Schwerpunkt by ignoring repeated calls to action from von Bock, the three panzer generals and many others. The Ostheer had yet another huge force defending Moscow, ripe for the taking, but it could not pull off this penultimate Vernichtungsschlacht. German exhaustion and strategic overstretch, weak logistics, Soviet resistance plus climate and terrain all conspired to deny the blitzkrieg its punch. It came up short with the perfect target for another operational victory to its immediate front. For the Second Panzer Army the glory days were over, the last three and a half years of the war would be drudgery by comparison.

General Zhukov had been husbanding reserves around Moscow and starting on 5 December he loosed them on Army Group Center in an increasing torrent. He succeeded in turning the tables of operational maneuver against the Ostheer. A major goal of Stalin's counteroffensive was the destruction of the two panzer spearheads north and south of Moscow. In view of the greater threat posed by Third and Fourth Panzer Armies north and northwest of the capital, Zhukov began there. Knowing it would soon be Second Panzer's turn, on the 6th, von Bock gave Guderian permission to withdraw to better defensive positions as far back as the Don and Shat Rivers, slightly east of Tula. For his part, Guderian had already been considering pulling back to the Plava River, west of the city. However, Zhukov struck on 8 December, before Guderian had a chance to withdraw. The 10th and 50th Armies of Zhukov's Western Front aimed straight at Second Panzer headquarters and its only railhead at Orel.[36]

The 10th Motorized Division, guarding Guderian's long and exposed eastern flank was partially encircled but largely managed to escape. However, Zhukov created a huge gap between the XXIV Panzer and XLIII Corps through which poured twenty-two rifle divisions and the 1st Guards Cavalry Corps. By 10 December, von Bock seemed on the verge of losing his nerve and began to speak in terms of a general retreat of 'Napoleonic proportions'. The OKH had no help to give although decisions now came fast and furious. On the 14th, with the entire Tula front about to implode, von Brauchitsch, in one of his last official acts as Army Commander in Chief, flew to Roslavl to meet von Kluge and Guderian. The following day Hitler ordered Second Panzer to hold its ground, although he would permit it to 'straighten out' the Tula Line. But Hitler could not make up his mind and for two more days issued conflicting guidance. That all changed around midnight on the 16th when the Führer finally decided on his defensive strategy. As he told von Bock: fanatical resistance and not one step back. On 19 December, von Bock went on medical leave and von Brauchitsch tendered his resignation.[37]

The day before, Hitler ordered Second Panzer to plug the gap between XXIV Panzer and XLIII Corps. The latter formation had stubbornly stuck to Fourth Army and had therefore swung northwest, while XXIV Panzer and the mass of Second Panzer fell away to the southwest down the Tula–Orel road. Boldin's advanced units occupied Kaluga and the 10th Army reached Belev, both on 20 December. In his vanity, Guderian still believed he had significant influence with Hitler, so on that same day flew to Führer headquarters on his own initiative (and over the head of von Kluge, von Bock's replacement). There, instead of showing the expected fighting resolve, he presented withdrawal plans, and for his pains received a viscous dressing down for his 'insane scheme'. The general saw no way out; his men were forced into making do with a mere 360 tons of supplies per day. His panzer strength had dropped from a 970 (initial issue plus reinforcements) to 70 machines in running order and another 168 in various stages of repair. Unbeknownst to the Germans, this mid–December crisis coincided with the end of Phase I of the Soviet counteroffensive (Stavka now considered Moscow out of immediate danger). To complicate matters, Zhukov recreated the Bryansk Front, and in Phase II, planned to smash through Guderian's right, and cut off Army Group Center near Mstensk.[38] Guderian's problems were not over.

A change of organizational boundaries on 21 December made Kaluga the Fourth Army and von Kluge's problem. But Guderian's personal crisis neared its finale. He spent all day on the 22nd with the 296th Infantry Division, the front of which had been penetrated in many places. On the following day, he unilaterally pulled the division behind the Oka River. Within 24 hours, von Kluge told him that Hitler would not allow such a retreat. The army group commander in turn telephoned Halder, explaining that Guderian had begun to withdraw the entire Second Panzer, and if that formation pulled back, the neighboring Second Army would have to as well. Halder recommended a court martial for Guderian. By Christmas Day, Hitler had had enough, and gave von Kluge permission to 'do what is necessary' with the panzer expert. The field marshal cashiered Guderian that same day, while Hitler prohibited a farewell message to the panzer army.[39]

Armeegruppe Guderian became Armeegruppe Schmidt the following day, named after acting Second Army commander, General of Panzer Troops Rudolf Schmidt. Schmidt tried to accomplish Hitler's orders to his predecessor but had only one division, 4th Panzer, even remotely capable of closing the gap with Fourth Army. It duly attacked toward Belev on the 27th, got stuck in the deep snow and had to turn back having accomplished nothing. Making better progress than Zhukov expected, the 10th and 50th Armies continued west toward Sukhinichi. In view of these Soviet successes, it looked for a while as though Schmidt might have to give up both Orel and Kursk. However, by the first week of January 1942, after nearly a month on the offensive, the Red Army ran out of steam just as German defenses began to stabilize. For the next eighteen months, both sides could only manage to launch tactical operations of barely a couple divisions' strength. The gash in the German lines had grown to almost 80km wide at its mouth and over 100km deep, but Zhukov lacked the reserves to exploit this success. By 9 January, the Second Panzer and Fourth Army fronts trailed off toward Kirov in the west, and this town marked 10th Army's limit of advance. Headquarters XXIV Panzer – soldiers of the actual corps headquarters – manned a portion of the line. In the middle of a sea of red, 216th Infantry Division plus some support troops occupied a now-isolated outpost at the Sukhinichi railroad junction.[40]

Despite Stavka's exhortations that German resistance at Sukhinichi 'at all costs had to be broken down', the 216th Infantry managed to survive on hard fighting and random air-dropped supplies. On 15 January, Hitler ordered Sukhinichi rescued, originally in a combined Second Panzer and Fourth operation (but the Fourth was otherwise occupied and did not participate). A day later, Schmidt gave XXIV Panzer Corps the mission of relieving the beleaguered garrison. At Zhizdra, von Schweppenburg assembled portions of 18th Panzer (fresh from chasing down rampaging Red cavalry and partisans near the city of Bryansk, but down to only a dozen panzers) and 208th Infantry Divisions to attack northeast along the rail line to Moscow. This tiny task force took the 323rd Rifle Division by surprise and in general, the Soviets reacted slowly. By the 24th, the Kampfgruppe had opened a 50km corridor and managed to evacuate 1,000 German wounded. Even Zhukov panicked over the possible threat to his hard-won salient and ordered Rokossovsky to retake the town with his 10th and (newly created) 16th Armies. Initially Hitler insisted on keeping Sukhinichi, but later relented, requiring only that Schmidt keep it within artillery range. Red Army troops liberated the town on the 29th.[41]

With Soviet exhaustion and the coming spring rasputitsa, action along the Army Group Center front began to resemble First World War positional warfare. On 6 February, von Kluge ordered Schmidt to change direction to the northwest and attack to close the hole in army group lines at Kirov. But with only forty-five operational panzers and XXIV Panzer stuck in exposed positions fewer that 10km from Sukhinichi, this was impossible. A month later von Kluge and Schmidt met and agreed to withdraw from the Belev and Sukhinichi salients, which indeed happened by early April. That spring of 1942, the Wehrmacht reoriented its efforts to the southern theater so that reinforcements dried up and many units deployed to Army Group South. The winter counteroffensive had certainly shocked the Germans, caused massive casualties and saved Moscow from danger. However, the Soviets were not easy on themselves. They identified three main reasons for not accomplishing all they set out to achieve: 1. Overestimating their chances of success; 2. Failure to concentrate reserves so that there were seldom enough at breakthroughs, and; 3. Failure to concentrate tank and cavalry forces to develop a main effort, therefore allowing the Germans to reestablish their defenses.[42] During the autumn of 1942 they would show how well they had learned these lessons.

The Second Panzer's rear areas between the cities of Bryansk and Kirov were heavily forested and had become a massive sanctuary for partisans that required much effort by Schmidt's men to combat. One major cleansing operation was Operation Vogelsang. Led by XLVII Panzer Corps headquarters, 6,000 men from the 339th Infantry and 707th Security Divisions tried to clear 12,000 square miles of marches and forests. These men fought in terrible conditions against hidden enemies, mosquitoes as much as partisans and accomplished little during the period 6 June to 4 July 1942. Another major mission that spring was participation in the Wehrmacht's deception plan to trick the Soviets into thinking the Germans planned to renew the assault against Moscow. With Army Group Center occupying approximately the same area it had in November 1941, Operation Kremlin was not so far fetched. Phony orders went out to Second Panzer to recapture Tula. Stavka continued to expect an attack on Moscow even weeks after Operation Blau should have indicated to them that Hitler really wanted the Caucasus oil region and Stalingrad.[43]

Once the Soviets realized their mistake, they planned their own attacks along the northern and central theaters in order to attempt to take pressure off the more critical southern. On 5 July, elements of 16th, 61st and 3rd Armies attacked against the 18th and 19th Panzer and 52nd Infantry Divisions around Belev and Zhizdra. The common (at that time of the war) Red Army handicaps, weak coordination and poor combined arms tactics, condemned the effort. After losing 446 tanks, they called off the attack. Von Kluge tried his hand attacking with Operation Wirbelwind, 11–24 August. This shoestring operation suffered from many false starts and constant draining off of assault forces to threatened sectors elsewhere within Army Group Center. Eventually, four panzer divisions operating in two pairs launched an attack on either side of Ulyanovo, part way between Belev and Kirov, aiming past the old Sukhinichi battle-field. The 11th Panzer gained 12km on the first day, the other three divisions, just 2km. By 14 August, one panzer division had a small bridgehead over the Zhizdra River. Von Kluge's pep talk at the panzer army's command post that day did little to change things. This time the Soviets were not deceived and did not overreact: they boxed in the bridgehead with a large minefield. When 16th Army counterattacked on the 24th, the Germans evacuated the bridgehead.[44] Except for these anti-partisan operations, both sides settled down to many months of static defense and mutual harassment.

To the south, the German summer offensive of 1942, the Soviet counterattack that autumn and the German reaction in the winter of 1943 dominated fighting between the two titans. By early February 1943, the far right wing of Red Army forces punching west after their victories at Stalingrad hit the Second Army and levered it out of Kursk. This made the Orel bulge occupied by Second Panzer even more dangerous. At this time, Schmidt's command consisted of XXXV, LIII Infantry and XLVII Panzer Corps and the army reserve (442nd and 707th Infantry Divisions).[45] On 22 February, the 13th and 48th Armies of the Bryansk Front hit Second Panzers' north flank along the oft-contested Zhizdra sector. Von Kluge dispatched reinforcements from the Rzehv and Viazma sectors. By the end of the month the Soviets had gained only about 20km and called off the attack. Accordingly, Rokossovsky moved his efforts south to the boundary between the Second and Second Panzer Armies. His men gained a little ground until OKH ordered Schmidt to counterattack toward the south and regain contact with his neighbor. The 4th Panzer led the way over the exact same Novgorod-Seversky battlefield it fought over during the opening phases of the Kiev pocket maneuver a year and half earlier. On 12 March, the Soviets tried to reorganize but the endeavor came too late. By the 21st, Red Army forces went over to the defensive, thus creating what would be the north face of the Kursk bulge in the next great campaign in the Nazi-Soviet War, Operation Citadel. Until then, that spring Second Panzer Army had to defend its 250km front with its 160,000 men in 14 weak divisions.[46]

As the original choice to lead the northern pincer in Citadel, Second Panzer Army had an opportunity to regain some lost glory and again become an operational force to be dealt with. Instead, that honor went to the Ninth Army, and Second Panzer remained the whipping boy of the Soviet Bryansk and Western Fronts along with partisans intent on making the occupiers regret their invasion. Stavka had been planning Operation Kutuzov against the Orel bulge since April. When it became clear in its early stages that Citadel was going nowhere, especially its northern attack, the Soviets pounced. The Western Front (211,000 men, 745 tanks and self-propelled guns, 4,285 tubes of indirect-fire weapons) and Bryansk Front (170,000 men, 350 AFVs) attacked at 0300 hours on 12 July. The Western Front's move split the 56th from the 262nd Infantry Division northeast of Bolkhov. It achieved success unexpected by the high command, which did not have reserves nearby with which to exploit the good fortune. Schmidt immediately rushed the relatively fresh 5th Panzer Division to the main point of rupture near Kroma. By noon on that first day, von Kluge first sent two divisions from Ninth Army, then later in the day dispatched a further two panzer divisions. If there had been any doubt before, with the loss of these assets, Citadel's northern attack was over for certain. Hitler now put Model in temporary command of the combined Second Panzer and Ninth Armies with orders to restore the earlier lines.[47]

However, Second Panzer's front in turn suffered three penetrations: two east of Orel and another up near Sukhinichi. The XXXV Corps (left to right: 34th, 56th, 262nd and 299th Infantry Divisions) took the brunt of the punishment between Mstensk and Orel. The Germans brought up reinforcements, the arrival of which, fortunately for the defenders, the Red Army Air Force could not halt. The Soviets set about enlarging the cracks they had created in the Second Panzer lines and expanded their attacks into the Ninth Army Sector; Model could foresee more trouble ahead. The 8th Panzer Division and other units came forward and halted the 1st Guards Tank Corps. German success was short-lived, because on the 20th, Stavka committed the 698 tanks of the 3rd Guards Tank Army. Even General PS Rybalko's massive force stalled before the two panzer divisions. Two days later Stalin personally telephoned 3rd Guards Tank headquarters and asked the chief of staff, 'Why has Rybalko not yet taken Stanovoi-Kolodez? Tell the commander that I am not pleased with the handling of the tank army.'[48]

While Stalin cajoled his commanders forward in order to freeze Second Panzer units as far east as possible, the Germans were considering the unthinkable: a phased withdrawal. On 16 July, Model had ordered increased exertion on the Hagen Line, a set of field works at the base of the Orel salient, just east of Bryansk. On the 20th, Hitler ordered Ninth and Second Panzer Armies not to retreat, but two days later gave Model approval to form an 'elastic defense'. Hitler giving such latitude to a commander had become very rare during the eighteen months following the Moscow counteroffensive, and it is certain few generals besides Model would have received this permission. On 28 July, OKH ordered Operation Herbstreise, the withdrawal from Orel to the Hagen Line. On the last day of July, Second Panzer units began to move west. Soviet units arrived in Orel on 5 August, just as XXXV Corps units left. By the 6th, both German armies were on the run, closely pursued by many units of the Red Army. Partisans mercilessly hounded their every step. Its first units arrived at the Hagen positions on 14 August, and the last closed in three days later. The Second Panzer Army executed a skillful withdrawal, complete with scorched earth tactics. The 129th Infantry Division received the unenviable mission to serve as the rear guard, ably assisted by 8th Panzer Division.[49] Upon reaching its new lines, the army's units were distributed to other formations, while its headquarters moved to a new theater of war, complete with a new mission and a new commander. After having the eyes of the world fixed on its operational maneuvers during Barbarossa, Second Panzer slipped into the background for the next two and a half years. When it was not involved in static warfare or retreating, the most it could accomplish was a counterattack by four divisions.

As the Red Army finished its first great lunge westward following Citadel, Headquarters Second Panzer Army traveled by rail to occupied Yugoslavia. It redeployed, far from the main front, to combat partisans, disarm – and often fight – Germany's erstwhile Italian, Bulgarian and Rumanian allies and guard the Adriatic coast from expected Allied landings. An Austrian, General of Infantry Lothar Rendulic, whose XXXV Corps had defended unexpectedly so well against Operation Kutuzov, ascended to command the panzer army. In late August and early September, the Second Panzer's headquarters arrived in the Balkans to lead the main striking force of Army Group F there. With its command post at Kragujevac, Yugoslavia, it commanded fourteen divisions but had only two battalions of tanks. For much of the next few months, most of its 'panzers' were captured Italian models. The Germans estimated that at the beginning of 1943, Tito's partisans numbered 150,000 men organized into 9 divisions and 36 brigades. The Yugoslav partisans were better led, armed and motivated than their Greek comrades, so Second Panzer spent much of the campaign on the defensive.[50]

Rendulic commanded many fine organizations, such as the fabled 1st Mountain Division. But he also had the 297th Infantry, rebuilt after destruction at Stalingrad with a base of 1,000 men returning from leave and collected from various hospitals. One of the Second Panzer's first missions was to disarm Italians in the Balkans. A month before Rendulic took over the theater, on 25 July, General Vittorio Ambrosio overthrew Mussolini. On 9 September, Hitler launched Operation Achse to disarm the Italian military, including a quarter of a million occupation troops in the Balkans. Most Italians gave up without a fight, but many resisted according to Marshal Pietro Badaglio's orders, resulting in casualties on both sides. Still others remained with the Germans, figuring that was a better alternative than returning to their own country. Rendulic's men had alternately to protect their Italian charges from communists and partisans, take the surrender of Italian divisions and corps or fight large groups loyal either to the Italian king or the partisans. One major operation against 'Badaglio' Italians took place in the second half of September, between the 7th SS Mountain Division, Prinz Eugen and the garrison of the old fortress at Split. Stukas pounded the fort, while Allied warships in the harbor countered with fire in support of the Italians. The Wehrmacht reported Split captured on the 27th. Likewise, the 1st Mountain conducted Operation Spaghetti to disarm Italians on the island of Korfu and the 100th Jäger and 297th Infantry Divisions did the same in Albania.[51]

Infantry

By far the bulk combat power of all Second World War armies (even the American) was marching infantry. The blitzkrieg and Panzerwaffe would have failed without infantry, mounted or dismounted. Fighting as a combined arms team of infantry, cavalry, artillery and other branches was a hallmark of successful combat since before Frederick the Great. Although often forced to make do with the bottom of the manpower pool, the infantry nevertheless carried the heaviest load of all armies during the war. Despite this, the number of infantry officers who became successful practitioners of the blitzkrieg or who commanded panzer armies is impressive. German armaments engineers and manufacturers gave the infantry a wide variety of excellent weapons and equipment.

Even the mass of panzer and panzergrenadier units fighting in the USSR were made up of infantry. The Germans had a number of vehicles to get the Landsers into combat, but once engaged, they fought dismounted. Often the infantry rode to battle on trucks, artillery prime movers, panzers or whatever vehicles were available. Best known of the purpose-built armored personnel carriers were the half-tracks. The medium model (SdKfz 251 family, of which over 15,000 were produced) was developed in the mid-1930s as the concept of the panzer division was being explored. In addition to its main function, throughout the war the army created many variants: command, mortar, ammunition resupply, ambulance, rocket launcher, anti-tank, pioneer, signal, anti-aircraft and even infrared searchlight models. Later, the Wehrmacht ordered a light version (SdKfz 250), and over 7,200 of these rolled off German production lines.

For individual weapons, the German soldier in 1939–45 used many of the same armaments as his father, including the Model 98 rifle (Gewehr 98) and carbine (Karabiner 98k) firing a 7.92mm shell and the Luger P08, plus the newer Walther P38 9mm pistols. These could not produce the amount of firepower required against the Red Army, and so machine pistols (automatic weapons firing pistol ammunition) became popular with soldiers (and postwar movie makers). The MP38 and MP40 were originally intended for small unit leaders, but later could be found in regular rifle sections. Their short range prompted the development of the MP43 and MP44 Sturmgewehr, an adaptation of Soviet assault rifles, firing 'short' rifle ammunition. Hand grenades were a staple for close combat. The German 'stick grenade' is one of the most recognizable weapons of the period, although they also had an egg-shaped version.

The Germans excelled in the design of machine-guns, the best known being the MG34 and MG42. Both fired 7.92mm rifle ammunition and were reliable, easy to maintain and had high cyclic rates of fire. Either could be employed in light (bipod) or heavy (tripod) mode and in anti-aircraft defense. These weapons were superior to contemporary Allied weapons in rate and weight of fire.

The infantry had two main indirect fire weapons for use at the regimental level and below: infantry guns and mortars. The lightweight (but still horse drawn) short-barreled 75mm Infantriegeschutz was common early in the Nazi-Soviet War but later weapons superseded it. On the other hand, the Germans employed mortars throughout the war. A 50mm model proved to be ineffective and was phased out. The 81mm type was constantly improved over time. The Germans copied the heavy 120mm Soviet mortar, and mounted it on two-wheeled trolleys or on the back end of trucks and half-tracks. These proved to be excellent close-support weapons and could be found in large numbers in both line and motorized (later panzergrenadier) regiments.

Anti-tank weapons were another critical piece of military hardware near and dear to the heart of the infantry. With the introduction and improvement of shaped-charge explosives, individual anti-tank weapons became very common, especially late in the war. The best known are the Panzerfaust and Faustpatrone series grenade launchers, effective to a range of 150m. A true bazooka-type weapon, commonly known as the Ofenrohr or Panzerschrek, fired rocket-propelled projectiles, accurate to 120m.

Rendulic, who once said, 'When things look blackest and you don't know what to do, beat your chest and say, "I'm a National Socialist!" that moves mountains!'[52] would lead Second Panzer in a losing effort in the Balkans. For the most part, the Germans owned the villages and some roads, but the partisans owned the countryside. The numerous anti-partisan operations it conducted give this period of the army's history a useful framework. A constant fear for Army Group F was the threat of Allied landings along the Adriatic coast; to paraphrase Mussolini, the Adriatic Sea could now be called 'an Allied lake'. The Second Panzer discovered this unhappy fact when they launched Operation Herbstgewitter, intended to clear the coast line. In late October, partisans, reinforced by Italians and supported by Allied naval gunfire and CAS, put up a tenacious defense. On 8 November, the Volksdeutsche of Prinz Eugen tried to assault the Italian fort at Jasen, but lacked the requisite training and pioneer support or equipment. The entire operation yielded little. Next came Operation Kugelblitz, conducted by V SS Mountain Corps under Lieutenant General of Police and SS Gruppenführer Hermann Behrens. The corps consisted of Prinz Eugen, 1st Mountain, 369th and 187th Infantry

Divisions, the 24th Bulgarian Division and the 1st Croatian Mountain Division. Against partisans plus over 2,000 Italians, the operation in central Bosnia lasted from 2 to 17 December. At the end of Kugelblitz, one SS man said, 'We had great respect for Tito.'[53]

The day after Kugelblitz ended, Prinz Eugen and other units advancing under Stuka CAS launched Operation Schneesturm. Fought near Srebenica in eastern Bosnia, it pitted Germans against the 1st Proletariat Division, 'Tito's best troops', and lasted until 27 December. For most German troops, the winter of 1944 compared favorably to the Stalingrad winter a year earlier. By 9 March 1944, OKW Operations Staff had identified 11 partisan corps (10–15,000 men each) and over 30 divisions (2–4,000 men), by far the bulk of which operated out of Croatia. Supreme Commander Southeast, Luftwaffe Colonel General Alexander Lohr (another Austrian) wrote, 'The classification of the enemy as bandits and the fighting against them as bandit warfare is incorrect. They are operationally and tactically well led, equipped with heavy weapons and the constantly increasing number of units cannot be over-estimated.'[54] This growing danger caused Army Group F Commander von Weichs to order another massive strike at the partisans.[55]

Accordingly, the XV Mountain Corps, under General of Infantry Ernst von Leyser, would lead Operation Rösselsprung against Tito's headquarters near Drvar in western Bosnia. Under command were three infantry divisions, the reinforced Motorized Grenadier Regiment 92, elements of the Brandenburger Regiment 1 and the 500th SS Parachute Battalion. Defending were over 12,000 partisans and representatives of various Allied countries in barricaded positions supported by tanks from nearby Petrovac. Von Leyser's plan envisioned CAS preparation, followed by the first wave of nearly 650 SS paratroopers, Brandenburgers and Abwehr men and a second wave of over 200 paratroopers. Then on d-day, 25 May, the 373rd Infantry Division and Regiment 92 would then come overland to relieve the special forces units. But weeks before the attack, partisans attacked a train and captured documents indicating that the Germans knew of Tito's Drvar hideout so were somewhat forewarned.[56]

After softening up by Stukas and fighter-bombers (the Luftwaffe flew 440 sorties that day, a significant number for a backwater theater so late in the war), the first wave arrived by parachute and glider at 0700 on the 25th. The second wave arrived 5 hours later. Despite their advanced intelligence captured on the train, the assault surprised the partisans, who fled into the mountainous countryside. Soon, however, they regrouped and counterattacked. That day, the commander of the SS paratroopers, Hauptsturmführer Kurt Rybka was wounded during hand-to-hand combat. His men created a 360 degree defense at the local cemetery that night. More Luftwaffe CAS arrived at 0500 on the

26th and advance elements of the 373rd showed up 2 hours later. Still, once the partisans recovered from the initial shock, they put up a stout defense, complete with Allied CAS flying from Italy. Rendulic kept a firm hand on the operation, at one point overhearing a radio transmission: 'Wherever we are, that is the front!' On the 29th, panzer army headquarters told von Leyser, 'The commander expects decisiveness and cleverness from all leaders. The chances of success depend on speed of maneuver.'[57] But they did not act fast enough for the wily partisans. On the 31st, SS men found Tito's marshal's jacket hanging over a chair and Randolph Churchill's backpack – obvious signs the partisans left in a hurry. The wounded Tito escaped in a Soviet DC-3 to Italy with members of the British mission. After the war, in 1974, he admitted it had been a very close call at Drvar. Nevertheless, Second Panzer Army had reason to be satisfied with Rösselsprung: they had destroyed Tito's headquarters and communication gear, mauled his 1st and 6th divisions and captured 6,000 of his men. That was Rendulic's last major event at head of the Second Panzer; on 24 June he turned over command to fellow Austrian, General of Mountain Troops, Franz Böhme. Böhme only lasted three weeks before giving up the post to yet another Austrian, General of Artillery Maximilian de Angelis.[58]

During the early summer of 1944, Operations Waldrausch and Freie Jagd in Bosnia followed. A final major operation, Rübezahl, also in Bosnia, took place between 12–30 August. Participating were Prinz Eugen, the 181st and 369th Infantry Divisions plus the 13th SS Handschar and 21st SS Skanderbeg Mountain Divisions. The two last named formations consisted mainly of non-Germans, respectively Croatians and Albanians, and were of doubtful military value. Numerous smaller anti-partisan operations also took place that usually lasted only a few days: Zeitgenosse, Herbsternte, 1828, Freibeuter, Roter Mann, Otto, Seydlitz and Horrido 1, 2, 3. Second Panzer Army also disarmed Bulgaria's I Corps in Macedonia, when that nation changed sides in September, kept a weary eye on Romania when it did the same and assisted in Operation Schwartz, the evacuation of one-third of a million Volksdeutsche through the 'Vardar Corridor' and back to the Reich.[59] A year of fighting partisans had little to do with being a 'panzer army' and even less to do with the operational level of warfare.

By autumn 1944, the Red Army had liberated the Ukraine and began its victorious march through the Balkan Peninsula. The Second Panzer's experiences became more conventional. Yugoslav partisans also continued to evolve toward a more conventional fighting force, and by late in the war can almost be considered an auxiliary of the Soviets. In view of the approaching danger from the east, on 5 October, Army Group F commander von Weichs reoriented

Second Panzer toward the mountains in central and northern Yugoslavia. He gave de Angelis, centered on the confluence of the Tisza and Danube Rivers, the twin missions of guaranteeing Croatian loyalty and of defending Belgrade. But the Soviet 57th Army, moving from the Iron Gate up the Morava River (the same route taken by First Panzer Army in April, 1941), soon overcame the weak Armeeabteilung Serbia. This maneuver cut off both German formations from Belgrade, which the Soviets 'liberated' on the 19th, with help from Tito's 1st Proletarian and 12th Corps (four and three divisions respectively). Once the Belgrade bridgehead evacuated, the German position in Yugoslavia collapsed. During the latter half of October, von Weichs ordered Second Panzer to resist along the next natural defensive line to the north, the Danube, Sava and Drava Rivers. At precisely this time, however, de Angelis' men received a much-needed pause when Marshal FI Tolbulkin's 3rd Ukrainian Front swerved north into Hungary, leaving Tito alone facing Second Panzer. By 2 November, de Angelis stabilized his front, even linking up with the Hungarian 2nd Army, creating a solid line with other Axis units for the first time in months.[60]

Von Weichs could not discern the Soviet main effort so was indecisive about what to do next. During the first week of November, Second Panzer received its new mission: defend the oil fields in southwest Hungary. A week later, on 15 November, Tolbulkhin attacked with his 3rd Ukrainian Front assisted by the Bulgarians and Tito's partisans. They levered the Second Panzer and 2nd Hungarian Armies off the Danube and reached the Pecs (Fünfkirchen) Line five days later. The 1st Mountain and 44th Infantry (Reichs Hoch und Deutschmeister) Divisions fought a skillful rearguard action. In accordance with the new situation on the ground, on 1 December, Hitler transferred Second Panzer from Army Group F to Army Group South. Under increasing pressure from the 57th Army, his new boss, General of Infantry Josef Freissner, kept de Angelis moving northwest toward the southern tip of Lake Balaton. Here Second Panzer received significant reinforcements and occupied part of the Margarethe Line and Drava River guarding Nazi Germany's sole remaining natural oil field at Nagykanizsa.[61]

The Germans devised numerous operations to guard their last ally, Hungary, and keep the Soviets off balance. In most cases the Sixth SS Panzer Army acted as the army group's Schwerpunkt, with Second Panzer, and sometimes Sixth Armies in supporting roles. Army Group South launched Operation Eisbrecher on 19 January 1945. On the 24th, de Angelis contributed by attacking with 1st Mountain, 71st Infantry, 118th Jäger Divisions plus elements of SS 16th Panzergrenadier Division, Reichsführer SS, in the direction of Kaposvar. The XXII Mountain Corps launched another assault on 30 January, but by the last day of the month German strength had played out at a cost of

500 killed and 3,000 wounded. The Germans had doubts over the reliability
of their allies, as one Landser wrote, 'In every German regiment, in every
division, the question is always the same: "whose units are to the right and left
of us, German or Hungarian?" '[62]

Operation Frühlingserwachen followed in early February as Hitler tried to
pre-empt a major Soviet offensive. He sent Second Panzer the 297th Infantry
and 117th Jäger Divisions plus 14th SS Division, Galician #1, as reinforcements. De Angelis' mission was to attack first, again in the direction of
Kaposvar, and draw Red Army reserves away from the Sixth SS Panzer Army.
As earlier, his target was the 57th Army, now augmented by the 1st Bulgarian
Army. Group Konrad (reinforced LXVIII Corps) struggled forward against
a stout defense. The 71st Infantry Division with the Hungarian Bakony
Regiment also made progress in very poor terrain. An assault by Sturmgeschütze
of Reichsführer SS accomplished little due to a lack of ammunition and no
promised Luftwaffe CAS. Second Panzer's contribution to the entire operation
was a small salient 10km across its base and not even that distance in depth.
Kaposvar once again proved too distant an objective. Soviet artillery especially
brutalized de Angelis' men. Although they lost the town of Nagykanizsa on
29 March, the Germans kept the oil region to the west for a few more days.[63]

By mid-April the Second Panzer, plus Sixth SS Panzer and Sixth Armies,
all occupied positions in the western Alps. The Reichs Schutzstellung
along the Austro–Hungarian border was formidable in name only. A Second
Panzer Army officer, the commander, 7th Company, Grenadier Regiment 523
(297th Infantry Division) had this to say about the last days of the war:

> Together with our comrades from Regiment 524 we closed on the
> Hungarian-Yugoslav border and we crossed the Mur River bridge
> into the southern Steiermark ... As we reached our Regiment 522
> again, the 7th Company had fifty-three men. In the afternoon we
> slept for a few hours in a meadow because we marched all night. In
> the morning twilight we stood before a turnpike: the German border.
> On the one side: the lost war. On the other side: a still peace, then we
> were in our homeland again!
>
> On 7 April, thirty replacements arrived in our 7th Company,
> although they wore flight suits. All the men were over 40, they struck
> us as sorry. Everyone of them had to begin an infantry education
> 'on the fly:' assault carbines, hand grenades and machine guns. These
> were ground crewmen from the Agram (Zagreb) airfield – they had
> hardly fired a shot in anger during the entire war.

We are supposed to occupy the East Wall, so-called Reich Defense Position. We all had one crazy wish: That the Soviets wouldn't attack! A withdrawal from this position over the open area to the west was not possible so long as it was light. We were in combat on the 9th. By the 11th only three of our former flier comrades were still with us. Our 1st Platoon has almost entirely vanished. On the 12th, we had to abandon our position. Of those who retreated from Albania, only a few remain; we receive men from the rear services as replacements. Because of numerous casualties we are completely despondent . . .

On 16 April, Captain Thiel, our battalion commander, was severely wounded and died during evacuation. Now First Lieutenant Konhäuser leads both battalions. We remain in the area between Stridovar and Schützendorf. On the 22nd, Major Wegener took over our position. Tomorrow night we'll march west. We saw our division rear services for the first time since Good Friday . . . In the evening [of the 25th] we marched to Radkersburg. We occupied positions near Schloss Mureck; it would be our last shots of the Second World War, as we shot from the castle windows over the Mur behind us.[64]

On 5 May, de Angelis met with Field Marshal Kesselring in Graz. All both men wanted to do was surrender to the Western Allies. The Soviets did not press too hard; the Second Panzer Army slipped west toward the Americans advancing through Austria.[65]

Chapter 4

Third Panzer Army

Third Panzer Army began Operation Barbarossa as the mirror image of Second Panzer. Under the equally skilled but less flamboyant Colonel General Herman 'Papa' Hoth, Third Panzer ran parallel to Guderian to the north of the old Post Road route, taking part in the Minsk and Smolensk encirclement battles. In the late summer it contributed some units to Army Group North's drive on Leningrad, and during Operation Typhoon, formed the far left wing in the Viazma and Moscow battles.

From late 1941 through mid-1944, it fought swarms of partisans while slowly giving ground and eventually retraced its steps taken during Barbarossa. When the Red Army set out to destroy Army Group Center in June 1944, it chased Third Panzer back to the Baltic coast, and to positions centered on the port of Memel. That fall and winter, Third Panzer withdrew through East Prussia, eventually holding the lower Oder River Line north of Berlin for the final defense of Germany. By the end of the war it was streaming westward, and its units surrendered to both the Soviets and the Western Allies.

Campaign	Battles and Engagements
Barbarossa, **22 June–5 December 1941**	Dvina River crossings, Bialystok, Vitebsk, Stalin Line, Minsk, Smolensk, Nevel, Velikie Luki, Viazma, Kalinin, Klin, Moscow Canal
Defense of Army Group Center, **5 December 1941–12 December 1943**	Kalinin, Velikie Luki, Demidov, Dogorobush, upper Dvina, Yartsevo, Nevel, anti-partisan action
Defense of White Russia, **December 1943–15 August 1944**	Vitebsk, lower Niemen, Kaunas, Dubissa
Defense of Baltic coast, **16 August 1944–8 February 1945**	Siualiai, Tukums, Tauroggen, Memel, Tilsit, Insterburg, Königsberg
Defense of the Reich, **21 February–8 May 1945**	Pomerania, Oder River, Mecklenburg

Third Panzer began Barbarossa subordinated to Ninth Army in the Suwalki 'peak', with two panzer and two infantry corps assigned (the XL Panzer Corps, recovering from the Balkan campaign, would join in August). Its orders for the campaign read,

> break through the enemy's border forces in the area north of Grodno in cooperation with the Ninth Army and, by quickly advancing into the region north of Minsk, make contact with the Second Panzer Group [*sic*], which is advancing on Minsk from the southwest, to create conditions for the destruction of those forces located in the Bialystok and Minsk region.[1]

Soviet defenders consisted of Western Front units occupying the dangerously exposed Bialystok salient. This 125km-deep protrusion into German-occupied Poland came into being when Stalin invaded the eastern portion of that country in 1939. He considered it one of the USSR's prime interwar acquisitions and insisted it be defended without compromise.

Because of sympathetic Lithuanians on both sides of the frontier, Hoth had good intelligence about enemy dispositions. Though his men had to contend with thick woods and trackless terrain, Red Army defenders generally melted away in the face of German pressure as occurred all along the line on Barbarossatag. Marshal Timoshenko radioed Western Front deputy commander Lieutenant General IV Boldin first thing that morning, saying 'comrade Stalin has forbidden to open artillery fire against the Germans'. The main effort of holding Hoth back fell on Lieutenant General VI Kuznetsov's 3rd Army, one of whose first reports read, 'Germans crossing the border, Grodno being bombarded. Telephone contact with border interrupted, two radio stations down'.[2] As bad as the situation might have sounded to Soviet high command, reality on the ground was worse. The defenders' plan had been to demolish the bridge over the Niemen River at Alytus by 1700 hours on the first day, but Hoth's men arrived there earlier than expected and pioneers of Infantry Regiment 5 captured the bridge intact. Colonel Rothenburg's Panzer Regiment 25 (7th Panzer Division) lost half of its vehicles to 5th Tank Division's T-34s in good, hull-down fighting positions, but the Germans had established a bridgehead on the east bank of the river. The Germans retained possession of the battlefield after most of these engagements, and their workshops were able to repair and return to duty many damaged panzers. The 7th Panzer managed to destroy nearly seventy tanks by nightfall and continued the advance eastward the next day.[3]

As impressive as Guderian's thrust to the south had been, strategically Hoth's was by far more important. The Soviets' problems compounded when the 11th Army, southernmost component of the Northwestern Front, failed to withdraw due east, but instead swung northeast. This maneuver only opened the door for Hoth all the wider. Within two days, the gap dividing the two fronts measured 100km wide. By 24 June, elements of 7th Panzer approached Vilnius. Pavlov reacted as best he could: on 22 June he ordered Boldin to organize a counterattack by the 6th and 11th Mechanized Corps[4] plus the 6th Cavalry Corps northward against Hoth's southern flank. By the time they were ready on the 24th, Third Panzer had long since moved on to the east, so Boldin's stroke hit the Ninth Army, surprising Strauss. As many a French general had discovered to their chagrin a year earlier, just doing the right thing, in this case launching a sizeable counterattack against an exposed flank, did not always achieve the desired results. Luftwaffe reconnaissance had been looking deep into the Soviet rear so missed the Soviet build-up closer to the front. Over 200 Stuka sorties and a handful of 88s helped the infantry blunt Boldin's attack. Around 2100 hours Boldin's men stalled only 1 mile from downtown Grodno, out of fuel. The assault, despite the large number of units involved, suffered from the usual Red Army shortcomings: poor command and control, weak CAS, no combined arms tactics and under-resourced logistics. The commander of the 6th Mechanized was killed and a day later the cavalry had sustained 50 percent casualties. By the night of 25/26 June, Boldin received an order to withdraw, but his units were too engaged so could not make a clean get-away and made easy targets for the Germans to mop up.[5]

Violating the accepted tenants of the blitzkrieg, two days into Barbarossa, a dangerous dispersal of Army Group Center's panzer force began. In part this was due to lack of clarity and agreement among the German generals over Barbarossa's initial ways and means. Halder wanted to close the inner (infantry) and outer (mechanized) arms of the Minsk encirclement. Von Bock disagreed because he wanted to keep plunging to the east, but he obeyed. Von Brauchitsch offered a compromise, allowing the army group, meaning the panzer armies, to push east with strong security forces. In Hoth's case, this meant toward Vitebsk and Polotsk, both important crossing sites over the Dvina River and therefore keys to the Soviets' defensive arrangements.[6] Not only did the Army's Commander in Chief permit the panzers to fan out and lose the benefits of concentration, this also meant fewer German units would be available to 'digest' trapped Red Army forces. The Ostheer did not need more worthless territory: it needed to eliminate (Vernichten) thoroughly the enemy it had already caught. This was not a case of the amateur, dilettante Hitler interfering with the professional generals of the German Army; this was a case of the generals ignoring centuries of Prussian/German military tradition and development and allowing themselves to get caught up in a land grab of questionable utility.

With von Richthofen's VIII Fliegerkorps overhead, Third Panzer pushed on, having earned 'operational freedom' and so free of Ninth Army's control. The 7th Panzer's motorcycle battalion captured the Vilnius airfield, complete with fifty intact planes, and then entered the city proper. This maneuver opened the road into the Red Army's rear echelons, one of von Bock's operational objectives. A bit south, on 25 June, another of Hoth's units over-ran the 13th Army's command post, complete with numerous documents of high-intelligence value. That night, his vanguard, Rothenburg's regiment and 1st Battalion, Infantry Regiment 6, cut the Minsk–Moscow highway about 20km northeast of the Belorussian capital.[7] Von Bock wanted to send more of Third Panzer towards Polotsk than just the security elements allowed by von Brauchitsch. Again, OKH denied the request: Hoth was to move against Minsk and wait for Guderian in order to seal properly the Kessel: at least somebody was home, minding the store in term of faithfulness to the Vernichtungskrieg philosophy. In accordance with OKH orders of 1130 hours, 26 June, Hoth obediently sent XXXIX Panzer Corps south toward Minsk and the expected rendezvous with Second Panzer. The 12th and 20th Panzer Divisions closed on the city later that day, with 14th Motorized following not too far behind. Elements of 12th Panzer entered Minsk in the evening of the 27th, and completed taking the city the next afternoon. Still back to the west near Novogrudek, the dividing line between Bialystok and Minsk cauldrons, LVII Panzer guarded the northern flank of the pocket until marching infantry arrived. With most trapped Red Army units trying to escape to the southeast, Guderian admittedly would have had a tougher time containing the pocket than Hoth, even if he had been inclined to do so. In any event, as was proper for higher headquarters, OKH looked forward in time to the next battle, at Smolensk.[8]

On the 28th, Hoth sent the 7th Panzer, leading XXXIX Panzer Corps, toward Borisov on the Berezina River, his next major obstacle to overcome. However, about this time, higher headquarters became nervous about the growing gap between Army Groups Center and North. So, in early July, Third Panzer received the mission to turn back toward Molodechino, then advance northeast to an eventual link-up with von Leeb. Regardless of how one feels about the necessity of capturing Moscow, this represented a possibly fatal dispersal of Third Panzer Army. As a result of this and other strategic decisions, the drive on the Soviet capital seemed to be suffering, so Guderian flew to Hoth's headquarters on 2 July. The panzer leaders made two decisions: first, they basically conspired to circumvent their new Fourth Panzer Army commander, von Kluge, (see p. 65) and secondly, on their own initiative, they agreed to continue toward Moscow. With that decision, 7th Panzer (with 20th Panzer close behind) angled away from Polotsk and instead toward Lepel further south and on a much more direct line to the great city. The LVII Panzer took the high road, reaching the Dvina River at Dissna (19th Panzer, after covering 180km in 24 hours) and Polotsk (18th Motorized). Again, VIII Fliegerkorps lent invaluable assistance. All this maneuvering put the Soviets at a disadvantage, but it also meant that Third Panzer had lost the appearance of the armored fist favored by the blitzkrieg and instead looked like fingers on a spread-out hand.[9]

None of this was lost on Stavka, which considered Hoth a greater danger to Moscow than Guderian. It noticed the 100km gap between XXXIX and LVII Panzer Corps. Therefore, on 4 July, Stavka ordered Timoshenko to 'organize a reliable defense ... concentrate reserves ... deliver counterstrokes along the Lepel, Borisov and Bobruisk axes'. The marshal intending on taking advantage of the fact that neither of Hoth's spearheads were within supporting distance of the other, threw three new armies across the Dvina–Dnepr gap: 22nd, 19th and 20th Armies at Polotsk, Vitebsk and Orsha, respectively. With 7th Panzer spread out along the Borisov–Lepel road, it made an inviting target and Timoshenko ordered 22nd Army to attack with 5th and 7th Mechanized Corps (300 and 400 tanks, respectively): 'go over to a decisive offensive to destroy the Lepel enemy concentration'.[10] They came dangerously close to splitting the seam between Second and Third Panzer Armies as part of the bargain, and in fact, pushed 7th Panzer back 20km. In response, von Kluge added the 12th Panzer to the 7th, 17th and 18th Panzer Divisions[11] already fighting below von Richthofen's Stukas and Bf-110s. By 6 July, a massive and swirling battle between opposing mechanized forces occurred around the town of Senno. After five days, Timoshenko lost over 800 tanks, the offensive's cohesion was shot and his scattered formations made easy picking for the panzers. At the same time, 70km to the north and unrelated to the armor battle, two divisions of LVII Panzer, 20th Panzer and 20th Motorized, had already breached the Dvina downstream at Ulla. The XXXIX Panzer reached the river in force on 8 July. Crossing the one remaining railway bridge was slow going for the panzers, where a centimeter mistake one way or the other would result in a 20m plunge to the river below. A day later, smoldering Vitebsk fell to Panzer Regiment 21 and the 92nd Motorcycle and 92nd Antitank Battalions. Within 24 hours, panzer units approached Disna, with the Ninth Army's XXIII and VI Corps close behind. During the second week of July, the Dvina–Dnepr River Line, a mainstay of the Soviet defensive structure, had been punctured in numerous places. On the 13th, the Germans captured an order from Timoshenko instructing his units to hold the river line and in fact, assault to regain any positions already lost.[12] The seized papers indicated the Soviets had absolutely no intentions of conducting a general withdrawal.

By the middle of July, the Smolensk pocket began to take shape. The freewheeling 7th Panzer was again on the move; on 15 July, 1st Battalion, Panzer Regiment 25 (commanded by a captain) cut the highway to Moscow near Yartsevo. This came as a surprise to Timoshenko, Hoth was much farther east than the Soviets thought possible. The only way Rokossovsky's men could make sense of this situation was to report an imaginary large-scale paratroop landing up the chain of command to Stavka. At this time, Guderian's 29th Motorized stood only about 30km to the south. Despite the fact that Stalin's orders to Lieutenant General MF Lukin to defend Smolensk with his own 13th Army plus remnants of the 19th and 20th Armies played into the Germans' hands, von Bock did a poor job of executing the Smolensk Kessel for two reasons: 1. As discussed in the previous chapter, Guderian allowed personal objectives to override organizational goals, so did not take the time to reduce the pocket properly, and; 2. Alluded to above, was that OKH sent Third Panzer (and Ninth Army) too far north in an attempt to create a continuous front with Army Group North. Hoth had to compensate for these contradictory instructions by driving his men in two, nearly opposite directions. Further, one of Hoth's two panzer corps, LVII, was still fighting in the Nevel and Velikie Luki regions and missed the Smolensk battle completely.[13] It can be seen that one month into the campaign, unlike Poland, France or Yugoslavia, the massive size of the USSR had deprived the blitzkrieg of much of its punch.

Hoth's men occupied a great arc west, north and east of Smolensk: 12th Panzer practically surrounded at Rudnya, Training Brigade 900 at Demidov, 20th Panzer occupying an Igel (hedgehog, or 360-degree defense) near Prechistoe and 7th Panzer still at Yartsevo where Infantry Regiment 7 took a severe beating, including a rude introduction to the new Katyusha rocket artillery. A 7th Panzer Division report read:

> On 18 July, the Russians attack against the division's positions in the afternoon with approximately eighty tanks, followed by strong infantry attacks. Our artillery fire causes the attack to collapse immediately to the front of the rifle regiment. In the evening a new attack by another 100 tanks or so, also halted by artillery. Thirty tanks remain burning. At the same time, in the dark we attack traffic on the highway and railroad. An enemy tank platoon is destroyed, detonations go on for two hours. The enemy continues to attack energetically against the

division's north flank, a section of twenty-five tanks remains in front of our positions.[14]

Hoth had his hands full, especially since he simultaneously commanded the Ninth Army for the temporarily ailing Strauss. Help arrived in the form of V Corps, which relieved 12th Panzer, but the infantry soon found themselves in uneven combat against the 23rd, 46th, 134th, 144th, 153rd and 229th Rifle Divisions. The VII Corps also showed up to join the fighting. Near Solovevo, bits and pieces of the Soviet 19th and 20th Armies, plus the rump of the 5th Mechanized Corps, managed to keep open an escape route from Smolensk through the weak cordon. Inside the pocket, Lukin's men put up a stiff defense, while NKVD troops policed the rear areas and managed to scrape together over 100,000 stragglers, deserters and other 'lost' Red Army troops to stiffen the defenses.[15]

Artillery

Artillery (to include rocket launchers, etc.) is the greatest casualty producing weapon on the modern battlefield. However, second only to horse fodder, artillery ammunition took up the bulk of rail and other logistical capacity. During Barbarossa, by far the mass of German artillery was horse drawn. This proved to be a considerable liability, both in attack and defense. However, in mechanized units, prime mover vehicles, normally half-tracks, towed artillery in order to keep pace with the panzers. These in turn often gave way later in the war to indirect-fire weapons actually mounted on armored vehicle chassis. Soviet artillery has been described as 'The Red God of War', and the Wehrmacht could never hope to match the number of tubes employed by the enemy. The Germans countered this mass with speed and accuracy.

The standard German divisional piece was the 105mm leFH 18 gun. Early versions fired a 15kg shell over 10,000m, but by 1943 the weapon had been lightened and improved, now with a range closer to 13,000m. Corps and army artillery units for general support missions fired the 150mm sFH 18. Midway through the Nazi-Soviet War, the Germans introduced the 'stinging insect' family of vehicles. The Wespe (Wasp) mounted the 105mm gun on a PzKw II chassis, and proved to be a very effective and widely used self-propelled (SP) artillery piece. The larger Hummel (Bumblebee, a name later forbidden by Hitler) mounted the 150mm sFH 18/1 on various PzKw III/IV chassis. The Germans had their own answer to the Soviet Katyusha, the 150mm rocket launcher Nebelwerfer ('smoke projector,' a code name meant to conceal its real purpose from enemy intelligence). Less accurate than tube artillery, these area weapons caused widespread damage and terrorized troops in its impact zone.

The Germans made all types of panzer chassis into turretless anti-tank or assault gun Sturmgeschütze. First conceived by von Manstein during the 1930s, these weapons realized the Napoleonic goal of having artillery accompany infantry in the attack. As such, assault guns belonged to the artillery branch rather than the Panzerwaffe. They were cheaper and faster to make and could mount larger caliber guns than corresponding panzer variants, in all cases due to the lack of relatively delicate turret mounting and traverse considerations. As the war dragged on, armored support often came in the form of these simple vehicles rather than panzers.

Anti-aircraft artillery (Flak) played a critical role in the blitzkrieg as early as Guderian's move through the Ardennes in 1940. The Red Army Air Force proved undaunted by the Germans, and soon recovered from the beating it took in Barbarossa's opening days. By 1943, the Luftwaffe was seldom seen over the battlefield, and Flak became ever more important for protecting troops on the ground. Here too, earlier slow and towed models gave way to guns mounted on fully or half-tracked vehicle chassis. Calibers ran the gauntlet from 20mm, 37mm, 50mm all the way to 88mm. Of these, the 37mm struck the best balance of size, firepower and economy. Guns were mounted singly, in pairs and in quad versions.

In 1941, 37mm Pak 35/36 (anti-tank) guns had already been revealed to be completely useless against Allied tanks and the 50mm Pak 38 was not far behind in becoming obsolete. For much of the war, the 75mm Pak 40 took over most of the anti-tank duties, although in later years, they too were growing inadequate. They were frequently augmented by captured Soviet 76mm weapons. The most famous German anti-tank gun was the dual-purpose 88mm Flak 36/37, initially mounted on the high-profile Luftwaffe version, but later attached to a low-slung and therefore, more easily concealed, army model, the Pak 43. A later development was the Raketenwerfer 43, a crew-fired recoilless rifle system, deadly out to 700m. Again, these weapons were frequently mounted on panzer chassis. Two of the best-known SP anti-tank AFVs were the 75mm Jagdpanzer 38(t) (based on the Czech tank, unofficial nickname, Hetzer) and the 88mm Hornisse (Hornet – also called Nashorn, Rhinoceros – built on a PzKw III/IV chassis). After the war, the Swiss Army purchased 150 Hetzer, and these continued to serve until 1970. The Hornisse were employed in heavy anti-tank battalions and over 1,200 were made.

On 20 July, Stavka decided to launch a large counteroffensive in order to encircle the Germans trying to encircle Smolensk. Stalin told Zhukov he wanted 'operations by larger groups', while the attackers were occupied fighting in and around Smolensk. Four of the five groups attacked Third Panzer Army:

Group Maslinnikov (29th Army: 252nd, 256th, 243rd Rifle Divisions plus the 31st Aviation Group and Armored Trains 52 and 82), attacking from the Toropets area on 23 July.

Group Khomenko (30th Army: 242nd, 251st, 25th Rifle Divisions, supported by 122nd Fighter and 190th Aviation Assault Regiments), the main effort, also beginning on the 23rd, aiming for Dukhovshchina.

Group Rokossovsky (38th Rifle and 101st Tank Divisions, forty old tanks) attacking toward Yartsevo.

Group Kalinin, (24th Army: 89th, 91st and 166th Rifle Divisions) with orders to exploit Khomenko's 'success'.

As usual, things were not as easy as they seemed, and the 'Timoshenko Offensive' got off to a slow and staggered start. Khomenko and Kalinin attacked on 24 July; Rokossovsky ran into the 7th Panzer supported by VIII Fliegerkorps, halted, then started again on the 28th; Maslinnikov finally moved out on the 29th. For a change, German intelligence was good and they knew of Timoshenko's plans; the Luftwaffe interdicted Soviet assembly areas before the offensive even began. Due to the delays, the attacks were uncoordinated and piecemeal. Hoth managed each successive crisis and by the evening of 27/28 July, he and Guderian had completed the Smolensk Kessel. Stavka gave all concerned a new mission: get the encircled garrison out of danger. Although a few Soviet soldiers managed to escape until about 4 August, by the end of July Stavka realized the offensive had no real chances of success and quietly called it off.[16]

Stalin had grown weary and saw the futility of tactical counterattacks of only a couple of divisions. Although Timoshenko employed fourteen divisions (granted, of uneven size), the fact that the offensive spanned nearly a 300km front drastically weakened its impact. Meanwhile, in Third Panzer's northern area of operations, the Germans had been expanding their salient near Nevel since 7 July. LVII Panzer Corps received orders to push on past Nevel and on to Velikie Luki. Only the 19th Panzer and half of the 14th Motorized Divisions could participate. The 19th moved out on 13 July. Roads through the terrible terrain were practically non-existent. Relatively heavy panzers routinely collapsed weak bridges, but pioneers could find no timber in the swamps with which to make repairs. The division took Nevel two days later. General of Panzer Troops Adolf Kuntzen left the 14th there while 19th Panzer continued northeast. The 53rd and 54th Cavalry Divisions, newly arrived from the Caucasus, had little will to fight but nonetheless frustrated the Germans. Seldom a team player, von Bock wanted no part in this 'useless venture' to help Army Group North. He therefore directed von Kluge and Hoth not to take part in an attack against Velikie Luki. Too late: by 20 July the 19th Panzer had already taken the city.

Von Bock ordered it abandoned; the city would have to be recaptured a month later by the same men at a much higher cost.[17]

Answering the question 'What to do next?' had vexed the German high command even before the conclusion of the Battle of Smolensk. In its original concept, Barbarossa would halt along the central axis while Hitler eliminated the politically valuable objective of Leningrad in the north plus the economically (and politically) valuable objective of the Ukraine in the south. He therefore issued directives in late July and early August, that in relevant part, sent portions of Third Panzer northeast to assist Army Group North. Specifically, Hoth lost XXXIX Panzer Corps, or one-third of his mechanized strength. Part of the reason OKH did not send more Third Panzer assets to von Leeb was the difficulty Hoth's men had in containing the various Soviet counterattacks. It is interesting to contemplate, if instead of the half measure as executed, the impact that all of Third Panzer, or even the bulk of its forces, would have had on the fighting for Leningrad. In late August and early September, while Second Panzer and Second Army headed for Kiev and the Ninth Army struggled around Yelnia, Third Panzer enjoyed relative quiet. Except for refighting the battle for Velikie Luki by Group Stumme (newly arrived XL Panzer Corps under Lieutenant General Georg Stumme), Hoth's sector of the front remained uneventful. Velikie Luki netted 34,000 POWs and 400 guns captured when the town fell on 22 August, and 20th Panzer occupied the important nearby communications center of Toropets a week later,[18] but these maneuvers only left Third Panzer's strength spread out just when it needed most to be massed. Time for the penultimate assault on Moscow grew nigh.

Another debate broke out among the fractious German leadership over the depth of the encirclement that marked Operation Typhoon's opening stages. Von Bock (with Guderian's backing) wanted a deep penetration and a larger pocket. Hitler and OKH wanted a shallower maneuver, one that would close near Viazma. The latter argument won out. With the Soviets defending along the Smolensk–Moscow highway, von Bock would go around those positions to the north (Hoth) and south (Hoepner's newly arrived Fourth Panzer Army). As usual, the plan was to destroy the defenders before they could retreat. Down at the troop level, more mundane questions arose: Landsers of the 6th Infantry wondered if they were going into winter quarters or not? The answer came on 26 September with orders to march on Moscow. In fact, far from going to winter quarters, the 6th would lead the breakthrough attempt. Hoth commanded the familiar V and VI Corps plus the new XLI and LVI Panzer Corps. Both panzer corps had just arrived from Army Group North after a 700km march over poor terrain. There had been no time for maintenance so operational rates for panzers were terrible and that for artillery prime movers was similarly bad.[19] Third Panzer would be subordinated again to Ninth Army, giving both responsibility for the far northern pincer of Typhoon. Von Bock scheduled d-day for 2 October.

Third Panzer's front that day opened with 100 tubes per kilometer artillery barrage. By 0530 hours Hoth's men were on the move, ably supported overhead by the VIII Fliegerkorps. The Soviets had not yet recovered from the Timoshenko Offensive and were ill-prepared for a defensive struggle. By twilight (approximately 1700 hours at that latitude), the 7th Panzer's reconnaissance battalion won a bridgehead over the Vop River (again!) and 6th Panzer was even more successful. A lieutenant in the 6th Panzer's artillery regiment remembered that day:

> Peacefully, the first light hit positions of both sides. The troops talk about the cold night. Then suddenly death and ruination spews from the throats of countless batteries upon the rows of unsuspecting enemy. Furiously but uncoordinated, the enemy artillery shoots back. Our own heavy artillery of all calibers plus waves of bombers and Stukas cover the enemy batteries. The infantry succeeds in overcoming the front lines of the enemy to clear the extensive minefields and clear the way for the panzer's main attack.[20]

The 1st Panzer Division had also achieved a breakthrough by evening. Hoth scored an operational coup by ripping apart the 19th and 30th Armies, pitting 12 German divisions (including 415 panzers), against 4 Soviet. Southwest of Bely the assault stalled temporarily as it struck well-prepared positions held by stubborn defenders. To compound matters, near that same town, Konev's Western Front hit Hoth's flank with the 126th and 152nd Rifle, 101st Motorized and 126th and 128th Tank Divisions. To no avail, however; XLI Panzer requested permission to bypass this obstacle to the south and Hoth approved. By the second day of Typhoon, Third Panzer had penetrated into Konev's second echelon and reached the upper Dnepr. By 4 October, LVI Panzer Corps managed to lever the 103rd Tank Brigade away from the river and establish a bridgehead. At precisely this time, Hoth's formations ran out of fuel and had to wait over 24 hours for resupply. Although Third Panzer Army resumed its advance the next day, Konev used the pause to request permission to withdraw from his exposed positions. The 5th also marked Hoth's last day at the helm of the panzer army. He departed for Army Group South that day to take command of the Seventeenth Army. Reinhardt moved up from XLI Panzer Corps, while Model in turn succeeded him.[21]

Red Army Chief of Staff, Marshal Shaposhnikov, concurred with Konev's request and on 6 October, Konev passed down the order for 16th and 19th Armies to withdraw. He sent a similar order to the remainder of the Western Front the next day. As usual, the blitzkrieg moved too fast for the Soviet command and control mechanism. On the morning of 7 October, Reinhardt's 7th Panzer and Hoepner's 10th Panzer linked up at Viazma, bagging elements of the 16th, 19th, 20th and 32nd Armies. Rokossovsky, commanding the 16th Army, received the unrealistic order to keep the neck of the bottle open so his comrades could escape. He could not. Also on the 7th, OKH ordered von Bock to take up pursuit operations toward Moscow while the Red Army struggled to regain its footing. The field marshal believed he could do both that mission and reduce the twin pockets. At Viazma and Bryansk, Army Group Center had ripped a 450km hole in Moscow's defenses. Neither side quite knew how Zhukov would plug that gaping hatchet wound or with what. But it soon became evident to the Germans at least, that clearing each Kessel would take more time and manpower than previously assumed. Autumn rains began in the northern portion of the army group's sector on the 7th and 8th,[22] slowing the army, grounding much of the Luftwaffe and worsening the logistic situation.[23]

The Soviet State Defense Committee realized on 6 October that they could not halt the inevitable defeat at Viazma and Bryansk. Two days later, Stavka mandated the next defensive effort along a line centered on the town of Mozhaisk. As history would have it, this was where the real Battle of Moscow would be fought. On the 10th, Zhukov took over command of Reserve and Western Fronts. Simultaneously across the front, on 7 October OKH ordered Reinhardt to attack along the Gzhatsk-Sychevka to Kalinin axis. There, if everything went according to plan, it would repeat its success at Viazma by creating another Kessel, again presumably with Fourth Panzer. Unfortunately for the Germans, any lessons about the benefits of shallow pockets gained at Viazma and Bryansk were evidently now forgotten. On the 11th, OKH ordered Second and Fourth Panzer Armies to execute a ridiculously deep encirclement hundreds of kilometers east of Moscow. The dangerous dispersal of effort that had bedeviled Third Panzer for much of Barbarossa continued. Reinhardt now had three tasks: continue reducing the Viazma Kessel, drive towards Kalinin as part of the developing battle for Moscow and push toward Rybinsk to help close the 80km-wide gap with Army Group North.[24]

Despite the impossible-sounding combination of conflicting missions, Third Panzer drove on against the 22nd and 29th Armies of Konev's Kalinin Front. Low fuel supplies and muddy terrain conspired with unrealistic higher headquarters' expectations and Red Army defenses to slow Reinhardt's men to a crawl. Nevertheless, while 36th Motorized and 6th Infantry Divisions guarded the growing flank from Soviet probes, SS Motorized Division Reich captured Gzhatsk on the 8th and other units took Sychevka the next day. For all the new troops who had only left the Leningrad fighting the month before, the terrain around Moscow seemed much different: fewer trees and flatter topography. Now the Red Army Air Forces owned the skies, flying from numerous permanent airfields around the Soviet capital, complete with heated hangers and concrete runways; the Luftwaffe, planes parked out in ice storms and using earthen airstrips, was seldom seen. Nevertheless, Zubsov fell to Reinhardt's men on the 11th and Staritsa the next day; both towns sat on the upper reaches of the Volga. Third Panzer's appearance managed to surprise the Soviets, but the latter still managed to launch counterattacks against the panzer army flanks. Requirements for German security outriders, including Brigade 900, to deal with these threats meant weakened spearheads. On 14 October, 1st Panzer Division became Reinhardt's first element to reach Kalinin. With this maneuver he cut the Moscow–Leningrad rail line and created an oblique threat to Moscow that Zhukov could not ignore. Reinhardt had two courses of action open to him: at any time Third Panzer might wheel right, either on Moscow or behind the Mozhaisk Line. While Model reinforced the success of the 1st Panzer with more XLI Panzer Corps formations – 36th Motorized, 6th, 26th and 129th Infantry Divisions plus Brigade 900, Konev dispatched his chief of Staff, Lieutenant General NF Vatutin, in an attempt to stabilize the situation.[25] The danger to Moscow's northern flank seemed real enough.

Third Panzer, with the help of Ninth Army (now through clearing the Viazma Kessel), fought a running battle in Kalinin until 29 October, when it finally prevailed over Group Vatutin. A counterattack on 24 October, by Siberian battalions of the 29th Army versus Reinhardt's left accomplished little, but as always, indicated Stalin's desire to contest every meter of the country. On the 26th, a corporal in 6th Panzer wrote, 'Rumors are everywhere that we only have a few weeks to deliver a death blow to the Soviet giant. In reality nothing looks so rosy.'[26] Meanwhile, on the panzer army's right, LVI Panzer (6th and 7th Panzer, 14th Motorized Divisions), in conjunction with the Ninth Army's XXVII Corps (86th and 162nd Infantry Divisions), moved on Volokomansk. Reinhardt was putting tremendous pressure on the Moscow defenses. However, by the end of the month, due to defenders, weather, logistics and pure exhaustion, Operation Typhoon had come to rest, generally along the Mozhaisk Line. The plan for the final assault on Moscow as approved by Hitler on 30 October had Third Panzer attacking beyond Klin and over the Volga–Moscow Canal, starting by the middle of November. Reinhardt still embodied the main threat to Moscow and von Bock had such high hopes for the operation's success he parked his command train behind the Schwerpunkt: Third and Fourth Panzer Armies. Quite correctly, Zhukov worried little about his center opposite the methodic and lethargic von Kluge, and concerned himself instead over Moscow's flanks, especially the northern.[27]

Zhukov hoped to launch a preemptive attack, but except for a small effort by Rokossovsky's 16th Army, the Germans got the jump on him on 15–16 November with Operation Schneesturm. The attackers counted approximately 233,000 men, 1,880 guns, 1,300 panzers and 800 aircraft. The defenders fielded a like number of men, 1,254 guns, 502 tanks and 600–700 aircraft. With 7th Panzer in the lead, the panzer army promptly split Rokossovsky from Leliushenko's 30th Army. Leliushenko further obliged Reinhardt by swinging away to the north instead of facing Third Panzer directly. Germans poured through the growing hole as Reinhardt outpaced Hoepner. On the 23rd, Klin (with Rokossovsky personally in charge of the defense) fell to a combined force of 7th Panzer and 14th Motorized troops. Soviet counterattacks failed to dislodge them. Reinhardt exhorted his men eastward and two days later, Panzer Regiment Rothenburg and Infantry Regiment 6 reached Yakhroma. They cut the Volga–Moscow Canal and the 7th Panzer created a small bridgehead on the eastern bank. Although the Germans did not realize it, with Colonel Hasso von Manteuffel's men only 35 km from the Kremlin, 27 November was the Soviet's nadir. Stalin sent all available reserves to his northern flank and directed all Red Army Air Force assets in that direction. Zhukov sent the winter-equipped 1st Shock and 20th Armies into the gap between the 16th and 30th Armies. By the 28th, just 24 hours after its creation, Army Group Center ordered the Yakhroma bridgehead evacuated. That same day, the 1st Shock Army launched its attack.[28] As the history of the half-frozen 7th Panzer Division states,

> On 29 November, the higher command ordered withdrawal from the bridgehead and creation of defensive positions on the west bank of the canal. The withdrawal crushed all members of the division, especially members of the Kampfgruppe on the far bank that, with exemplary preparation and bravery, had won the bridgehead in the expectation of an advance over the canal towards Moscow.[29]

Model's XLI Panzer Corps, its troops still in their temperate uniforms, edged to within 25 km of Moscow on the canal's west bank, but basically the threat to Moscow had passed. By the last day of November, its panzer strength stood at 77 (1st Panzer: 37, 6th Panzer: 4, 7th Panzer: 36). At the same time, Zhukov had over 1,000 tanks divided among 1 tank division, 16 tank brigades and over 20 independent tank battalions. Even the perpetually optimistic Model realized that with the infantry down to thirty men per company, no food, no ammunition or fuel coming forward and with Soviet counterattacks getting bolder, the drive on Moscow was over. On 5 December, Reinhardt wrote in his diary, Third Panzer Army was 'completely exhausted and, for the first time in the campaign, combat ineffective'.[30]

So long as it could act in a concentrated manner, Third Panzer Army contributed mightily to Operation Barbarossa. Through the Battle of Smolensk, it received much more of the Soviets' attention, including being attacked by over three-fourths of the Red Army forces involved in the Timoshenko Offensive. However, by the beginning of August, demands placed on Hoth by higher headquarters meant it lost the advantages of mass. Regrouped again for Typhoon, by late November, Third Panzer caused Zhukov his most anxious moments. However, the panzer army's operational excellence could only bring it to the outskirts of Moscow and no closer.

The Soviets' general counteroffensive began on 5 December with no less ambitious an objective than the total destruction of Army Group Center. North of Moscow, from 5 to 7 December, that meant blasting through Third and Fourth Panzer Armies in concert with a similar subsequent effort against Guderian to the south. If Stalin had had his way, Zhukov would have created an encirclement on the scale of Kiev three months earlier.

The 30th, 1st Shock, 20th and 16th Armies combined to attack the bulge created by the Third and Fourth Panzer Armies. Elements of Konev's Bryansk Front overran the LVI Panzer Corps headquarters. Manning the canal just south of Yakhroma, stood the 1st Panzer Division. Unable to resist the 1st Shock Army, at 2130 hours that first day of the offensive, the division commander, Major General Walter Krüger, radioed his command post from his vantage point with the fighting troops, 'We're going back! Turn the division around!' The 1st Panzer lost or abandoned all of its panzers so the crewmen had to fight with rifles and grenades like 'common' Landsers. Further north, the 30th Army split the seam between the 14th and 36th Motorized Divisions and made for Klin. Reinhardt ordered 1st Panzer in that direction and by 7 December the Germans temporarily stabilized the situation and maintained their hold on the city. Behind the 1st followed the 2nd, 6th and 7th Panzer, 14th and 36th Motorized and 23rd Infantry Divisions, plus corps and army troops in three side-by-side convoys. Red cavalry and partisans hounded their every step, picking off stragglers. A 6th Panzer soldier recorded in his diary, 'In long rows, unnaturally silent, the three companies moved back at night.'[31] But the Germans' grasp on Klin could only be temporary, and the panzer army commander told von Bock that Third Panzer would have to order a general withdrawal. Luftwaffe transport aircraft flew in supplies, mainly fuel, originally allocated for Guderian. Krüger led a mishmash of units with three Sturmgeschütze, five Panzer IIIs, nineteen Panzer 38(t)s, division musicians, Luftwaffe aircrew and maintenance personnel, army and Luftwaffe Flak units plus a few panzers from the maintenance shops. By 11 December, LVI Panzer security lines had been penetrated in numerous places and the corps was in danger of encirclement. Pioneers detonated massive amounts of special Christmas rations warehoused in the city. Despite Reinhardt's exhortations on the 13th to hold Klin, by the next night his men were streaming south-west, heading back along the roads they had just covered days earlier. They left 800–1,000 wounded in the hospital that they could not evacuate. Soviet infantry, T-34s and CAS aircraft chased the survivors.[32]

The 6th Panzer had the unenviable job of covering the panzer army's rear as it withdrew. The next logical place for Third Panzer to halt and offer resistance was along the Lama River. On 18 December, Reinhardt said he doubted his men could do it. Strength of XLI Panzer stood at 1,821 Kämpfer (fighters), while LVI Panzer had 900 combat troops. The four panzer divisions possessed thirty-four operational panzers between them. Reinhardt could count on sixty-three light and twenty-one heavy artillery pieces and a dozen PAKs in his entire panzer army. His men reached the Lama on the 19th and faced east against Zhukov's avenging frontovicki. By the end of 1941, Reinhardt believed he could defend the river position indefinitely, and besides, Third Panzer was almost frozen into place so he doubted he could withdraw in good order even if instructed to. The 6th Panzer's 1st Battalion, Infantry Regiment 4 (all thirty men of it), spent New Year's Eve capturing a small hut, putting the frozen dead outside then drinking some wine, while Red Army soldiers did about the same in another house only 50m away. A week into 1942, the panzer division, called by its men the 6th Division zu Fuss (Foot Division) felt it had earned a breather.[33] Like almost every similar unit in the Wehrmacht in Russia, it had been de facto de-mechanized by the exertions of a five-month campaign.

On the Third Panzer's left flank, however, the Soviets pressed hard along the boundary with the Ninth Army. To the west, the VI Corps of the Ninth, since 29 December under General of Aviation von Richthofen, held Rzhev, the 'corner post', against the 39th, 29th and 31st Armies. Von Richthofen, simultaneously still commanding VIII Fliegerkorps, made sure his Stukas continued to fly on 2 January despite the −40° F temperatures. Three days later, the 3rd Shock Army forced its way between Reinhardt and von Richthofen, creating a 12km wide gap. A lame counterattack attempt by the SS Cavalry Brigade on 7–8 January failed to neutralize the threat or seal the break. A week later, Hitler approved a retreat to the Königsberg Line, running along the Volga to Gzhatsk and thence southeastward. Von Kluge withheld his concurrence for three days, finally permitting the Third and Fourth Panzer Armies to retreat to the new line between 18 and 25 January. At about this time, in mid-January, Stavka ordered Belov's 1st Guards Cavalry Corps to advance against Viazma, close to the seam between the two panzer armies, a maneuver calculated to threaten Reinhardt's only rail connection, his army's lifeline. Belov could count on the help of the 4th Airborne Corps (4th, 8th and 201st Airborne Brigades) dropped between Viazma and Yartsevo, plus countless partisans.[34] Though this force rampaged in the army group rear unchecked for weeks, huge snow drifts hampered German rail movement as much as the Red cavalry. A 7th Panzer soldier described the winter fighting that January thus:

> Day and night the men stayed at their posts without chance for warmth or rest. They try to improve their positions daily, schlepping around materials for bunkers. There are few supplies, one can hardly speak of 'organizing' materials taken from homes and burnt-out huts. It is very easy for the Russians to break through our thin lines. Our men become exhausted going through the snow from one bunker to another. How can one describe this fighting? The Russians attack in a completely mulish and senseless manner, and think nothing of it if ten, thirty, forty or fifty men fall. In every combat we have two-three men in fighting positions without any communications with neighbors on the right or left. The wind blows against the observation posts so one's tears freeze in his eyes. Nose, ears and chin have no feeling from the cold and are often frozen. Who among them doesn't have frozen feet? Who has hands that move? Who does not have intestinal problems? Who is not frozen?[35]

During the third week of the month, Third Panzer Army headquarters moved west by aerial transport to the Velikie Luki–Bely sector in an attempt to contain the 4th Shock Army. There, in an effort to create his own battle of annihilation, Zhukov endeavored to envelop Army Group Center by exploiting the break between it and Army Group North. Reinhardt's new area of responsibility did not have a solid front line, but instead consisted of division-sized Igel fighting positions at Velikie Luki, Velizh and Demidov, all randomly linked by screening forces. His neighbor to the north, Sixteenth Army, had a similar arrangement, with its southern-most fortified location at Kholm. In between, Red cavalry units and bands of partisans were everywhere. Soon however, the Soviets fell victim to many of the same limitations as the Germans a month earlier: exhaustion, overstretch, German resistance, the rasputitsa and, perhaps most significantly, Stalin's interference, which meant the end of the winter counteroffensive without exterminating Army Group Center.[36]

To the Germans, the spring of 1942 meant more than just the return of the seasonal rain and mud, it signaled the change from defense to offense. Specifically, the Wehrmacht made preparations for its summer offensive, Operation Blau, the attack on the southern front toward Stalingrad and the Caucasus oil region. Headquarters, Fourth Panzer Army would be one of Blau's main players and it deployed to the Ukraine, so on 1 April, Third Panzer returned to the familiar Gzhatsk and Viazma sector in its place. In addition to the deception plan to convince the Soviets that the main German blow that year would once more aim at Moscow, Army Group Center formations reinforced their defenses and endeavored to clear their rear areas of Soviet conventional and partisan forces. One such operation was Hannover, conducted by Fourth Army from 24 May to 21 June. Reinhardt contributed elements of the IX Corps to mop up remains of Belov's 1st Guards Cavalry, 4th Airborne Corps and their partisan comrades, which had stubbornly remained behind German lines. Third Panzer also lost the 20th Panzer Division to Ninth Army for its anti-partisan mission, Operation Seydlitz, which lasted from 2–12 July. Some major conventional combat operations took place along the central theater that summer as well. On 13 August, as part of a larger action to pinch off the bulge at Gzhatsk, the 33rd Army attacked Third Panzer's right along the Vorya River. They hit the seam between the 183rd and 292nd Infantry Divisions in battalion strength, and soon added tanks in waves of twenty to forty. German artillery fired at tanks over open sights and Stukas added their bomb loads to the mix. On the 15th, a one-division counterattack surrounded the enemy's main body. Reinhardt visited the command post of the 292nd and received a report from commander of 2nd Battalion, Infantry Regiment 507:

> We succeeded in surprising the enemy. He had sought shelter from the rain and had security only in the north. After short but very lively house-to-house fighting, the Russians lost their heads and fled into the woods. His losses must have been great. But before daybreak we arrived at the new defense line as ordered with all of our elements intact and only slight losses.[37]

Reinhardt's men counterattacked and mastered the situation. Move and counter-move by both sides did not venture into the operational realm, but were limited to tactical harassment operations. Soon both sides settled down to the routine of static defense, with the usual partisan activity bedeviling the Germans in increasing intensity.[38]

Attention remained riveted on the south that autumn and winter: the great battles around Stalingrad and the Caucasus, the Soviet Operations Uranus, Little Saturn and Ring and finally, von Manstein's counter stroke that eventually ended only in March 1943. By far the most serious fighting in von Kluge's area had been against the Ninth Army's salient at Rzhev. A second hot spot was at Velikie Luki, on the army group's extreme left, defended by the corps-sized Group von der Chevallerie. On 16 January, under the blows of the 3rd Shock Army, the Germans lost the town. To master that situation, two weeks later, von Kluge once again pulled Third Panzer Army out of the line facing Moscow and returned it to the Velikie Luki area. As before, Reinhardt also assumed the mission of maintaining contact with Army Group North. Within days of arriving, he tried to recapture the town, but failed owing to the 'appalling condition' of the troops he had inherited.[39]

Fighting on the front lines ebbed and Third Panzer turned its attention to partisans in the rear. Its 'front line existed mainly on maps, but in reality was a porous set of strongpoints',[40] often occupied by Luftwaffe field divisions of doubtful quality; partisan bands roamed free in the large gaps in between. At Surazh, near the center of his sector, Reinhardt launched Operation Kugelblitz with two security divisions against approximately 4–5,000 partisans. Between 15 February and 8 March, the Germans claimed 3,700 partisans killed. The focus in the spring and summer again shifted south, this time to Operation Citadel on the boundary of Army Groups Center and South. Reflecting the continued decline in the stature of panzer armies, Reinhardt's command played no part in the fighting around the Kursk salient. With the unmitigated failure of the 1943 offensive, and in recognition of the swing in momentum from the Wehrmacht to the Red Army, on 12 August Hitler ordered work begun on a series of defensive works stretching the entire length of the eastern front. In Third Panzer's area, this 'Panther position' ran north–south along a line east of Vitebsk and Nevel and west of Velikie Luki.[41] However, the concept of such an 'East Wall' represented the Führer's wishful thinking of a most dreamy nature. The Soviets had no intention of allowing the invaders such a comfortable luxury.

The Red Army wasted absolutely no time transitioning from strategic defense to strategic offense as soon as Citadel had shot its bolt in mid-July. Its first target in von Kluge's area was the Orel bulge where the Second Panzer and Ninth Armies were soon overwhelmed. The scope of the Soviet assault soon spread north, first with the Western Front's attack against Heinrici's Fourth Army and then when Eremenko's Kalinin Front attacked Reinhardt. During the second half of September, Eremenko overwhelmed the Third Panzer's right flank, taking Velizh on 20 September and Demidov two days later. Not many hours after, VI Corps troops arrived at Surazh and the under-construction Panther position. Eremenko thereupon switched his main effort north to the junction of Army Groups Center and North. This was the weakest point in the already weak German line and the terrain was equally terrible for attacker and defender alike. On 6 October, his 3rd and 4th Shock Armies hit the Luftwaffe's 2nd Field Division near Budnitsa. After offering resistance against four rifle divisions and two tank brigades for a couple of hours, the division vaporized, creating an 18km gap between the two army groups. Reinhardt sent the 129th Infantry and some of his panzer army assets to buttress what was left of the II Luftwaffe Field Corps. Over 500 sorties of CAS flew in support of their brethren in blue, fighting for their survival on the ground. Nevel fell that same day and it had lost all contact with Army Group North, but Third Panzer seemed to be holding its own for the time being.[42]

On 9 October, Eremenko paused, allowing the Third Panzer to regain its footing. Field Marshal Ernst Busch, new Army Group Center commander, helped by sending the 20th Panzer Division and the 505th Heavy Panzer Battalion (Tiger tanks), while also authorizing a withdrawal to the Panther position. Toward the end of the month, the 1st Baltic Front (as Eremenko's command was renamed on 1 October) launched some preparatory assaults that dented Reinhardt's line. Its attacks began in earnest on 2 November. They promptly succeeded in cutting the Nevel–Polotsk rail line and by the 6th had reached Pustoshke on the panzer army's left. Reinhardt assembled a counter-attack force based on the 252nd Infantry Division, reinforced with a Nebelwerfer regiment, two battalions each of Sturmgeschütze and PAKs, plus one battalion each of pioneers and heavy artillery. The 20th Panzer participated as well, but when Army Group North did not contribute from the north as planned, Busch called off the attack after gaining barely 8km in 24 hours. That same day, 8 November, Eremenko again shifted his main effort, this time toward Vitebsk. The 206th Infantry stood alone against 8 rifle divisions, 2 rifle brigades, 2 tank brigades and a mechanized brigade. A relief counterattack by the 211th Security Division had to be cancelled when fog grounded the scheduled Luftwaffe CAS. By the 11th, the 3rd Guards Cavalry Corps broke through Reinhardt's right and made for Gorodek, thus threatening the panzer army's line of communications. Meanwhile, 4th Shock had penetrated as far as Dretun, 50km in Third Panzer's rear and dangerously close to Polotsk.[43]

The greater threat was connection to the strained right flank of Army Group North. With Gorodek and Vitebsk both in danger, Third Panzer had its share of worries. Reinhardt sensed another exposed salient developing around Vitebsk and requested permission from Busch to pull out of that town. The army group commander refused. Reinhardt told his men: 'In this anxious hour, each of us has been called upon by the Führer to hold our positions until the last. Difficult weeks lay behind us. In spite of this, we will hold in the decisive hour. I believe in each of you. We must and will succeed!'[44]

On 24 November, Third Panzer received a break from an unexpected source: unseasonable warm weather occurred, causing a thaw that turned the country-side to mud. Both sides waited for the next frost, which came on 9 December. Four days later, the 4th Shock and 11th Guards Armies renewed their attacks, this time against the IX Corps at the Third Panzer's northernmost extremity. Again Reinhardt requested to withdraw his almost-trapped elements. Again Busch told him 'No'. By the 15th, enemy tanks stood behind IX Corps, now encased around Lobok. Only then did Hitler relent, but now it was too late for the two divisions inside. What two days earlier would have simply been an extremely difficult escape, turned into a very low-odds breakout. As happened with the Ostheer countless times, an encircled garrison marched out across enemy territory, leaving behind over one-quarter of its men and most of its heavy equipment. The final straw came on 17 December, when the 5th Tank Corps split the 20th Panzer from the 129th Infantry Division. On his own initiative, starting that day, Reinhardt ordered Third Panzer back.[45]

For the next few days, the Soviets probed 14th Panzergrenadier Division positions in front of Vitebsk. Then, on 23 December, 1st Baltic Front launched a new assault on the town from due east, sending portions of his 4th Shock, 11th Guards, 39th and 43rd Armies right between the 206th and 246th Infantry Divisions. On Christmas Eve, 5th Tank Corps achieved another penetration and rushed the town of Gorodek. Three days later, Busch sent one division each from Second and Ninth Armies to Reinhardt as reinforcements, but these were small consolation in the face of thirty-eight Soviet divisions and fifteen tank brigades. The newly arrived Feldherrnhalle Panzer Grenadier Division managed to put up a credible defense astride the Vitebsk–Orsha road in order to prevent the enemy from breaking any deeper into the German rear area. Into the first week of 1944, the Soviets lavished attention on Feldherrnhalle, but the division generally held its ground with the help of the 256th and 246th Infantry Divisions. A week later, another attack hit the Luftwaffe's 6th Field Division, now down to 436 men.[46] The Soviets refused to cut the panzer army any slack and kept up relentless pressure.

By 17 January, however, the 1st Baltic Front could go no farther. From left to right Reinhardt's line included IX, LIII and VI Corps, but only one panzer division, the 20th, in this 'panzer army'. He had between 60 and 80 additional operational AFVs in 3 Sturmgeschutz and Hornisse (Hornet) battalions. On 3 February, 1st Baltic Front was ready to try Vitebsk again. After 2½ hours of artillery preparation, elements of the 11th Guards, 4th Shock plus 5th, 33rd, 39th and 43rd Armies combined against the 131st and 206th Infantry Divisions to the southeast of the city (the Soviet main effort) and the 12th Infantry and part of the 20th Panzer to the northeast. Heavy fighting raged for days.

Red Army forces achieved a breakthrough on the 12th, but could not exploit their success due to deep snow drifts. Five days later, the Soviets called off the attack: Reinhardt's men had held. A month later, on 13 March, Hitler's Order #11 added Vitebsk to his list of Fester Platz cities that could not be surrendered. That spring, Third Panzer Army participated in anti-partisan operations Regenschauer (11–16 April) and Frühlingsfest (16 April–10 May) around Ushachi and Kormoran across a large area generally north and northeast of Minsk (22 May–20 June).[47]

Reinhardt had demonstrated tactical skill in the unfamiliar role of the defense, especially considering the Ostheer's deteriorating position and the Red Army's growing confidence. Like the Second Panzer to the south, Third Panzer had hardly played an operational role in the eighteen months following Barbarossa. All it could do was to observe the Soviet build-up across the front and wonder what would happen next?

'Next' came the destruction of Army Group Center, a disaster, in terms of German men and matériel lost, worse than Stalingrad. The Soviets had numerous reasons to emphasize the central theater: 1. Many German units were defending there (or to put it another way, many German units could be destroyed there); 2. Since an offensive in this area would directly threaten the German Reich and put Army Groups North and North Ukraine in a position of severe disadvantage, Hitler was bound to send reinforcements there, and these would also be ripe for the picking; 3. Soviet forces elsewhere, especially in the northern Ukraine, had taken a bad beating, despite recovering much territory since the previous summer; 4. The partisan movement was very strong in this region and would assist the Red Army, and; 5. It was unexpected by the Germans. Busch's headquarters knew the Soviets were preparing an offensive, it just did not know in what strength. Intelligence officers of the Third Panzer and other armies in the area saw unmistakable signs of an impending attack.[48] Considering the massive violence Stalin threw at Army Group Center that summer, this foreknowledge would only help so much.

By the time of the Soviet summer offensive, Operation Bagration, the panzer army had no panzer divisions under command. In fact, higher headquarters had siphoned off many of Reinhardt's units, assuming there would be no major enemy attacks and, as had previously been the case, he could handle any crises thrown his way. However, his seven infantry and two Luftwaffe field divisions manning a 220km front would face an overwhelming array of adversaries of long standing: 4th Shock, 6th Guards, 43rd, 39th, 5th, 11th Guards, 5th Guards Tank Armies of the 1st Baltic and 3rd Belorussian Fronts, with 24 and 28 divisions and 3 and 10 tank brigades respectively (plus numerous other combat and support units). Soviet maskrovka (deception) plans worked on both the strategic and operational levels: Busch felt secure enough to travel back to Germany on the eve of Bagration, while Reinhardt's intelligence staff fell for the feint towards Polotsk and missed indications of the real attack on Vitebsk.[49]

For the men of IX Corps the first attack on 22 June, the third anniversary of Barbarossatag, felt real enough. That day, the 43rd and 6th Guards Armies overran the 206th and 252nd Infantry Divisions. The 5th and 39th Armies had similar success against VI Corps south of Vitebsk and brushed aside a feeble counterattack by the 95th Infantry. Busch arrived back at his headquarters that afternoon and for the next 24 hours tried to rally a defense. The two divisions Reinhardt received as emergency reinforcements could not hold the Soviets back. By the second day of the offensive, VI Corps had fallen back and now it was Busch who requested permission to abandon Vitebsk. On that day and again on the 24th, OKH told him 'No'. Two days later, Busch flew back to Obersalzberg to see Hitler in person, only to be refused again. Everywhere Red Army units took advantage of the chaos. On 25 June, they cut the rail line at Bogushevsk and continued on to the former Barbarossa battlefield (and high ground) at Senno, which essentially meant that LIII Corps had become trapped in Vitebsk. Now that it was too late, Hitler agreed to let LIII Corps escape. Four of five German divisions departed, while 206th Infantry remained to anchor the city's defense.[50]

As a Fester Platz, a flawed concept for the defensive battles dating from the previous winter, the commander of Vitebsk gave his personal word to defend as long as possible. Ammunition and food had been stockpiled for the better part of four divisions plus the Luftwaffe's 10th Flak Brigade now holed up there. Third Panzer lacked sufficient reserves to execute a viable counterattack; the three-division-strong relief effort that Reinhardt managed to hobble together came within 5–6km of the Vitebsk perimeter, but could get no closer. The LIII Corps commander, Lieutenant General Friedrich Gollwitzer, did pull off a breakout of sorts. In the end, approximately 8,000 men made it to the relative safety of the Third Panzer Army's lines, while nearly 20,000 perished when the worthless 'fortress' fell on the 27th. A 40–50km gap now existed, into which the 3rd Belorussian Front sent the 5th Guards Tank Army and 3rd Guards Mechanized Corps. By 28 June, Hitler had had enough of Busch's mediocre leadership and replaced him at the top of Army Group Center with the trusty Model. By the end of the month, the panzer army consisted of the weak IX Corps of three divisions with a total of about seventy artillery pieces: VI Corps had drifted south in an effort to maintain contact with Fourth Army, while LIII Corps had been obliterated at Vitebsk.[51]

The 5th Panzer Division raced by rail to Borisov, the site of the worst breech, but its counterattack was too small to achieve more than limited, tactical gains. At this stage of the war it was the Germans' turn to mount tiny, ineffectual tactical counterattacks, when only larger operational assaults could possibly make a difference. By early July, crumbs of the once-proud panzer army trickled west to try and establish a legitimate defense along the Dvina and Ulla Rivers. That line could not hold the Soviets back, however. By 7 July, their advanced elements had already reached Vilnius. At this point, novel strategic factors came into play that complicated the entire northern portion of the Nazi-Soviet War. On 10 July, Grand Admiral Karl Dönitz, Kriegsmarine commander, met Hitler at the latter's East Prussian headquarters. He explained that Army Group North could not continue to fall back to the southwest along with Army Group Center. Instead it would have to withdraw, on its own if absolutely necessary, to the northwest and toward the mouth of the Dvina. His navy needed the port of Riga if the Baltic Sea was to remain a 'German lake': essential for U-boat training, merchant shipping, and as Hitler noted, the continued participation of Finland as an Axis co-belligerent. In the first two weeks of Operation Bagration, Third Panzer had lost ten divisions; Reinhardt thought only of his army's survival and fought on accordingly. Therefore, from this time onward, Third Panzer's connection to the southern end of Army Group North grew ever more tenuous. As the summer continued, and despite the best efforts of many, the army group drifted north basically to 'fight its own war' until May 1945.[52]

By the second week of July, fighting in the Third Panzer Army area centered on encircled Vilnius. This Fester Platz had a 4,000-man garrison of assorted army units plus some Luftwaffe flak batteries (including 10 88s). Reinhardt created a relief force, 'Kampfgruppe 1067', consisting of a couple of field replacement battalions, and sent it towards Vilnius. When it too became encircled, Reinhardt now had two pockets to rescue. However, he said that he would not squander any more strength trying to save the stronghold, even if directly ordered by Hitler: 'Constantly acting against my better judgment is more than I can do.'[53] He told Model he had only enough strength for one mission: link up with Army Group North or relieve Vilnius: which would it be? Model told him to save the city. For the sake of his trapped men, he sent the 6th Panzer (with twenty Panthers), which had just arrived by rail, plus a tank battalion from Grossdeutschland (the division also began to arrive in the panzer army sector after a furious rail 'blitz' transport across Germany). This force reached Kampfgruppe 1067 about the same time that Hitler gave the men in Vilnius permission to escape – 2,000 of them made it back to friendly lines, while Red Army troops entered the city on 13 July. A week later, the 2nd Guards

Army caved in the panzer army's southern flank when six guards rifle divisions surrounded one German division. The defense 'fell apart' as the Soviets created a penetration almost 60km wide and the same distance deep. Somehow, toward the end of July, the Third Panzer coalesced along its new line, running generally along the middle Niemen River, anchored at Kaunas and Grodno and even made solid contact with Fourth Army on the right. Its 13,850 men combat strength equaled that of an undernourished infantry division. Facing it were 18 rifle divisions, 3 tank corps, 1 mechanized corps and 3 tank brigades.[54] Sadly, it seemed that with this correlation of forces there could be but one outcome to the upcoming battle.

On 29 July, about half of this Soviet force plunged over the Niemen, south of Kaunas. By the next day, they had advanced to Mariampol, but then halted of their own accord. Two divisions plus Fallschirmjäger Regiment 16 held out, defending the old First World War fortifications around Kaunas, but were soon in danger of being entrapped like so many other German units. Model would not acquiesce to Reinhardt's request to evacuate the city. The panzer army commander neared the limit of his endurance. 'Very well, if that is how things stand,' he told Model, 'then *I* will save my troops.' At ten minutes past midnight on the 30th, he unilaterally ordered his men to abandon Kaunas. One can see that nearly three years of commanding many of the same units and men over much of the same ground was having an effect on Reinhardt. It was clearly time for Reinhardt to move on, and on 16 August, Colonel General Erhard Raus arrived to take command of Third Panzer. Reinhardt did not go far, however, he ascended to command of Army Group Center, where he would have to work all the more closely with Hitler.[55]

Colonel General Erhard Raus

Born in 1889 in Moravia, Raus became a lieutenant in the Austro-Hungarian Army in 1912. He fought in light infantry and bicycle units on the Russian Front during the First World War: an excellent example of the type of Wehrmacht officer whose First World War experience should have better prepared the Ostheer for the environment encountered from 1941–45. Following the Anschluss between Austria and Nazi Germany, Raus received a colonel's rank in 1938. He sat out both the Polish and French campaigns.

Raus took command of Rifle Regiment 4 in July 1940, and then Rifle Brigade 6 in April 1941. Often at the front of XLI Panzer Corps, Raus led the way toward Leningrad, earning both classes of Iron Cross within two weeks and the Knight's Cross after four months. Von Leeb failed to exploit Raus' Luga River bridgehead, and soon the 6th Panzer transferred to the central sector to participate in

Operation Typhoon. Often serving as acting division commander during that offensive, Raus' men came very close to Moscow only to fall back, defending with his last two operational panzers. During the winter of 1941–42, Ninth Army commander Model put Raus in charge of defending the army's rear areas. In April 1942, the 6th Panzer Division transferred to France to refit, with Raus now officially its commanding general. That November, disaster at Stalingrad cut this training short as 6th Panzer hurriedly railed east. Raus organized his rail shipment by 'combat trains' rather than for bureaucratic convenience, which minimized casualties upon arrival.

The 6th Panzer Division played a central role in the failed Sixth Army rescue effort. After this operation, von Manstein heaped praise on the 'experienced old panzer division' under its 'admirable commander'. After retreating to the Ukraine, his new command, XI Corps (sometimes called Provisional Corps Raus) took part in the third Battle of Kharkov, in March 1943. He commanded the same headquarters during Citadel, the last Battle of Kharkov and the defense of the eastern Ukraine. With Raus now wearing Oak Leaves, XI Corps held open the Eighth Army's bridgehead over the Dnepr River that autumn.

Hitler replaced Hoth with Raus at the head of Fourth Panzer Army on 1 November 1943. Determined not to retreat as had been his predecessor's downfall, Raus organized the counterattacks by army and SS units at Fastov and Zithomir. Raus arranged his formations to absorb Vatutin's winter offensive, but nevertheless had to give ground in the face of superior force. He did succeed in keeping his panzer army intact and in preventing the Soviets from achieving a breakthrough. On 1 May 1944, Raus moved south to take command of the First Panzer Army, now backed up to the Carpathian Mountains. At times during this period, he also had command of Hungarian and Slovak units.

Raus took over Third Panzer Army in the Baltic region on 16 August. Here he led a quick counterattack to regain contact with Army Group North in Courland (northwest Latvia) and also served under SS leader Heinrich Himmler. Hitler relieved Raus on 12 March, and the general spent the years 1945–47 as a POW. After the war, Raus authored a number of monographs for the US Army Historical Division. Raus was fluent in Italian, Czech and Slovenian and spoke some French. Raus proved his worth in the tactical and operational levels and in both attack and defense. He died in 1956.

The Third Panzer's right stabilized after the loss of Kaunas, but less than 20km from German territory in East Prussia. In early August, the defenses of Army Group North on its left began to fall apart. Raus' first day on the job as panzer army commander proved to be eventful. For starters, he had inherited a poorly planned operation, Doppelkopf, an effort to rejoin the two army groups along the Baltic coast, that involved more panzer divisions than the 'panzer' army had seen in years. Next, his relief force would have to cover 130km of rivers, forests and marsh. However, thanks in large part to the German Army's new Chief of Staff, Guderian, quite a number of panzer units massed in northern Lithuania. The XXXIX Panzer Corps (General of Panzer Troops Dietrich von Saucken, 4th, 5th and 12th Panzer Divisions) and Panzer Unit Strachwitz (SS Brigade Gross and 101st Panzer Brigade) assembled near the port town of Libau. The XL Panzer (General of Panzer Troops Otto von Knobelsdorff, 7th and 14th Panzer, 1st Infantry Divisions and Grossdeutschland) started from Tauroggen and attacked north toward Siauliai. With so many panzer thrusts, the Soviets had difficulty discerning Raus' Schwerpunkt, if there even was one. After some initial success, the Germans ran into 10 rifle and 3 artillery divisions supported by 4 anti-tank brigades of 1st Baltic Front that were fully prepared and 2 lines deep. The XL Panzer halted on the Venta River, having gained only 40km.[56]

With 14th Panzer Division covering its exposed right flank, Grossdeutsch-land made it to Siauliai on 18 August. And 2 days later, XXXIX Panzer and Major General Hyazinzh Graf von Strachwitz's formation moved out again, this time supported by 284 rounds of naval gunfire provided by the heavy cruiser *Prinz Eugen*, and destroyers *Z-25* and *Z-28*. Red Army units at Siauliai held out, but von Strachwitz prevailed at Tukums on the Gulf of Riga against elements of the 51st Army. When his men finally linked up with the 281st Security Division on the 20th, they opened an 18km-wide corridor to Army Group North. The first truck convoys headed north the very next day. Nearly simultaneously, Raus fought a small, sharp action to firm up the corridor's shoulder. He withdrew his 400 remaining AFVs to Auce and then attacked toward the high ground near Doblen, where Red Army units overwatched the newly won strip of land. The assault surprised the 51st Army, and on the second day carried the heights with the help of Sixteenth Army's Provisional Corps Kleffel (81st and 93rd Infantry Divisions), which attacked south from Riga.[57] Occasionally, the Germans could pull off a small victory, but this armor concentration on the Baltic coast meant that somewhere else along the front opportunities to create a panzer grouping with operational significance were lost.

The 3rd Belorussian Front had a second welcome for Raus on 16 August. The 5th, 33rd and 11th Guards Armies attacked Third Panzer's right and drove to Vilkavishkis, practically on the East Prussian frontier. A few Soviet units even conducted the first raid into German territory, but these were soon defeated. Raus kept his head, and did not allow himself to be distracted from his main mission to help Army Group North.[58]

Indeed, action again switched north in mid-September. On the 16th, Raus launched a three-division attack under the command of XXXIX Panzer Corps to relieve enemy pressure on Army Group North. In the area south of Riga, they gained 15km and managed to destroy about 100 tanks and 200 guns. However, the 1st Baltic Front was just too strong for those relatively small losses to make much of a dent in its order of battle. With the bulk of Third Panzer in the Courland anyway, on 20 September, Hitler transferred it to Army Group North. Into early October, Raus, without 'a single panzer at [his] disposal', continued to guard the 160km-wide corridor linking Army Groups North and Center. The road to Riga had been blasted open, but at a heavy cost. Losses were high from fighting a defense in the open country. Strength in Grossdeutschland's infantry companies again sank to forty men.[59] Obergefreiter Sachs, 5th Company, 1st Battalion of the division's Füsilier Regiment described the fighting thus:

> As our 1st Battalion attacked toward the east, we had the mission of destroying the Soviets that we had pinned down in the woods. As I got my group into position, I wondered how the infantry and tanks were arrayed over there. I didn't have long to find out. Nothing, then Ivan storms against us with a loud 'Hurrah!' There was wild confusion but we remained and were not deceived.
>
> A comrade destroyed a tank in close combat, but we could not determine how many other Soviets were knocked out in the rush. 'The situation is favorable' I thought, and so we pushed further and without much concern about the Ivans came across a supply column with prima Studebakers!
>
> We took out fifteen Soviets in close combat and captured a heap of booty and supplies. From some POWs we learned we were not far from their supply area. I left my men in position with instructions and worked my way forward to see what was up. I hadn't gone far when I came upon an entire Soviet company right by our position. I thought, 'In I go!'
>
> Then it happened so fast I didn't have time to think about it. As I fired my last shot and could finally get my bearing I found at least twenty-five dead, eighteen wounded, two mortars, one heavy- and three light machine guns and many rifles and pistols.
>
> I never would have thought that I would have earned a Knights Cross for that.[60]

German intelligence assumed the Soviets still needed many days to reorient their forces south from the Riga sector prior to any attack in the direction of East Prussia. Instead, on 5 October, 1st Baltic Front began a new offensive from the vicinity of Siauliai toward Memel. Raus, with never enough infantry, had to make do with the new Volksgrenadier divisions deployed in this previously quiet portion of his defenses. The 549th and 548th Volksgrenadier Divisions, with the help of the newly arrived 5th Panzer, took the brunt of an attack by 29 rifle divisions and over 500 tanks. Even with the favorable defensive terrain – marshes and bogs made up most of the landscape – it was amazing that they held out at all. It took two days for the Soviets to smash the defenses and two more days for the 5th Guards Tank and 43rd Armies to reach the Baltic coast (they also overran the panzer army command post, although they did not know it and therefore Raus and his staff escaped). When these two armies encircled Memel on 9 September they also cut off Army Group North from the rest of the war. A day later, Hitler transferred Headquarters Third Panzer Army from Courland back to East Prussia. Raus left one corps with Army Group North and another trapped at Memel, so had only one corps with which to fight on the main front.[61]

Memel enjoyed a stout defense: Grossdeutschland, the 7th Panzer, 58th Infantry, 551st Volksgrenadier Divisions, Luftwaffe Flak Regiment 6, 502nd Heavy Panzer Battalion (Tiger tanks), the Kriegsmarine's 217th and 227th Flak Battalions and a myriad of smaller formations, including students from the U-boat school. Perhaps its greatest asset was the sea to its back, which the Germans used 1. To resupply the besieged port, in one case removing the wheels from railroad tank cars, filling them with fuel and towing them from East Prussian ports; 2. Transporting troops into and out of the city, and; 3. To provide naval gunfire from *Prinz Eugen*, destroyers, torpedo boats and now even the armored ship *Lützow*. Stuka ace Hans Ulrich Rudel flew overhead. Considering the Red Army's 600,000 men, 400 armored vehicles – giving them a staggering five-to-one superiority, the defenders needed every advantage available. Soviet attacks began in earnest on 14 October, and were beaten back. Three days later, OKH decided Grossdeutschland and 7th Panzer could do more good on the main front, so these units evacuated by sea in numerous vessels (large and small) and with many losses. At the same time, the 95th Infantry Division arrived from Army Group Courland (formerly Army Group North). Both sides eventually settled into a stalemate, and the city's garrison remained unbowed into 1945.[62]

At the same time on the approaches to Königsberg, the Red Army kept up the pressure. Even though the weather had turned bad (the rasputitsa arrived as always), the Soviets had by this stage of the war developed the ability to conduct operations almost any time of year and with much improved logistical support. Guarding the northern face of the East Prussian defenses, Raus once again had three corps of eleven divisions, under command. On 16 October, forty rifle divisions and several tank brigades of the 1st Baltic and 3rd Belorussian

Fronts attacked Third Panzer in the direction of Tilsit and stove in the defensive lines 11km on the first day. Schirwindt, the keystone of the entire 'East Prussian Defense Position', fell on the 17th. But as their comrades were doing in the west around the city of Aachen (the first major city in Germany proper to come under direct attack in that theater), Raus' men put up a furious defense of their own homeland. It took the frontovicki of 3rd Belorussian Front four days just to penetrate the Germans' tactical defenses. The second defensive line was so strong that the Soviet commander committed his exploitation force to the (attempted) breakthrough battle. Red Army Air Force CAS dominated the skies. By the 20th, the enemy had reached Gumbinnen. Führer Headquarters could not let this stand, so sent to Raus the Army's 5th Panzer and the Luftwaffe's Hermann Göring Parachute Panzer Divisions to attack the penetration from the north. Starting on 21 October, along with the Führer Grenadier Brigade attacking from the Fourth Army area in the south, they cut off the attacking Soviets. Around the Prussian town of Goldap, a huge armored battle developed. The Red Army spearhead was isolated, and in a week's fighting, the Germans destroyed 616 tanks. Fourth Army took over responsibility for the line, and by the first week of November, the front stabilized in a fairly straight fashion. By the end of November, Third Panzer was arrayed north to south thus: XXVIII, XI, XL Panzer and XXVI Corps.[63] It would basically stay that way for the next two months.

Stavka's plan for the January 1945 offensive into East Prussia was to split Fourth and Third Panzer Armies and then destroy each in detail. The panzer army's old nemesis, 3rd Belorussian Front, with four armies and two tank corps under command, would drive on Königsberg. From there the Soviets planned to finish the war in forty-five days. On the eve of the attack, Third Panzer counted nine infantry divisions: its last panzer division, the 20th, had already departed for Hungary (although the 5th Panzer, with fifty operational panzers, soon returned from Fourth Army in its place). Included in the defenders strength were eighteen battalions of Volkssturm, armed civilians which the soldiers judged as 'absolutely useless'. The only thing the Germans had in their favor were 'elaborate prepared defenses'. On 13 January, the 3rd Belorussian Front attacked with 44 rifle divisions, 3,000 guns and 800 tanks. The main effort took the Insterburg–Königsberg axis into the center of Third Panzer's line. Forewarned, Raus had abandoned his most forward lines so that except for a few rear guards, Red artillery fell mainly on empty positions. German Nebelwerfer units exacted a toll on the Soviet infantry, but when that happened, Soviet tanks merely took over the advance. Red Army Air Force aircraft shot at anything that moved. Army Group Center sent reinforcements, in the form of Sturmgeschutz Battalion 190, which launched a counterattack

towards Kettenau. By the end of the 13th, the Germans had regained their
original lines, in the process destroying 122 tanks at Kettenau alone.[64]

The Soviets renewed their attacks on 14 January, but with less enthusiasm
and coordination. The Kettenau heights changed hands many times that day,
and the Germans destroyed a further 200 tanks there. As happened in October,
creating a Red Army penetration took longer than predicted; the zone defense
worked as well as could be expected. By the 18th, the Soviets had battered the
defenders to the point where their lines began to buckle. Raus ordered his men
back toward Königsberg and the Heilsberg Fortified Region. During the next
two days, fighting centered on Schlossberg, where pioneers and Sturmgeschütze
saved the day. On 20 January, the Soviets tried to turn the German flank
by swinging north near Kreuzingen. Raus organized a counterattack led by
5th Panzer, plus whatever other units he could find, into the flank of the offending
tank corps. This small crisis mastered, the panzer army continued withdrawing
towards Königsberg 'according to plan'. On the 24th, the Soviets punched over
the Pregel River, creating a real danger of cutting off the East Prussian capital
from the south. A day later they were less than 20km from the city.[65]

A greater threat came from the west where, starting on 23 January, the
2nd Shock Army and Raus raced toward the Baltic. Past German Eylau and then
to Osterode, the Germans came in second. The Soviets established a blocking
position to hold the Third Panzer, and continued to Marienburg and finally to
Ebling. This put Raus at a severe disadvantage. When the 5th Guards Tank
Army reached that town on the 26th, Third Panzer, Fourth and a portion of
the Second Armies were all trapped in East Prussia. Starting the following
day and for a few days beyond, Reinhardt tried to orchestrate a breakout to
the west. This 'treason' caused him to run afoul of Hitler one last time and
lose his job as commander of Army Group Center. The Führer demanded the
Königsberg pocket, now renamed Armeeabteilung Samland, hold at all costs.
As had often been the case, the mere existence of such a large force on its
flank and rear represented a thorn in the side of Soviet forces advancing west.
Therefore, the Germans trapped in East Prussia actually delayed Stavka's
Berlin operation. Starting in late January and running through mid-February,
4th Panzer, numerous infantry divisions and other formations evacuated
Königsberg aboard Kriegsmarine warships and merchant vessels. Headquarters,
Third Panzer was among them. On 21 February it appeared at the front again,
this time in Pomerania as part of Army Group Vistula.[66]

Third Panzer managed to escape much of the destruction meted out by
the Red Army during the second half of 1944. Many of its losses were due
to Hitler's insistence that Reinhardt leave corps-sized garrisons in hopeless
situations: Vitebsk, Vilnius, Courland and Memel. The counterattack toward

Riga possessed moments of the old blitzkrieg flair, but ultimately accomplished little of lasting (or operational) significance.

Earlier in February, Himmler, the unlikely commander of the new Army Group Vistula, had created the Eleventh SS Panzer Army out of ten divisions under a former corps headquarters. In its only combat mission prior to arrival of Raus and his staff, it had gained perhaps 5km in two days of attacking. After this lackluster performance, Raus took over most of that corps' responsibilities. Sandwiched between the Second Army and the Oder River, the new Third Panzer Army manned a 240km-wide front with 3 infantry divisions and 2 fortification regiments defending forward, 3 more infantry and 2 motorized divisions in reserve, 4 brigades and some independent regiments and other units in its order of battle. It could muster about 250 artillery pieces and 70 AFVs. Along each kilometer of front it had 1 artillery piece, 1 heavy and 2 light machine-guns and 40 men. The day after Raus arrived, the Soviets attacked with two objectives: split Third Panzer and Second Armies, and take Stargard on Raus' western extremity. The first attack, conducted mainly by the 2nd Belorussian Front, managed to achieve a breakthrough on 22 February, and reached Bublitz two days later. This thrust separated the SS 15th Latvian and 33rd Charlemagne Divisions away from Second Army and toward Third Panzer. The Soviets continued to press along the seam until the 3rd Guards Tank Corps reached Koeslin on 1 March, effectively isolating Second Army to the east. Hitler's order on the 4th for Raus to counterattack to regain contact with Second Army was not based on reality and could not be carried out.[67] The Second ended the war with its back to the Baltic, a German island centered on the Vistula delta, surrounded on three sides by the Red ocean.

In the Stargard area, Marshal Rokossovsky's attack did not do as well against the 5th Jäger Division. On 1 March, he therefore shifted his main effort slightly east to Reetz. His 1st and 2nd Guards Tank Armies led the way, followed by 3rd Shock. Within three days, 1st Guards Tank Army reached the Baltic coast, isolating the fortress city of Kolberg, famous for Napoleon's siege and Gneisenau's defense in 1807. Remnants of the 163rd and 402nd Infantry Divisions plus Kriegsmarine, Luftwaffe, Volkssturm, Hitler Youth forces held the city of 35,000, now swollen by 50,000 refugees fleeing the avenging Red Army. Against the 2nd Belorussian Front, these defenders and the Kriegs- marine worked miracles for 10 days as nearly 80,000 escaped by sea. The last soldiers followed them in a destroyer on 18 March. By then, Third Panzer, a collection of 'isolated formations and detachments' had lost all of Pomerania except for the 90km Altdamm bridgehead just east of Stettin and Raus had lost his job. On 5 March, after Hitler had taken 'a sudden dislike' to the general, he brought in Hasso von Manteuffel to be the Third Panzer Army's last commander. One of the new general's first accomplishments was to talk Hitler into abandoning the hopeless bridgehead on 19 March (but left much of its heavy equipment on the far bank).[68]

Although the Germans had long since given up that river, Third Panzer and Ninth Armies' higher headquarters was still named Army Group Vistula, now commanded by defensive specialist Heinrici. He and his men would have to hold the direct route to Berlin. The heaviest load fell on the Ninth Army, while the Third Panzer's eleven weak divisions fought on Berlin's far northern margin. Von Manteuffel's command also included Volkssturm men from Stettin and Potsdam, foreign volunteers, Hungarians, Soviet ex-POWs under Vlassov, Hitler Youth and other para-militaries for a total of about 105,000 men. The panzer army had no artillery and 242 AFVs. Facing them was the 2nd Belorussian Front with 33 rifle divisions, 4 tank and mechanized corps that included 6,642 tubes of indirect fire weapons and 951 tanks and assault guns. Stavka made clear one of its main missions: prevent Third Panzer from contributing to the defense during the Battle of Berlin.[69]

Soviet artillery and CAS preparation of the battlefield began on 19 April. At 0400 hours on the next day, Hitler's fifty-sixth birthday, Rokossovsky's 65th and 70th Armies came across the Oder which stood, at that time, approximately 3km wide (including its flooded plains). The 49th Army, scheduled to participate in the assault, inexplicably did not move. Under the cover of smoke, the Soviets claimed numerous small bridgeheads. But the marshy ground reduced their artillery's effects. The defense held reasonably well under the circumstances. On the 21st, Rokossovsky reinforced the 65th Army's success, but it would still take another day to fight through the initial defensive lines.[70]

Still under the delusion that he could somehow hold off the Soviet onslaught, Hitler put great faith in a planned counterattack by Group Steiner, based on the III SS Panzer Corps (SS 27th Langemarck and 28th Wallonie Panzer-grenadier Divisions) plus other units. Felix Steiner had the mission of clearing 'every last bridgehead on the Oder and get ready to attack south [to rescue Berlin]'.[71] After 24 hours and no counterattack (by an SS Obergruppenführer no less), Hitler broke down during the daily conference in his bunker. Heinrici ordered Steiner to attack on the 23rd, ready or not, which the SS general did. However, threatening moves by the 2nd Guards Tank Army caused the attack to be cancelled and Group Steiner redirected toward Oranienburg 'at once'. The whole affair caused Hitler to lash out again at the 24 April situation conference: 'The Russian success against the Third Panzer Army can only be attributed to German military incompetence.'[72]

Somehow von Manteuffel maintained his panzer army's sketchy defensive line at places along the Oder as late as 25 April, but his defenses were about to cave in. That day, Hitler ordered von Manteuffel to 'prevent expansion of the Oder bridgehead', but that afternoon the 2nd Belorussian Front shoved its way past the panzer army's last reserves and advanced as far as Prenzlau. Rokossovsky had been especially successful in the north, around Stettin, and planned to swing north and separate Third Panzer from Berlin for good. Von Manteuffel pulled in his flanks so he could concentrate on defending his center. Even Group Steiner forsook its mobile mission and manned the defensive line. A day later, after another Soviet push, Jodl commented, 'The enemy has clearly broken through Third Panzer Army at Prenzlau.'[73] That night, von Manteuffel telephoned Heinrici to say his army had quit fighting and 100,000 men were trying to escape west. He had seen nothing like this before, not even in 1918. Just 24 hours later, on the 28th, Keitel tried to relieve Heinrici (and replace him with von Manteuffel!) because commanders would no longer obey the Führer's orders.[74] The German military had begun to implode.

General of Panzer Troops Hasso-Eccard Freiherr von Manteuffel

Born in Potsdam in 1897 to an old Prussian military family, von Manteuffel entered the Kaiser's army in February 1916 as a lieutenant in Hussar Regiment 3. In the 1930s he was drawn to the new panzer branch, serving as commander of a motorcycle battalion in Guderian's 2nd Panzer Division and teaching at the Kramnitz Panzer School. He commanded Motorcycle Battalion 3 during the Polish campaign. He began Barbarossa as a lieutenant colonel, commanding a motorized rifle battalion in the 7th Panzer Division. Despite his small stature (he was shorter than even Hoth), he rose throughout the general ranks like few other German officers and served in every major German theater of the Second World War.

During Barbarossa, von Manteuffel led from the front in the central sector, advancing through Lepel and Vitebsk as part of Third Panzer Army. Two months into the campaign he took command of Rifle Regiment 6 (also of 7th Panzer) when the original commander fell in battle. He led his regiment farther east in the northern pincer against Moscow that first winter than any other Army Group Center unit, a maneuver that earned him the Knight's Cross. Fritz Kurowski wrote that von Manteuffel 'was first in attack and last to retreat'. He became commander of the 7th Brigade of the 7th Panzer during the division's refit in France during the summer of 1942. By early 1943, he commanded a Kampfgruppe named 'Division von Manteuffel' in combat against the British in Tunisia. In the spring of that year, he collapsed on the battlefield due to illness and exhaustion and evacuated North Africa by hospital ship. After recovery and promotion to major general, he returned to the 7th Panzer Division, again under Hoth's command, now fighting west of Kiev. His leadership in the battles of Fastov and Zithomir earned him the Oak Leaves to his Knight's Cross.

In January 1944 von Manteuffel took command of Panzergrenadier Division Grossdeutschland (adding that cuff title to his Afrika Korps version), and was promoted to lieutenant general a month later. For most of that year he commanded the elite formation during defensive battles in the Ukraine, Romania, East Prussia and the Baltic States. On 1 September, he took the helm of the battered Fifth Panzer Army fighting George Patton's forces near Arracourt. He led that panzer army during the Ardennes Offensive in December. There, von Manteuffel achieved significant gains on the southern flank of the bulge, despite its supporting role, bringing him the Diamonds. In March 1945, von Manteuffel was given command of Third Panzer Army, another battered outfit, which he led for the last two months of the war in hopeless combat north of Berlin. Von Manteuffel survived the fighting and postwar captivity to become a Bundestag deputy from 1953–57, but later served a couple of months in prison for war crimes. Throughout the 1960s, he wrote and lectured about his experiences, and was praised by former colleagues and foes alike. He died in 1978.

Nonetheless, Third Panzer still managed to fight a delaying action among the many canals in northern Germany. The 7th Panzer Division arrived by boat from Danzig and joined the fight. The Germans, Soviets and British all raced for Lübeck. On 28 April, at a famous and apocryphal meeting between three generals at a Neubrandenburg crossroads, it became clear that the end of the 'Thousand Year Reich' was near. Keitel ordered Heinrici to halt the headlong retreat of von Manteuffel's command. At the top of his lungs, Heinrici screamed at Keitel that he would not order Third Panzer to stand fast. The panzer army's commanding general in turn yelled at Keitel, 'the Third Panzer Army listens only to General Hasso von Manteuffel!' When Keitel challenged his subordinate, the panzer general replied, 'The von Manteuffels have served Prussia for 200 years.' The shouting match solved nothing. The mass exodus continued for days. By 2 May, the Third Panzer and neighboring Twenty-first Army had been squeezed into a strip of land 25–30km wide. The 2nd Belorussian Front, British 21st Army Group and US Ninth Army surrounded them near Wittenberge and Parchim. That night, von Manteuffel surrendered to the Americans.[75]

Chapter 5

Fourth Panzer Army

Of all the panzer armies, the story of the Fourth is probably the most interesting. Its combat trail begins with attacks on both Leningrad and Moscow. Through the second half of 1942, it was a major component of Operation Blau against Stalingrad, which it almost conquered, from which it barely escaped and for which it was the main hope for rescue. In 1943, Fourth Panzer parried Soviet drives into the heart of the German line, led the way in Operation Citadel and then avoided destruction once more trying to defend Kiev and the western Ukraine that autumn and winter.

For the last eighteen months of this period, Hermann Hoth commanded the Fourth. After the war's momentum irreversibly switched to the USSR, the panzer army withdrew through southern Poland. During the second half of 1944, it manned the middle Vistula River. Beginning in January 1945, the Red Army shoved the Fourth west through Lower Silesia. It ended the war in Saxony, squeezed there between Soviet and American forces. The Fourth Panzer Army fought on nearly every sector of the eastern theater at one time or another, providing invaluable service to the Reich.

Campaign	Battles and Engagements
Barbarossa, 22 June–5 December 1941	Dvina crossings, Stalin Line, Luga River, Staraya Rusa, Leningrad, Narva, Novgorod, Viazma, Mozhaisk, Istra
Defense of Army Groups Center and South, 4 December 1941–27 June 1942	Gzhatsk, Viazma, Kharkov
1942 Offensive, 28 June–30 December 1942	Middle Don, Voronezh, Millerovo, southern Stalingrad
Retreat and Defensive Battles, 31 December 1942–3 July 1943	Stalingrad relief, Rostov, Kharkov, Belgorod
Citadel and Defense of Ukraine, 4 July 1943–26 March 1944	Prokhorovka, Kharkov, Achtyrka, Kiev, Fastov, Zithomir, Lutsk, Ternopol, Kovel
Poland and middle Vistula, 27 March 1944–11 January 1945	Bug River, Cholm, Lubin, Baranow
Lower Silesia and Saxony, 12 January–8 May 1945	Breslau, Steinau, Neisse River, Görlitz, Torgau

Unlike Moscow, capturing Leningrad did figure prominently in Barbarossa's planning. Taking the USSR's second city would deprive the Soviets of a huge industrial center, a massive naval base and control of the Baltic Sea, while simultaneously giving Hitler a solid connection to Finland and possession of Bolshevism's birthplace. Unfortunately for Fourth Panzer Army, charged with leading the way, the same sanguine German planning that condemned all of Barbarossa 'hoped' that getting close to the great metropolis was as good as its outright capture.

Army Group North published its campaign orders on 29 May. Colonel General Erich Hoepner's mission was to attack to Dünaburg and Jekabpils to gain crossings over the Dvina River, push on to the Pskov–Opotshka Line and from there toward the southern approaches of Leningrad. Along with the Dnepr to the south, both sides believed that the Dvina held the key to success. Speed, mainly getting to the bridges as quickly as possible, was of the essence. Accordingly, Field Marshal Wilhelm Ritter von Leeb did not tie Hoepner to an infantry army as had been the case with the other three panzer armies. As intended, this meant Fourth Panzer would not have to wait for the marching Landsers to catch up. It was difficult to conceal the tremendous build-up of German troops in the congested Memelland, especially Hoepner's, but his men disguised themselves as Lithuanian farmers and reconnoitered the frontier. The panzer army had other limitations as well. It belonged to the smallest army group, which had the smallest complement of Luftwaffe support. The terrain was an infamous mixture of woods and marshes, once across the Dvina it turned into a 'thick green jungle'. Many panzer army wheeled vehicles were commercial and French made, and 42 percent of Hoepner's panzers were of Czech manufacture. For example, the 6th Panzer Division's 155 PzKw 35(t)s were among the oldest panzers in the Wehrmacht inventory. Their 37mm main gun had been rendered obsolete by newer armor, and along with other problems, its pneumatic steering made the vehicle nearly useless in freezing weather. As soon as Germany captured the Czechoslovak arsenal in 1938–39, they declared the 35(t) 'no longer suitable for combat.'[1]

After moving into their attack positions north of the Nieman River during the shortest night of the year, Barbarossa began for the men of Fourth Panzer at 0305 hours with an artillery preparation fire that for some divisions lasted 3 hours. The LVI Panzer fired 550 tubes of artillery, Nebelwerfer and railway guns at the defenders. The Germans attacked through a thick morning fog and immediately hit swampy ground. All the Panzertruppen knew their army commander's motto: 'Surprise, then forward, forward, forward!' The Sixteenth Army on von Leeb's right reported some resistance, but initially the enemy opposite Hoepner's men appeared disjointed. The 8th Panzer Division broke free of the Soviet defenses, covered 80km that day and crossed the Dubyussa River at Ariogala. Von Manstein's LVI Panzer had avoided all Red Army units sent to intercept him and was in the open country deep in the enemy rear. Unfortunately for Reinhardt, his lead division, the 6th Panzer encountered stiffer defenses. The heavy combat meant logistics support could not safely get forward. On the very first day of what would be nearly a four-year-long war the division ran out of ammunition. It failed to accomplish its daily mission, securing a bridgehead across the steep valley of the Dubyussa. Such are the fortunes of war, however. While von Manstein made spectacular advances thanks to splitting the 8th and 11th Armies, XLI Panzer Corps was stymied despite destroying 186 tanks in the war's first armored battle.[2]

The campaign's second day was much the same, von Manstein facing little organized opposition and Reinhardt coming up against significant resistance. In Tauroggen, site of the famous Prussian–Russian neutrality pact of 30 December 1812 and the 1st Panzer Division's first Knights Cross of Barbarossa, every building could be considered a small fort. In his diary, von Leeb noted 'heavy tank movement' toward Rossieni from the north. This turned out to be a 100-tank counterattack against the 6th Panzer Division, to the right of 1st Panzer. These were lead elements of the 3rd Mechanized Corps, the super-heavy KV 1s that presently demolished the 6th Panzer's motorcycle infantry battalion in about 20 minutes. The 1st Panzer Division halted and its 1st Brigade turned east to attack into 6th Panzer's tormentors, beginning a three-day armored battle there. The sand and moor slowed movement. Due to superior Soviet equipment, panzers had to close to within 30–60m of a tank or else shoot it from behind if the Germans hoped to win. Artillery and 88mm guns took a heavy toll on the Soviet monsters. Logistics still posed a problem, and by the 23rd, Luftwaffe bombers had to fly supplies to panzer units, a terrible misuse of that asset. On the other hand, German aerial reconnaissance could not locate any Red Army units in front of LVI Panzer, and even the official Soviet history admits that von Manstein caught Stavka flat-footed.[3] Regardless of the fact that Reinhardt had originally been Hoepner's Schwerpunkt, blitzkrieg tactics demanded he switch his emphasis to reinforce von Manstein's more successful drive. There was no end to the interference from higher headquarters: Hitler, Halder, Keitel, von Leeb and others all had good ideas about where Hoepner's panzers should go next.

Soviet counterattacks around Rossieni continued on 24 June. The Germans, despite being surprised by the attacks from such unexpected directions, managed every crisis. The 6th Panzer (surrounded for two nights and a day) tangled with the 2nd Tank Division (which also became trapped) and the battlefield was strewn with smashed vehicles and mutilated bodies. As the division's operations officer commented that day:

> Before our own attack began the enemy attacked with strong tanks and infantry forces from his bridgehead over the Dubyussa in the direction of Rossieni. Despite the surprise, his infantry did not succeed in a breakthrough, even though he renewed the attack many times. Suddenly the day led to a crisis of massive proportions. That came from the appearance of numerous completely unknown super heavy tanks, the so-called 52-tonners.[4]

Although the Germans had been aware of the T-34 since at least December 1940, these encounters represented their first exposure to the even heavier KV 1 and 2 tanks. Although the troops on the ground would not have agreed, higher headquarters welcomed the counterattacks as signs that the Soviets were not withdrawing into the interior of the country. If the Army Group had been stronger and if Hoepner had had more to work with, perhaps he could have sprung his own Kessel on the Northwestern Front. This was not the case, however, although by the 25th the battle around Rossieni had definitely gone the Germans' way. By then, Reinhardt had also committed both the 36th Motorized and the 269th Infantry to the fighting. The 12th Mechanized was on its way to losing 90 percent of its tank strength in one week, half those losses to maintenance, fuel, ammunition and communications problems. To the east, von Manstein's men lived a relatively charmed life, reaching Ukmerge on the 24th. The LVI Panzer exploited the huge hole created when the 8th Army fell back towards Riga and the 11th Army drifted southeast behind Vilnius.[5] Essentially, no defenses worthy of the name barred von Manstein's advance.

Hoepner's men pulled off the first of many coups on their way to Leningrad on the morning of 26 June. Led by members of the 8th Company of the Brandenburg Regiment dressed in Red Army uniforms and riding in captured Soviet trucks, the 8th Panzer captured the Dünaburg crossings. Behind the commandos came 3rd Company, 59th Engineers and a combined arms Kampfgruppe under the 29th Panzergrenadier Regiment's commander. In the early dawn they raced past Soviet units that had no clue the Germans could possibly be so deep in the Northwestern Front's hinterland. Shortly after 0600 hours, the Germans had the main road bridge in the suburb of Griva. Demolitions experts disarmed explosive charges while firefighters put out flames started by Soviet guards. At the site of the railroad bridge a smaller assault group had a more difficult time. The guards there managed to set off their explosives, but the slight damage caused surprised both sides and left the bridge perfectly serviceable. Within half an hour the battlegroup's main combat units arrived and established an all-round defense in order to secure the hard-won bridges from Red Army counterattacks which now began in earnest. By noon, more 8th Panzer elements showed up, followed by those of the 3rd Motorized. Soviet counterattacks came from forces on both sides of the Dvina, including 27th Army units moving down from the north on their way to the front and the 21st Mechanized Corps, falling back after encountering von Leeb.[6] The Germans had scored a massive success reminiscent of that at Sedan thirteen months earlier.

What remained to be seen was whether the Wehrmacht could translate this operational-level achievement into strategic victory as in the earlier war with France; tragically for them they would not. Hitler immediately saw the bridge-head's larger potential, and von Manstein agreed. As the Führer told Keitel at Rastenburg, 'Concentrate Hoepner's panzers at Dünaburg, open Jekabpils from the east and drive through Ostrov.'[7] It was imperative to get past the town, the gateway to Leningrad south of Lake Peipus, before Stavka could adequately defend it. Cautiously, von Brauchitsch and von Leeb demurred and so it was: von Manstein sat at Dünaburg until the Sixteenth Army marched up. The same day LVI Panzer took that city, Reinhardt was finishing up around Rossieni and resuming his movement towards Jekabpils, which he reached on the 28th. He too wasted time holding a bridgehead while waiting for the infantry. This conservatism was completely antithetical to the blitzkrieg doctrine and, as will be demonstrated, hamstrung the push on Leningrad just as it would have wrecked the drive across northern France. Army Chief of Staff Halder rationalized the crippling loss of initiative this way: the panzer army would be 'in danger of being encircled and destroyed in the vast forests in front of Leningrad, unless it has the support of closely following infantry divisions'.[8] While von Leeb dawdled thus, Stavka ordered Colonel General FI Kuznetsov to attempt to reestablish a viable defense further east.[9] Supreme headquarters wanted him to hold the Velikaya River Line south of Pskov, since, as any soldier who could read a map knew, this would be Hoepner's next objective. Fortunately for the USSR, the Northwestern Front faced von Leeb and only one panzer army, otherwise its northern flank would be staring at disastrous collapse rather than merely a poorly executed attack and an even more incompetent defense.

While Hoepner waited for permission to continue, the Soviets launched numerous counterattacks on the ground, supported by Red Army Air Force planes above: none enjoyed any success (the future German Chancellor Helmut Schmidt was a lieutenant in the flak battalion of the 1st Panzer Division here). The panzer army expanded some bridgeheads, created others – such as the one won by Brandenburgers and 1st Panzer at Lievenhof, and conducted aggressive patrols to the east. Kuznetsov had a big counterattack planned against Dünaburg for the 29th, but von Manstein got the jump on him by attacking first, at 0500. Fighting around the bridgeheads continued unabated, with von Leeb's men taking advantage of masses of supplies captured at Dünaburg and elsewhere. The SS Motorized Division Totenkopf, late to reinforce Dünaburg, took particularly heavy losses. Also on the 29th, von Leeb published his order to continue operations toward Opotshka and Ostrov. Two days later he paid a visit to Hoepner's command post, where Barbarossa's Achilles heel again came to the fore: the inability of commanders to agree on objectives. Whereas von Leeb spoke of the upcoming assault as part of an 'attack east of Lake Il'men', Hoepner, and most others, thought only in terms of Leningrad.[10] Not to worry, the renewed offensive would begin again soon enough and these matters would take care of themselves.

After Kuznetsov's relief on the last day of June, Marshal Timoshenko temporarily led the Northwestern Front's defensive efforts until the 4 July arrival of the new front commander, Lieutenant General PP Sobeninikov, formerly of 8th Army. Early on 2 July, Fourth Panzer moved out along a string of old forts built by the Teutonic Knights, but now roles were reversed for the two panzer corps: von Manstein's ran into stout resistance and terrible terrain along the road to Rezekne, while Reinhardt's had a relatively easy go of it and covered over 100km that first day. The 6th Panzer described the enemy's morale as 'very high', and with LVI Panzer bogged down, Hoepner reinforced success by transferring the 3rd Motorized Division from von Manstein to Reinhardt. Nevertheless, the Soviets' new defensive structure collapsed after barely 24 hours as Hoepner split the old 8th and new 27th Armies. The Soviet plan called for the 27th to retreat promptly back to the Velikaya River and take up new positions, but the Germans moved faster and got there first. Two days after leaving the Dvina behind, XLI Panzer reached Ostrov and made contact with the 24th Rifle Corps defensive position along the Velikaya.[11] Hoepner's panzers, with the remainder of Army Group North close behind, stood ready to defeat the Stalin Line and enter Russia proper.

For Reinhardt's men this took one day: on 4 July the 1st Panzer entered, occupied and prepared to defend Ostrov, its two bridges and masses of captured supplies. About 30km to the south, KG Raus of the 6th Panzer did basically the same, meaning that XLI Panzer Corps now had a two-division lodgment in the Stalin Line. Overhead, Ju-88s of Kampfgeschwader 1, 76 and 77 provided CAS. On land and in the air, the Soviets launched fierce counterattacks and the city was in flames. With their PAKs nearly useless against the KV tanks of the 27th Army, the Germans withdrew to the burning town but still managed to hold. On the panzer army's right, however, von Manstein's men struggled mightily, mainly against the upper Velikaya's marshes. The OKH, proving it too could send panzers on missions and into terrain they had no business going, ordered von Manstein to take the 'high ground' near Opotshka by the most direct route. The entire region was barely serviced by any roads worthy of the name. Von Leeb did not dispute the poorly conceived maneuver and evidently, neither did Hoepner. The LVI Panzer Corps literally chopped and sawed its way through thick wilderness on its way to nowhere. Its advance averaged about 10km per day, causing even Hoepner to doubt the wisdom of the advance on Lake Il'men.[12] Once out of this abysmal landscape, von Manstein, discovered, to his dismay, that his next objective was not the cradle of Bolshevism, but more terrain completely unsuited to armored warfare far to the south and southeast of Leningrad.

Between the time Hoepner punctured the Divna and Velikaya Lines, Stavka decided Leningrad would need another defensive position. Therefore, Northern Front deputy commander Lieutenant General KP Pyadychev received the mission to survey a more close-in line for his new command, the Luga Operational Group (LOG). In the first half of July he decided on the Narva–Luga River system, anchored on one end by the Gulf of Finland and at the other by Lake Il'men, with the position's keystone being the actual town of Luga. By 8 July, Reinhardt was ready to move again and on the next day, echoing his rallying cry 'Open the gates to Leningrad!', XLI Panzer had taken Pskov. On the 10th, Hoepner had met what he believed to be all the pre-conditions for the final thrust to Leningrad. He would send Reinhardt up the middle on the road through Luga, while von Manstein made a wide eastern enveloping move via Novgorod and Chudovo. Assuming little resistance and good conditions, Fourth Panzer thought it could cover the last 300km in four days.[13] Perhaps if the entire panzer army had followed Reinhardt's advise and lead, it could have.

As it was, that proved to be a completely unfounded assumption, especially for LVI Panzer Corps. Reinhardt at least had some reasonable terrain in front of him. But Luftwaffe reconnaissance had missed the Soviet build-up representing the Luga Line. On the other hand, von Manstein only ran into more marshes in addition to Red Army defenders. The men of LVI Panzer encountered increasing resistance well short of Luga so Hoepner had them turn 90 degrees northwest at Zapole. This meant that instead of the two panzer corps travelling roughly parallel courses where they could offer mutual assistance if necessary, they were instead sent on divergent axes with hundreds of kilometers of wilderness separating them. Already, the tailing infantry armies were nearly 100km distant to the rear. To Hitler, Hoepner's actions constituted an 'undesirable maneuver'. The panzer army's Schwerpunkt, Reinhardt as usual, planned to move toward the eastern shore of Lake Peipus until reaching the dry ridge south of Kingisepp where he would turn towards Leningrad. The XLI Panzer's right-angle turn back at Zapole also meant 6th Panzer had leapfrogged in front of 1st Panzer to become Reinhardt's vanguard. With Colonel Erhard Raus again leading the Kampfgruppe that bore his name, the 6th worked its way through the unmapped, medieval, swampy world toward the Luga. He was so far ahead of Reinhardt's main body that he had to send a radio truck back 60km in order to regain communications with corps headquarters. At 2100 hours on the 13th, the division commander told Raus, 'The Luga bridge must be taken tonight.' By 0400 the morning of 14 July, with the help of some Brandenburgers, Raus' small command (5,000 men in 7 infantry companies, 2 machine-gun companies and 1 pioneer company, about 60 panzers, a battery of howitzers and various other units) had established a perimeter around the 2 200m bridges at Porechye – one of which was not even on the Germans' maps. Further south, at Sabsk, 1st Panzer also achieved a bridgehead and 36th Motorized occupied the gap between them. All supplies for Raus had to be air dropped, a situation exacerbated by the fact that the farther the Germans advanced, the closer they got to Leningrad and its excellent airport facilities. A 1st Panzer Division wit composed a poem to show the frustration with his own flyboys:

> *Der Russenflieger über uns sehr viele,*
> *Sie suchen uns im Tiefangriff zum Ziele,*
> *Wo bleibt Professor Messerschmitt?*
> *Wir machen sonst hier nicht mehr mit!*

> There are so many Russians above us,
> They dive low to make us their targets,
> Where is Professor Messerschmitt?
> We'll make do down here without 'im[14]

Red Army counterattacks grew in intensity, but with little more than Leningrad militia and factory new tanks driven by the workers who built them to throw into the fight, Reinhardt's veterans held on despite heavy losses. Von Leeb had two panzer divisions across the Luga, the last natural barrier before Leningrad, now barely 100km to the northeast. Soviet defenses were correspondingly weak and disorganized.[15] Could the Germans pull it off?

The answer it seems is no, they could not. The only formation in the Ostheer that could have kept up with the XLI Panzer Corps, brought it relief and combined with it to march on Leningrad was Hoepner's other half, LVI Panzer. But von Manstein was over 150km away from the Luga bridgeheads – straight-line distance; there is no telling how much space separated the two when swamps, enemy and unmapped dead-end trails are taken into account. Nor could Reinhardt help von Manstein. The latter's 8th Panzer Division had become dangerously strung out on the road from Ostrov to Novgorod. Badgered by Stavka over its handling of the defense of greater Leningrad, Northwestern Front chief of staff Lieutenant General NF Vatutin developed a counterattack by the resuscitated 11th Army against the vulnerable and at times completely cut off LVI Panzer. On 15 July, the 8th Panzer, essentially in a single-file column on a narrow forest track near Stolcy, was separated from the rest of von Manstein's corps when hit on three sides by the 10th Mechanized Corps plus parts of the 21st Tank and 70th Rifle Divisions. It hunkered down in a division-sized Igel close to Stolcy to await reinforcement. That came 24 hours later in the form of a regiment from the Panzer army reserve, SS Totenkopf, and later from elements of the 3rd Motorized, involved in its own struggle near Gorodishche. By 17 July, the 8th Panzer had broken out to the west, a tactical retreat for the proud panzers. During the battle, 8th Panzer lost 70 out of 150 panzers, damaged or destroyed. The crisis took four days to master, required commitment of many panzer army assets and even the Sixteenth Army's I Corps to stabilize.[16] While putting neither Fourth Panzer nor von Leeb's drive on Moscow in mortal danger, Vatutin's counterstroke did divert scarce German resources and cause consternation up and down their chain of command.

Barely one month into Barbarossa, during the second half of July, the same command paralysis struck Army Group North that has already been mentioned previously in regard to Center and South. Hitler's attitude to von Leeb's conduct of the campaign waxed and waned, generally corresponding to Hoepner either pulling off another successful panzer raid or sitting and waiting. In fact, the Führer even made a quick visit to see von Leeb on 21 July, which was generally viewed as a tremendous disappointment by members of the army group command group. A combined operation with Third Panzer Army against Leningrad at this point had been assumed as early as the previous December. Halder fought this idea since he believed it would siphon off resources from his pet project: the assault on Moscow. He schemed to bolster his argument by sending his operations deputy, and so-called panzer expert Lieutenant General Paulus to Army Group North. As would happen almost one month later when Halder tried to use Guderian against Hitler, Paulus returned in full agreement with the commanders on the scene; Halder's plan had backfired. As laid out in the various Führer Directives, plus the discussions and studies that surrounded them, Hitler ultimately concluded von Leeb could not go it alone. In the end the high command reached a compromise and

Hoepner would receive temporary help in the form of Hoth's XXXIX Panzer Corps.[17] This half measure predictably produced only partial results. One has to wonder instead, what would have become of the northern theater if the Wehrmacht had been fully committed as it was in the south when it sent all of Second Panzer to Kiev?

While the German high command deliberated and von Manstein parried in isolation, Reinhardt stewed. Von Leeb could not choose whether to strengthen one flank or the other in order to create a Schwerpunkt; in the end he resolved not to decide and left his forces as they were. For the last two weeks of July, after taking the Luga bridgeheads in such a brilliant coup, his men merely occupied space, fighting back Soviet counterattacks and swatting giant mosquitoes. In one day, 6th Panzer fired 150,000 rounds defending its hard-won gains. By the end of the month, Reinhardt's diary is full of comments such as 'This is dreadful . . . the decisive opportunity has passed' and 'More delays. It's terrible . . .'.[18] He tried to resign over the failure to rush Leningrad when his panzer corps was 100km distant and Soviet defenses were negligible. Reinhardt's bold move at Ivanovskoye, just east of Porechye, anticipated Model's action at Novgorod Severesky weeks later and hundreds of kilometers south, except for one critical point: the absence of resolute leadership above that could exploit the opening. Meanwhile, through the end of the first week of August, Red Army defenses received reinforcement including fourteen rifle and four cavalry divisions plus numerous brigades and regiments and militia (DNO) formations.[19] The defenders also had a new leader, Marshal KE Voroshilov, who infused them with a determination to win.

After five delays in fifteen days, on 8 August, reinforcement, supply and weather conditions had improved so that von Leeb's assault of the Luga River Line could begin. He had been substantially buttressed by the Luftwaffe: Luftflotte One, VIII Fliegerkorps and elements of Luftflotte Two. Hoepner began the attack with Reinhardt on the left, with 1st Panzer and 36th Motorized charging out of the Sabsk bridgehead, the 6th Panzer and 1st Infantry at Ivanovskoye and 8th Panzer, recently taken from von Manstein, in reserve. Moving out in driving rain, they hit well-prepared defenses interspersed in deep woods, with mutually supporting man-made and natural obstacles. On the second day of the offensive the two lead panzer divisions began to work together and the Soviet cause suffered accordingly. The breakthrough moment came when 1st Panzer punctured the Red Army lines, and swung behind the enemy forces holding 6th Panzer. As Raus remembered that day:

> On 10 September, the bulk of 6th Panzer Division advanced along the road toward the northern bridgehead. I detached some elements

to mop up the remaining Russian forces on the plateau west of Krasnogvardeysk, while others finished rolling up the enemy's forest position that forced us to keep a strong flank guard the previous day. In this manner the entire assault sector south of the Leningrad Line was cleared of the enemy before noon. Along the northern edge of the forest area alone, 40,000 Soviet mines had to be disarmed and removed.[20]

After a further two days, Reinhardt broke out from the woods that generally followed the Luga and into the relatively open country leading to Leningrad, now only 40km to the northeast. Hoepner's right wing, von Manstein, did not do so well against the 41st Rifle Corps; weather, terrain and defenders all conspired to slow LVI Panzer for another fortnight. The commanding general of the Polizei Division (not yet called SS) died in combat, and von Manstein lost his only other mechanized outfit, 3rd Motorized, when Hoepner reinforced success by shifting that division to Reinhardt.[21] This shifting of forces, reinforcing the Schwerpunkt, was all critical to the blitzkrieg, and served to keep the Soviets off balance.

The Soviets had completely lost control of the battle on the most direct axis of advance on Leningrad and against Hoepner's Schwerpunkt. The Luga Line, upon which the defense hung its hopes, delayed Reinhardt barely four days. When Leningrad Front commander Lieutenant General MM Popov shifted forces to deal with this threat he gave von Manstein an opening. Ideally, Hoepner would now reinforce success and keep the LOG on its heels, tumbling back towards the great metropolis. However, on von Leeb's far right a Soviet counterattack diverted the attention of the senior German leadership, just when it should have been fixed on Lenin's city. On 12 August, the 34th Army (eight divisions, later reinforced to twelve) struck the weak and exhausted X Corps (Sixteenth Army) south of Staraya Russa. Within 48 hours they had punched a hole nearly 100km deep and 60km wide. At about that same point, von Leeb took two motorized infantry divisions, SS Totenkopf from his own reserve, and 3rd Motorized, at the time preparing to assault the town of Luga (100km south of Leningrad), and redirected them to Staraya Russa. These units soon arrived and stabilized the situation. At Rastenburg Hitler fretted and Halder fumed: the first wanted to dispatch a panzer corps to the scene, the second railed against overreacting to such pinpricks. As might be expected, the dictator won this debate and on the 16th, the XXXIX Panzer (General of Panzer Troops Rudolf Schmidt, 12th Panzer, 18th and 20th Motorized Divisions) began to transfer from Hoth's Third Panzer Army. By the 18th, X Corps seems to have mastered its situation with the help of I Fliegerkorps and probably no longer needed to be rescued. Further, a day later, long before Schmidt's arrival, von Manstein had completed preparations for a counterattack during the night and smashed into the overextended 34th Army's left flank. Within four days they encircled four rifle divisions and the threat to Staraya Russa and the 16th Army's lines of communications had passed. The situation stabilized but at a terrible cost: the last real chance von Leeb had to attempt to march into Leningrad. For the price of one infantry army Stavka derailed Hitler's best opportunity in the north: the Germans weakened Reinhardt's promising effort, turned von Manstein 180 degrees and brought up XXXIX Panzer too late to make an impact. Blitzkrieg theory and practice suffered a crushing blow as a flank attack caused Hitler and von Leeb to lose their nerve just when Hoepner and the Sixteenth Army had begun to make progress against the Luga Line.[22]

With von Manstein sent southeast as part of Sixteenth Army, Reinhardt continued on toward Leningrad as Hoepner's sole representative. From now on, XLI Panzer took part in a relatively uncoordinated, three-pronged attack against the city: Reinhardt with the support of Eighteenth Army coming from the west, XXXIX Panzer and Sixteenth Army to the south, and the Finns attacking from Karelia. For Hoepner, this required a slower and more deliberate approach than normally associated with the blitzkrieg. Von Leeb had promised him XXXIX Panzer after the battles along the middle Luga, but later changed his mind. Reinhardt's men would go it alone when the final assault on Leningrad began at 0930 on 9 September. The whole weight fell on Reinhardt (left–right: 36th Motorized, 1st and 6th Panzer), attacking out of the southwest corner of the German line, with 8th Panzer in reserve. According to Hitler himself, the attack would not go all the way into the city, but only as far as the last defensive positions; the city would be starved to death instead of being conquered outright. In the direction of the Duderhof plateau, 36th Motorized quickly achieved surprise and success, and 1st Panzer moved adroitly behind and to the right. The 118th Motorized Infantry Regiment captured the old tsarist barracks and nearby Hill 143. The distance to Leningrad was barely 10km. But with 6th Panzer occupied to the south and von Leeb jealously holding on to 8th Panzer, Hoepner could not build his Schwerpunkt large enough or fast enough. Subordination of XXVIII Corps to the panzer army did not help to the degree anticipated. Fourth Panzer units in the lead enjoyed success again on the 10th, but as before, the 8th Panzer could not exploit.[23]

On that same day, Hitler's order arrived for von Leeb, telling him to dispatch XLI Panzer to the Moscow sector. This only motivated Hoepner to try harder during his last days in Barbarossa's far north. Though supported all the way by VIII Fliegerkorps, however, the most he could accomplish was the conquest of Pushkin by 1st Panzer and the Polizei Division on 1 September. The Soviet defenses, under Zhukov since the 11th, stiffened, with brand new T-34 tanks rumbling out of the factory at Kolpino and straight into the fighting. The 6th Panzer had entrained for Army Group Center on 15 September, 1st Panzer left four days later and the 36th Motorized and corps headquarters on the 20th.[24]

Reinhardt's departure left Army Group North with one panzer corps, XXXIX, on the Leningrad front. Although it had a couple of flashes of glory, von Leeb's flawed campaign ultimately failed to isolate the city completely or to subdue it. Clearly, part of the blame also goes to Hitler, with his changing priorities and guidance and to the Reich's co-belligerent, Finland, which did not have 'total war' aspirations and so did not contribute fully. As with the entire army group, Fourth Panzer fought what the field marshal called 'a poor man's war' with only one panzer army of only two corps. In terrain mostly unsuited for mechanized operations, Reinhardt's men struggled even though blessed with a bungling enemy commander. The very nature of Leningrad insured it possessed an essential feature of a blitzkrieg objective: a massive army defending it, ripe for the taking by the skilled panzer leader.[25]

Unfortunately for the Germans, Fourth Panzer Army was not the weapon, and von Leeb was not the commander, required for such daring success. Although Leningrad surely suffered, it never fell. However, Fourth Panzer Army was an operational weapon, although not in the sense of the other three. It never participated in the huge, six-digit encirclement battles, but on more than one occasion threw open the door to the USSR's second city. It created opportunities that neither Hitler, Halder nor von Leeb could exploit. After the departure of Hoepner and the panzer army, the entire northern theater settled down to a three-year tug-of-war.

After long road and rail movement across the northern tier of the Ostfront, the reorganized Fourth Panzer arrived in the middle of Army Group Center's sector. Hoepner's command would be ad hoc from the start: units thrown together on the eve of combat, some had been manning the Desna Line for nearly two months and others arriving by rail from the Leningrad front after operations had begun. Von Bock's plan called for the usual pairing of infantry and panzer armies during the initial, breakthrough phase of a large operation. For Operation Typhoon Hoepner's new formation would be attached to von Kluge's Fourth Army, the Schwerpunkt, heading east on the southern highway and eventually directly into the center of Moscow's defenses. Exhausted and attritted, at the end of a long and inadequate logistical tail, with bad weather approaching and with the Red Army surely prepared to fight hard for its capital, only Moscow could justify the risks the Ostheer was about to take.[26] Stalin had provided that prerequisite for a successful Vernichtungsschlacht: a massive defensive force tied down in front of a valuable target. Typhoon represented the penultimate battle that Halder, von Bock and many other German generals had wanted so badly for over a year. What would they do with the opportunity now that they finally had it?

For Hoepner, the final offensive against Stalin's capital began at 0530 on 2 October, a beautiful autumn day. The XLVI Panzer Corps commander, General of Panzer Troops Heinrich von Vietinghoff published this Order of the Day:

> The 2nd of October is the birthday of the late General Field Marshal von Beneckendorff und von Hindenburg. His was the first, the great victory over the Russians, and hindered their invasion in search of empire. On his birthday we begin the decisive crusade against the last large group of Russian forces. The passwords for the panzer corps on 2 October are: Hindenburg-Forward-Victory![27]

His XL Panzer and XII Corps made short work of the defenses, augmented by the Desna River, but weakened after the Timoshenko Offensive of late summer. The Germans soon earned numerous bridgeheads, and by the end of the first night 10th Panzer occupied positions 30km deep into the Soviet lines. Fourth Panzer had managed to work the seam between the Reserve and Bryansk Fronts and within a couple of days turned the left flank of the 43rd Army. Three days into Typhoon, 10th Panzer took Yukhnov and Hoepner sent the rest of XL Panzer northwest with the ultimate goal of reaching Gzhatsk, all of which came as a surprise to the Soviets. The LVII Panzer Corps (late in returning from Velikie Luki sector) fell in behind them, ready to exploit in the direction of Moscow. (But as happened to Third Panzer Army on its left, Fourth Panzer also outran its fuel, ammunition and food supplies.) Of equal concern to Stavka, was XLVI Panzer at Spas Demyansk, turning north in concert with the Fourth Army's VII and XX Corps, pressuring the left flank of Reserve Front forces holding the main road from Smolensk through Viazma. Field Marshal von Kluge stood at the Vishody bridgehead over the Ugra River, cheering the 5th Panzer onward. As had been the case throughout Barbarossa, Stalin's orders to stay put played into the Germans' hands. By the 5th, Stavka could not help but see that XL Panzer coming up from Yukhnov meant disaster to these defenders, now counting the bulk of 19th, 20th, 24th and 32nd Armies plus other formations. The Soviets intended withdrawal to subsequent positions 25km east came to naught when panzer units began to arrive in their rear. On 7 October, XL Panzer linked up with units from Hoth's Third Panzer

Army at Viazma, closing the door on the northern portion of the massive double encirclement. On the same day, XLVI Panzer reached Nikolskoye, barely 15km south of Gzhatsk.[28] The three panzer armies and their infantry consorts had ripped a giant hole in Moscow's first line of defense and sent another two-thirds of a million frontovicki to captivity. Could even Zhukov, that master of improvisation and the new commander of the combined defenses of Moscow, save the city?

By 10 October, Hoepner's men prepared to continue on towards the east as the winter arrived in earnest; from here on, weather would have a tremendous effect on operations. The 710 panzers he had available outnumbered those of Guderian (271) and Reinhardt (259) combined, by a wide margin, but it is difficult to see how he made full use of his advantage. The SS Reich took Gzhatsk, but because XL Panzer was still involved clearing the Viazma Kessel, it had to hold on against two Soviet armies alone. Star shells routinely illuminated the night since it was then that Red Army soldiers tried to slip the noose. Fourth Panzer advanced but slowly during the second half of October. Eventually the 2nd, 5th and 11th Panzer Divisions arrived and continued east past the Napoleonic battlefield of Borodino, capturing Mozhaisk on the 19th. The Germans did not know it at the time, but this town represented the center of Zhukov's defensive structure for Moscow. As Soviet defenses stiffened, Hoepner skirted around to his left, searching for a weak point in Moscow's perimeter. By 20 October, Hoepner's line ran from 3rd Motorized near Yermolino in the south to XLVI Panzer's outposts at Klementyevo in the north. He sent 10th Panzer over the Moscow River, which on the 25th captured the town of Ruza on the river of the same name, while 2nd Panzer neared Volokolamsk on the panzer army's far northern flank. Like most of Army Group Center, Fourth Panzer made slow but steady progress, but not nearly enough to win Moscow or even bring Typhoon, much less Barbarossa, to a successful conclusion. As Soviet resistance and mud continued to stymie the advance, Hitler searched in vain for a decision on von Bock's flanks, therefore resources and effort went to Guderian and Reinhardt instead of Hoepner.[29]

So it went through the first half of November, as well. Fresh baked bread had to be brought forward 50km on panzers or other tracked vehicles, while winter uniforms were back in Roslavl and fuel was as far away as Smolensk. Fourth Panzer pushed eastward very gradually and in his diary, von Bock scarcely mentions it or Hoepner for an entire month. When the ground finally froze solid, both army group and OKH had high hopes for Hoepner, who would attack along with the Fourth Army due east to Moscow during Typhoon's second phase. He issued a rousing Order of the Day on the 17th: 'The time for waiting is over. We can attack again. The last Russian defense before Moscow is defeated. We must stop the beating of the heart of the Bolshevik movement in Europe . . . The panzer group [*sic*] has the good fortune of leading the decisive attack!'[30]

Hoepner's command was arranged north to south, V Corps (2nd Panzer, 35th and 106th Infantry Divisions), XLVI Panzer (5th and 11th Panzer), XL Panzer (10th Panzer, SS Reich), IX Corps (78th and 87th Infantry) and VII Corps (7th, 197th and 267th Infantry). With V Corps leading, they got off to a slow start, partly as a result of pre-emptive Red Army attacks and much to von Bock's annoyance, but by 17 November he had 5th Panzer just short of Novopetrovskoye against Rokossovsky's 16th Army. A couple of days later Hoepner's right flank units driving for Zvenogorod gave Zhukov cause for concern. It took other elements of the panzer army five days to get close to the town of Istra, a testament to both the Germans' fatigue and the Siberians' determination. By the 23rd, on Hoepner's left, the 2nd Panzer had cut the railroad from Leningrad to Moscow near Solnechnogorsk and four days later reached a point only 35km from Moscow. In the center, his Schwerpunkt of the two panzer corps astride the main Istra road made respectable progress. Die Afrikaner (The Africans) of 5th Panzer and Brigade 900 had the sensitive mission of capturing the Istra Reservoir dam before the enemy could demolish it, but the Soviets succeeded. The 10th Panzer and SS Reich, largely leading the panzer army since the beginning of Typhoon, took the town of Istra on the 26th. With Guderian clearly stalled south of the capital, the Germans switched their emphasis to the northern flank – as it turned out, one last time. With Reinhardt also advancing to his left, Hoepner urged his men to their final effort. Despite the enemy (and his scorched earth tactics), the weather, the disappearance of the Luftwaffe and the lack of supplies, the 2nd Panzer reached Krasnaye Polnaya, 22km northwest of Moscow, on the 27th. On the first day of December, Panzer Engineer Battalion 62 (directly under panzer army control) reached Chimniki, 15km from the city.[31]

Engineers

Engineers (often 'pioneers' in Europe) are frequently neglected from consideration as members of the combined arms teams of modern armies. This is a serious mistake: engineers are among the hardest working soldiers on the battlefield, often covered in dirt from before dawn until after dark, clearing or breaching minefields and other obstacles in front of the other combat troops, or continuing to improve strongpoints and other positions to the rear. During the Nazi-Soviet War, German engineers helped the blitzkrieg forward by assaulting over rivers, making, repairing and improving bridges, creating corduroy roads through marshes and performing other mobility improving tasks. During the second part of the war, when the Germans were largely on the defensive, engineers also made and improved field works, bunkers and other survivability assets for friendly troops. During the Second World War, the German Army considered engineers elite troops.

Throughout Barbarossa, the Soviets employed extensive systems of anti-tank ditches and massive numbers of mines wherever they chose to make a stand; these all had to be negated by engineers. Tactical bridging units made light (*c.* 10 ton) and medium (up to 20 ton) capacity bridges. Army level bridging columns (complete with their own self-sufficient saw-mill detachments) made pontoon bridges and even heavy duty 'permanent' bridges of 50- to 60-ton capacity.

German engineers employed over forty types of mines during the war. Early anti-tank mines were called Tellerminen ('plate' mines). Later, they developed wooden mines filled with Amatol to confound mine detectors and to save metal. The Germans also used anti-personnel 'S-mines' filled with shrapnel and often used as booby traps. The Germans also had a few models of remote-controlled demolition vehicles, but these were used in small numbers and had a limited effect. In the Wehrmacht, engineers also had responsibility for flame throwers, both man packed and AFV mounted.

But the panzer armies could not do it alone, they needed the attack's Schwerpunkt, von Kluge, to act. Unfortunately no power on earth could move the stodgy old Prussian. The three panzer army commanders each begged von Bock to give them command of the main effort (the Ostheer only had enough resources for one) – they and their men wanted the honor! But not even the army group commander could cause von Kluge to bestir himself. Halder wanted the increasingly ill von Brauchitsch to give the Fourth Army commander a direct order to attack. In the end, the Fourth made a half-hearted effort on either side of Naro-Fominsk during the first three days of December, which can only be charitably described as too little, too late. Zhukov's men easily parried the attempt. Hoepner would later say that von Kluge abandoned Fourth Panzer Army.[32] It was effectively the end of Typhoon and ultimately the end of Barbarossa. Since the Fourth was a latecomer to the central front, it is little wonder that its impact may be considered less than the other two panzer armies. Despite arriving late for Typhoon, it did smash the Desna River Line, did give Stavka quite a shock as it made for Yukhonov and did come closest to Moscow of any German formation. It seems that the panzer army had a difficult time escaping mopping up duty following the Viazma battle and one has to ask, with significantly more than 50 percent of the panzers participating in Phase II of Typhoon, why did it not have a bigger influence? Surely attacking into the center of Zhukov's shield before Moscow and being 'unequally yoked' to a weak leader such as von Kluge is part of the reason. Coupling of Third and Fourth Panzer Armies together immediately after the Viazma operation, and sending the combined force around Zhukov's right is exciting to contemplate. With adequate logistical support (and Hoth still as commander?), the twin panzer armies would have been a force to reckon with. Of course, a German defeat of the USSR probably still remained outside the realm of possibility.

On 3 December, on his own initiative, Hoepner called a three-day halt to operations. The pause was much needed, and his men expected to renew their attacks on Moscow's defenses on the 7th. That was not to be. The Soviets' winter general counteroffensive began slowly on 5 December and began to take off the next day. It began in the north, where Third and Fourth Panzer Armies posed a greater danger to Moscow than did Guderian's Second Panzer the south. On 7 December, von Bock noted in his diary that the enemy was especially active opposite Fourth Panzer. Hoepner and Reinhardt requested permission to withdraw, and on 7 December, not understanding the full implication of events, Hitler agreed. The two armies pulled back without allowing potentially disastrous breakthroughs. The following day, von Bock finally did what he should have done two months earlier, join the two panzer armies. Zhukov ordered the 5th, 16th and 20th Armies to encircle Third Panzer Army plus Hoepner's adjoining XLVI Panzer Corps. Reinhardt, in the more exposed salient, began to retreat. As it did so, Fourth Panzer had to do the same so as not to offer an exposed left flank, and therefore Fourth Army had to do likewise. Only a weak performance by the Soviets in the offensive's opening stages, as noticed at the time by Zhukov and admitted to in their official history a dozen years later, saved Army Group Center from greater calamity. Logistics, a weakness since Barbarossatag, continued to bedevil the Germans when Hoepner received a train of fuel-tank cars that were all empty. As the general feared, slow-moving artillery would be lost during any improvised movement such as an unexpected withdrawal in the worst conditions imaginable. By the end of the second week of December, a dangerous penetration in the VII Corps sector developed. On the 15th, Hitler agreed in theory to allow Fourth Panzer to return to the Ruza River Line, which in any event Hoepner doubted his men could hold for long. Already his units had begun to evacuate non-essential matériel, including, in the case of 11th Panzer Division, the markers from its field graveyard, but not the corpses under the crosses.[33]

At midnight on 16 December, Hitler believed he could halt the rout with a new 'stand fast' order, but Stalin's offensive had not yet run its course. An SS man in Motorized Division Reich penned these lyrics, sung to the tune of 'Lili Marlene':

> *Auf der Strass' von Moskau zieht ein Battalion*
> *es sind die Letzten Reste von unser Division.*
> *Wir sehen Moskau schon von ferne stehen*
> *jedoch wir musten stiften gehen.*
> *Wie einst Napoleon, wie einst Napoleon ...*

> A battalion on the road to Moscow pulls away
> From our division it is all that remains.
> From afar we see Moscow standing
> Nevertheless we must get going.
> Like Napoleon once, like Napoleon once ...[34]

On the right, 78th and 267th Infantry divisions were smashed. 'Hiwis', Soviet POWs now working with the Germans, no longer simply drove trucks and cooked food, they fought at the front and manned artillery pieces. Landsers wore women's sweaters to ward off the cold. Another SS man, Sturmbahn-führer Dr Roschmann, wrote about his experiences as a physician in a field hospital in mid-December:

> There was no rest day and night. We got lice from the infected wounded. There were many severely wounded, many amputations, stomach and lung shots, fractured bones. We had the tragic certainty that all of them, despite their need for quiet, must shortly be transported in unfavorable conditions. That, and the uncertainty about the right time to order transport, wore heavily on my nerves ... We quickly eat in the operating room, a bite of bread and a gulp of coffee, because we have to take a break until the new wounded are brought in. The excised scraps of skin, the blood-stained uniforms and amputated members have to be taken away. Our eyes are teary, heavy and drooping, our legs have no feeling, we are sick from the bloody work and the lice bites. When the next wounded is brought in it is understood that we have to concentrate on him like he was the first one when we were fully rested. We can cut through the air because it is so heavy from the heat and instrument sterilizer, and because of the many bodies that work so close together. The smells and the haze ...[35]

By the 19th, both von Brauchitsch and von Bock were gone, Guderian and Hoepner and others would soon follow. Recalling his combat during the First World War, Hitler took direct command of the Army in addition to his many other duties. Only the day before, Hoepner had warned his superiors that Fourth Panzer was at risk of being vaporized by the Soviet onslaught, leaving a gaping hole in the front. But exactly the opposite occurred: on the same day the Führer took over the Army, the panzer army quickly managed to take new positions along the Ruza after breaking contact with the 5th and 33rd Armies near Solnechnogorsk. About 24 hours later it looked like five Soviet armies had ground to an ignominious halt. However, by 20 December, Hoepner's V Corps, battered from its direct assault on Moscow and long retreat east, managed to hold the 15km space between the Ruza and Lama Rivers southeast of Volokolamsk. Its parent organization and left neighbor, Fourth and Third Panzer Armies respectively, helped to shore up the corps and secure the line. Somehow, the line held past Christmas Day, reinforced by a battalion flown directly to the front from Germany armed only with pistols and wearing regular shoes. That it managed to retain its positions past New Year's Day almost defies explanation. Perhaps the three best reasons are that Hitler's 'stand fast' order had some merit, that Stalin had overreached Soviet capabilities and that the assaulting Red Army formations had also suffered tremendous losses.[36]

The Fourth Panzer's positions on 1 January 1942 projected dangerously on either side of the Warsaw–Moscow highway, centered on Mozhaisk. Its Ruza and Nara River Line stood firm as Third Panzer and Fourth Armies faded away to the west. Amazingly, they still stood within 70km of Moscow's center. When, on the next day Hoepner asked about the possibility of a planned withdrawal, a 'categorical' denial came back as the answer. On the day after that, von Bock's replacement as Army Group Center commander, von Kluge ordered Fourth Panzer to launch a counterattack to regain contact with Fourth Army's left flank, now wide open near Maloyaroslavets. Hoepner needed five days to make preparations for the attack. By that time the situation had changed, Soviet forces now threatened the panzer army's right but von Kluge insisted the assault go off as planned. The commander of the now-endangered XX Corps told Hoepner his corps would perish if forced to continue attacking as it had on 7–8 January and not withdraw. Von Kluge, not the type of general to make a decision or take responsibility himself, said he would phone Halder who in turn said he would contact Hitler. By January 1942, the Führer had not yet reached the point where he would throw corps away like so much spare change (that only came later in the war), so all concerned figured they had a fifty-fifty chance XX Corps could be saved. However, when no permission arrived, Hoepner authorized the withdrawal of the corps' slower troops on his own authority. There is reason to believe that von Kluge misrepresented Hoepner's case to OKH. And 24 hours later, about midnight on the 9th, von Kluge telephoned Hoepner to say that Hitler had relieved the panzer army commander of his duties. General of Infantry Richard Ruoff, until then commanding the embattled V Corps, took over Fourth Panzer.[37]

The 35km withdrawal that cost Hoepner his career meant Fourth Panzer relinquished the Nara portion of its line. On 13 January, Führer Headquarters authorized the exact same withdrawal that Hoepner advocated, anticipating a bizarre command behavior common later in the war that brutally punished a field commander for some misdeed, then in a prudently retroactive manner approved of the same course of action hours or days later. The following day, von Kluge gave the army group permission 'in principle' to withdraw to the Königsberg Line (when he gave the word), which so far as Fourth Panzer was concerned, meant either side of the highway, just east of Gzhatsk. He allowed movement to begin on the 18th, but then he micromanaged the entire operation. He would not allow a clean break that might make a retreat under enemy pressure, one of the more difficult military maneuvers, any easier. The large (eight divisions and four brigades) 5th Army captured Mozhaisk on 20 January but then the advance slowed. Other Red Army formations pursued, initially somewhat energetically, but later much less so: they too had taken a severe beating along the Nara–Ruza Line. Despite 33rd Army's movement (itself eight divisions) and a sizeable cavalry presence in the rear and along the boundary between Fourth and Fourth Panzer Armies, Ruoff generally honored the Königsberg Line. In this, on 21 January, Stavka greatly aided Army Group Center by withdrawing the 1st Shock and 16th Armies. On 3 February, the 20th Panzer, attacking south from Gzhatsk, met the Fourth Army's XII Corps coming north from Yukhonov, closing the gap in the middle of the army group's front.[38]

The 33rd Army represented the Soviet effort along the Moscow theater in microcosm: while it had reached suburbs of Viazma, deep in Army Group Center's rear and a key rail junction with lines going in all four cardinal directions, the 33rd became isolated from its comrades and the Germans eventually whittled it away. Stavka used every asset at its disposal: conventional forces, cavalry raids, partisan activities and even airborne operations. In this last case, in late January the Soviets made many numerous parachute jumps into the Viazma area, often into the Fourth Panzer Army sector. The 3rd Motorized Division history records this action:

> We pushed into the town, and could tell that the partisans had left and had gone south into the next village. We had to change our

tactics: we had to go quickly into a village so that the partisans had no time to leave and alert the other villages. On the third day our entire battalion was 'motorized' on sleds. Each sled had hay on its undercarriage and on the hooves of the horses, and besides a Russian driver, a crew of two to three men. The crew was ready and aimed right and left behind the horses. We were able to fire on the move. That day was supposed to be our first attempt ... While one company went wide right another went left through the next village to keep the Russians from escaping while the main column attacked straight ahead into Semeshkovo. A platoon of the Brandenburger company rushed the village, opened fire and surprised the Russian's security. We lamented three dead and five to six wounded, including the lieutenant and a platoon leader. In despair, the rest of the men took cover behind dead horses and overturned sleds until we had taken the villages. We settled in for the night.

At midnight, suddenly alarm. The Russians attacked. Shots go through windows and walls of the wooden houses. Everyone out and into the prepared positions in the snow. Finally quiet reigned. Then we heard the familiar sound of the motors of the Russian bombers. Quite slow and low over the snow, barely a hundred meters overhead. Their dark shadows rush over us. On the next day we saw impressions in the snow but no parachutes. Interrogation of POWs confirmed the suspicion [the Soviets had jumped without parachutes]. Dark spots reveal sacks thrown out full of welcome provisions. In the distance is a bi-plane on its nose, it had a hard luck crash landing.[39]

Phase II of the Stalin's winter counteroffensive ended like the first: the Germans farther away from Moscow and pounded mercilessly, but the Soviets over optimistic and over extended. By early March, the 'Africans' of 5th Panzer busied themselves clearing up pockets in the panzer army's rear, first the 1st Guards Cavalry Corps and later remnants of the 33rd Army. Then in mid-March, the springtime half of the bi-annual rasputitsa struck. As the snow melted, Ziemke and Bauer relate how 'corpses of men, animal cadavers, garbage and human waste that been frozen for weeks ... began to thaw thus ... raising the threat of an epidemic' for both armies.[40] Zhukov kept up the pressure, despite the conventional wisdom that operations came to a halt during that season. By mid-April even these threats diminished as the combined factors of casualties, enemy action, weather, insufficient logistics, illness and others brought both sides to a halt.[41]

Of the six German armies that the Soviets brutally shoved back from Moscow that winter, Fourth Panzer perhaps fared best. Like the other three panzer armies during Stalin's winter offensive, it can hardly be considered to have played a significant operational role. It had fought to maintain itself on the battlefield, despite losses, non-existent logistic support, the weather and the Red Army. While it was not employed as an operational-level weapon in the sense used in this book, it had remained intact, had not allowed any major breaches in its lines and, in fact, had negated a significant danger to Army Group Center's lines of communications. The OKH pulled out the panzer army headquarters and sent it back to the Army's reserve where it would refit and assume command of new and refurbished divisions in preparation for its next campaign: Operation Blau.

The strategic background for the Wehrmacht's 1942 campaign against the Caucasus oil region and Stalingrad has been explained in Chapter Two. The experience of Fourth Panzer in 1942 would be very different from its sister panzer armies. Toward the end of April, Seventeenth Army commander Hermann Hoth prepared to go to Germany on leave, when he was told that upon his return he would take command of a new Fourth Panzer Army. When he did come back, he once again fell under von Bock, now commanding general of Army Group South. Hoth's first mission would be to first attack to seize Voronezh, then turn hard right behind the main Soviet defenses to Korotoyak on the Don River. The assumed start date was approximately 15 June, and within thirty days of that, OKH expected to have laid the groundwork for a massive, Barbarossa-style Kessel. During Phase II, it would continue along the Don to the area of Millerovo, link up with First Panzer and Sixth Armies a month later. In Blau III, First and Fourth Panzer Armies would come under Army Group A for the drive on Stalingrad and then capture the oil-rich Caucasus. As in the year before, the panzers would be joined with an infantry army, in this case von Weichs' Second, into Armeegruppe Weichs, which also included the Hungarian 2nd Army.[42]

After nearly two weeks of delays due to other operations, weather and security breaches, Operation Blau began on 28 June. Near midnight on the eve of the offensive, the panzer army commander visited the assembly area of 1st Company, Fusilier Regiment 2 of Motorized Division Grossdeuschland. The company commander wrote:

> I just had a meeting with my platoon leaders in a hut when one of my men reports, 'The colonel general is here!' I ran to report as my

men, some sleeping, some getting ready, some lying with weapons in foxholes call from group to group, 'The colonel general is coming!' and jump up to report. The small general on foot with his orderly at least two heads taller, came into our assembly area and winks, 'Stay seated boys, don't get up!' (Bleibt sitzen, Kinder, bleibt liegen!) He recognized me when I reported and asked in a friendly manner if we are ready to advance and if we took casualties from the enemy air activity. By this visit we see that he is a man in motion. His eyes are constantly moving between the men. He is open-faced about thanking us about the expected massive attack and the unavoidable losses. Somewhat abruptly he asks, 'Do you think all will go well?' I answer, 'What we can control will go well, and everyone will do the best he can.' With that a thought occurred to me for the first time because of the colonel general's question: the attack will go for sure the next morning. Colonel General Hoth indicated it would not be easy and then said quite literally, 'Hopefully everything will go well!' Once more he offered me his hand and wished me personally and my men, 'Break a leg!' (Hals und Beinbruch!)[43]

A couple of hours later, at 0215, Blau began for the men of Fourth Panzer Army. Hoth's Schwerpunkt, XLVIII Panzer punched through the first Soviet defenses and by noon had gone 16km, crossed the Tim River, then went another 16km to cross the Kschen. The XXIV covered the left flank, and the 16th Motorized (part of Hungarian 3rd Corps, and the only element of that formation to cross the Tim) covered the right. The death and destruction all around as Hoth's men passed over the shattered Soviet defenses was welcomed news: the enemy did not seem to be withdrawing as he had earlier during Fridericus II and Wilhelm. Rain on Blau's second and third days slowed XLVIII Panzer, but not so much that it could not overrun 40th Army headquarters. Operationally and strategically the Red defenses were uncoordinated and hamstrung by logistics woes. On 1 July, Grossdeutschland passed 24th Panzer to take the lead of XLVIII Panzer and reached the Olym River, 60km from Voronezh. In the first six days of the campaign, Grossdeutschland destroyed 100 tanks without losing a single panzer. The 16th Motorized continued to guard the right flank of General of Panzer Troops Werner Kempf's panzer corps. Stalin and his staff urged an attack against Hoth's spearhead, in the area around Gorshechnoye, where the Soviets believed that they had a 2:1 superiority over Fourth Panzer's 500 AFVs. After much milling around by 1st, 4th, 16th, 17th and 24th Tank Corps, a small engagement did occur south of the town on 1 July. None of this did much to slow down Hoth, and by the 2nd, even Stavka admitted their Voronezh defenses had deteriorated.[44] Not that it would matter all that much in the end, Stalin and the rest of the Soviet high command had already decided that this year they would give up space if it meant keeping its army in the field.

Hoth continued toward Voronezh according to original OKH plans. By the 5th, XLVIII Panzer had three bridgeheads over the Don quite near the city, while 9th Panzer and 3rd Motorized Divisions of XXIV Panzer began a spirited five-day armored battle against the 5th Tank Army. Over 800 KVs and T-34s attacked half that number of panzers, the latter supported by Luftwaffe CAS. But the Wehrmacht was still the master of the blitzkrieg and could run circles around the still inexperienced Soviet commanders, so the tank army counterattack achieved little. Kempf's men approached Voronezh that same evening of 5 July, but initially were told not to enter the city. The next day, elements of 24th Panzer, Grossdeutschland and 3rd Motorized occupied the western portion of city from the west and north anyway, and later that day von Bock asked permission to do what had already been accomplished. The battle for Voronezh would shortly cost von Bock his job. As for the Soviets, loss of the city and the ineffectiveness of the 5th Tank Army's attack, seem to have confirmed to Stavka at least, that the time for the general retreat had arrived. An overall loss of firm control by various Red Army field units over their organizations led to an unorganized retreat around the same time. The end result was that by 6–7 July, much of Bryansk and Southwest Front pulled back and the Germans, specifically von Bock, noticed the weakening resistance immediately. Unfortunately, Hitler only partially understood the meaning of this, even thought it was happening before his eyes and Halder missed it completely.[45] However, the Germans seemed to be losing some of their mental alacrity, perhaps Stalin's staff was now operating within a faster decision loop, so the German high command had real difficulty adjusting to the new reality. Von Bock suggested OKH needed to reconsider Blau's objectives. In other words, unless they made some changes fast, the opportunity for the intended Vernichtungsschalcht might soon slip away.

Von Bock therefore ordered much of Fourth Panzer (XLVIII and XXIV Panzer Corps) south on 6 July, for an intended link up with Sixth Army forces at Rossosh. Three days into the operation reality intruded, the recurring nightmare of logistics, and derailed his grandiose plans. Some mobile units sat at Voronezh and waited to be relieved (3rd and 16th Motorized), while others were stranded all over the steppe without fuel (23rd and 24th Panzer, Grossdeutschland). By 11 July, Hoth's van met Sixth Army's XL Panzer and VIII Corps and absorbed them into his panzer army. In fact, they now became the Fourth Panzer's main striking force since the organizations with which he began Blau were waiting to be refueled. Fourth Panzer received orders on the 12th to continue past Millerovo and another junction, this time with von Kleist. Von Bock accurately predicted that two panzer armies' worth of combat power clustered around the town to no advantage. Again, the massive Kessel with its huge haul of POWs failed to materialize, making false any analogies between Lochvitsa ten months earlier and Millerovo. That von Bock was right made no impact on higher headquarters, which changed Hoth's direction of attack from east (possibly Stalingrad) to south (probably Rostov). On the next day von Bock made a counter offer to Halder, a drive on Morozovsk, well over 100km east, as the field marshal believed, with a real chance of catching more than just a few retreating Southwest Front troops. Meanwhile at Rastenburg, Hitler got involved and within a very short time that same day von Bock was out of a job – again. Von Bock took the fall, probably justifiably, for poor planning and execution that hamstrung Blau. Suffice it to say, four reasons for this are: 1. Inadequate logistics planning and preparations; 2. Too much effort expended on empty victory at Voronezh; 3. Failure to keep panzers concentrated; and 4. Hitler sensed a victory in the making and did not want to share credit with von Bock.[46] Barely a fortnight into Blau (or what was left of it), however, the operation bore little resemblance to its original conception.

On that same fateful 13 July, new instructions came down calling for another giant trap at Rostov. Hoth would cover von Kleist's left flank as the two panzer armies drove south-southwest, even brushing by Morozovsk as suggested by von Bock. Then Fourth Panzer would cross the Don and follow the river west, presumably trapping prodigious numbers of Soviets. Indeed, First and Fourth Panzer Armies joined hands near Millerovo on the 15th, and a day later Hoth reached the Don at Tsimlyansky. Two days later, Hitler overrode Halder's objection to the concentration of so much armor to so little purpose[47] and thereafter, Hoth was not to cross the Don, but try to close the supposed encirclement north of the big river. Just 48 hours after that, on the 19th, the Führer changed his mind again: now half of Hoth's army would remain to the north of the Don and participate in the Rostov battle, while the other half crossed over, but would move first east then west or southwest! Fourth Panzer, which had grown quite large when it absorbed two mechanized divisions from the Sixth Army on the 11th, eight days later gave Paulus the XIV Panzer (one panzer and two motorized divisions near Millerovo) and LI Corps (three infantry divisions by Morozovsk) for the evolving Stalingrad attack. Jerked first one way and then the other, Hoth never figured prominently in the battle for Rostov, and on the 24th, handed over XXIV Panzer (one panzer division) to the Sixth Army. In the wide open spaces of the steppe, pulled along two operational axes and countless tactical axes, the Germans violated most tenants of their own blitzkrieg doctrine, with no concentrated mass of panzers and no large enemy force to vernichten (destroy) even if there had been.

One reason there was no sizeable Soviet force ready to be destroyed is that Stavka could not divine where Hitler and Blau were going. Besides deliberately avoiding a repetition of the disasters of 1941, Operation Kremlin (see Chapter 2) had worked so well that through early July Stalin expected a German turn north toward Moscow at any moment. Also, with two divergent main axes and panzer armies zigzagging throughout the great Don bend, Stavka did not know where to make a serious stand. But while First Panzer and Sixth Armies had clear missions following Führer Directive 45 (Caucasus and Stalingrad, respectively), Hoth, greatly reduced in size, continued to drift. On 21 July his men moved to the south bank of the Don in order to advance against the oil region, only to be redirected a short time later toward Stalingrad. In the meantime, Fourth Panzer kept heading toward the Caucasus, roughly between the Manych and Don Rivers. At a meeting at Führer headquarters on the last day of the month, Hitler revised his eight-day-old directive (much as he had done a year earlier with Directives 33 and 34). Forthwith, Hoth's headquarters plus the XLVIII Panzer, IV Corps and Romanian VI Corps were reoriented toward Stalingrad. Here, even the robust Sixth Army was not strong enough to overcome ever-growing Soviet resistance. So the panzer army made yet another 90 degree turn and headed northeast. This surprise move caught the Soviets unaware again, and against 51st Army's disorganized defenses, Fourth Panzer reached Kotelnikovo, about 150km from Stalin's city on 2 August. By 4 August, what was left of the panzer army crossed the Aksay R. River and semi-officially entered the Battle for Stalingrad from the city's relatively unprotected southern side.[48]

As happened so often during the Nazi-Soviet War, inadequate German logistical arrangements came to the Red Army's rescue while Hoth waited for Paulus. Arranged Romanians, XLVIII Panzer and IV Corps (left to right), Hoth came to a halt along the Aksay R. River. Over the next fortnight his men barely advanced 20km. To the north, Paulus' LI Corps won a surprise bridgehead over the Don which was then exploited by his XXIV Panzer. With this new development, during the last week of August, Army Group B commander von Weichs ordered Fourth Panzer and Sixth Armies to unite for a final drive on Stalingrad. That was easier said than done, especially for two armies hanging tenuously at the end of fragile logistical threads. By 26 August, Hoth had made only modest progress against the 64th Army, now part of the Southeast Front, commanded by one of the Ostheer's chief nemeses, Eremenko. (On that same day another general, his name even more dreadful to German ears, became Deputy to the Supreme Commander (Stalin) and 72 hours later arrived in Stalingrad: Zhukov.) A day later the first rain in five weeks came to the desert. At the same time, a Red Army attack came out of the region of Lake Sarpa into Hoth's right flank. Two days later, undeterred by the ineffective threat and well supported by the Luftwaffe, XLVIII Panzer reached the Karpovka River, which it overcame on 30 August. With the forward movement of Paulus, the two inner armies of both Soviet fronts defending Stalingrad needed to be pulled back to the city to avoid encirclement. Here, the stubborn defense against the Romanians worked against them. But while Soviet resistance against the Romanians and in front of the Sixth Army stood firm and made a junction of the two armies impossible, Fourth Panzer could see no enemy to its front. Therefore on 2 September, von Weichs ordered Hoth to drive on Stalingrad, with or without Paulus. Within 24 hours, Hoth and Paulus linked up at Goncharry, fewer than 20km from the city center. Kempf's 14th Panzer and 29th Motorized Divisions pushed aside the 62nd and 64th Armies and 29th Motorized Division reached the Volga at Kuperosnoye on the 10th. Simultaneously, LI Corps pulled along side to the left, at the very edge of Stalingrad. The 29th lost its foothold with the Volga to Soviet counterattacks that same day and the battle for that tiny suburb raged for four days. Hoth then directed Kempf to continuing assaulting northward, all the while telling von Weichs that combat in Stalingrad exceeded anything yet experienced in the USSR by the Wehrmacht.[49]

On 13 September, Hoth's 14th and 24th Panzer plus the 29th Motorized Division joined by some Sixth Army units, attacked the 62nd Army. They reached the railroad station and Tsaritsa River the next morning and even the Volga that afternoon. Hoth lost XLVIII Panzer to Paulus on the 15th, and here our detailed account of the Battle for Stalingrad will end, its story has been told too well, too often elsewhere. Suffice it to say, Fourth Panzer would hardly behave like a panzer army for the next two months. As is well known, the urban fighting was gruesome, casualties mounted inexorably, life was miserable, the wounded did not receive adequate care, the men had to eat their horses, camels and whatever other scraps they could forage. In short, life during the Rattenkrieg (war of the rats) of Stalingrad was no life at all, and death lurked around every corner, 24 hours a day, seven days a week. After the war von Kleist wrote that Hoth 'could have taken Stalingrad without a fight at the end of July', but Hitler diverted Hoth toward the lower Don where no need existed. At the end of August and in early September, Stalin, Zhukov and the rest of the Soviet high command worried about their ability to hold Stalingrad with only 40,000 defenders in the city and Hoth and Paulus so close. Both points of view are probably correct.[50] As had been the case with Moscow the year earlier, if Hitler had really wanted to take Stalingrad and if the Wehrmacht had really been focused on a single objective, the Germans probably could have done it. But that is another story. On 17 November, a memorandum from the Führer came down the panzer army's chain of command to the men of the 297th Infantry Division:

> I know of the difficulties of the struggle for Stalingrad and of the sinking combat strength. But the difficulties for the Russians are greater, especially with the Volga iced over. If we use this time now we will save blood later. Therefore, I expect leaders to use conspicuous energy, and troops, demonstrable dash, and as a minimum to stake all on attacking through the weapons factory and metallurgy works to the Volga, and to capture these parts of the city.[51]

For Hitler to use the word 'dash' (Schneid) to describe any part of the Stalingrad fighting indicates he actually had no clue 'of the difficulties of the struggle' there. Paulus' Landsers almost granted Hitler's wish and got close to the Volga in numerous places. Not that it mattered, two days after Hitler's missive the Soviets launched Operation Uranus.

Logistics

The military witticism that 'amateurs talk about tactics while professionals speak of logistics' may not apply to the Wehrmacht. Throughout modern military history, the Germans have given scant consideration to matters not directly connected with 'operations', especially logistics, but also military intelligence and other less-sexy aspects of making war. From the Barbarossa's earliest planning stages, logistics was dealt with as an afterthought: troops were forced to forage for food and even Luftwaffe maintenance officers had to scour the Russian countryside for wrecked aircraft in order to scrounge repair parts. When Landsers were freezing to death in front of Moscow during the winter of 1941–42, it was not because the Wehrmacht did not possess warm clothing; many hundreds of rail cars full of winter equipment sat idle back in Germany. The high command could not – or would not – ship them forward to the fighting front. So it would be for much of the Nazi-Soviet War, although retreating toward their homeland did shorten German lines of communication.

Despite the First World War experience of many German leaders, the Soviet Union's crude and under-developed infrastructure 'surprised' and confounded them. Fortunately for the panzer armies, the best of the Russian roads were reserved for their use. Sand or snow, but especially mud, reduced speeds while multiplying fuel and maintenance estimates absolutely wreaked havoc with pre-Barbarossa staff calculations. The Polish, Western and Balkan campaigns had poorly prepared the Wehrmacht for Russia. Civilian Reichsbahn rail authorities had responsibility of getting supplies to the main depots in the army group or army rear echelons. From there a complicated intermediary system called the Gross-transportraum brought stores from railheads to corps or divisional supply points. Here responsibility fell on the Kommandeur der Divisions Nachschubtruppen (Kodina or Commander of the Division Support Troops) to put together truck or quite often native panje horse and cart convoys to the fighting troops. While fighting in the Caucasus, First Panzer Army even made extensive use of camel caravans! All this work was complicated by partisans, climate and terrain, nearly 100 vehicle types in the Wehrmacht inventory (indigenous Axis makes, plus plundered equipment from all over occupied Europe), draft horses dying by the tens of thousands and inaccurate maps. Bizarre Nazi notions about biology and race (i.e., 'blood') further complicated the overtaxed medical care system.

Civilian buses intended for the streets of Berlin and simply given a coat of gray paint failed in Russia. Maintenance troops were overwhelmed by the sheer destructiveness of the Nazi-Soviet War, and countless AFVs littered the battle-field even when the Germans were victorious: repair parts were in short supply and recovery assets were swamped with work. The differing railroad gauges between Germany and the USSR is a well-worn trope in the litany of excuses dragged out by the Germans to explain their logistical failures against the Soviets. As before, this situation was common knowledge to a generation of First World War veterans and should have been known by the youngest captain on the general staff. Equally important was the wanton destruction of Soviet rolling stock and roadbeds by over zealous panzer commanders or Stuka pilots. Once the Nazi-Soviet War shifted from the hoped-for ten-week stroll in the park to a struggle of attrition, German logisticians must have rued such wasteful sport.

Strategically, Germany could not sustain a war against most of the rest of the world. Its manpower pool, the capacity of its industry to produce enough Flak shells and panzers, its petroleum stocks and countless other measures never added up.

Fourth Panzer Army's contribution to Operation Blau was limited by the same factor that had bedeviled Barbarossa: the Germans' inadequate resources plus their inability to stick with a set of objectives and to work toward that goal as a team. When the Red Army did not stand and fight when the odds against them were overwhelming, Blau began to unravel, and Hoth's men paid the price by wastefully wandering over the steppe. Through no fault of their own, they spent the summer of 1942 mainly consuming massive quantities of precious fuel to little advantage and ended the campaign in temporary possession of Stalingrad's southern suburbs.

Eremenko launched his Stalingrad Front's portion of the offensive on 20 November. As also happened northwest of the city, in Hoth's southern sector the 51st and 57th Armies singled out Germany's less than totally committed allies as targets, in this case the Romanian VI and VII Corps. The Romanian VII Corps had only arrived in the panzer army area about three weeks before. His one remaining German outfit, IV Corps itself had one Romanian division out of three in total. All of his allied units suffered from 'tank fright' and fell apart on the first day, despite Hoth's efforts to stiffen their resolve. The Romanian 20th Division fought bravely, but stood little chance against the waves of enemy tanks. The panzer army had no panzer corps or divisions and only about twenty panzers in its two motorized divisions. The best units Hoth had under command soon became trapped in Stalingrad, IV Corps and 29th Motorized. Only trepidation on the part of Red Army commanders across the front from Fourth Panzer saved the remnants. In fact, excessive Soviet concern about reducing the Stalingrad pocket may have been the main thing that prevented the destruction of more German forces in the area. By the end of November Hoth's command was renamed Armeegruppe Hoth (Fourth Panzer plus Romanian Fourth Armies), with only one German formation in its order of battle, 16th Motorized. It was backpedaling south toward Kotelnikovo, from whence it had come just three months earlier, gingerly pursued by the overcautious 51st Army. By early December, however, Fourth Panzer began to receive some much-needed reinforcements. First, the new Army Group Don under von Manstein assigned LVII Panzer Corps (6th Panzer, its refit in France cut short by the crisis, and 23rd Panzer, coming north from the Caucasus but quite beat up) and later the reliable old XLVIII Panzer (currently 11th Panzer, 336th Infantry and 7th Luftwaffe Field Division). Soon Hoth had assembled 232 panzers (most of which belonged to 6th Panzer), including a battalion of the brand new Tigers. Paulus was to prepare to break out and meet Hoth anytime after 8 December. Threatening Soviet activity near the Chir River first diverted XLVIII Panzer, and then delays in assembling LVII Panzer forced sequential postponement of the rescue operation, named Operation Wintergewitter (Winter Storm). Stalingrad was over 100km distant.[52]

General Hoth received orders to attack on 12 December, regardless of weather and the availability of 17th Panzer. General of Panzer Troops Friedrich Kirchner's LVII Panzer got off to a good start, back over the familar ground between Kotelnikovo and the Aksay River, which it crossed at 0800 hours the next day with VIII Fliegerkorps CAS. Raus' 6th Panzer took the lead, with 23rd Panzer providing flank security with its remaining thirty panzers. With XLVIII Panzer struggling to keep contact with Hoth's left-hand neighbor, it could not assist Kirchner, whose men would have to go it alone. Raus described Soviet efforts to halt the relief operation:

> the Russians attacked the southern bridgehead three more times with newly-arrived tank and infantry forces – twice on 14 December and once on 15 December. Each time, our panzergrenadiers in their narrow trenches and deep dugouts were overrun by tanks without suffering the slightest injury. As veteran eastern front campaigners, they had long since become immune to the shock effects of tanks. As soon as the black monsters had trundled past, the heads of the German infantry reappeared, directing devastating machinegun fire across the battlefield. This suppressive fire threw the Russian troops following in the wakes of the tanks back to their line of departure or forced them to remain motionless in shallow depressions until nightfall ... Out of nearly a dozen enemy tanks that penetrated into Saliyevsky during each attack, not a single machine survived to return to its line of departure. The village street was blocked by the burnt-out wrecks of their predecessors ...[53]

Hitler finally freed up 17th Panzer on the second day of the attack (it had been sent to bolster the XLVIII Panzer on the 10th, but it would not return until the 17–18 December) and Hoth made steady but unspectacular progress against 57th Army. During a three-day battle at Verkhne-Kumsky nearly 200 panzers and Sturmgeschütze faced between 450–500 tanks of Rokossovsky's 4th Mechanized and 13th Tank Corps; in normal times the Germans considered these good odds. By the 19th, Kirchner had overcome the Red Army defenses and Raus crossed the Mishkova River, half way to Paulus' outpost. Though the assault by one battle-weary panzer corps progressed slowly, it was having a major effect on Soviet operational planning; during the third week of December Stavka downgraded Operation Big Saturn (attack to Rostov) to Little Saturn (attack to Morozovsk), largely based on the impression created by Hoth. Risk-taker that he was, even this reduced effort was more than von Manstein could handle. He nevertheless had to strip Kirchner of his strongest element, 6th Panzer. By 21 December, Hitler, evidently frozen in inaction, could not bring himself to order Paulus to break out of the trap and the general would not make the decision on his own. On Christmas Eve, 2nd Guards Army pushed LVII Panzer back over the Aksay for the last time. Hoth was now even in danger of becoming encircled himself near the river by elements of the 2nd and 51st Armies. The 7th Tank Corps stove in Fourth Panzer's left flank, being held by the Rumanian VII Corps, endangering Kirchner's corps. Hoth pulled back to Kotelnikovo with 17th and 23rd Panzer and newly assigned Viking

SS Motorized Divisions being chased by 43 enemy units of at least brigade size, supported by 635 tanks and 1,500 guns. Whatever slim chance Fourth Panzer had of succeeding with Wintergewitter was gone. Von Manstein kept retreating, pulling the panzer army over the Sal River on the 28th. A week later Hoth occupied a line of strongpoints on the south bank of the Manich facing north, between Prolyetarskaya and the river's confluence with the Don.[54]

Stavka devoted most of its attention to subduing the Stalingrad pocket or else the plight of German units on the outside would have been much worse. Fourth Panzer Army of von Manstein's Army Group Don and all of von Kleist's Army Group A (see Chapter 1) depended on rail lines routed through Rostov for sustenance. Hoth's lines stretched well over 300km along the Manich, but ironically were weaker the closer they got to Rostov. One week into the new year, the 5th Shock and 2nd Guards Armies stood mere kilometers from von Manstein's command post at Novocherkassk. Hitler pinned his hopes on the ability of the battalion of new Tigers to destroy the entire 3rd Guards Tank Corps. On 21 January, the Soviets began their attack anew across a broad front, worked their way behind the panzer army and were soon only 15km from Rostov. First Panzer would not be through the city until the end of the month and Hoth's men had the mission of holding the door open. Von Mackensen duly extricated his panzer army through Rostov, and then it was Hoth's turn, with Armeeabteilung Hollidt barring the way of the Red Army. During the first half of February these two formations withdrew over 150km, west of the Mius, with the 3rd Guards Mechanized on their heels. Hoth kept moving west toward the Dnepropetrovsk and Zaporozhe. As this occurred, the lead elements of the follow-on maneuvers to Saturn, Operations Gallup and Star were closing on the river crossing sites. If Mobile Group Popov and 25th and 1st Guards Tank Corps, driving through a nearly 300km hole in von Manstein's defensive front, could reach these two cities on the Dnepr bend and hold them, he would lose the foundation of his army group's logistical support and the entire southern tier of the German line would become unhinged.[55]

The field marshal had other plans, however, and Fourth Panzer Army represented their centerpiece. On 17 February, Hitler and his retinue arrived at army group headquarters at Zaporozhe, fully intending to replace von Manstein with Model. With the two fresh tank corps 50km distant, no German forces between them and with the sound of combat as a backdrop, von Manstein explained to the Führer how Hoth would counterattack into the void between First Panzer and Armeeabteilung Kempf, recapture Kharkov and regain the Donets River Line. Since Stavka had mistaken the Fourth Panzer's reorientation to the west as a general retreat, it had imprudently pushed its tank forces to pursue without regard to its separation from Vatutin's main body. Hitler liked the risky but bold plan, basically the same idea von Manstein presented at Rastenburg on 6 February, and the next day Fourth Panzer received its orders. It would be the main force in a broadly conceived move involving First Panzer and Army Detachment Kempf, respectively south and north of the Soviet salient. Before he left on the 19th, Hitler released seven weak mechanized divisions from his reserve and agreed to reduce greatly the Taman bridgehead opposite Kerch on the Crimea, and fly tens of thousands of troops to von Manstein's potentially fatal main front. Von Richthofen's Luftflotte Four accomplished this mission and would be instrumental in the upcoming battle, where his 950 aircraft (over half the total available on the eastern front) contributed an average of 1,000 sorties per day. However, the key to the entire operation was undoubtedly the new SS Panzer Corps (Das Reich and Totenkopf SS Panzer Divisions), the most powerful organization the Soviets were to encounter since the heyday of Operation Blau, eight months earlier. In addition to Obergruppenführer Paul Hausser's SS, Hoth commanded LVII Panzer (6th and 17th Panzer) and eventually XLVIII Panzer Corps, while von Mackensen and Kempf contributed numerous mechanized formations on the flanks.[56]

Soviet intelligence noted the concentration of German armor, but incorrectly assumed its purpose was to cover a continued retreat. So when von Manstein's men counterattacked on the evening of 19 February, their surprise was complete. With panzers to the front and Stukas overhead, the Germans painted a picture of the good old days of the blitzkrieg. By the offensive's second day, the danger to the Dnepr crossing had already passed. Three days later, the 6th and 17th Panzer Divisions (the latter down to eight panzers and eleven assault guns) advanced east of Pavlograd, while SS Totenkpof crossed the Samara River on its way north. Hoth's main objective was destroying Popov's three corps (greatly weakened, as were most Soviet formations at this time, with only twenty-five operational tanks in total). By 26 February, his advance elements closed on Lozovaya, and 2 days later nearly 400 panzers reached Petrovskoye, aided by Vatutin's stubborn refusal to allow his men to escape danger. On the 28th, von Manstein ordered Fourth Panzer north towards Kharkov, which Hausser had disobediently (but fortuitously) abandoned just two weeks earlier. With the SS in the lead and XLVIII Panzer on a parallel course to the north, despite signs of an early rasputitsa thaw, the panzer army covered over 70km in five days. By 5 March, it stood barely a dozen kilometers from the Soviet Union's fourth city. The exhausted 1st Guards Army tried to mount an effective defense, but as the Germans noted, did not fight with much enthusiasm; its 12th and 15th Tank Corps were each the size of battalions. Likewise, the bulk of the 3rd Tank Army succumbed when pincers launched by Hoth's SS and

XLVIII Panzer Corps and Kempf's Grossdeutschland met near Rogan. When temperatures dropped again on 7 March, Hoth decided to march on Kharkov, swinging clockwise in order to maintain communications with Kempf. By the 9th, the SS Panzer Corps reached the city's western suburbs and Hausser announced his intention to take Kharkov by storm. He had only 105 panzers still operational out of the original hundreds. Hoth ordered him not to, but as the SS general had done a month earlier to his then commander, General of Mountain Troops Hubert Lanz, he disobeyed and sent his men into Kharkov from the west and north. After a three-day battle, Kharkov fell on 14 March. By the 18th, the SS men had covered the additional 50km to Belgorod, which they captured along with Kempf's Grossdeutschland, despite fierce resistance from the NKVD rear guard. In the process, numerous 40th and 69th Army units were trapped between Hausser and 'Corps Raus' (based on the 6th Panzer, under Kempf's command) in the so-called Udy Kessel.[57] By this point the rasputitsa had arrived in earnest, and compounded by exhaustion, the Germans' planned elimination of the Kursk bulge died a natural death and both sides settled down to four months' stalemate. For most of that spring of 1943, the Wehrmacht pulled Fourth Panzer Army out of the line, and as twelve months earlier, it prepared for a leading role in the upcoming summer offensive.

The six months preceding Operation Citadel had been both eventful and an emotional rollercoaster for Hoth's men. Their under-resourced attempt to break into the Stalingrad pocket had not been to help the Sixth Army escape, but to make it so Paulus could continue attacking once reconnected to the rest of the Ostheer. Their early start surprised the Soviets but could not assure success. Likewise, the loss of Rostov was not due to overwhelming pressure on Fourth Panzer and Armeeabteilung Hollidt, but because von Manstein wanted to withdraw these units over the Mius River and eventually use the panzer army for his planned 'castling' maneuver. In February, 1943, Hoth's command numbered about 125,000 men and approximately 250 panzers, and it was ready to restore the caved-in eastern front. These were operational tasks of great significance befitting a panzer army. By March, it had largely repaired the damage caused by Stavka's post-Stalingrad offensives, and in four weeks had destroyed 567 tanks, 1,072 guns, killed 40,000 Red Army men and captured a further 12,000. The Soviets had lost 30 percent of their 1942–43 gains.[58] How would the upcoming operations go?

By mid-1943, the Wehrmacht already spoke of the Defense of the Fatherland, even though they were still hundreds of kilometers deep inside the Soviet Union. Operation Citadel started off as just part of a coherent and somewhat reasonable campaign plan for 1943. The plan underwent numerous delays, and if von Manstein had had his way, the offensive would have been cancelled in favor of husbanding Germany's valuable, and limited, mechanized reserves for the Soviet offensive all knew was coming. Fourth Panzer Army was given pride of place as Citadel's Schwerpunkt. Barely a week prior to its start date, Hoth's headquarters opined that with each delay, chances of success declined. Nevertheless, the panzer army commanded an impressive mass of panzers, with Kempf's two panzer corps covering its right flank and Ninth Army launching a supporting attack from the north, the whole enterprise was well buttressed by Luftwaffe CAS. Hoth wielded a massive armored hammer: II SS Panzer Corps with SS Leibstandarte (100 Pz III/IVs, 13 Tigers and 34 Sturmgeschütze), SS Das Reich (113 Pz III/IVs, 14 Tigers, 34 Sturmgeschütze), SS Totenkopf (104 Pz III/IVs, 15 Tigers and 27 Sturmgeschütze) plus XLVIII Panzer Corps with Grossdeutschland (67 Pz III/IVs, 46 Tigers and 34 Sturmgeschütze), 11th Panzer (74 Pz III/IVs), 3rd Panzer in reserve near Kharkov (56 Pz III/IVs and 32 'older' panzers) plus a new (formed only on 23 June) and massive formation, 10th Panzer Brigade (1 battalion of 45 Tigers and Panzer Battalions 51 and 52, with a total of 200 Panthers) and Assault Gun Battalion 911. The LII Corps (57th, 255th and 332nd Infantry Divisions) covered the panzers' left.[59] Hoth's 1,176 AFVs faced 1,699 of the Voronezh Front. Luftflotte Four and VIII Fliegerkorps contributed 1,100 aircraft, including 7 Stuka Geschwader. To their front, the Red Army had provided the ideal target for a blitzkrieg operation: a massive defensive force. Unfortunately for the Germans, they were clueless about the sophistication, depth and strength of the defense. Thanks to their spy network, on the other hand, the Soviets were well informed regarding German intentions.[60]

In the predawn hours of 5 July Hoth visited his troops in their jumping-off positions. To 11th Panzer he stressed the seriousness of the coming offensive: the Germans had always held the enemy's toughness in high regard, but after Stalingrad they had new respect for his skill, too. The day started with the usual artillery barrage and CAS missions, but the Soviets sent counterbattery fire back over the German lines and the Red Army Air Force was also very active. Weather became a factor as well, but Hoth's men advanced through the first Soviet defenses and into the second. They used better techniques than did Model, leading with their Tiger and Panther tanks in order to protect the older marks of panzers and half-tracks from the devastating power of the extensive and well-positioned anti-tank defenses. The two forward Soviet armies, 6th Guards and 7th Guards, deployed nearly sixteen anti-tank guns per kilometer in their first echelon and fourteen guns per kilometer in their second. Towed by American lend-lease trucks, these deadly weapons, up to 76mm in caliber, were mobile and difficult to nail down. Vatutin withdrew according to plan without suffering massive losses usually expected in the first phases of a German offensive. Fourth Panzer, applying armored wedge tactics, achieved a penetration 30km deep and 30km wide at its base, but was outpacing Kempf's flank guard which struggled forward without much Luftwaffe support. That first night, Voronezh Front rushed the 1st Tank Army behind the 6th Guards, facing Hoth. The Landsers were skeptical that the 'wonder weapon' Panthers would have the desired effect. Sure enough, on 5 July, Panzer Battalion 52 (formerly 1st Battalion of Panzer Regiment 15 – 11th Panzer Division) lost 30 percent of its Panthers to all causes, mostly due to enemy action and mechanical failure. On the 6th, a Pz IV of the 3rd Battalion, Panzer Regiment 15, destroyed a Panther because the crew did not recognize the new vehicle as German.[61] Despite Citadel's inauspicious start, the Germans had high hopes.

Surprising the Soviets with Citadel had been out of the question, the salient and the German preparations against it had just been too obvious, therefore a prime consideration of blitzkrieg operations was forfeited from the beginning. By the second day, Hausser's progress of a mere 5km was described as 'good'. Slow progress of Armeeabteilung Kempf continued to arouse concern, and necessitated diverting SS Totenkopf from II SS Panzer's spearhead to security duties on Hoth's increasingly insecure right. Luftwaffe sorties dipped from 1,958 on Citadel's first day to 899 on the second. Conversely, the number of Soviet sorties rose to 1,632. Grossdeutschland took the lead of von Knobelsdorff's XLVIII Panzer in an attempt to create a Kessel deep in the Soviet rear by linking up with II SS near Iakovlevo. Kursk was still well over 100km away and Model's progress paled even compared to Fourth Panzer's modest advances. On the morning of 7 July, Hoth threw 700 AFVs against the 1st Tank Army, at one point cramming 500 vehicles onto a front 6km wide. Stukas from VIII Fliegerkorps darkened the sky above, but Sturmoviks wreaked havoc among the attackers as well. Luftwaffe losses in 2 days amounted to greater than 100 aircraft, but the Germans had blasted a sizeable hole in Vatutin's lines and were deep into his second echelon (of 8 belts). The Army's XLVIII Panzer could not move as quickly as the better equipped SS divisions and failed to spring the trap at Iakovlevo, allowing three Soviet corps to escape. They approached Oboyan, the lynchpin of Vatutin's defenses. The 8th represented the last day of meaningful German progress as von Manstein tried to lever the Soviets out of their stout positions. But even on that day, vigorous counterattacks by mobile reserves released by Stavka forced the Germans back in a number of places. Soviet CAS was overwhelming, and all defensive efforts seemed to concentrate on Hausser's spearheads. German intelligence calculated they had destroyed over 500 tanks in 4 days but that Vatutin still had 1,500 remaining.[62]

Von Manstein thought he could overpower the Soviet's defenses by widen-ing the breech, so on 9 July ordered Hoth to send Grossdeutschland peeling off to the left in attempt to destroy the 6th Tank Corps. On the same day the panzer army commander decided to change plans and shift his main effort northeast, and have II SS Panzer attack toward Prokhorovka. To Hoth this option represented the indirect approach to Kursk, and if he could secure the cooperation of Kempf's III Panzer Corps, could enjoy decent chances of success. Little did he know that he would be turning his forces directly into the 5th Guards Tank Army; Soviet intelligence had noticed the switch from Oboyan to Prokhorovka. The little railroad station gave its name to the engagement that is often considered the signature of the Kursk battle. Hausser got off to a slow start on the morning of 10 July, because a few hours were not enough to concentrate his three divisions. No assistance came from Kempf, nor would von Manstein acquiesce to Hoth's request that Second Army launch a supporting attack in order to draw off Soviet forces. Poor weather on the second morning minimized Luftwaffe CAS, so the struggle became one of tank versus tank. The Germans considered 400 of their panzers against 800 Red tanks even odds. While Leibstandarte and Totenkopf made acceptable progress, Das Reich lagged. The Germans initially enjoyed range and killing power advantages from the Tiger's 88mm guns and the Stuka's 37mm 'tank-busting' cannons. Therefore Rotmistrov's 5th Guards Tank lined up, fender-to-fender, and raced forward in order to close with the Tigers and allow their greater numbers to shift the odds. Prokhorovka became a graveyard: 400 tanks and 320 panzers and Sturmgeschütze littered the countryside. Fourth Panzer now calculated it had destroyed over 1,000 tanks in a week. The SS had won bridgeheads over the Psel and Donets. To Hoth this was even more a reason to slip around to the east with Kempf's III Panzer Corps. Again, Hitler would not hear of it. Hoth could not even use his own XLVIII Panzer; just as von Knoblesdorff was about to add his strength to Hausser's, Vatutin sent the 22nd Guards Rifle Corps into his flank. Hitler knew what von Manstein, Hoth, Kempf and others did not: Citadel was dead. He told von Manstein and Model as much when he summoned them to Rastenburg on the 13th.[63]

While Germany had no more reserves, it seemed that the Soviets had an endless supply. Citadel, like the Ardennes Offensive over a year later, can technically be considered an operational-level maneuver. Forfeiting surprise and attacking into the Soviets' defensive strength, Fourth Panzer had only the slimmest chances of success, odds that a few hundred Tigers and Panthers could not appreciably improve. Hoth may have believed that with a bit more will power he could have prevailed, but he could not see the big picture across the front. And for Germany the war had just taken a serious strategic turn: on 9 July the western Allies invaded Sicily, their first incursion onto the home territory of a major Axis power.

Operation Citadel had been a German failure by any and every measure. It did not meet any of its objectives. It greatly weakened the Ostheer, especially in mechanized forces and did not appreciably damage the Red Army. The Soviets promptly came back with a vengeance and the German retreat would not end for twenty months until they reached Berlin and could go no farther. In fact, Citadel had been so non-threatening to the Soviets that Stavka had been able to deflect its feeble blows and then almost immediately counterattack. The fact that its plan closely mirrored that of von Manstein was not lost on many Germans. On 14 August, Hoth told his men to assume a defensive posture, dig in, cinch down their helmets and destroy any panzers that could not be towed to repair shops. Within a week of Hitler's cancellation of Citadel, the Soviets launched attacks of their own in the Orel and Mius River sectors. During the last week of July, the Italian king arrested and replaced Mussolini so Hitler stepped up the transfer of military formations from the USSR to Italy, further weakening already stretched German forces there. During the second half of the month, Vatutin made good many of the losses incurred during Citadel, and completed his own preparations and made ready for his next move. For his Operation Rumantsev, he commanded 980,000 men to the panzer army's 210,000, plus 12,627 guns and 2,439 AFVs, practically 10 times the 250 panzers and Sturmgeschütze available to Hoth. At 0500 hours on 3 August, elements of the Voronezh, Steppe and Southwest Fronts attacked (Stavka 'coordinator': Zhukov), obliterating the 167th Infantry Division on the Fourth Panzer boundary with Armeeabteilung Kempf. Though poorly trained, the masses of frontovicki easily created a 16km gap, and by 1300 hours Vatutin could confidently deploy his exploitation force: the reconstituted 1st and 5th Guards Tank Armies. Rumantsev completely caught German intelligence by surprise (they had figured the Soviets would need months to recover from Citadel), so von Manstein had quickly to recall SS Das Reich and Totenkopf from the Mius, plus XXIV and XLVIII Panzer Corps from elsewhere in the army group, where he had sent them just weeks earlier. Two days into the new counteroffensive 1st Tank Army had raced far ahead of its infantry and support elements, and in conjunction with the 6th Guards and 27th Armies, had created a small encirclement near Graivron.[64]

About the same time, Grossdeutschland started showing up at Achtyrka (joining combat as soon as its vehicles rolled off the rail cars) and the 3rd Panzer also joined Hoth's order of battle. Between 7–9 August, XLVIII Panzer counterattacked to save their trapped comrades. Vatutin's men had slowed down and were not creating any new penetrations, but the hole separating Hoth from Kempf had grown to over 50km. The men of Fourth Panzer put up a stout defense and Vatutin sought a way around this obstacle. The Soviets crossed the Merchik River near Valki, where Breith's III Panzer had dug in well to the west of Kharkov. Vatutin kept up slow but steady progress and by the 11th had cut the Poltava–Kharkov rail line in numerous places. The commander of Grossdeutschland's assault-gun battalion described the fighting east of Achtyrka on 12 August:

> In the morning, it must have been 0300, a sentry reported tank engine noise on the north edge of the village. I went immediately on a motor-cycle and determined that it must be Russian T-34s. I strengthened security on the north edge with two Sturmgeschütze. Mainly, I alerted the rear services to be ready to march. I made the remaining guns ready for action. I clarified the situation in the morning twilight. I could see a task force of twenty to thirty T-34s with mounted infantry north of us getting ready to attack Achtyrka. In any case, more Russian T-34s are deployed with security in the grain fields to the west. Some of the crews have dismounted to rest. Since we have no infantry support, I decide to escape to Achtryka. I figure that this enemy battle group, especially the infantry, can pursue us, and since we are alone we are not ready to fight in a village. Since our reconnaissance did not report any enemy movement from the south of Achtyrka, I ordered my adjutant, Lieutenant Bauer, to take our wheeled elements to the town, being careful to avoid any combat. I would take the assault guns and attempt to relieve the situation in front of Achtyrka from the northern route. So we raced from the north part of the village west toward Achtyrka. As soon as we were undetected 200–300 meters from the flanks of the enemy tanks, we opened fire. We shot up the totally surprised T-34s. I counted five of them burning. The T-34s further back took up the fight. One of our guns was hit on the flank and destroyed ... We broke off the engagement and fled under heavy fire to Achtyrka where we had cover from friendly PAKs and panzers.[65]

Von Manstein put together a counterattack plan with the objective being the base of the Soviet penetration near Boguduchov. Kempf (after 14 August: Wöhler) would attack northward with III Panzer Corps while Hoth came down with an ad hoc collection of units under the new XXIV Panzer: 7th (17 panzers) and 11th (6 panzers) Panzer Divisions and Grossdeutschland (70 AFVs, including Tigers and Panthers) plus the 52nd and 503rd Heavy Panzer Battalions (13 Tigers and Panthers, total). Vatutin's 47th Army launched its own preemptive strike early on 17 August against the 57th and 68th Infantry Divisions. Hoth was not to be deterred by the uncoordinated effort and attacked as planned the next morning. However, that day the unheard of occurred, 57th Infantry broke and ran after suffering the same treatment 167th Infantry had experienced a fortnight earlier. Hoth's mechanized units kept driving, and on the 20th linked up with Totenkopf west of Kharkov.[66]

Vatutin ordered counterattacks everywhere along the endangered sector. The cordon created by XXIV and III Panzer Corps proved too thinly held and the bulk of the 4th and 5th Guards Armies managed to escape. Hoth claimed to have taken 32,000 POWs and to have destroyed over 2,000 tanks and almost that many artillery pieces. These numbers sound impressive and it is clear that Zhukov and Vatutin had underestimated the strength of the Fourth Panzer Army. But Rumantsev had had limited objectives all along and had deliberately eschewed the overambitious penetrations and encirclements that had marred similar operations earlier that winter. The Soviets had generally avoided becoming encircled themselves and suffered from no breakdowns in discipline at the front. On the German side of the front, numerous infantry regiments and divisions had been obliterated either by the massive preparation fires of the Red artillery or uneven combat when their remnants came up against strong Soviet forces. Although Hoth's net panzer strength was about the same at both ends of August, his men had been forced to destroy many Panthers and Tigers that could not be repaired.[67] Through 22 August, the Germans fought the fourth and final Battle of Kharkov, and then began the long retreat to the Dnepr River.

In the second half of August, Stavka ordered operations continued in order to build upon their success in the Kharkov area. The battles around Achtyrka and Bogoduchov sapped Fourth Panzer strength, while Hoth became increasingly frustrated by the slow trickle of promised reinforcements. The fact that the Soviets had consumed most of their stockpiled fuel and ammunition helped the Germans. Nevertheless, to the north, Hoth lost contact with Army Group Center and as Rokossovsky renewed his attacks on the 26th, Soviet wedges began to break Fourth Panzer into three groups. By the first week of September, Stalin saw his chance to split the seam between Fourth Panzer and Eighth Armies, gain some crossings over the Dnepr and seriously threaten Kiev. With Rokossovsky to the north of the Ukrainian capital and Vatutin to the south, it was a race, all the while the Germans drove herds of cattle before them and left scorched earth behind. Hoth's men broke contact and thereby earned some freedom of maneuver on 16–17 September. In Hitler's mind the Dnepr represented a solid defensive line, part of what he wishfully called the East Wall. On the main southern sector, both Soviet fronts reached the river on 21st, and near Kanev Vatutin's 3rd Guards Tank Army crossed the next day. Tiny bridgeheads up and down the Dnepr soon swelled, with those at Pereyaslav and Sorokoshichi (where the Pripet joins the Dnepr) being most threatening to Hoth.[68]

Twenty-four months minus a week earlier, the two combatants had discovered how even a massive river like the Dnepr (between 500–1,000m wide in the area defended by Fourth Panzer) could not halt a modern army. Granted, the west bank was generally up to 100m higher than the east, giving the Germans more of a defensive advantage in September 1943 than Kirponos enjoyed two years earlier. But at that later date, the defenders were exhausted and weakened by years of combat, perhaps at no time worse than the preceding ten weeks. At their bridgeheads near Kanev, Pereyaslav and also Burkin, the Dnepr makes a very sharp bend, and here is where Vatutin planned to expand three small encroachments into a massive one. He would take an existing 40th Army bridgehead and drop in three airborne brigades and some glider-borne troops. On the night of 24/25 September, slightly fewer than 5,000 parachutists (less than half of planned number) landed scattered all over the bridgehead, and right in the middle of Wöhler's XXIV Panzer Corps and Hoth's 19th Panzer and 72nd Infantry Divisions. Most of the Soviet soldiers were killed or rounded up within 24 hours, although many escaped to join partisans or otherwise continue to fight the Germans. The bottom line so far as von Manstein was concerned was that this potential threat was neutralized and contained. Rokossovsky and Vatutin continued to expand existing lodgements on the west bank and create new ones. By the second week of October, elements of three armies crowded into the Burkin–Kanev bridgehead, but lacking heavy weapons, failed in two attempts to break out during the middle of the month. Meanwhile, Vatutin, his command renamed 1st Ukrainian Front, cast about for a way to break the Dnepr stalemate. His attention settled on Lutezh, immediately north of Kiev, where the 38th Army and the redeployed 3rd Guards Tank would have better success. Supported in this instance by 2,000 tubes of artillery, and with a tank corps present, Vatutin attacked on 3 November. By the end of the day, Hoth's lines suffered from a 6km deep gash. Within two days – precisely according to Vatutin's ambitious time plan – his men rudely pushed aside Hoth's VII Corps and liberated Kiev. Not content with that single accomplishment, the 3rd Guards Tank with 38th Army in tow made for the important rail junction of Fastov, where the 25th Panzer Division was just arriving from France.[69]

Both Stavka and the OKW/OKH realized the importance of Kiev as a stepping stone to both southern Poland and the Carpathian Mountains and one of the Reich's last allies, Hungary. The city's loss was too much for Hitler, who had soured on Hoth despite the general's exemplary service since the invasion of Poland. Hoth left for home leave in November; Hitler made the departure permanent and never recalled the short Brandenburger to service. The XLVII Panzer Corps commanding general, Raus, took over the reins of Fourth Panzer Army that same month. In the midst of this turmoil at the top of the panzer army, von Manstein tried to regain the initiative in the Fastov area. Raus' new organization was stretched from Korosten near the fringe of the Rokitno Marshes (LIX Corps), arcing around the Kiev salient (VII and XIII Corps) then coming to rest on the Dnepr upstream from Burkin (XXIV Panzer) and its component parts were dispersing as if by centrifugal force. An old friend, XLVIII Panzer Corps, was arriving near Fastov from the First Panzer area. During the second week of November, the new 25th Panzer struggled in the mud and winter against the veterans of the 3rd Guards Tank Army. In the meantime, XLVIII Panzer assembled major portions of its three divisions (1st and 7th Panzer plus Leibstandarte) and counterattacked on 12 November to the northwest and into the 38th Army's rear. The objective was to continue on to Zithomir, but Balck's men could not make it on the first go. They cut off the three lead tank brigades of 3rd Guards, but 1st Guards Cavalry Corps defenses halted them short of the city. Two days and some reorganization later, XLVIII Panzer tried again, this time with the experienced 7th Panzer in place of the green 25th. General von Manteuffel, commanding Rommel's old division, had this to say:

On 18 November, I tried the entire day to penetrate the Zithomir, but could not find any weakness in the enemy's defensive system. I tried to come around the city from the south. It didn't succeed – crossing the Tetrev into Zithomir was only possible with riflemen because the bridge was destroyed. With a different Kampfgruppe of the division I tried a similar attempt from the east and then in the evening from the northeast. There was a weak spot where our forces could break through. We also had to establish security from the east because our reconnaissance reported enemy forces on the Kiev–Zithomir highway, that our security elements had stopped. About an hour before dark we receive a radio call: 'All stations, Manteuffel to Schultz as soon as possible!': That was discomforting and I feared that this fact indicated some disaster because just two hours earlier I had spoken to Schulz in his command post. When I met Lieutenant

Colonel Schulz he told me that a local advance in the direction of the
city had overwhelmed a drunken antitank gun crew. (We later found
many empty champagne and cognac bottles there.) This signaled to
me that we should attack as soon as it became dark. I sent an 'All
stations' message that everyone should attack the city and follow
Schulz and me. Further, I said on the radio, 'The Christmas gifts are
in Zithomir!' We, in other words, Lt. Col. Schultz with six panzers,
me in my APC and a panzer grenadier battalion of about 100 men,
pushed ahead, meter by meter, into the city ... We began at 1700 hours
and by 0300 the next day (19 November), we had broken the Red
Army resistance and had begun to clear the houses of its men.[70]

The Leibstandarte went on to capture Bruislov on the 23rd. To the north,
after a seesaw battle the LIX Corps took Korosten on the next day, which
reopened the rail connection to Army Group Center. In spite of unseasonably
warm weather and rain, everywhere Raus' men were successful in pushing
the Soviets back toward Kiev. Vatutin assumed a defensive posture while the
Germans figuratively beat themselves up fighting both the Red Army and
the mud.[71]

In early December, as freezing weather returned, von Manstein may have
even believed that Fourth Panzer could recapture Kiev. Again XLVIII Panzer
with nearly 200 panzers would be the main assault force against the 60th Army
on Vatutin's right. After achieving total surprise, it advanced from north of
Zithomir on 6–10 December, in the process creating a 25km penetration and
eliminating five Soviet bridgeheads over the Tetrev. The numerous Panthers
present put on an impressive show, as did the IL-2 Sturmoviks (nicknamed
'the butcher' by the Germans). In this operation the 18th Artillery Division, a
replica of similar Soviet organizations (9 artillery and 1 infantry battalion, with
60 light guns and 40 medium guns and 24 Sturmgeschütze) provided valuable
support. The XLVIII Panzer attacked again from the 19th to the 21st but with
much less success. At that point, Raus ordered his men to take up a defensive
posture. Between 8–28 November, Fourth Panzer had killed an estimated
20,000 frontovicki and captured another 5,000, while destroying 603 tanks and
1,305 guns. From 6–13 December it killed a further 11,000 and sent another
4,000 POWs to the rear, while destroying 254 tanks and nearly 900 guns. These
figures are not staggering like those from Barbarossa, yet they demonstrate
the Ostheer's continued ability to cause damage when ever it could create a
convergence of a healthy panzer corps set up against a Soviet force that had
reached its culminating point. But while the XLVIII Panzer appeared to be
having its way blunting Vatutin's spear tip, Stavka was creating a new striking

force with the objective of crushing the panzer army and indeed, the Germans' entire southern defensive structure. On Christmas Day 1943, the Soviets launched a new offensive with forces they had been assembling for weeks, thus initiating what they call the third, and last, period of the war.[72]

Vatutin made his opening move the day before, moving against Zithomir, the principal Ukrainian city west of Kiev. Instead of heading due west in the most direct route to Poland and Germany, the 1st Guards and 3rd Tank Armies veered south toward another rail junction, Kazatin, and the site of von Manstein's headquarters, Vinnitsa. The blow fell squarely on the XXIV Panzer (8th and 19th Panzer Divisions). These transportation nodes, plus Zhmerinka, on the main lines of communication for both Army Group South and A, had to be held if Hitler's southern front was to remain viable. Von Manstein told the OKH that without serious reinforcement (five or six divisions), Fourth Panzer could not survive. Since these reinforcements could only come from a withdrawal somewhere else in the army group's lines, OKH replied that there was little chance such a move could be made; in other words, he would have to fight on the cheap, with what he had. By the offensive's second day Vatutin began to reinforce the original southward thrust with 40th Army and also push west toward Korosten with the 3rd Guards Tank, 1st Guards, 13th and 60th Armies. This time XLVIII Panzer did not have the strength to launch a meaningful counterattack, but could only plug holes. The twenty-five Tigers of Leibstandarte and ten from Das Reich could only do so much. On the 30th, the Germans, including the 18th Artillery Division, lost Kazatin and a huge amount of logistical assets to marauding tanks. And 24 hours later, on the last day of the year, Zithomir changed hands for the last time in the war. Vatutin threw 47 rifle divisions and 9 tank and mechanized corps at Raus' 14 infantry, 1 motorized, 8 panzer and 1 artillery divisions. However, for von Manstein to strengthen his left, or possibly even counterattack there, he would have to retreat elsewhere to create the necessary surplus of forces. This caused an explosion at Führer headquarters where Hitler railed against the field marshal. He insisted that the VII and XLII Corps maintain their hold on the Dnepr, meaning that Fourth Panzer stretched back west nearly 200km, before turning sharply northwest the same distance to Novgorod-Volynsky.[73]

Fortunately for Raus, Vatutin did not push too hard against LIX Corps, which had fallen back into pre-war Poland by the beginning of 1944. The Fourth Panzer's large central force (XXIV and XLVIII Panzer plus XIII Corps) held the Berdichev–Vinnitsa Line with twelve divisions. XLVIII Panzer, since New Year's Day under Lieutenant General Nikolas von Vormann, shifted northwest of Berdichev in order to make an effort to reach out to LIX Corps, while also preventing Vatutin from coming in behind the panzer army. This mission devolved onto XIII Corps, now the main obstacle to the Soviets simply moving due west through the area around Rovno, Kovel and Lutsk, towns from the Barbarossatag battles thirty months earlier. With the help of XLVIII Panzer the Germans held Dubno, but could not appreciably narrow the 50km gap to LIX Corps. At the same time, III Panzer Corps, on temporary loan from Eighth Army, had come to Vinnitsa to shore up XLVI Panzer, another temporary expedient. By the second half of January, three weeks of constant offensive operations has taken its toll on Vatutin's 1st Ukrainian Front at the same time Raus concentrated the few reinforcements von Manstein could spare. Soviet tank formations made general progress along most of the 500km front, notably toward Uman, but achieved no crippling penetration or encirclement against Fourth Panzer. Strategically Stalin was concerned with his far northern and southern flanks, and operationally, Zhukov (coordinating efforts of 1st and 2nd Ukrainian Fronts) had to deal with the protrusion between those two elements: what became the Korsun Pocket (see p. 51).[74] For most of February, the panzer army had a much-needed break between two storms.

Through late February, the main Soviet movement in the Fourth Panzer sector had been in the direction of Sheptovka, possibly with an end goal of L'vov. As von Manstein's staff correctly surmised, Stavka planned for the heavily reinforced 1st Ukrainian Front to attack his north, right on the seam between Fourth and First Panzer Armies through Proskurov and into the Carpathians. Zhukov, now commanding the front, moved on 4 March, both along the boundary and in the Lutsk–Dubno area. Within two days the space between the two panzer armies had grown to over 130km as Zhukov pushed his commanders to advance even at night. All Raus had to counter with and keep the rail line open were remnants of XLVIII Panzer and two inexperienced divisions rushed in from Germany. Fighting raged around Ternopol for days with 7th Panzer (no operational AFVs) and Leibstandarte putting up a credible defense against vastly superior numbers. First Panzer also stiffened, and by the second week of March, Zhukov's efforts had been frustrated. He therefore shifted his main effort north, the 13th Army taking both Dubno and Lutsk on the 16th and later investing Kovel. To this last-named town von Manstein dispatched the XXXII Corps (131st Infantry and SS Viking, the latter very weak and trying to recover from the Korsun pocket), although chances were slim for both of these depleted formations to have any dramatic effect. After a week of preparation, Zhukov was ready to try again at Ternopol, attacking on the 21st with 200 tanks of the 1st and 4th Tank Armies. Two days later the two panzer divisions plus the 68th Infantry were falling back in tiny, uncoordinated packets. Ternopol of course was garrisoned in accordance with Führer Order 11, which codified the concept of 'fortified places'. It was at this point that Raus (in particular, the briefly assigned II SS Panzer Corps) assisted First Panzer Army in escaping its trap near Kamenets-Podolsky (see p. 54). Likewise, Fourth Panzer's right flank defensive positions provided a safe haven for Hube's retreating masses.[75]

The end of March also meant the end of von Manstein's tenure and the arrival of Model to command the new Army Group North Ukraine. These moves had no bearing on Zhukov, who kept advancing into early April. After taking Dubno he pushed down the rail line to L'vov (Army Group headquarters), eventually hitting the small town of Brody, designated by Hitler as another Fester Platz. A tug-of-war battle developed, and Raus recalled one counterattack to break the siege:

> They did succeed in encircling the town on several occasions, but the traps were broken each time by provisional Kampfgruppe Friebe made up of one battalion of PzKw VI Tigers and one of PzKw V Panthers. This KG, augmented by a Nebelwerfer Brigade equipped with 900[!] late-model launchers, struck the enemy while he was still in his assembly areas preparing for the final all-out attack. This mass concentration of firepower resulted in the creation of a mass grave. As far as the eye could see, men, guns, smoldering stumps of trees and clumps of earth lay in ghastly confusion. The margin of the forest had vanished down to the roots.[76]

Colonel General Hans Valentin Hube

Hube was born in Silesia in 1890, and joined the Imperial Army's Infantry Regiment 26 in 1909. Two months into the First World War he received severe wounds, causing his left arm to be amputated. Later, he also spent one year convalescing in a hospital after being gassed in April 1918. Retained by the Reichsheer despite his wounds, during the interwar period he instructed at the Infantry Schools in Dresden and Doberitz and authored works on infantry tactics. In 1939–40, Hube commanded Infantry Regiment 3, and on 1 June 1940 took over the 16th Infantry Division from Gotthard Heinrici. Throughout the second half of 1940 and early 1941, Hube oversaw the conversion of his outfit into the 16th Panzer Division.

During Barbarossa, Hube led the 16th through the Dubno and Stalin Line battles, earning the Knight's Cross in early July. The division participated in the fighting for Uman, Nikopol and the Kiev Pocket, where it spearheaded von Kleist's panzer group in linking up with Guderian at Lockvitsa. Hube then spun around to the south, taking part in the Sea of Azov encirclement battle in

October, and reached the Don River the following month. During Operation Blau, his 16th Panzer again led the way, being the first German outfit to reach the Volga River, in this case north of Stalingrad. On 15 September 1942, Sixth Army commander Paulus placed Hube in charge of XIV Panzer Corps. During the Battle of the Stalingrad, Hube flew in and out of city numerous times, reported directly to Hitler to describe conditions inside the pocket and finally had to be ordered to leave his beleaguered comrades. During the last few weeks of that battle he helped lead the Luftwaffe resupply effort.

Hube was in command in Sicily during the summer of 1943, organized the Etna Line defenses and managed the evacuation of German forces from that island to the Italian mainland, earning praise even from Churchill. Back on the Eastern Front, Hitler wanted new leadership for the First Panzer Army, and put Hube in command on 29 October. By March 1944, First Panzer was cut off behind Soviet lines. Initially Hube refused to withdraw, and relented only when ordered by von Manstein. He created the classic 'wandering pocket', and in April regained German positions, although at a cost of half his men and most of his equipment. Hitler flew the general to Berchtesgaden to promote him and award the Diamonds to his Knight's Cross. On the following day, taking off from Salzburg, his He-111 crashed into a mountainside, killing Hube and all aboard.

Hube's nickname throughout the German Army was der Mensch (the Man). Hitler admired his 'old warhorse', and Hube impressed his men with his powerful build and black-gloved prosthetic hand. He inspired confidence with his unflappability, taking a daily nap in the middle of battle and eating regular meals regardless of the combat situation. Some subordinates criticized him, however, for falling too easily under Hitler's mesmerizing spell, the infamous 'sun-ray cure'.

A similar struggle centered on Ternopol, the other 'fortified place' in Raus' area of responsibility. The SS Panzer Division Hohenstaufen, detached from II SS Panzer Corps, attempted a relief attack starting on 11 April but only made modest progress. On the 14th, Model replaced the enthusiastic but un-professional SS officers commanding the panzers with more experienced Army officers. In 24 hours this group advanced close to the city but could not break in. The city fell on the 16th. That spring, both sides were concerned with strategic developments: the fates of Hungary and Romania and the upcoming invasion of western Europe. Also, Stavka cast and recast plans for its series of summer offensives, the cornerstone of which was the destruction of the Army Group Center bulge. Fourth Panzer, shifted north by Model to cover the Chelm–Lubin axis in southern Poland, braced for the next onslaught. Surprisingly, given Hitler's insistence on holding every square meter of ground, he allowed

Harpe (who assumed command on 18 May) to give up Brody, Kovel and Torchin with hardly a whimper. Straightening the panzer army line eliminated costly to defend salients and freed up units for both defense and counter-attack.[77]

Koniev, the new 1st Ukrainian Front commander, launched his offensive a day ahead of schedule on 13 July with 4 armies, 3 guards (relatively better resourced and considered 'all arms') armies, 3 tank armies, 2 cavalry corps and 2 air armies following a 170,000-round artillery barrage. Their first target was the 291st Infantry Division on the far right of Harpe's line, again on the boundary with First Panzer. Koniev's 13th Army had more success the next day as two other armies joined in to pound the panzer army to the south. A counter-attack south by the XLVI Panzer Corps (16th and 17th Panzer Divisions) ran afoul of T-34s and the Red Army Air Force. Model pulled both back to the Prinz Eugen Line, but with Koniev on their heels these new positions did not hold out long. The 1st Guards Tank Army crossed the Bug at Krystynopol on the 18th, on the same day the newly organized 1st Belorussian Front (Rokossovsky) attacked along the road to Chelm. The 8th Guards Army forced the Bug on the 21st, causing Harpe to withdraw the entire Fourth Panzer behind the river. His 20 operational panzers and 154 assault guns were completely outmatched. On 22 July, the Soviets took Chelm in the morning and Lubin in the evening; when Hitler designated the latter a Fester Platz, he basically condemned its 900-man garrison. A last-ditch rescue effort by 17th Panzer came up short when the division ran out of fuel and had to destroy its AFVs in place. The Germans clearly saw that the 2nd Tank Army was exploiting into central Poland. Harpe told Model that if he were to save his panzer army it would have to withdraw to the Vistula–San River Line as soon as possible. Days later, the Fourth Panzer represented a German island in Poland surrounded on three sides by the Red Army, there were nearly 100km between it and its neighbors to the north and south. By the 28th, Harpe reached the Vistula and managed to beat back Soviet attempts to cross to the west bank. Fourth Panzer held near Sandomeriez but the 1st Tank and 13th Armies created a bridgehead on either side of Baranow. At the beginning of August, counterattacks by Fourth Panzer and its new neighbor to the south, Seventeenth Army, failed to slow significantly Koniev. Then, almost inexplicably, the one infantry and three tank armies crowded into Baranow became lethargic.[78]

Throughout the remainder of 1944, the central theater's front-line trace did not change much. While the Polish Home Army first rose up and then perished and while Himmler's extermination camps murdered millions, Stavka directed its attention elsewhere. It seems that in the center, the offensive operations of June and July had exhausted the Red Army; most activity that autumn and early winter took place in the Baltic and Balkan regions. However, Stalin knew the war would have to be won on the central front and so ordered his commanders to continue with a New Year's offensive along the length of the Polish front. Fourth Panzer Army held the middle Vistula, and had successfully contained the Baranow bridgehead. Its primary mission was to protect Krakow and the upper Silesian industrial area, still working full-blast in place of the bombed out Ruhr. For this General of Panzer Troops Fritz-Hubert Graeser (commander since September) had 7 infantry divisions, 96 guns, 474 AFVs spread across 190km of front. The Soviets created another massive attack force: compared to the Fourth Panzer, 1st Ukrainian forces outnumbered the Germans between 9–10:1 in the key categories of infantry, armor and artillery. Vatutin's initial objective was Radomsko, 150km northwest, from which he would then turn north and south to assist his neighboring fronts destroy German formations attempting to block their way. The 1st Ukrainian's intermediate goal would be the same Breslau that Graeser had to defend and then it was on to Berlin.[79]

The XLVIII Panzer Corps (with no panzer divisions) had the misfortune of occupying the ground over which Vatutin planned to attack. At 0300 hours on 12 January, the Red artillery began a 3-hour barrage by approximately 300 guns per km. The Germans called this 70,000 shell-per-hour fire raid a 'Hurricane'. Following penal battalions clearing the way, Soviet infantry created a penetration 6–8km deep when Vatutin committed his tanks. By the end of the day, the three German divisions ceased to exist, a gap 20km deep and 35km wide had been created and the road was open for the 3rd Guards and 4th Tank Armies and 52nd Army. The Soviets reached the Nida River on the 13th, and Army Group A sent what was left of its reserve, XIV Panzer (16th and 17th Panzer Divisions, approximately 200 panzers under Nehring), to Kielce to try and stop them. Vatutin's men took Kielce on 15 January, cutting the Warsaw–Krakow rail line. The XXIV Panzer tried to keep a corridor westward for the XLII Corps to escape through. Completely lacking mobility, Graeser's Landsers were cut to pieces in the open countryside. Orders to halt Vatutin at Czestochowa were useless. Graeser's two forlorn corps made up a 'wandering pocket' that drifted towards Germany, hounded every meter of the way by the Soviets. By the 21st, what was left of Fourth Panzer reached a bridgehead over the Warte being held open by Grossdeutschland (now a panzer corps of its own). A week later the panzer army received its next mission: hold Breslau. This Graeser did, holding a small outpost there as Vatutin crossed the Oder River on either side of the Silesian capital.[80]

Fourth Panzer had two bridgeheads east of the Oder, at Breslau and Glogau (army headquarters), while Vatutin had many on the west bank. By 0600 hours on 8 February, the 1st Ukrainian Front was ready to move again. Some Soviet units advanced 60km by nightfall. Within days, instead of two bridgeheads, Graeser had two surrounded 'fortresses' at Breslau (116,000 civilians and 35,000 military) and Glogau (7,800 and 4,100). A turn south by 3rd Guards Tank Army briefly left the flank of 4th Tank Army unguarded, a situation exploited by the Brandenburger and 20th Panzergrenadier Divisions' brief counterthrust near Sagan on the Bober on 14–15 February. Graeser's six weak divisions fell back to the Neisse. When 1st Ukrainian pulled up to the river on the 21st, Vatutin called a halt. Back in Breslau, ensconced behind First World War fortifications (medieval ones had been destroyed by Napoleon) parts of five divisions manned a 120km-long defensive line, and held on in the face of numerous Soviet attempts to reduce the fortress. For over three months, until VE Day, this collection of Army, Navy, SS, Police, Volksturm and Hitler Youth held out. However, this thorn in Vatutin's side did not stop the 1st Ukrainian Front from exceeding Stavka's expectations for it. As attrited were the Germans after five and a half years of war, the Red Army was also in bad shape. While fighting raged in Hungary during the late winter and early spring, Soviet forces along the Oder River prepared for the final lunge on the core of Hitler's Reich. Koniev would attack through three Neisse bridgeheads at Forst, Bad Muskau and Görlitz into Saxony for an anticipated junction with the Americans and possibly, a supporting attack into Berlin's southern defenses.[81]

The last crumbs of the once-proud Fourth Panzer Army occupied relatively strong (for April 1945) positions in three successive lines: 1. The Neisse itself; 2. The Peitz–Weisswasser complex, which included numerous open-pit coal mines; and 3. The upper Spree River. Koniev had no established bridgeheads over the Neisse so would have to create them on day one. That day came on 16 April, when over 7,700 guns opened fire at 0615 hours along a 400km front. By evening the Soviets had numerous crossing sites up and down the river, many up to 10km deep. What was left of the Luftwaffe went up against the Red Army Air Force, and promptly went down in glorious defeat. Graeser counterattacked with what panzer reserves he did possess, 20th Panzer (including twenty-five Panthers), the new Bohemia Panzergrenadier Division and even a force of captured T-34s, under LVII Panzer Corps. Hitler held out hope that 1st Ukrainian was running out of steam. Knowing that Fourth Panzer had no reserves left, Koniev threw in his exploitation force of two tank armies. With Stalin urging them on, Koniev's men took terrible casualties. Between Fourth Panzer's defensive lines swirling battles took place as Koniev shifted his main effort from 4th Guards Tank to 3rd Guards Tank Armies (combined strength of 963 AFVs). The Germans falsely assumed the enemy would need existing Spree bridges, not knowing they had saved their heavy bridging equipment for just that purpose. Telling them to avoid well-defended urban areas such as at Cottbus, held by V Corps, soon Koniev's men crossed the Spree at Spremburg and Bautzen. Fighting was particularly intense on the Dresden axis near the southern bridgeheads beyond Gorlitz, where the Germans counterattacked with some success. 'Fortress Dresden', already thrashed by the Royal Air Force, fell without a fight on 24 April. By the third week of April, all major Fourth Panzer points of resistance had been overcome as Soviet and American soldiers met on the 25th. On that same date, Graeser's command had been broken into two, widely separated pieces: an encirclement including elements of Ninth Army northwest of Cottbus and another near the Saxon capital. A small counterattack near Dresden by 20th Panzer and SS Frundsberg (and even the Luftwaffe's Herman Göring Panzer Division) only delayed the inevitable.[82] By early May, all eyes were on Berlin and other sectors, such as that occupied by Fourth Panzer Army no longer counted for much. Fourth Panzer Army, perhaps the most storied of the four, a veteran of Barbarossa, Blau, Stalingrad, Backhand Blow, Citadel, the long retreat and on the fringe of the Battle of Berlin, fizzled out in the rolling countryside of Saxony.

Chapter 6
Conclusions

The fates of the four panzer armies described here largely mirrored that of the German Reich. In the early stages of the war, fighting in France, Yugoslavia and during Operation Barbarossa, they carried all before them. Neither terrain, weather, sanguine German logistical planning nor the enemy could seriously slow the panzer armies. These slashing formations, their clever commanders and dedicated Panzertruppen seemingly could not be stopped. The panzer armies made things happen, they created undreamed of opportunities for the German high command by laying Dunkirk (1940), Leningrad, Moscow, Rostov (1941), Stalingrad and the Caucasus Mountains (1942) at Hitler's feet.[1] However, with its small size and paucity of strategic thinkers, Germany could not exploit the openings that these moves presented. As Hitler surrendered the strategic initiative, the panzer armies became just like any other army in the German arsenal.

This trend began around Moscow, especially in regards to the Second and Third Panzer Armies. In June of 1941, Germany attacked all along the massive Soviet frontier, but it could only sustain that level of activity for five months. The First and Fourth Panzer Armies enjoyed a renaissance of operational significance in 1942. But by this stage in the war, Germany could only impose its will over the southern half of the front. By 1943, only Fourth Panzer enjoyed anything close to the freedom of maneuver that panzer armies had come to expect, and then in a sector covering a mere few hundred square kilometers and for one short week. From mid-July of that year until VE Day, all four panzer armies would reel back like an exhausted boxer, retreating into his corner under a hail of blows from his opponent who could smell victory at any moment. The Second Panzer Army disappeared to near obscurity in the Balkans. In 1944, the First (March–April) and Third (June–July) were fortunate to avoid total destruction. Ironically, the panzer army closest to the central theater during the last few months of the war, the Fourth, survived largely intact.

By the middle stages of Operation Blau, infantry armies, the Sixth in particular, were commanded by panzer generals (Paulus in this case) and often had as many panzer divisions under command as did the panzer armies themselves. The same happened during Operation Citadel, when an infantry army, the Ninth (although commanded by a panzer general, Model), had the second most-powerful panzer force in the Ostheer. Germany never regained the strategic, or even operational, initiative for the remainder of the Nazi-Soviet War.[2] For the last two years of the Second World War, panzers hardly operated together in units larger than a panzer corps, and on only a handful of occasions, with two panzer corps fighting together. By that stage of the war, the Red Army's tank and 'all arms' guards armies behaved more like the panzer armies of yore, than even the actual panzer armies did at the end of the war.

The reasons for this juxtaposition are not material; it is common knowledge that the Panzerwaffe fought outnumbered yet prevailed with inferior weapons and numbers starting in May 1940. In the later stages of the war, once Germany finally adopted the semblance of a total-war economy, its industry produced prodigious numbers of AFVs (and fighter aircraft and flak guns and ...) which allowed the Wehrmacht to deploy a massive armored arsenal. Unfortunately for them, numbers of panzers did not equal the campaign-winning concentration that carried Germany to victory after victory until Stalingrad. Panzers and assault guns were spread over the continent of Europe in huge amounts, fighting on every front. But they were employed in small, tactical groups like divisions and brigades and, as often as not, danced to the tune of the Allies, in the case of this book, the Red Army.

The temptation to break up the panzer armies and use them as tactical weapons in pin-prick operations had always been there. Within weeks of Barbarossatag, Army Group South received pressure to divide First Panzer, but von Rundstedt steadfastly refused. By late summer, Third Panzer was being split into corps and the decline of the panzer armies began down the slippery slope. During Operation Blau, there were two panzer armies worthy of the name, during Citadel one, and from August 1943 onwards, none. By Stalin's 1941 general winter offensive, reacting to this and that crisis, Hitler, the OKW and OKH, army group commanders and others had seemingly unlearned the lessons about the power of concentrated armor. Of course at that moment, they no longer possessed a mass of panzers, but that fact does not diminish my argument. With the Red Army killing the Ostheer via both their own application of concentration and the death by a thousand cuts techniques, panzer formations became just so many bandages. In other words, like the French and Soviets earlier in the war, the Germans succumbed to treating the immediate symptoms, **not** the root problems themselves.

The fact that the panzers armies spent the bulk of the war on the defensive and reacting to Soviet moves should in no way detract from their earlier accomplishments. Their feats during 1941–42 will remain legendary in the annals of military history. In a well-known anecdote, during a 1944 visit to the Soviet Union, French General Charles De Gaulle toured the Stalingrad battlefield. Initially his comments about 'magnificent soldiers' were wishfully misinterpreted by his hosts as praise for the victors. Upon further clarification, it was explained that he was referring to the fact that a medium-sized country like Germany had made it so far against such improbable odds. Credit for whatever successes Germany did enjoy on the battlefields of Europe goes both to the performances and endurance of the long-suffering Landsers and to the headline-grabbing panzers.

Appendix I

Panzer Army Commanders

Rank[1]	Name	Date Took Command	Highest Award[2]	Birth Year[3]	Remarks
First Panzer Army					
Colonel General	Kleist, Ewald von	3 May 1940	RK+EL+Sch	1881	Captured by Western Allies, tried by Yugoslavs, died in Soviet captivity
General of Cavalry	Mackensen, Eberhard von	November 1942	RK+EL	1889	
General of Panzer Troops	Hube, Hans Valentin	29 October 1943	RK+EL+Sch+Br	1890	Died in aircrash day after promotion and receiving Diamonds to Knights Cross
Colonel General	Raus, Erhard	1 May 1944	RK+EL+Sch	1889	Austrian
Colonel General	Heinrici, Gotthard	15 August 1944	RK+EL+Sch	1886	
General of Panzer Troops	Nehring, Walther	20 March 1945	RK+EL+Sch	1892	
Second Panzer					
Colonel General	Guderian, Heinz	16 November 1940	RK+EL	1888	
Colonel General	Schmidt, Rudolf	26 December 1941	RK+EL	1886	
Colonel General	Model, Walter	15 July 1943	RK+EL+Sch+Br	1891	
General of Infantry	Rendulic, Dr Lothar	15 August 1943	RK+EL+Sch	1887	Austrian lawyer
General of Infantry	Boehme, Franz	25 June 1944	RK	1885	Austrian, committed suicide in 1947 during Nuremberg trial
General of Artillery	Angelis, Max de	18 July 1944	RK+EL	1889	Austrian
Third Panzer					
Colonel General	Hoth, Hermann	16 November 1940	RK+EL+Sch	1885	
General of Panzer Troops	Reinhardt, Georg-Hans	8 October 1941	RK+EL+Sch	1887	
Colonel General	Raus, Erhard	16 August 1944	RK+EL+Sch	1889	
General of Panzer Troops	Manteuffel, Hasso von	10 March 1945	RK+EL+Sch+Br	1897	Previously commanded Seventh Panzer Army in West

Rank[1]	Name	Date Took Command	Highest Award[2]	Birth Year[3]	Remarks
Fourth Panzer					
Colonel General	Hoepner, Erich	17 February 1941	RK	1886	Executed after July 1944 Attentat
Colonel General	Ruoff, Richard	8 January 1942	RK	1883	
Colonel General	Hoth, Hermann	31 May 1942	RK+EL+Sch	1885	
General of Panzer Troops	Raus, Erhard	15 November 1943	RK+EL+Sch	1889	
Colonel General	Harpe, Josef	1 May 1944	RK+EL+Sch	1887	Previously commanded Fifth Panzer Army in West
General of Panzer Troops	Balck, Hermann	28 June 1944	RK+EL+Sch+Br	1893	
General of Panzer Troops	Graeser, Fritz Hubert	30 September 1944	RK+EL	1888	

Basic information: Wolf Keilig, *Das Deutsche Heer, 1939–1945*, Podzun Verlag, 1956
1. Rank when assumed command.
2. Awards: RK=Knights Cross; EL=Oak Leaves; Sch=Swords; Br=Diamonds.
3. Birth year information provided to show relative ages.

Appendix II

Panzer Army Orders of Battle

Abbreviations

Bde — Brigade	Gren — Grenadier	Korueck — Rear Area HQs	Rom — Romanian
Cav — Cavalry	Grp — Group	LAH — Leibstandarte Adolf Hitler	SS — Schutz Staffel
Div — Division	Ho — Hohenstauffen	Lw — Luftwaffe	Ski — Ski mounted troops
DR — Das Reich	Hung — Hungarian	Mar — Marine	T — Totenkopf
Est — Estonia	HQs — Headquarters	Mot — Motorized	Tng — Training
Fest — Festung	HW — Horst Wessel	Mtn — Mountain	V — Viking
Fld — Field	Inf — Infantry	Ned — Nederland	VG — Volksgrenadier
Fr — Frundsberg	Ital — Italian	PE — Prinz Eugen	Vol — Volunteer
Gal — Galician	IR — Infantry Regiment	Pz — Panzer	
GD — Grossdeutschland	Jg — Jaeger	R — Reich	

First Panzer Army

22 June 1941[1]	XIV Pz Corps	SS Mot Div V	16 Pz Div	9 Pz Div	
	III Pz Corps	14 Pz Div	298 Inf Div	44 Inf Div	
	XIX Corps	299 Inf Div	111 Inf Div		
	XLVIII Pz Corps	11 Pz Div	75 Inf Div	57 Inf Div	13 Pz Div
	Reserve	16 Mot Div	25 Mot Div	SS Mot Bde LAH	
1 July 1941	XIV Pz Corps	SS Mot Div V	9 Pz Div	13 Pz Div	
	III Pz Corps	25 Mot Div	14 Pz Div	11 Pz Div	
	XLVIII Pz Corps	16 Mot Div	16 Pz Div		
	Reserve	SS Mot Div LAH			
7 August 1941	III Pz Corps	57 Inf Div	60 Mot Div	SS Mot Div V	
	XIV Pz Corps	25 Mot Div	9 Pz Div	16 Pz Div	14 Pz Div
	XLVIII Pz Corps	16 Mot Div	11 Pz Div	SS Mot Div LAH	
	XLIV Corps	297 Inf Div	24 Inf Div		
3 September 1941	Italian Fast Corps	Ital 52 Torino	Ital 3 Celere	Ital 9 Pasubio	
	Hungarian Fast Corps	1 Hung Mot Bde	2 Hung Mot Bde	1 Hung Cav Div	
	XLVIII Pz Corps	16 Pz Div	SS Mot Div V	60 Mot Div	
	III Pz Corps	198 Inf Div	25 Mot Div	13 Pz Div	
	XIV Pz Corps	9 Pz Div	16 Mot Div	14 Pz Div	

Date	Corps	Col 1	Col 2	Col 3	Col 4	Col 5
2 October 1941	**Italian Fast Corps** **III Pz Corps** **XIV Pz Corps** **Reserve**	Ital 52 Torino Slovak Fast Div 16 Pz Div 60 Mot Div	Ital 3 Celere SS Mot Div V 14 Pz Div 198 Inf Div	Ital 9 Pasubio 13 Pz Div		
4 November 1941	**Italian Fast Corps** **XLIX Mtn Corps** **XIV Pz Corps** **III Pz Corps** **Reserve**	Ital 52 Torino 198 Inf Div 16 Pz Div SS Mot Div LAH 60 Mot Div	Ital 3 Celere 4 Mtn Div 14 Pz Div 13 Pz Div	Ital 9 Pasubio 1 Mtn Div SS Mot Div V		
4 December 1941	**Italian Fast Corps** **XLIX Mtn Corps** **XIV Pz Corps** **III Pz Corps** **Reserve**	Ital 52 Torino 198 Inf Div Slovak Fast Div 13 Pz Div 125 Inf Div	Ital 3 Celere 4 Mtn Div SS Mot Div V 14 Pz Div 100 Lt Div	Ital 9 Pasubio 1 Mtn Div 16 Pz Div 60 Mot Div	SS Mot Div LAH	
1 January 1942	**Italian Fast Corps** **XLIX Mtn Corps** **XIV Pz Corps** **III Pz Corps** **Reserve**	Ital 52 Torino 198 Inf Div Slovak Fast Div 125 Inf Div XI Corps HQs	Ital 9 Pasubio 4 Mtn Div SS Mot Div V 13 Pz Div 73 Inf Div	1 Mtn Div 100 Lt Div 14 Pz Div Rom 6 Cav Bde	Ital 3 Celere 16 Pz Div 60 Mot Div Rom 5 Cav Bde	SS Mot Div LAH
6 February 1942	**Italian Fast Corps** **XLIX Mtn Corps** **XIV Pz Corps** **Reserve**	Ital 52 Torino 198 Inf Div Slovak Fast Div 73 Inf Div Rom 5 Cav Bde	Ital 9 Pasubio 4 Mtn Div SS Mot Div V 60 Mot Div	1 Mtn Div 16 Pz Div SS Mot Div LAH	Ital 3 Celere 125 Inf Div	13 Pz Div
10 March 1942	**Italian Fast Corps** **XLIX Mtn Corps** **XIV Pz Corps** **Reserve**	Ital 52 Torino 198 Inf Div Slovak Fast Div 73 Inf Div Rom 5 Cav Bde	Ital 9 Pasubio 4 Mtn Div SS Mot Div V SS Mot Div LAH Rom 6 Cav Bde	Ital 3 Celere 16 Pz Div HQs Rom Cav Corps	125 Inf Div	13 Pz Div
5 April 1942	**Italian Fast Corps** **XLIX Mtn Corps** **XIV Pz Corps** **Reserve**	Ital 52 Torino 198 Inf Div Slovak Fast Div 73 Inf Div Rom 5 Cav Bde	Ital 9 Pasubio 4 Mtn Div SS Mot Div V SS Mot Div LAH Rom 6 Cav Bde	Ital 3 Celere 16 Pz Div HQs Rom Cav Corps	125 Inf Div	13 Pz Div
11 May 1942	**Italian Fast Corps** **XLIX Mtn Corps** **XIV Pz Corps** **Reserve**	Ital 52 Torino 198 Inf Div Slovak Fast Div SS Mot Div LAH Rom 5 Cav Bde	Ital 9 Pasubio 4 Mtn Div SS Mot Div V Rom 6 Cav Bde	Ital 3 Celere 125 Inf Div HQs Rom Cav Corps	13 Pz Div	73 Inf Div

Date	Corps	Divisions
8 June 1942	XI Corps (Strecker)	454 Sec Div, 1 Mtn Div, 1 Rom Div
	VI Rom Corps	2 Rom Div, 20 Rom Div, 4 Rom Div
	XLIX Mtn Corps	384 Inf Div, 97 Jg Div, 101 Jg Div, 257 Inf Div, Rom 4 Div
	Reserve	68 Inf Div, 100 Lt Div
24 June 1942[2]	XLIV Corps	257 Inf Div, 101 Jg Div, 97 Jg Div, 68 Inf Div, 71 Inf Div
	XI Corps (Strecker)	1 Mtn Div, 1 Rom Div, 454 Sec Div, Rom VI Corps
	III Pz Corps	14 Pz Div, 16 Pz Div, 22 Pz Div (–), 60 Mot Div
	LI Corps	Rom 20 Div, Rom 2 Div, 62 Inf Div, 44 Inf Div
	Reserve	1 Pz Div, 384 Inf Div, 297 Inf Div
4 July 1942	III Pz Corps	SS Mot Div LAH, 22 Pz Div, 16 Pz Div
	XIV Pz Corps	14 Pz Div, 60 Mot Div
	XI Corps (Strecker)	2 Rom Div, Rom 20 Div
	Rom VI Corps	Rom 1 Div, 97 Jg Div, Rom 4 Div
	XLIV Corps	68 Inf Div, 454 Sec Div, 101 Jg Div, 257 Inf Div
	Reserve	1 Mtn Div
5 August 1942	XL Pz Corps	23 Pz Div, 3 Pz Div
	XLIV Corps	101 Jg Div, 97 Jg Div
	III Pz Corps	13 Pz Div, 16 Mot Div
	LII Corps	370 Inf Div, 111 Inf Div
	LVII Pz Corps	Slovak Fast Div, SS Mot Div V
	Reserve	GD
2 September 1942	LII Corps	370 Inf Div, 111 Inf Div
	XL Pz Corps	13 Pz Div, 23 Pz Div, 3 Pz Div
	III Pz Corps	Rom 2 Mtn Div
8 October 1942	XL Pz Corps	3 Pz Div, SS Mot Div V, 23 Pz Div
	LII Corps	111 Inf Div, 13 Pz Div
	III Pz Corps	370 Inf Div
	Grp Steinbauer	Rom 2 Mtn Div
5 November 1942	XL Pz Corps	3 Pz Div, SS Pz Gren Div V
	LII Corps	111 Inf Div, 13 Pz Div
	III Pz Corps	370 Inf Div, 23 Pz Div, Rom 2 Mtn Div
	Reserve	50 Inf Div
1 December 1942	XL Pz Corps	3 Pz Div, 111 Inf Div, 50 Inf Div, 23 Pz Div
	LII Corps	370 Inf Div, 13 Pz Div, Rom 2 Mtn Div
	III Pz Corps	SS Pz Gren Div V

Date	Corps	Divisions
1 January 1943	XL Pz Corps	3 Pz Div, 111 Inf Div, 50 Inf Div
	LII Corps	370 Inf Div, Rom 2 Mtm Div
	III Pz Corps	13 Pz Div
	Reserve	5 Lw Div
3 February 1943	III Pz Corps	27 Pz Div, 19 Pz Div, 7 Pz Div
	XXX Corps	335 Inf Div
	Reserve	XL Pz Corps HQs, 8 Lw Div
4 March 1943	XL Pz Corps	7 Pz Div, SS Pz Gren Div V, 333 Inf Div, 62 Inf Div
	III Pz Corps	3 Pz Div, 19 Pz Div
	XXX Corps	335 Inf Div, 304 Inf Div
9 April 1943	LVII Pz Corps	17 Pz Div, 15 Inf Div, 38 Inf Div, 46 Inf Div, 257 Inf Div
	XL Pz Corps	7 Pz Div, SS Pz Gren Div V, 3 Pz Div
	XXX Corps	333 Inf Div, 62 Inf Div
	Reserve	III Pz Corps HQs, 19 Pz Div
1 May 1943	LVII Pz Corps	17 Pz Div, 15 Inf Div, 46 Inf Div, 38 Inf Div
	XL Pz Corps	SS Pz Gren Div V, 257 Inf Div, 62 Inf Div
	XXX Corps	387 Inf Div, 333 Inf Div
	Reserve	19 Pz Div, 3 Pz Div
1 June 1943	LVII Pz Corps	17 Pz Div, 198 Inf Div, 15 Inf Div, 62 Inf Div
	XXIV Pz Corps	SS Pz Gren Div V, 3 Pz Div, 19 Pz Div
	XL Pz Corps	257 Inf Div, 46 Inf Div
	XXX Corps	333 Inf Div, 387 Inf Div
7 July 1943	LVII Pz Corps	328 Inf Div, 15 Inf Div, 198 Inf Div, 62 Inf Div
	XL Pz Corps	257 Inf Div, 46 Inf Div, 333 Inf Div
	XXX Corps	387 Inf Div, 38 Inf Div, 62 Inf Div
	Reserve	XXIV Pz Corps HQs, 23 Pz Div, 17 Pz Div
5 August 1943	LVII Pz Corps	328 Inf Div, 15 Inf Div, SS Pz Gren Div V, 17 Pz Div, 387 Inf Div
	XL Pz Corps	257 Inf Div, 46 Inf Div, 62 Inf Div
	XXX Corps	333 Inf Div, 38 Inf Div
5 September 1943	LVII Pz Corps	328 Inf Div, 15 Inf Div, 23 Pz Div, 16 Pz Gren Div, 387 Inf Div
	XL Pz Corps	257 Inf Div, 46 Inf Div, 62 Inf Div
	XXX Corps	333 Inf Div, 38 Inf Div
4 October 1943	LVII Pz Corps	23 Pz Div, 8 SS Cav Div, GD, 306 Inf Div, 62 Inf Div, 38 Inf Div
	LII Corps	293 Inf Div, 161 Inf Div, 355 Inf Div, 328 Inf Div, 294 Inf Div
	XXX Corps	15 Inf Div, 387 Inf Div, 46 Inf Div, 257 Inf Div
	XL Pz Corps	9 Pz Div, 125 Inf Div, 16 Pz Gren Div, 123 Inf Div
	XVII Corps	304 Inf Div, 335 Inf Div, 333 Inf Div

Date	Corps	Divisions				
8 November 1943	LII Corps	SS Pz Div T	17 Pz Div	23 Pz Div	9 Pz Div	306 Inf Div
	LVII Pz Corps	8 SS Cav Div	14 Pz Div	16 Pz Gren Div	62 Inf Div	14 Pz Div
	XXX Corps	355 Inf Div	328 Inf Div	38 Inf Div	GD	294 Inf Div
	XVII Corps	293 Inf Div	387 Inf Div	11 Pz Div	257 Inf Div	
	XIX Corps	15 Inf Div	125 Inf Div	46 Inf Div	333 Inf Div	
	Reserve	304 Inf Div		123 Inf Div		
3 December 1943	LII Corps	384 Inf Div	76 Inf Div	SS Pz Div T	62 Inf Div	328 Inf Div
	LVII Pz Corps	23 Pz Div	355 Inf Div	161 Inf Div	293 Inf Div	17 Inf Div
	XXX Corps	9 Pz Div	GD	16 Pz Gren Div	304 Inf Div	
	XVII Corps	38 Inf Div	15 Inf Div	306 Inf Div	333 Inf Div	
	IV Corps	387 Inf Div	46 Inf Div	257 Inf Div	111 Inf Div	
	XIX Corps	125 Inf Div	123 Inf Div	294 Inf Div		
	Reserve	302 Inf Div, 79 Inf Div, 335 Inf Div, HQs XL Pz Corps	3 Mtn Div	258 Inf Div		
1 January 1944	Assigned to Army Group South					
1 February 1944	XLVI Corps	101 Jg Div	18 Art Div	254 Inf Div	4 Mtn Div	1 Inf Div
	VII Corps	6 Pz Div	75 Inf Div	34 Inf Div	198 Inf Div	
	Reserve	82 Inf Div	16 Pz Div	SS Pz Div LAH		
3 March 1944	LIX Corps	SS Grp Lang	6 Pz Div	SS Pz Div DR	291 Inf Div	96 Inf Div
	XXIV Pz Corps	19 Pz Div	208 Inf Div	20 Pz Gren Div	25 Pz Div	168 Inf Div
	XLVI Corps	371 Inf Div	18 Art Div	254 Inf Div	1 Inf Div	
	Reserve	101 Jg Div	17 Pz Div	1 Pz Div	III Pz Corps HQs	
15 April 1944	II SS Pz Corps	19 Pz Div	16 Pz Div	100 Jg Div	SS Pz Gren Div Fr	96 Inf Div
	XLVI Corps	208 Inf Div	168 Inf Div	75 Inf Div	82 Inf Div	371 Inf Div
	LIX Corps	68 Inf Div	20 Pz Gren Div	25 Pz Div	1 Pz Div	367 Inf Div
	III Pz Corps	7 Inf Div	18 Art Div	6 Pz Div	17 Pz Div	
	Reserve	291 Inf Div, 101 Jg Div, 1 Inf Div, XXIV Pz Corps HQs	SS Pz Div LAH			
15 May 1944	XXIV Pz Corps	100 Jg Div	75 Inf Div	371 Inf Div	208 Inf Div	Hung 20 Inf Div
	LIX Corps	82 Inf Div	254 Inf Div	291 Inf Div	17 Pz Div	20 Pz Gren Div
	XLVI Corps	1 Inf Div	168 Inf Div	367 Inf Div		
	Reserve	III Pz Corps HQs	6 Pz Div	7 Pz Div		

Date	Corps	Divisions
15 June 1944	XLVIII Pz Corps	349 Inf Div, 357 Inf Div, 96 Inf Div, 359 Inf Div, 17 Pz Div
	XXIV Pz Corps	100 Jg Div, 75 Inf Div, 371 Inf Div
	LIX Corps	254 Inf Div, 208 Inf Div, Hung 20 Inf Div
	XLVI Corps	1 Inf Div, 168 Inf Div, 367 Inf Div
	Reserve	III Pz Corps HQs, 1 Pz Div, 7 Pz Div, 20 Pz Gren Div
15 July 1944	XIII Corps	454 Sec Div, 361 Inf Div, 8 Pz Div, 254 Inf Div
	III Pz Corps	1 Pz Div, 75 Inf Div, 371 Inf Div
	XXIV Pz Corps	100 Jg Div, 96 Inf Div, 359 Inf Div
	LXVIII Pz Corps	349 Inf Div, Hung 20 Inf Div
	LIX Corps	208 Inf Div
	Hung First Army	SS Vol Div Gal
	Reserve	20 Pz Gren Div
31 August 1944	XXIV Pz Corps	208 Inf Div, 68 Inf Div, 96 Inf Div, 75 Inf Div
	XI Corps	168 Inf Div, 254 Inf Div
	Hung First Army	Hung 6 Inf Div
16 September 1944	XXIV Pz Corps	357 Inf Div, 208 Inf Div, 1 Pz Div, 75 Inf Div, 68 Inf Div, 8 Pz Div
	XI Corps	96 Inf Div, 254 Inf Div, 168 Inf Div
	Hung First Army	
	Reserve	154 Inf Div
13 October 1944	XXIV Pz Corps	253 Inf Div, 1 Ski Div, 8 Pz Div, 357 Inf Div, 75 Inf Div
	XLIX Mtn Corps	68 Inf Div, 100 Jg Div, 101 Jg Div
	Hung 1 Mtn Bde	168 Inf Div
	Reserve	Hung 1 Mtn Div
5 November 1944	XI Corps	68 Inf Div, 75 Inf Div, 253 Inf Div, 1 Ski Div, 357 Inf Div, 168 Inf Div
	XLIX Mtn Corps	97 Inf Div, 254 Inf Div, 100 Jg Div, 101 Jg Div
	Reserve	154 Inf Div
26 November 1944	XI Corps	253 Inf Div, 1 Ski Div, 168 Inf Div, 75 Inf Div
	XLIX Mtn Corps	97 Jg Div, 254 Inf Div, 100 Jg Div, 101 Jg Div
	Reserve	154 Inf Div
31 December 1944	XI Corps	253 Inf Div, 75 Inf Div, 100 Jg Div
	XLIX Mtn Corps	101 Jg Div, 254 Inf Div, 97 Jg Div, 1 Ski Div
	Hung First Army	Hung 5 Res Div, 2 Hung Res Div
	Reserve	154 Inf Div

19 February 1945

Grp Sieler	168 Inf Div	344 Inf Div	253 Inf Div	544 VG Div	359 Inf Div
LIX Corps	68 Inf Div	75 Inf Div	1 Inf Div	3 Mtn Div	545 VG Div
XI Corps	371 Inf Div	97 Jg Div	4 Mtn Div		
XLIX Mtn Corps	320 VG Div	78 VG Div			
Reserve	154 Inf Div	SS Vol Pz Gren Div HW			

1 March 1945

Grp Silesia	Waff Gren Div SS Est #1	168 Inf Div	97 Jg Div	1 Ski Div	
XI Corps	344 Inf Div	371 Inf Div	253 Inf Div	544 VG Div	
LIX Corps	68 Inf Div	75 Inf Div	320 VG Div		
XLIX Mtn Corps	78 VG Div	4 Mtn Div			
Reserve	154 Inf Div	SS Vol Pz Gren Div HW			

12 April 1945

XXIV Pz Corps	344 Inf Div	254 Inf Div	78 VG Div	10 PzGren Div	68 Inf Div
XI Corps	158 Inf Div	1 Ski Div	97 Jg Div	371 Inf Div	4 Mtn Div
LIX Corps	544 VG Div	16 Pz Div	19 Pz Div	715 Inf Div	320 VG Div
XLIX Mtn Corps	3 Mtn Div	253 Inf Div	304 Inf Div	Hung 16 Inf Div	
Group Bader					
XXIX Corps	76 Inf Div	8 Inf Div	15 Inf Div	153 Inf Div	
Reserve	154 Inf Div	8 Pz Div	75 Inf Div	17 Pz Div	

5 May 1945

XI Corps	Feldhernhalle Pz Gren Brandenburg	715 Inf Div	10 Pz Gren Div		
LIX Corps	254 Inf Div	78 VG Div	304 Inf Div	153 Inf Div	76 Inf Div
LXXII Corps	4 Mtn Div	3 Mtn Div	97 Jg Div	46 VG Div	711 Inf Div
XLIX Mtn Corps	271 VG Div	19 Pz Div	8 Inf Div	320 VG Div	253 Inf Div
XXIV Pz Corps	15 Inf Div	6 Pz Div	544 VG Div		
Reserve	10 Fallschirm Div	8 Pz Div	371 Inf Div		

Except as noted, all data www.bundesarchiv.de/findbuecher/ma/rh21-1/index.htm

1. Horst Boog et al., *Germany and the Second World War*, Vol. IV, *Attack on the Soviet Union*, Clarendon Press, 1998, appendix 2.
2. Hans-Adolf Jacobsen, *Kriegstagebuch: das Oberkommando der Wehrmacht*, Vol. II (2), Bernard & Graefe, 1965, pp. 1372–73.

Note on all OBs: The Germans often arranged their units north to south, hence the seemingly random listing of formations.

Second Panzer Army

22 June 1941[1]

XLVI Pz Corps	IR GD	10 Pz Div	SS R	18 Pz Div	
XLVII Pz Corps	29 Mot Div	167 Inf Div	17 Pz Div		
XII Corps	31 Inf Div	45 Inf Div	34 Inf Div		
XXIV Pz Corps	10 Mot Div	3 Pz Div	4 Pz Div	1 Cav Div	267 Inf Div
Reserve	LIII Corps HQs	293 Inf Div			

Date	Corps	Div 1	Div 2	Div 3	Div 4	Div 5	Div 6	Div 7
1 July 1941	XLVI Pz Corps	IR GD	10 Pz Div	SS R	10 Pz Div	268 Inf Div		
	XLVII Pz Corps	29 Mot Div	17 Pz Div	18 Pz Div				
	XXIV Pz Corps	3 Pz Div	4 Pz Div					
	Reserve	1 Cav Div	10 Mot Div					
7 August 1941	XLVII Pz Corps	18 Pz Div	29 Mot Div	17 Pz Div				
	XLVI Pz Corps	IR GD	SS R	15 Inf Div				
	IX Corps	292 Inf Div	263 Inf Div	137 inf Div				
	VII Corps	197 Inf Div	23 Inf Div	78 Inf Div				
	XXIV Pz Corps	10 Mot Div	3 Pz Div	4 Pz Div				
	Reserve	HQs XX Corps						
3 September 1941	XLVII Pz Corps	29 Mot Div	18 Pz Div	17 Pz Div	3 Pz Div			
	XXIV Pz Corps	IR GD	10 Mot Div	4 Pz Div				
	Reserve	1 Cav Div	SS R					
2 October 1941	XLVII Pz Corps	29 Mot Div	17 Pz Div	18 Pz Div	1 Cav Div			
	XXIV Pz Corps	4 Pz Div	3 Pz Div	10 Mot Div				
	XLVIII Pz Corps	9 Pz Div	25 Mot Div	16 Mot Div				
	XXXV Corps	95 Inf Div	296 Inf Div	293 Inf Div				
	XXXIV Corps	45 Inf Div	134 Inf Div					
4 November 1941	XLIII Corps	131 Inf Div	31 Inf Div	IR GD	17 Pz Div			
	LIII Corps	112 Inf Div	167 Inf Div	25 Mot Div	18 Pz Div			
	XLVII Pz Corps	3 Pz Div	4 Pz Div					
	Reserve	29 Mot Div	10 Mot Div	56 Inf Div				
4 December 1941	XLIII Corps	131 Inf Div	31 Inf Div	IR GD	17 Pz Div			
	XXIV Pz Corps	3 Pz Div	4 Pz Div	167 Inf Div				
	LIII Corps	29 Mot Div	112 Inf Div					
	XLVII Pz Corps	10 Mot Div	18 Pz Div					
	Reserve	25 Mot Div	56 Inf Div					
2 January 1942	XXIV Pz Corps	Lisinger	Eberbach	167 Inf Div	112 Inf Div	56 Inf Div	4 Pz Div	10 Mot Div
	LIII Corps	IR GD	296 Inf Div	18 Pz Div	17 Pz Div			
	XLVII Pz Corps	25 Mot Div	29 Mot Div					
6 February 1942	XXIV Pz Corps	18 Pz Div	208 Inf Div	211 Inf Div	167 Inf Div	112 Inf Div	25 Mot Div	
	XLVII Pz Corps	134 Inf Div	17 Pz Div					
	LIII Corps	IR GD	56 Inf Div					
	XXXV Corps	29 Mot Div	293 Inf Div					
10 March 1942	XXIV Pz Corps	339 Inf Div	4 Pz Div	18 Pz Div	403 Inf Div	208 Inf Div	211 Inf Div	25 Mot Div
	XLVII Pz Corps	134 Inf Div	56 Inf Div	296 Inf Div	167 Inf Div	112 Inf Div	17 Pz Div	
	LIII Corps	IR GD	293 Inf Div	262 Inf Div				
	XXXV Corps	29 Mot Div						

Date	Corps	Divisions
5 April 1942	XXIV Pz Corps	339 Inf Div, 17 Pz Div, 4 Pz Div, 18 Pz Div, 208 Inf Div, 211 Inf Div
	XLVII Pz Corps	134 Inf Div, GD, 112 Inf Div, 25 Mot Div
	LIII Corps	56 Inf Div, 296 Inf Div, 262 Inf Div
	XXXV Corps	29 Mot Div, 293 Inf Div
	Reserve	167 Inf Div
11 May 1942	XLVII Pz Corps	339 Inf Div, 17 Pz Div, 18 Pz Div, 208 Inf Div, 211 Inf Div, 4 Pz Div
	LIII Corps	134 Inf Div, 56 Inf Div, 296 Inf Div, 112 Inf Div, 25 Mot Div
	XXXV Corps	29 Mot Div, 293 Inf Div, 262 Inf Div
	Reserve	707 Inf Div
8 June 1942	XLVII Pz Corps	339 Inf Div, 17 Pz Div, 18 Pz Div, 208 Inf Div, 211 Inf Div
	LIII Corps	134 Inf Div, 56 Inf Div, 296 Inf Div, 112 Inf Div, 25 Mot Div
	XXXV Corps	4 Pz Div, 293 Inf Div, 262 Inf Div
	Reserve	707 Inf Div
4 July 1942	XLVII Pz Corps	707 Inf Div, 339 Inf Div, 56 Inf Div, 17 Pz Div, 296 Inf Div, 18 Pz Div, 208 Inf Div, 211 Inf Div
	LIII Corps	216 Inf Div, 293 Inf Div, 262 Inf Div
	XXXV Corps	134 Inf Div, Hung 108 Div
	Reserve	4 Pz Div, Hung 102 Div
5 August 1942	Gp. Gilsa	Hung 102 Div, Hung 108 Div, 18 Pz Div, 208 Inf Div, 211 Inf Div, 216 Inf Div
	XLVII Pz Corps	707 Inf Div, 339 Inf Div, 134 Inf Div, 296 Inf Div, 112 Inf Div, 25 Mot Div
	XLI Pz Corps	52 Inf Div, 19 Pz Div, 56 Inf Div
	LIII Corps	26 Inf Div, 11 Pz Div
2 September 1942	Gp. Gilsa	Hung 102 Div, Hung 108 Div, 208 Inf Div, 216 Inf Div, 211 Inf Div, 9 Pz Div
	XLVII Pz Corps	339 Inf Div, 18 Pz Div, 19 Pz Div, 11 Pz Div, 134 Inf Div, 25 Mot Div
	XLI Pz Corps	52 Inf Div, 56 Inf Div, 17 Pz Div, 296 Inf Div, 112 Inf Div
	LIII Corps	20 Pz Div, 26 Inf Div, 262 Inf Div
	XXXV Corps	4 Pz Div, 293 Inf Div
	Reserve	707 Inf Div
8 October 1942	Korueck 532	Hung 102 Div, Hung 108 Div, 216 Inf Div, 208 Inf Div, 211 Inf Div
	XLVII Pz Corps	339 Inf Div, 18 Pz Div, 52 Inf Div, 293 Inf Div
	XLI Pz Corps	134 Inf Div, 19 Pz Div, 112 Inf Div, 26 Inf Div
	LIII Corps	25 Mot Div, 296 Inf Div, 56 Inf Div, 262 Inf Div
	XXXV Corps	17 Pz Div, 4 Pz Div
	Reserve	707 Inf Div, 20 Pz Div
5 November 1942	Korueck 532	Hung 102 Div, Hung 108 Div, 216 Inf Div, 208 Inf Div, 211 Inf Div, 112 Inf Div
	XLVII Pz Corps	339 Inf Div, 18 Pz Div, 293 Inf Div, 25 Mot Div, 296 Inf Div
	LIII Corps	134 Inf Div, 52 Inf Div, 56 Inf Div, 262 Inf Div, 17 Pz Div
	XXXV Corps	26 Inf Div, 4 Pz Div
	Reserve	707 Inf Div, 19 Pz Div

Date	Corps	Divisions
1 December 1942	Korueck 532	Hung 102 Div, Hung 108 Div
	XLVII Pz Corps	339 Inf Div, 18 Pz Div, 208 Inf Div, 211 Inf Div, 112 Inf Div
	LIII Corps	134 Inf Div, 52 Inf Div, 293 Inf Div, 25 Mot Div, 296 Inf Div
	XXXV Corps	26 Inf Div, 4 Pz Div, 56 Inf Div, 262 Inf Div
	Reserve	707 Inf Div
1 January 1943	Korueck 532	Hung 102 Div, Hung 108 Div
	XLVII Pz Corps	339 Inf Div, 18 Pz Div, 208 Inf Div, 211 Inf Div, 112 Inf Div
	LIII Corps	134 Inf Div, 293 Inf Div, 25 Mot Div, 296 Inf Div
	XXXV Corps	4 Pz Div, 56 Inf Div, 262 Inf Div
	Reserve	707 Inf Div
3 February 1943	Korueck 532	Hung 102 Div, Hung 108 Div
	XLVII Pz Corps	339, 208 Inf Div, 211 Inf Div, 296 Inf Div, 112 Inf Div
	LIII Corps	134 Inf Div, 293 Inf Div, 25 Mot Div, 18 Pz Div
	XXXV Corps	34 Inf Div, 56 Inf Div, 262 Inf Div
	Reserve	707 Inf Div, 442 Inf Div
4 March 1943	Korueck 532	Hung 102 Div, Hung 108 Div
	Gp. Scheele	339 Inf Div, 208 Inf Div, 5 Pz Div, 9 Pz Div, 211 Inf Div, 251 Inf Div
	LIII Corps	134 Inf Div, 293 Inf Div, 25 Mot Div, 112 Inf Div, 296 Inf Div
	XXXV Corps	34 Inf Div, 56 Inf Div, 262 Inf Div, 299 Inf Div
	LV Corps	216 Inf Div, 383 Inf Div, 18 Pz Div, 78 Inf Div
	XLVI Pz Corps	20 Pz Div, 258 Inf Div, 12 Pz Div
	XLVII Pz Corps	137 Inf Div, 707 Inf Div
	Reserve	442 Inf Div, 45 Inf Div
9 April 1943	Korueck 532	Hung 102 Div, Hung 108 Div
	LV Corps	339 Inf Div, 110 Inf Div, 296 Inf Div, 134 Inf Div, 251 Inf Div
	LIII Corps	211 Inf Div, 293 Inf Div, 25 Mot Div, 112 Mot Div, 102 Inf Div
	XXXV Corps	34 Inf Div, 56 Inf Div, 262 Inf Div, 299 Inf Div
	XLI Pz Corps	216 Inf Div, 383 Inf Div, 86 Inf Div, 20 Pz Div
	XLVI Pz Corps	258 Inf Div, 7 Inf Div, 78 Inf Div, 72 Inf Div
	XX Corps	707 Inf Div, 45 Inf Div, 137 Inf Div
	XLVII Pz Corps	208 Inf Div, SS Cav Div, HQs XLVIII Pz Corps
1 May 1943	Korueck 532	Hung 102 Div, Hung 108 Div
	LV Corps	339 Inf Div, 110 Inf Div, 296 Inf Div, 134 Inf Div
	LIII Corps	211 Inf Div, 293 Inf Div, 25 Mot Div, 112 Inf Div
	XXXV Corps	34 Inf Div, 56 Inf Div, 262 Inf Div, 299 Inf Div
	XXIII Corps	216 Inf Div, 383 Inf Div
	XLI Pz Corps	86 Inf Div, 102 Inf Div, 137 Inf Div, 292 Inf Div, 20 Pz Div
	XLVI Pz Corps	258 Inf Div, 45 Inf Div, 208 Inf Div
	XX Corps	72 Inf Div, 78 Inf Div, 18 Pz Div
	Reserve	7 Inf Div, 12 Pz Div, 9 Pz Div, 251 Inf Div, 707 Inf Div, 2 Pz Div, 10 Mot Div, 4 Pz Div, 5 Pz Div

Date	Corps	Divisions
1 June 1943	Korueck 532	Hung 102 Div
	LV Corps	339 Inf Div, 110 Inf Div, 296 Inf Div, 134 Inf Div
	LIII Corps	211 Inf Div, 293 Inf Div, 25 Mot Div, 112 Inf Div
	XXXV Corps	34 Inf Div, 56 Inf Div, 262 Inf Div, 299 Inf Div
	XXIII Corps	78 Inf Div, 216 Inf Div, 383 Inf Div
	XLI Pz Corps	20 Pz Div, 86 Inf Div, 7 Inf Div, 4 Pz Div, 18 Pz Div
	XLVII Pz Corps	292 Inf Div, 10 Mot Div, 102 Inf Div, 251 Inf Div, 2 Pz Div
	XLVI Pz Corps	12 Pz Div, 285 Inf Div, 137 Inf Div, 6 Inf Div, 9 Pz Div
	XX Corps	72 Inf Div, 45 Inf Div, 5 Pz Div
	Reserve	707 Inf Div, 208 Inf Div
7 July 1943	LV Corps	339 Inf Div, 110 Inf Div, 296 Inf Div, 134 Inf Div
	LIII Corps	211 Inf Div, 293 Inf Div, 25 Pz Gren Div, 208 Inf Div
	XXXV Corps	34 Inf Div, 56 Inf Div, 262 Inf Div, 299 Inf Div
	Reserve	112 Inf Div, 707 Inf Div
5 August 1943	LV Corps	339 Inf Div, 110 Inf Div, 296 Inf Div, 134 Inf Div, 211 Inf Div, 183 Inf Div
	XXIII Corps	5 Pz Div, 95 Inf Div, 707 Inf Div, 8 Pz Div, GD, 112 Inf Div
	XLI Pz Corps	129 Inf Div, 213 Inf Div, 10 Pz Gren Div, 20 Pz Gren Div
	LIII Corps	253 Inf Div, 9 Pz Div, 34 Inf Div
	XXXV Corps	18 Pz Div, 26 Inf Div, 299 Inf Div
	Reserve	12 Pz Div, 78 Inf Div, 20 Pz Div, 25 Pz Gren Div
5 September 1943	LXIX Corps	187 Inf Div, 173 Inf Div, 297 Inf Div, 114 Inf Div
	XXI Corps	118 Inf Div, 100 Jg Div, 369 Inf Div
	XV Mtn Corps	373 Inf Div, SS PE, 11 SS Div
	Reserve	III SS Corps HQs
4 October 1943	LXIX Corps	1 Cos Div, 187 Inf Div, 173 Inf Div, 118 Inf Div
	XXI Corps	181 Inf Div, 100 Jg Div, 297 Inf Div, 373 Inf Div
	XV Mtn Corps	SS PE, 114 Inf Div, 369 Inf Div
	III SS Corps	11 SS Div
8 November 1943	LXIX Corps	1 Cos Div, 187 Inf Div, 173 Inf Div, 118 Inf Div
	XXI Corps	181 Inf Div, 100 Jg Div, 297 Inf Div, 373 Inf Div
	XV Mtn Corps	SS PE, 114 Inf Div, 369 Inf Div
	III SS Corps	11 SS Div, SS Ned Div, 367 Inf Div
	SS V Mtn Corps	SS V Corps HQs, 264 Inf Div
3 December 1943	LXIX Corps	187 Inf Div, 173 Inf Div, 367 Inf Div, 181 Inf Div
	XXI Corps	100 Jg Div, 297 Inf Div, 1 Cos Div
	V SS Mtn Corps	1 Mtn Div, 369 Inf Div, SS Ned Div, SS PE
	XV Mtn Corps	264 Inf Div, 114 Inf Div, 373 Inf Div, 371 Inf Div

Jan–Mar 1944 – Data incomplete: Arriving: Departing:	SS V Mtn Corps	XXI Corps	V SS Corps	118 Inf Div / SS PE / Brandenburger	181 Inf Div / 369 Inf Div	264 Inf Div	297 Inf Div
	42 Inf Div	373 Inf Div / 392 Inf Div / 100 Jg Div	1 Cos Div / 13 SS Div / 114 Inf Div	173 Inf Div	187 Inf Div	1 Mtn Div	SS Ned Div
	LXIX Corps					373 Inf Div	392 Inf Div
15 April 1944	XXI Corps	297 Inf Div / 369 Inf Div / 13 SS Div / 1 Cos Div	181 Inf Div / 118 Inf Div / 42 Inf Div / Brandenburger / 373 Inf Div	SS PE	187 Inf Div	264 Inf Div	
	V SS Mtn Corps						
	Syrmia Gp.						
	Reserve	264 Inf Div					
	XV Mtn Corps						
17 May 1944	XXI Corps	297 Inf Div / 369 Inf Div / 264 Inf Div / 13 SS Div / 1 Cos Div / Brandenburger	181 Inf Div / 118 Inf Div / 373 Inf Div	392 Inf Div			
	V SS Mtn Corps						
	XV Mtn Corps						
	Syrmia Gp.						
	LXIX Corps						
	Reserve						
17 June 1944	XXI Corps	21 SS Div / 118 Inf Div / Brandenburger / 373 Inf Div	297 Inf Div / 369 Inf Div / 264 Inf Div / 1 Cos Div	181 Inf Div / SS PE / 392 Inf Div	13 SS Div		
	V SS Mtn Corps						
	XV Mtn Corps						
	LXIX Corps						
15 July 1944	XXI Corps	21 SS Div / 13 SS Div / Brandenburger / 373 Inf Div	297 Inf Div / SS PE / 264 Inf Div / 98 Inf Div	181 Inf Div / 369 Inf Div / 392 Inf Div / 1 Cos Div	118 Inf Div		
	V SS Mtn Corps						
	XV Mtn Corps						
	LXIX Corps						
31 August 1944	LXIX Corps	1 Cos Div / 21 SS Div / 13 SS Div / 373 Inf Div / Brandenburger	297 Inf Div / SS PE / 264 Inf Div	181 Inf Div / 369 Inf Div / 392 Inf Div	118 Inf Div		
	XXI Corps						
	V SS Mtn Corps						
	XV Mtn Corps						
	Reserve						
16 September 1944	V SS Mtn Corps	13 SS Div / 392 Inf Div / 1 Cos Div	369 Inf Div / 373 Inf Div	SS PE / 264 Inf Div	118 Inf Div		
	XV Mtn Corps						
	LXIX Corps						
13 October 1944	IX SS Corps	13 SS Div / 369 Inf Div / 392 Inf Div / 1 Cos Div	Brandenburger / 118 Inf Div / 373 Inf Div	Boettcher / 264 Inf Div			
	V SS Mtn Corps						
	XV Mtn Corps						
	LXIX Corps						
5 November 1944	LXIX Corps	1 Cos Div / 13 SS Div / 392 Inf Div / 369 Inf Div / Brandenburger	373 Inf Div / 117 Inf Div	264 Inf Div / 1 Mtn Div	118 Inf Div		
	IX SS Corps						
	XV Mtn Corps						
	V SS Mtn Corps						
	LXVIII Corps						

Date	Corps	Divisions
26 November 1944	XV Mtn Corps	392 Inf Div, 373 Inf Div, 264 Inf Div
	LXIX Corps	1 Cos Div, 1 Mtn Div, 13 SS Div, 44 Inf Div, 31 SS Div, Brandenburger
	LXVIII Corps	117 Inf Div
	Grp Kuebler	118 Inf Div
	Reserve	HQs XXII Corps
31 December 1944	XXII Mtn Corps	3 Cav Div, 1 Mtn Div
	LXVIII Corps	71 Inf Div, 13 SS Div, 44 Inf Div
19 February 1945	XXII Mtn Corps	118 Inf Div, 1 Mtn Div
	LXVIII Corps	71 Inf Div, 13 SS Div
1 March 1945	XXII Mtn Corps	118 Inf Div, 1 Mtn Div
	LXVIII Corps	71 Inf Div, 13 SS Div
	Reserve	Bde 92
12 April 1945	I Cav Corps	16 SS Div, 14 SS Div, 3 Cav Div, 44 Inf Div, 4 Cav Div, 23 Pz Div
	XXII Mtn Corps	9 SS Div, 118 Inf Div, 71 Inf Div
	LXVIII Corps	297 Inf Div, 71 Inf Div
7 May 1945	I Cav Corps	3 Cav Div, 16 SS Div, 4 Cav Div, 23 Pz Div
	XXII Mtn B182 Corps	297 Inf Div, Hung St. Lasslo, 71 Inf Div
	LXVIII Corps	118 Inf Div, 13 SS Div, 71 Inf Div

Except as noted, all data www.bundesarchiv.de/findbuecher/ma/rh21-2/index.htm
1. Horst Boog et al., *Germany and the Second World War*, Vol. IV, *Attack on the Soviet Union*, Clarendon Press, 1998, appendix 2.

Third Panzer Army

Date	Corps	Divisions
22 June 1941[1]	VI Corps	26 Inf Div, 6 Inf Div
	XXXIX Pz Corps	14 Mot Div, 20 Mot Div, 20 Pz Div, 7 Pz Div
	V Corps	35 Inf Div, 5 Inf Div, 12 Pz Div
	LVII Pz Corps	18 Mot Div, 19 Pz Div
1 July 1941	XXXIX Pz Corps	14 Mot Div, 20 Mot Div, 20 Pz Div, 7 Pz Div
	LVII Pz Corps	18 Mot Div, 19 Pz Div, 12 Pz Div
7 August 1941	LVII Pz Corps	14 Mot Div, 18 Mot Div, 19 Pz Div, 20 Pz Div, 20 Mot Div, 129 Inf Div
	XXXIX Pz Corps	900 Tng Bde, 12 Pz Div, 7 Pz Div
3 September 1941	Part of Ninth Army, HQs only	
2 October 1941	VI Corps	110 Inf Div, 26 Inf Div, 6 Inf Div, 129 Inf Div
	XLI Pz Corps	36 Mot Div, 1 Pz Div, 7 Pz Div
	LVI Pz Corps	14 Mot Div, 6 Pz Div, 106 Inf Div
	V Corps	35 Inf Div, 5 Inf Div

4 November 1941	XLI Pz Corps	161 Inf Div	129 Inf Div	1 Pz Div	900 Tng Bde	36 Mot Div	6 Pz Div
	LVI Pz Corps	14 Mot Div	7 Pz Div				
	Reserve	110 Inf Div					
4 December 1941	LVI Pz Corps	36 Mot Div	14 Mot Div	7 Pz Div			
	XLI Pz Corps	6 Pz Div	1 Pz Div	23 Inf Div			
2 January 1942	XLI Pz Corps	36 Mot Div	1 Pz Div	2 Pz Div			
	LVI Pz Corps	7 Pz Div	14 Mot Div	900 Tng Bde			
6 February 1942	83 Inf Div	330 Inf Div					
	LIX Corps						
10 March 1942	LIX Corps	330 Inf Div	205 Inf Div	83 Inf Div			
5 April 1942	LIX Corps	330 Inf Div	205 Inf Div	83 Inf Div			
11 May 1942	XLVI Pz Corps	23 Inf Div	5 Pz Div	78 Inf Div	87 Inf Div	197 Inf Div	7 Inf Div
	IX Corps	35 Inf Div	252 Inf Div	183 Inf Div	255 Inf Div	20 Pz Div	
	XX Corps	258 Inf Div	292 inf Div				
	Reserve	17 inf Div					
8 June 1942	XLVI Pz Corps	23 Inf Div	5 Pz Div	78 Inf Div	7 Inf Div	20 Pz Div	
	IX Corps	35 Inf Div	252 Inf Div	183 Inf Div	255 Inf Div		
	XX Corps	258 Inf Div	292 inf Div				
4 July 1942	IX Corps	35 Inf Div	252 Inf Div	78 Inf Div	7 Inf Div		
	XX Corps	258 Inf Div	292 Inf Div	183 Inf Div	255 Inf Div		
5 August 1942	IX Corps	35 Inf Div	252 Inf Div	7 Inf Div	255 Inf Div		
	XX Corps	258 Inf Div	292 inf Div	183 Inf Div			
2 September 1942	IX Corps	35 Inf Div	252 Inf Div	7 Inf Div	258 Inf Div		
	XX Corps	31 Inf Div	183 Inf Div	255 Inf Div			
	Reserve	98 Inf Div					
8 October 1942	IX Corps	35 Inf Div	7 Inf Div	258 Inf Div	292 Inf Div	98 Inf Div	252 Inf Div
	XX Corps	31 Inf Div	183 Inf Div	255 Inf Div			
5 November 1942	XLVI Pz Corps	2 Pz Div	36 Mot Div	342 Inf Div	258 Inf Div	292 Inf Div	98 Inf Div
	IX Corps	35 Inf Div	252 Inf Div	7 Inf Div			
	XX Corps	31 Inf Div	183 Inf Div	255 Inf Div			
1 December 1942	XLVI Pz Corps	2 Pz Div	36 Mot Div	342 Inf Div	258 Inf Div	292 Inf Div	98 Inf Div
	IX Corps	35 Inf Div	252 Inf Div	7 Inf Div			
	XX Corps	31 Inf Div	183 Inf Div	255 Inf Div			
1 January 1943	XLVI Pz Corps+B93	5 Pz Div	36 Mot Div	342 Inf Div	258 Inf Div	292 Inf Div	98 Inf Div
	IX Corps	35 Inf Div	252 Inf Div	7 Inf Div			
	XX Corps	31 Inf Div	183 Inf Div	255 Inf Div			

Date	Corps	Divisions
3 February 1943	XLIII Corps	8 Pz Div, 20 Mot Div, 205 Inf Div, SS 1 Bde
	LIX Corps	291 Inf Div, 331 Inf Div
	II Lw Fld Corps	6 Lw Fld Div, 3 Lw Fld Div, 4 Lw Fld Div, 2 Lw Fld Div
	Reserve	12 Pz Div, 263 Inf Div
4 March 1943	XLIII Corps	331 Inf Div, 8 Pz Div, 20 Mot Div
	LIX Corps	291 Inf Div, 263 Inf Div, SS 1 Bde
	II Lw Fld Corps	6 Lw Fld Div, 3 Lw Fld Div, 4 Lw Fld Div, 2 Lw Fld Div
	Reserve	205 Inf Div
9 April 1943	XLIII Corps	331 Inf Div, 205 Inf Div, 20 Mot Div
	LIX Corps	291 Inf Div, 262 Inf Div, SS 1 Bde
	II Lw Fld Corps	6 Lw Fld Div, 3 Lw Fld Div, 4 Lw Fld Div, 2 Lw Fld Div
	VI Corps	83 Inf Div, 330 Inf Div, 206 Inf Div
	Reserve	201 Inf Div
1 May 1943	XLIII Corps	205 Inf Div, 20 Mot Div, SS 1 Bde
	LIX Corps	291 Inf Div, 263 Inf Div
	II Lw Fld Corps	6 Lw Fld Div, 3 Lw Fld Div, 4 Lw Fld Div, 2 Lw Fld Div
	VI Corps	83 Inf Div, 330 Inf Div, 206 Inf Div
	Reserve	201 Inf Div
1 June 1943	XLIII Corps	205 Inf Div, 20 Pz Gren Div, SS 1 Bde
	LIX Corps	291 Inf Div, 263 Inf Div
	II Lw Fld Corps	6 Lw Fld Div, 3 Lw Fld Div, 4 Lw Fld Div, 2 Lw Fld Div
	VI Corps	83 Inf Div, 330 Inf Div, 206 Inf Div
	Reserve	201 Inf Div
7 July 1943	XLIII Corps	205 Inf Div, 20 Mot Div
	LIX Corps	291 Inf Div, 263 Inf Div
	II Lw Fld Corps	6 Lw Fld Div, 3 Lw Fld Div, 4 Lw Fld Div, 2 Lw Fld Div
	VI Corps	87 Inf Div, 330 Inf Div, 206 Inf Div
	Reserve	201 Inf Div
5 August 1943	XLIII Corps	205 Inf Div, 83 Inf Div, 87 Inf Div
	LIX Corps	291 Inf Div, 263 Inf Div
	II Lw Fld Corps	6 Lw Fld Div, 3 Lw Fld Div, 4 Lw Fld Div, 2 Lw Fld Div
	VI Corps	330 Inf Div, 206 Inf Div
5 September 1943	XLIII Corps	205 Inf Div, 83 Inf Div
	LIX Corps	291 Inf Div, 263 Inf Div
	II Lw Fld Corps	6 Lw Fld Div, 3 Lw Fld Div, 4 Lw Fld Div, 2 Lw Fld Div
	VI Corps	87 Inf Div, 206 Inf Div
4 October 1943	II Lw Fld Corps	6 Lw Fld Div, 3 Lw Fld Div, 4 Lw Fld Div, 2 Lw Fld Div, 246 Inf Div
	VI Corps	87 Inf Div, 14 Inf Div, 256 Inf Div
	Reserve	HQs LIII Corps

8 November 1943	IX Corps II Lw Fld Corps VI Corps LIII Corps Reserve	87 Inf Div 3 Lw Fld Div 14 Inf Div 246 Inf Div 201 Inf Div	2 Lw Fld Div 4 Lw Fld Div 206 Inf Div 256 Inf Div 20 Pz Div	129 Inf Div	6 Lw Fld Div	6 Lw Fld Div	
3 December 1943	IX Corps LIII Corps VI Corps Reserve	252 Inf Div 3 Lw Fld Div 14 Inf Div 201 Inf Div	20 Pz Div 4 Lw Fld Div 206 Inf Div	252 Inf Div	129 Inf Div 246 Inf Div	2 Lw Fld Div 256 Inf Div	6 Lw Fld Div
1 January 1944	IX Corps LIII Corps VI Corps Reserve	211 Inf Div 6 Lw Fld Div 14 Inf Div 131 Inf Div 12 Pz Div	252 Inf Div 129 Inf Div 206 Inf Div Feldherrnhalle	20 Pz Div 2 Lw Fld Div 246 Inf Div	5 Inf Div 3 Lw Fld Div 256 Inf Div	87 Inf Div 4 Lw Fld Div	12 Inf Div 197 Inf Div
1 February 1944	IX Corps LIII Corps VI Corps	252 Inf Div 6 Lw Fld Div 131 Inf Div	5 Inf Div 4 Lw Fld Div 299 Inf Div	87 Inf Div 20 Pz Div 14 Inf Div	12 Inf Div 197 Inf Div 211 Inf Div	246 Inf Div 256 Inf Div	206 Inf Div
3 March 1944	IX Corps LIII Corps VI Corps Reserve	252 Inf Div 95 Inf Div 197 Inf Div 131 Inf Div	5 Inf Div 4 Lw Fld Div 299 Inf Div	6 Lw Fld Div 14 Inf Div	246 Inf Div 256 Inf Div	206 Inf Div	
15 April 1944	IX Corps LIII Corps VI Corps Reserve	252 Inf Div 246 Inf Div 197 Inf Div 201 Inf Div	4 Lw Fld Div 299 Inf Div	6 Lw Fld Div 14 Inf Div	206 Inf Div 256 Inf Div		
15 May 1942	IX Corps LIII Corps VI Corps Reserve	252 Inf Div 246 Inf Div 197 Inf Div 201 Inf Div	4 Lw Fld Div 299 Inf Div 95 Inf Div	6 Lw Fld Div 14 Inf Div	206 Inf Div 256 Inf Div		
15 June 1944	IX Corps LIII Corps VI Corps Reserve	252 Inf Div 246 Inf Div 197 Inf Div 201 Inf Div	4 Lw Fld Div 299 Inf Div 95 Inf Div	6 Lw Fld Div 256 Inf Div	206 Inf Div		
15 July 1944	IX Corps XXVI Corps	252 Inf Div 69 Inf Div	212 Inf Div 6 Pz Div	Pz Bde Werthen 201 Inf Div	Rothkirch		

Date	Corps	Units
31 August 1944	XXXIX Pz Corps	SS Gp Hirthes, GD, 4 Pz Div, 12 Pz Div
	XL Pz Corps	5 Pz Div, 201 Inf Div, 551 Inf Div
	XII SS Corps	7 Pz Div, 548 Inf Div
	IX Corps	252 Inf Div, 212 Inf Div, 69 Inf Div, 549 Inf Div, 52 Inf Div
	XXVI Corps	Pz Bde Werthen, 1 Inf Div, Schirmer
	Reserve	391 Inf Div, Pz Bde 103, Rothkirch, 561 Inf Div
16 September 1944	XXXIX Pz Corps	SS Gp Hirthes, GD, 12 Pz Div, 7 Pz Div, 4 Pz Div
	XL Pz Corps	5 Pz Div, 201 Inf Div, 551 Inf Div
	XII SS Corps	Pz Gren Bde 18, 548 Inf Div
	IX Corps	252 Inf Div, 69 Inf Div, 212 Inf Div
	Reserve	391 Inf Div, Rothkirch, 390 Inf Div
13 October 1944	XXVIII Corps	58 Inf Div, GD, 7 Pz Div
	Hermann Goering	Pz Bde 101, 1 Hermann Goering, Lanckert
	XL Pz Corps	5 Pz Div, 548 Inf Div, 549 Inf Div, 561 Inf Div, 61 Inf Div, Pz Bde 102
	IX Corps	21 Inf Div, 69 Inf Div, 95 Inf Div
	Reserve	390 Inf Div, 2 Hermann Goering, 551 VG Div
5 November 1944	XXVIII Corps	58 Inf Div, 7 Pz Div, GD
	XL Pz Corps	Pz Bde 18, Kempchen, Kontay
	IX Corps	548 VG Div, 95 Inf Div, 69 Inf Div
	XXVI Corps	56 Inf Div, 1 Inf Div, 349 Inf Div
	Reserve	390 Inf Div, 551 VG Div, 20 Pz Div, 61 Inf Div, Pz Bde 102, Pz Bde 103
26 November 1944	XXVIII Corps	58 Inf Div, GD, 607 Inf Div
	XL Pz Corps	West, Center, 551 VG Div
	IX Corps	548 VG Div, 561 Inf Div, 56 Inf Div
	XXVI Corps	69 Inf Div, 1 Inf Div, 349 Inf Div
	Reserve	95 Inf Div, 61 Inf Div
31 December 1944	XXVIII Corps	95 Inf Div, 58 Inf Div, 607 Inf Div, 561 Inf Div, 56 Inf Div
	IX Corps	286 Inf Div, 551 VG Div, 548 VG Div, 549 VG Div
	XXVI Corps	69 Inf Div, 1 Inf Div, 349 Inf Div
19 February 1945	Part of Army Group Vistula, HQs only	
1 March 1945	Group Tettau	15 SS Div, Baerwalde, Pommernland, 28 SS Div, 281 Inf Div, Voigt
	X SS Corps	163 Inf Div, 5 Inf Div, 402 Inf Div
	III SS Corps	11 SS Div, 23 SS Div, 27 SS Div
	Group Oder	9 Fallschirm, Deneke
	Reserve	33 SS Div, Pz Holstein

| 12 April 1945 | Gp Swinemuende
XXXII Corps
Group Oder
XLVI Corps
Reserve | 402 Inf Div
Voigt
610 Inf Div
547 VG Div
HQs, III SS Corps | 3 Mar Div
549 VG Div
Klossek
1 Mar Div
11 SS Div | Fest. Stettin
23 SS Div | 281 Inf Div
27 SS Div | 28 SS Div |

Except as noted, all data www.bundesarchiv.de/findbuecher/ma/rh21-3/index.htm
1. Horst Boog et al., *Germany and the Second World War*, Vol. IV, *Attack on the Soviet Union*, Clarendon Press, 1998, appendix 2.

Fourth Panzer Army

22 June 1941[1]	XLI Pz Corps LVI Pz Corps Reserve	1 Pz Div 290 Inf Div SS T	269 Inf Div 8 Pz Div	6 Pz Div 3 Mot Div	36 Mot Div
1 July 1941	XLI Pz Corps LVI Pz Corps	1 Pz Div 290 Inf Div	269 Inf Div 8 Pz Div	6 Pz Div 3 Mot Div	36 Mot Div SS T
7 August 1941	XXXVIII XLI Pz Corps LVI Pz Corps Reserve	58 Inf Div 1 Pz Div Polizei 8 Pz Div	1 Inf Div 269 Inf Div	6 Pz Div 3 Mot Div	36 Mot Div
3 September 1941	XLI Pz Corps L Corps	1 Pz Div 269 Inf Div	8 Pz Div Polizei	6 Pz Div	36 Mot Div
2 October 1941	LVII Pz Corps XLVI Pz Corps XL Pz Corps XII Corps	20 Pz Div 5 Pz Div 2 Pz Div 98 Inf Div	3 Mot Div 11 Pz Div 10 Pz Div 34 Inf Div	SS R 252 Inf Div 258 Inf Div	
4 November 1941	V Corps XLVI Pz Corps XL Pz Corps IX Corps VII Corps	106 Inf Div 2 Pz Div 10 Pz Div 87 Inf Div 267 Inf Div	35 Inf Div 11 Pz Div SS R 78 Inf Div 197 Inf Div	5 Pz Div 7 Inf Div	
4 December 1941	V Corps XLVI Pz Corps XL Pz Corps IX Corps VII Corps	2 Pz Div 11 Pz Div 10 Pz Div 257 Inf Div 267 Inf Div	106 Inf Div 5 Pz Div SS R 87 Inf Div 197 Inf Div	35 Inf Div 78 Inf Div 7 Inf Div	

2 January 1942	V Corps	23 Inf Div	6 Pz Div	106 Inf Div	35 Inf Div		
	XLVI Pz Corps	5 Pz Div	11 Pz Div	SS R	10 Pz Div		
	IX Corps	252 Inf Div	78 Inf Div	20 Pz Div	87 Inf Div		
	VII Corps	255 Inf Div	3 Mot Div	197 Inf Div	7 Inf Div	267 Inf Div	252 Inf Div
	IX Corps	23 Inf Div	106 Inf Div	35 Inf Div	3 Mot Div	10 Pz Div	
6 February 1942	IX Corps	23 Inf Div	106 Inf Div	35 Inf Div	3 Mot Div	11 Pz Div	10 Pz Div
	VII Corps	252 Inf Div	78 Inf Div	87 Inf Div			
	XX Corps	197 Inf Div	7 Inf Div	258 Inf Div			
	Reserve	15 Inf Div	267 Inf Div	255 Inf Div	183 Inf Div		
10 March 1942	V Corps	11 Pz Div	106 Inf Div	5 Pz Div	23 Inf Div	3 Mot Div	20 Pz Div
	IX Corps	35 Inf Div	252 Inf Div	78 Inf Div	87 Inf Div	197 Inf Div	
	VII Corps	7 Inf Div	258 Inf Div	15 Inf Div	255 Inf Div		
	XX Corps	267 Inf Div	292 Inf Div	183 Inf Div	20 Pz Div		
5 April 1942	V Corps	106 Inf Div	23 Inf Div	5 Pz Div	15 Inf Div	10 Pz Div	
	IX Corps	35 Inf Div	11 Pz Div	78 Inf Div	87 Inf Div		
	VII Corps	197 Inf Div	7 Inf Div	267 Inf Div	17 Inf Div		
	XX Corps	292 Inf Div	183 Inf Div	20 Pz Div			
11 May 1942	Recovery						
8 June 1942	XLVIII Pz Corps	377 Inf Div	9 Pz Div	82 Inf Div			
	Hung 2 Army	HQs XXIV Pz. Corps	HQs XIII Corps				
	Reserve	385 Inf Div					
24 June 1942[2]	XXIV Pz Corps	377 Inf Div	9 Pz Div	3 Mot Div	24 Pz Div		
	XIII Corps	82 Inf Div	385 Inf Div (-)	11 Pz Div			
	XLVIII Pz Corps	GD	24 Pz Div				
4 July 1942	XIII Corps	88 Inf Div	385 Inf Div	82 Inf Div			
	XXIV Pz Corps	11 Pz Div	377 Inf Div	9 Pz Div	3 Mot Div		
	XLVIII Pz Corps	16 Mot Div	GD	24 Pz Div			
5 August 1942	XLVIII Pz Corps	29 Mot Div	14 Pz Div	82 Inf Div			
	Rom VI Corps	Rom 1 Div	Rom 2 Div	Rom 20 Div	Rom 4 Div		
	IV Corps	94 Inf Div	297 Inf Div	371 Inf Div			
2 September 1942	XLVIII Pz Corps	29 Mot Div	14 Pz Div	24 Pz Div			
	Rom VI Corps	Rom 1 Div	Rom 2 Div	Rom 2 Div	Rom 20 Div		
	IV Corps	Rom 4 Div	94 Inf Div	297 Inf Div	371 Inf Div		

8 October 1942	IV Corps	371 Inf Div	297 Inf Div	Rom 20 Div			
	Rom VI Corps	Rom 4 Div	Rom 2 Div	Rom 1 Div			
	XLVIII Pz Corps	14 Pz Div	16 Mot Div				
	Reserve	29 Mot Div	71 Inf Div				
5 November 1942	IV Corps	371 Inf Div	297 Inf Div	Rom 20 Div	Rom 4 Div	Rom 5 Cav Div	
	Rom VI Corps	Rom 8 Cav Div	Rom 2 Div	Rom 1 Div			
	XLVIII Pz Corps	No units		Rom 18 Div			
	Reserve	16 Mot Div	29 Mot Div				
1 December 1942	Rom 4 Army	16 Mot Div	6 Pz Div				
	Reserve						
1 January 1943	LVII Pz Corps	16 Mot Div	SS V	23 Pz Div	17 Pz Div	Rom 2 Div	Rom 18 Div
	Reserve	15 Lw Fld Div	Rom 4 Army	Rom VI Corps	Rom 1 Div		
		Rom 4 Div	Rom 5 Cav Div	Rom 8 Cav Div (–)	HQs Rom VII Corps		
3 February 1943	LVII Pz Corps	17 Pz Div	SS V	23 Pz Div	15 Lw Fld Div	111 Inf Div	
	Special HQs	444 Inf Div	454 Sec Div	11 Pz Div			
	Reserve	3 Pz Div	16 Mot Div				
4 March 1943	SS Pz Corps	SS LAH	SS T	SS R			
	XLVIII Pz Corps	11 Pz Div	6 Pz Div				
	LVII Pz Corps	17 Pz Div	15 Inf Div				
9 April 1943	Army Group South, HQs only, not units						
1 May 1943	Army Group South, HQs only, not units						
1 June 1943	Army Group South, HQs only, not units						
7 July 1943	LII Corps	57 Inf Div	255 Inf Div	332 Inf Div	167 Inf Div		
	XLVIII Pz Corps	3 Pz Div	GD	11 Pz Div			
	II SS Pz Corps	SS LAH	SS T	SS R			
5 August 1943	VII Corps	88 Inf Div	75 Inf Div	323 Inf Div	68 Inf Div	167 Inf Div	
	XLVIII Pz Corps	7 Pz Div	57 Inf Div	11 Pz Div	6 Pz Div		
	LII Corps	255 Inf Div	19 Pz Div				
	Reserve	HQs III Pz Corps					
5 September 1943	XIII Corps	183 Inf Div	340 Inf Div	82 Inf Div	327 Inf Div		
	VII Corps	208 Inf Div	75 Inf Div	68 Inf Div	88 Inf Div		
	LII Corps	332 Inf Div	57 Inf Div	10 Pz Gren Div	34 Inf Div		
	XXIV Pz Corps	112 Inf Div	255 Inf Div	11 Pz Div			
	XLVIII Pz Corps	GD	19 Pz Div				

4 October 1943	XLII Corps	454 Sec Div	291 Inf Div	217 Inf Div	339 Inf Div	183 Inf Div	
	LIX Corps	8 Pz Div	208 Inf Div	82 Inf Div	327 Inf Div		
	XIII Corps	340 Inf Div	75 Inf Div	213 Inf Div	88 Inf Div		
	VII Corps	68 Inf Div	7 Pz Div				
	Reserve	332 Inf Div					
8 November 1943	XLII Corps	454 Sec Div	327 Inf Div	208 Inf Div	8 Pz Div	323 Inf Div	213 Inf Div
	LIX Corps	291 Inf Div	7 Pz Div	10 Pz Gren Div	88 Inf Div	82 Inf Div	112 Inf Div
	XIII Corps	340 Inf Div	25 Pz Div	SS R	75 Inf Div	19 Pz Div	
	VII Corps	68 Inf Div	10 Pz Gren Div	168 Inf Div	223 Inf Div		
	XLVIII Pz Corps	198 Inf Div	3 Pz Div				
	XXIV Pz Corps	34 Inf Div	SS LAH				
	Reserve	255 Inf Div	4 Pz Div				
3 December 1943	454 Inf Div	291 Inf Div	327 Inf Div	213 Inf Div	68 Inf Div	323 Inf Div	19 Pz Div
	LIX Corps	340 Inf Div	SS LAH	1 Pz Div	2 Fallschirm Div	SS R	
	XIII Corps	208 Inf Div	7 Pz Div	20 Pz Gren Div	20 Pz Gren Div	255 Inf Div	
	XLVIII Pz Corps	8 Pz Div					
	XLII Corps	25 Pz Div					
	VII Corps	198 Inf Div					
	XXIV Pz Corps	34 Inf Div					
1 January 1944	LIX Corps	291 Inf Div	147 Inf Div	454 Sec Div	68 Inf Div	7 Pz Div	
	XIII Corps	213 Inf Div	208 Inf Div	340 Inf Div	20 Pz Gren Div	17 Pz Div	
	XLVIII Pz Corps	SS LAH	1 Pz Div	82 Inf Div			
	XXIV Pz Corps	18 Art Div	168 Inf Div	6 Pz Div			
	VII Corps	88 Inf Div	198 Inf Div				
	XLII Corps	34 Inf Div	112 Inf Div				
	Reserve	SS Lang	8 Pz Div				
1 February 1944	XIII Corps	454 Sec Div	96 Inf Div	SS R	SS Lang	371 Inf Div	
	LIX Corps	291 Inf Div	8 Pz Div	20 Pz Gren Div	25 Pz Div	168 Inf Div	
	XLVIII Pz Corps	19 Pz Div	208 Inf Div	7 Pz Div			
	XXIV Pz Corps	1 Pz Div	340 Inf Div				
	Reserve	213 Inf Div					
3 March 1944	XLVIII Pz Corps	8 Pz Div	7 Pz Div				
	XIII Corps	340 Inf Div	454 Sec Div				
15 April 1944	XLII Corps	214 Inf Div	72 Inf Div	Brenner	361 Inf Div	213 Inf Div	454 Sec Div
	XIII Corps	340 Inf Div	8 Pz Div	SS Pz Div Ho	359 Inf Div		
	XLVIII Pz Corps	349 Inf Div	357 Inf Div				

Date	Formation	Div 1	Div 2	Div 3	Div 4	Div 5
15 May 1944	**XLII Corps**	214 Inf Div	72 Inf Div	361 Inf Div	454 Sec Div	
	XIII Corps	340 Inf Div	Lenz	96 Inf Div	359 Inf Div	
	XLVIII Pz Corps	349 Inf Div	357 Inf Div			
	Reserve	1 Pz Div				
15 June 1944	**LVI Pz Corps**	26 Inf Div	342 Inf Div	131 Inf Div	1 Ski Div	
	XLII Corps	214 Inf Div	72 Inf Div	88 Inf Div	291 Inf Div	
	XIII Corps	340 Inf Div	361 Inf Div		28 Inf Div	
	Reserve	454 Sec Div	4 Pz Div			
15 July 1944	**VIII Corps**	Hung 12 Res Div	211 Inf Div	5 Inf Div	340 Inf Div	
	LVI Pz Corps	26 Inf Div	342 Inf Div	1 Ski Div		
	XLII Corps	214 Inf Div	72 Inf Div	88 Inf Div		
	XLVI Pz Corps	16 Pz Div	17 Pz Div	291 Inf Div		
	Reserve	213 Inf Div	253 Inf Div			
31 August 1944	**LVI Pz Corps**	214 Inf Div	26 Inf Div	253 Inf Div	1 Ski Div	88 Inf Div
	XLII Corps	342 Inf Div	291 Inf Div	72 Inf Div	213 Inf Div	304 Inf Div
	XLVIII Pz Corps	23 Pz Div	3 Pz Div	1 Pz Div	20 Pz Gren Div	1 Ski Div
	III Pz Corps	17 Pz Corps	97 Inf Div	16 Pz Div	17 Pz Div	
	LVI Pz Corps	214 Inf Div	253 Inf Div	342 Inf Div	304 Inf Div	
	XLII Corps	291 Inf Div	72 Inf Div	88 Inf Div		
	XLVIII Pz Corps	97 Inf Div	16 Pz Div	20 Pz Gren Div		
13 October 1944	214 Inf Div	342 Inf Div	88 Inf Div	17 Pz Div	291 Inf Div	
	XLII Corps	72 Inf Div	20 Pz Gren Div	304 Inf Div		
	XLVIII Pz Corps	16 Pz Div				
5 November 1944	**LVI Pz Corps**	17 Inf Div	214 Inf Div	Hung 5 Res Div	342 Inf Div	
	XLII Corps	72 Inf Div	88 Inf Div	291 Inf Div		
	XLVIII Pz Corps	20 Pz Gren Div	304 Inf Div			
	Reserve	HQs XXIV Pz Corps				
26 November 1944	**LVI Pz Corps**	17 Inf Div	214 Inf Div	Hung 5 Res Div	291 Inf Div	
	XLII Corps	342 Inf Div	72 Inf Div	88 Inf Div		
	XLVIII Pz Corps	68 Inf Div	304 Inf Div			
31 December 1944+A56	**XLII Corps**	342 Inf Div	72 Inf Div	88 Inf Div	291 Inf Div	
	XLVIII Pz Corps	168 Inf Div	68 Inf Div	304 Inf Div		
19 February 1945	**XL Pz Corps**	Bde 100	36 SS Div	Div Matterstock	608 Inf Div	
	XXIV Pz Corps	342 Inf Div	72 Inf Div	16 Pz Div	25 Pz Div	
	GD	Brandenburg	1 Hermann Goering	20 Pz Gren Div		
	Grp Friedrich	21 Pz Div	6 Inf Div	17 Pz Div		

1 March 1945	XL Pz Corps	Bde 100	36 SS Div	Div Matterstock	608 Inf Div	25 Pz Div	35 SS Div
	V Corps	275 Inf Div	72 Inf Div	342 Inf Div		615 Inf Div	342 Inf Div
	GD	Brandenburg	1 Hermann Goering	20 Pz Gren Div	21 Pz Div		
	Reserve	16 Pz Div	Fest Glogau				
12 April 1945	V Corps	SS 35 Div	275 Inf Div	214 Inf Div	SS 36 Div	342 Inf Div	
	Grp Moser	463 Inf Div	404 Inf Div	193 Inf Div	615 Inf Div		
	GD	Brandenburg	Pz Div Bohemia	546 VG Div	615 Inf Div		
	LVII Pz Corps	72 Inf Div	6 Inf Div				
7 May 1945	LXXXX Corps	Brandt	Doepping	469 Inf Div	464 Inf Div		
	Hermann Goering	Luedecke	Dresden 1	1 Hermann Goering	2 Hermann Goering		
	GD	269 Inf Div	72 Inf Div	545 Inf Div	17 Inf Div		
	LVII Pz Corps	615 Inf Div	404 Inf Div	6 Inf Div			
	Reserve	SS R	20 Pz Div	SS Pz Div Fr			

Except as noted, all data www.bundesarchiv.de/findbuecher/ma/rh21-4/index.htm
1. Horst Boog et al., *Germany and the Second World War*, Vol. IV, *Attack on the Soviet Union*, Clarendon Press, 1998, appendix 2.
2. Hans-Adolf Jacobsen, *Kriegstagebuch: das Oberkommando der Wehrmacht*, Vol. II (2), Bernard & Graefe, 1965, pp. 1372–73.

Notes

Introduction

1. One panzer division had more radios (*c.* 500) than the entire German Army in 1914, Walther Nehring, *Die Geschichte der deutsche Panzerwaffe*, Propyläen Verlag, 1969, Appendix 6.
2. Isabel Hull, *Absolute Destruction: Military Culture and the Practices of War in Imperial Germany*, Cornell University, 2006, p. 160. The Germans 'glorified surprise', John English, *On Infantry*, Praeger, 1984.
3. Hull, *Absolute Destruction*, pp. 116–17, 145, 172. For the best discussion of Boyd, see Mike Spick, *The Ace Factor*, Avon Books, 1989.
4. Hull, *Absolute Destruction*, p. 166.
5. In this usage, *Vernichtung* (exterminate) does not refer to genocide.
6. Hull, *Absolute Destruction*, p. 12.
7. Nehring, *Die Geschichte der deutsche Panzerwaffe*, pp. 61, 79, 87. The French Army never eliminated this false heavy and 'legere' distinction. 'Light' in this case should not be confused with German light, or Jäger, divisions employed later in the war.
8. Many histories of the 1940 campaign instead merely perpetuate the Guderian and Rommel cults of personality.
9. Nehring, *Die Geschichte der deutsche Panzerwaffe*, Appendix 4.
10. Victor Madej, *Russo-German War, Summer 1944*, Fedorowicz, 1987, p. 1.
11. Horst Boog et al., *Germany and the Second World War*, Vol. IV, *Attack on the Soviet Union*, Clarendon Press, 1998, p. 313, speech 21 February 1941.

Chapter 1

1. Klaus Maier (ed.), *Germany and the Second World War*, Vol. II, *Germany's Initial Conquest of Europe*, Clarendon Press, 1991, p. 240. As it turned out, even the German's autumn 1939 plan could have probably beaten the French.
2. Armored strength favored the Allies 3,100:2,700, but the Germans dominated in the categories of aircraft (2,000:4,200) and flak (1,500:9,300). Nehring, *Die Geschichte der deutsche Panzerwaffe*, p. 109.
3. Martin Evans, *The Fall of France: Act with Daring*, Osprey, 2000, p. 48. Florian Rothbrust, *Guderian's XIX Panzer Corps and the Battle of France*, Praeger, 1990, pp. 26, 27.
4. The goal of Vernichtungskrieg was the destruction of enemy forces in the field, not the 'command paralysis' so often discussed by interwar theorists such as Fuller or Liddell-Hart.
5. CR Davis, *von Kleist: From Hussat to Panzer Marshal*, Lancer Militaria, 1979, p. 12; von Kleist's Panzer Group was the largest massed armor command in the

world at the time. Len Deighton, *Blitzkrieg*, Triad, 1980, p. 275; Maier, *Germany and the Second World War*, Vol. II, pp. 244, 247, 249; Alan Shepperd, *France 1940, Blitzkrieg in the West*, Osprey, 1990, p. 21

6. Karl-Heinz Frieser, 'Panzer Group Kleist and the Breakthrough in France, 1940, in Michael Krause and R Cody Philips (eds), *Historical Perspectives on the Operational Art*, Center for Military History, 2005, p. 171; Alistair Horne, *To Lose a Battle: France 1940*, Macmillan, 1990, p. 239.

7. Frieser, 'Panzer Group Kleist', pp. 169–70; Kurt Mehner (ed.), *Die Geheimen Tagesberichete der deutschen Wehrmachtführung im Zweiten Weltkrieg, 1939–1945*, Biblio Verlag, 1993, Vol. 1, p. 8.

8. Deighton, *Blitzkrieg*, pp. 273, 275; Peter Monsoor, 'The Second Battle of Sedan, May, 1940', *Military Review*, 26 January 1989; Shepperd, *France 1940*, pp. 37, 44.

9. Frieser, 'Panzer Group Kleist', p. 174; Rothbrust, *Guderian's XIX Panzer Corps*, p. 63; Edward Luttwak, 'The Operational Level of War', *International Security*, Winter 1980–81, p. 70; Shepperd, *France 1940*, p. 43.

10. Rothbrust, *Guderian's XIX Panzer Corps*, pp. 64, 67.

11. Deighton, *Blitzkrieg*, p. 289; Frieser, 'Panzer Group Kleist', p. 172.

12. Deighton, *Blitzkrieg*, pp. 290–91; Evans, *The Fall of France*, p. 51; Friesen, 'Panzer Group Kleist', p. 172; Horne, *To Lose a Battle*, p. 287; FW von Mellenthin, *Panzer Battles*, Ballantine Books, 1971, p. 18.

13. Evans, *The Fall of France*, pp. 53, 58, 60; von Mellenthin, *Panzer Battles*, pp. 17, 19.

14. Deighton, *Blitzkrieg*, p. 293; Evans, *The Fall of France*, p. 60; Frieser, 'Panzer Group Kleist', p. 173; Heinz Guderian, *Panzer Leader*, Ballantine Books, 1968, p. 83; von Mellenthin, *Panzer Battles*, p. 19. The 3rd Armored Division had only been in existence for six weeks.

15. Deighton, *Blitzkrieg*, pp. 286–87, 309; Freiser, 'Panzer Group Kleist', p. 174; Maier, *Germany and the Second World War*, Vol. II, p. 285; Mehner (ed.), *Die Geheimen Tagesberichete der deutschen Wehrmachtführung im Zweiten Weltkrieg*, Vol. 2, p. 13; Shepperd, *France 1940*, p. 59.

16. Shepperd, *France 1940*, pp. 62–3.

17. Evans, *The Fall of France*, p. 63; Frieser, 'Panzer Group Kleist', p. 176; Guderian, *Panzer Leader*, p. 86; Maier, *Germany and the Second World War*, Vol. II, p. 287; Rothbrust, *Guderian's XIX Panzer Corps*, p. 83; Shepperd, *France 1940*, p. 62. After the battle, a debate emerged as to whether or not Reinhardt had fully pressed his advantage, Deighton, *Blitzkrieg*, p. 288.

18. Deighton, *Blitzkrieg*, pp. 310–11; Horne, *To Lose a Battle*, pp. 332, 337; Rothbrust, *Guderian's XIX Panzer Corps*, p. 87; Shepperd, *France 1940*, pp. 64, 67, 69.

19. Davis, *von Kleist*, p. 12; Frieser, 'Panzer Group Kleist', p. 177; Horne, *To Lose a Battle*, pp. 419–20; Shepperd, *France 1940*, p. 75. German intelligence (*Fremde Herre West*) was correct in discounting the danger at Stonne, Horne, *To Lose a Battle*, p. 418.

20. Deighton, *Blitzkrieg*, pp. 312–13; Evans, *The Fall of France*, pp. 73–74; Maier, *Germany and the Second World War*, Vol. II, p. 287; von Mellenthin, *Panzer Battles*, p. 21. With the deception at the Ardennes complete, Hoepner's XVI Panzer Corps

transferred south. De Gaulle did not counterattack on the 16th as stated by Guderian, Horne, *To Lose a Battle*, p. 403.

21. Evans, *The Fall of France*, pp. 75, 122; Frieser, 'Panzer Group Kleist', p. 178; Horne, *To Lose a Battle*, pp. 422, 433, 468; Shepperd, *France 1940*, p. 80.
22. Deighton, *Blitzkrieg*, pp. 330–31; 487; Horne, *To Lose a Battle*, pp. 498, 508; Maier, *Germany and the Second World War*, Vol. II, p. 287; von Mellenthin, *Panzer Battles*, pp. 21–22. The southern, French pincer never materialized, Evans, *The Fall of France*, p. 92. By the 22nd, some German sources also refer to a Panzer Group Hoth, Mehner (ed.), *Die Geheimen Tagesberichete der deutschen Wehrmachtführung im Zweiten Weltkrieg*, Vol. 2, p. 21.
23. Davis, *von Kleist*, p. 13; Guderian, *Panzer Leader*, p. 91; Maier, *Germany and the Second World War*, Vol. II, pp. 289–90; von Mellenthin, *Panzer Battles*, pp. 22–23.
24. Maier, *Germany and the Second World War*, Vol. II, p. 291. It is interesting to compare panzer losses of the first 11 days, 10–20 May (Ardennes, Meuse, race across north-east France) – 127 destroyed, with the second 11 days, 21–31 May (action near the Channel coast) – 485 destroyed, nearly a factor of 4; Maier, ibid., p. 290.
25. Davis, *von Kleist*, p. 13, Deighton, *Blitzkrieg*, p. 350; Guderian, *Panzer Leader*, p. 100; Horne, *To Lose a Battle*, p. 556; Mehner (ed.), *Die Geheimen Tagesberichete der deutschen Wehrmachtführung im Zweiten Weltkrieg*, Vol. 2, pp. 27, 64, 70; von Mellenthin, *Panzer Battles*, pp. 24–25.
26. Mehner (ed.), *Die Geheimen Tagesberichete der deutschen Wehrmachtführung im Zweiten Weltkrieg*, Vol. 2, pp. 65, 70, 79, 82, 94.
27. Helmut Greiner et al., *The German Campaign in the Balkans*, US Army Center for Military History Publication (104–4), 1953, pp. 22–24, 30–32, 41. As Robert Citino has written in *The Death of the Wehrmacht: The German Campaigns of 1942*, University of Kansas, 2007, p. 20, the significance of Belgrade lay not only in its status as Yugoslavia's capital, but because of its strategic importance to Yugoslavia, therefore their army could not afford to lose the city and **had** to defend it.
28. Greiner et al., *The German Campaign in the Balkans*, pp. 51–52, 56; Mehner (ed.), *Die Geheimen Tagesberichete der deutschen Wehrmachtführung im Zweiten Weltkrieg*, Vol. 2, p. 56; von Mellenthin, *Panzer Battles*, p. 35.
29. Luttwak, 'The Operational Level of War', pp. 64, 67.
30. Ibid., pp. 68–70.

Chapter 2

1. Boog et al., *Germany and the Second World War*, Vol. IV, Appendix 2.
2. GW Schrodek, *Ihr Glaube galt dem Vaterland*, Schild Verlag, 1976, p. 119. A *Panzerstrasse*, sometimes called a (*Panzer*) *Rollbahn*, was a high-quality road reserved for the use of the panzers and their support units.
3. John Erickson, *Road to Stalingrad: Stalin's War with Germany*, Yale University, 1999, pp. 91, 160; James Sterrett, 'Southwest Front Operations, June–September, 1941', MA dissertation, University of Calgary, 1994; pp. 42, 50.
4. David Glantz (ed.), *The Initial Period of the War on the Eastern Front, 22 June–August 1941*, Frank Cass, 1993, pp. 255, 259, 261; Werner Haupt, *Army Group*

South: The Wehrmacht in Russia, 1941–1945, Schiffer Military History, 1998, p. 18; Eberhard von Mackensen, *Vom Bug bis zum Kaukasus*, Vowinkel, 1967, p. 11; Sterrett, 'Southwest Front Operations', pp. 51, 53.

5.   Glantz (ed.), *The Initial Period of the War on the Eastern Front*, pp. 261, 264, 268, 272; David Glantz and Jonathan House, *When Titans Clashed: How the Red Army Stopped Hitler*, University of Kansas, 1995, p. 54; Sterrett, 'Southwest Front Operations', p. 54.

6.   Boog et al., *Germany and the Second World War*, Vol. IV, pp. 549–51.

7.   Cajus Bekker, *Luftwaffe War Diaries*, Ballantine Books, 1969, p. 551; Glantz (ed.), *The Initial Period of the War on the Eastern Front*, pp. 276, 279; Glantz and House, *When Titans Clashed*, p. 54; Schrodek, *Ihr Glaube galt dem Vaterland*, pp. 133–34; Sterrett, 'Southwest Front Operations', p. 56; GK Zhukov, 'The War Begins: The Battle of Moscow', *Main Front*, Brassey's, 1987, p. 9. The Germans held the battlefield which greatly improved the recovery and maintenance rates of their damaged equipment and vehicles. Thanks to Göring's personal intervention no Stukas flew in support of von Kleist until 16 July, Boog et al., *Germany and the Second World War*, Vol. IV, p. 778; Charles von Luttichau, unpublished manuscript, US Army Center for Military History, n.d., Chapter X, p. 10.

8.   Boog et al., *Germany and the Second World War*, Vol. IV, pp. 555, 557; Erickson, *Road to Stalingrad*, pp. 165, 167; Glantz (ed.), *The Initial Period of the War on the Eastern Front*, p. 279; Werner Haupt, *Kiev*, Podzun Verlag, 1964, p. 26.

9.   Boog et al., *Germany and the Second World War*, Vol. IV, p. 556; David Glantz, *Barbarossa*, Tempus, 2001, n. 79; Glantz (ed.), *The Initial Period of the War on the Eastern Front*, pp. 282, 312; von Luttichau, unpublished manuscript, Chapter X, pp. 2, 9; Sterrett, 'Southwest Front Operations', p. 75.

10. Glantz (ed.), *The Initial Period of the War on the Eastern Front*, pp. 314–16; Haupt, *Kiev*, p. 29; von Luttichau, unpublished manuscript, Chapter X, p. 9; von Mackensen, *Vom Bug bis zum Kaukasus*, pp. 14–15; Sterrett, 'Southwest Front Operations', p. 74. As soon as III Panzer reached the Irpen, von Mackensen received notice that 'orders from the highest authority' (Hitler) were to halt immediately. The Führer had decided he wanted no part in urban combat, a wise lesson, but one he would apply very unevenly for the rest of the war.

11. Von Luttichau, unpublished manuscript, Chapter X, p. 12; von Mackensen, *Vom Bug bis zum Kaukasus*, p. 16; Sterrett, 'Southwest Front Operations', p. 75; Zhukov, 'The War Begins', p. 18. During the first three weeks of Barbarossa, First Panzer Army claimed 1,200 tanks destroyed, while Luftflotte Four claimed another 250, Glantz (ed.), *The Initial Period of the War on the Eastern Front*, p. 303; Samuel Mitcham, *Men of the Luftwaffe*, Presidio Press, 1988, p. 134.

12. Boog et al., *Germany and the Second World War*, Vol. IV, pp. 560–61; Erickson, *Road to Stalingrad*, p. 171; Glantz (ed.), *The Initial Period of the War on the Eastern Front*, p. 316; Haupt, *Army Group South*, p. 33; Haupt, *Kiev*, p. 36; von Mackensen, *Vom Bug bis zum Kaukasus*, p. 17; Sterrett, 'Southwest Front Operations', p. 79. The Eleventh Army was supposed to participate in the planned *Kessel*, but for many reasons could not make the rendezvous.

13. Erickson, *Road to Stalingrad*, p. 203; Haupt, *Army Group South*, p. 32; von Luttichau, unpublished manuscript, Chapter X, pp. 21–23, 26; Schrodek, *Ihr Glaube galt dem Vaterland*, p. 154, 'toy gun' refers to the dummy main armament

on a command tank. On 10 July, Stavka created 'Directions' to coordinate the efforts of two or more fronts, in this case, Southwestern and Southern plus the Black Sea Fleet.

14. Alan Clark, *Barbarossa*, William Morrow, 1965, p. 134; Haupt, *Kiev*, p. 45; Haupt, *Army Group South*, pp. 33, 37, 39; von Luttichau, unpublished manuscript, Chapter X, p. 26, Chapter XI, pp. 6, 23; Wolfgang Werthen, *Geschichte der 16. Panzer Division*, Podzun Verlag, 1958, p. 54. Originally First Panzer and Seventeenth Armies were to meet at Uman, but in view of delays incurred near Vinnitsa by the latter, the rendezvous was moved to Pervomaisk.

15. Boog et al., *Germany and the Second World War*, Vol. IV, pp. 563, 567; Martin van Creveld, *Supplying War: Logistics from Wallenstein to Patton*, Cambridge, 1977, p. 164; Erickson, *Road to Stalingrad*, p. 204; von Luttichau, unpublished manuscript, Chapter XII, pp. 7, 9; Sterrett, 'Southwest Front Operations', p. 76.

16. Boog et al., *Germany and the Second World War*, Vol. IV, pp. 596–97, 783; Walter Görlitz, *Paulus and Stalingrad: A Life of Field Marshal Friedrich Paulus with Notes, Correspondence and Documents from His Papers*, Greenwood, 1974, p. 129; Haupt, *Army Group South*, pp. 53, 55; von Luttichau, unpublished manuscript, Chapter XII, pp. 10, 12, 14–15, 17; Mitcham, *Men of the Luftwaffe*, p. 142; Werthen, *Geschichte der 16. Panzer Division*, p. 61. Both the Hungarian and Italian corps were far to the rear of the panzers and very low on supplies. Stavka gave Southern Front permission to evacuate the Dniester area so long as a garrison remained in Odessa. Earl Ziemke and Magda Bauer, *Moscow to Stalingrad: Decision in the East*, Military Heritage Press, 1988, p. 33.

17. Brian Fugate, *Operation Barbarossa: Stategy and Tactics on the Eastern Front, 1941*, Presidio Press, 1984, p. 262; von Luttichau, unpublished manuscript, Chapter XII, p. 25.

18. Boog et al., *Germany and the Second World War*, Vol. IV, p. 600; Haupt, *Kiev*, pp. 54–55, 63; von Luttichau, unpublished manuscript, Chapter XII, pp. 18, 24; von Mackensen, *Vom Bug bis zum Kaukasus*, pp. 26, 29; Samuel Mitcham and Gene Mueller, *Hitler's Commanders: Officers of the Wehrmacht, the Luftwaffe, the Kriegsmarine, and the Waffen-SS*, Scarborough House, 1992, p. 95.

19. Christer Bergstrom and Andrey Mikhailov, *Black Cross, Red Star: Volume 1, Operation Barabrossa 1941*, Pacifica Military History, 2000, p. 152; Boog et al., *Germany and the Second World War*, Vol. IV, pp. 600–1; Haupt, *Army Group South*, pp. 63, 70; Sterrett, 'Southwest Front Operations', pp. 87–88.

20. Boog et al., *Germany and the Second World War*, Vol. IV, pp. 783, 874–75; Erickson, *Road to Stalingrad*, pp. 207–8; Fugate, *Operation Barbarossa*, pp. 262, 265; Glantz and House, *When Titans Clashed*, p. 76; Haupt, *Army Group South*, pp. 65, 71, 73, 139, 141. Date for closing Kiev pocket at Lokhvitsa is alternatively given as 14 or 15 September. I have used date reflected in OKW War Diary, Hans-Adolf Jacobsen, *Kriegstagebuch: das Oberkommando der Wehrmacht*, Bernard & Graefe, 1965, p. 636.

21. Boog et al., *Germany and the Second World War*, Vol. IV, pp. 604–5, 608, 612–13; Following Kiev, Stavka abolished the Southwest Direction, the defenses reverted to Southwestern and Southern Fronts, Erickson, *Road to Stalingrad*, p. 210.

22. Boog et al., *Germany and the Second World War*, Vol. IV, pp. 607, 613; Erickson, *Road to Stalingrad*, p. 255; Haupt, *Kiev*, p. 89; Giovanni Messe, *Der Krieg im Osten*,

Thomas Verlag, 1948, pp. 123–24. In early October, panzer groups and motorized corps began to be renamed panzer armies and corps.

23. Bergstrom and Mikhailov, *Black Cross, Red Star*, p. 153; Boog et al., *Germany and the Second World War*, Vol. IV, pp. 607–8, 610, 1119–20; Helmut Breymayer, *Das Wiesel: Geschichte der 125 Infantrie Division, 1940–44*, Vaas Verlag, 1983, p. 158; van Creveld, *Supplying War*, p. 165; von Mackensen, *Vom Bug bis zum Kaukasus*, pp. 38–39, 41.

24. Boog et al., *Germany and the Second World War*, Vol. IV, pp. 617, 788; Messe, *Der Krieg im Osten*, pp. 129–30, 133, 135, 137.

25. Boog et al., *Germany and the Second World War*, Vol. IV, pp. 617–19; van Creveld, *Supplying War*, p. 165; Werthen, *Geschichte der 16. Panzer Division*, p. 74. The Motorized Brigade, later expanded to a division, was the one combat-worthy formation contributed by Slovakia.

26. Bergstrom and Mikhailov, *Black Cross, Red Star*, p. 241; *Germany and the Second World War*, p. 884; Erickson, *Road to Stalingrad*, p. 265; Werner Haupt, *Army Group Center: The Wehrmacht in Russia, 1941–1945*, Schiffer Military History, 1997, p. 102; Joel Hayward, *Stopped at Stalingrad: Luftwaffe and Hitler's Defeat in the East 1942–1943*, University of Kansas, 1998, p. 54; von Mackensen, *Vom Bug bis zum Kaukasus*, p. 42; Charles Messenger, *Hitler's Gladiator: The Life and Wars of Panzer Army Commander Sepp Dietrich*, Brassey's, 1988, p. 104.

27. Boog et al., *Germany and the Second World War*, Vol. IV, p. 61; Clark, *Barbarossa*, p. 178; John Ellis, *Brute Force*, Viking, 1990, p. 59; Erickson, *Road to Stalingrad*, p. 265; von Mackensen, *Vom Bug bis zum Kaukasus*, p. 46; Ziemke and Bauer, *Moscow to Stalingrad*, p. 54.

28. Boog et al., *Germany and the Second World War*, Vol. IV, pp. 622–26, 789; Ellis, *Brute Force*, p. 65; Erickson, *Road to Stalingrad*, p. 265; Görlitz, *Paulus and Stalingrad*, p. 44; Messenger, *Hitler's Gladiator*, p. 105; Ziemke and Bauer, *Moscow to Stalingrad*, pp. 54–57. For a different view of the Poltava meeting between Hitler and von Rundstedt, see John Toland, *Adolf Hitler*, Vol. II, Doubleday, 1976, p. 789.

29. Breymeyer, *Das Wiesel*, p. 164.

30. Ibid., p. 183; Hans Neidhardt, *Mit Tanne und Eichenlaub*, Stocker, 1981, pp. 152, 164. Light divisions were redesignated Jäger divisions on 1 April 1942, Neidhardt, *Mit Tanne und Eichenlaub*, p. 168.

31. Fedor von Bock, *The War Diary, 1939–1945*, Schiffer Military History, 1996, entries for most of February; Neidhardt, *Mit Tanne und Eichenlaub*, p. 156; Ziemke and Bauer, *Moscow to Stalingrad*, pp. 156, 159. As mentioned above, von Reichenau took command of Army Group South on 2 December. He suffered a stroke during lunch on 16 January, and died the next day. Von Bock was recalled from medical leave and reported to Hitler at Rastenburg on 17 January.

32. Ziemke and Bauer, *Moscow to Stalingrad*, pp. 288–89.

33. Anthony Beevor, *Stalingrad: The Fateful Siege, 1942–1943*, Viking, 1998, p. 65; Erickson, *Road to Stalingrad*, pp. 345–46; Haupt, *Army Group South*, pp. 139, 143; von Mackensen, *Vom Bug bis zum Kaukasus*, p. 71; Ziemke and Bauer, *Moscow to Stalingrad*, pp. 273, 276, 278–82.

34. Von Bock, *The War Diary*, 23 and 24 June 1942; Ziemke and Bauer, *Moscow to Stalingrad*, p. 318. Armeegruppe von Kleist was disbanded on 8 June as part of

the reorganization prior to Blau. (Since Operation Wilhelm was conducted by Sixth Army, it is not covered in detail here.)

35. Citino, *The Death of the Wehrmacht*, p. 174. Due to a security breach, on 30 June Blau I, II and III were all renamed, but for simplicity's sake the original names will continue to be used here. Ziemke and Bauer, *Moscow to Stalingrad*, p. 336.

36. Ziemke and Bauer, *Moscow to Stalingrad*, p. 346.

37 Von Mackensen, *Vom Bug bis zum Kaukasus*, p. 86; Ziemke and Bauer, *Moscow to Stalingrad*, pp. 347–48. Maximillian Freiherr von Weichs took over Army Group B after von Bock, while Hitler henceforth personally controlled both A and B.

38. Citino, *The Death of the Wehrmacht*, p. 177; Erickson, *Road to Stalingrad*, p. 362; Glantz and House, *When Titans Clashed*, p. 120; Ziemke and Bauer, *Moscow to Stalingrad*, pp. 348–51.

39. Erickson, *Road to Stalingrad*, p. 370; Haupt, *Army Group South*, p. 180; von Mackensen, *Vom Bug bis zum Kaukasus*, p. 89; Ziemke and Bauer, *Moscow to Stalingrad*, pp. 355–56.

40. Von Mackensen, *Vom Bug bis zum Kaukasus*, p. 91; Ziemke and Bauer, *Moscow to Stalingrad*, pp. 358–60. Fourth Panzer Army transferred to Army Group A on 30 July.

41. Citino, *The Death of the Wehrmacht*, pp. 228, 231–32; Haupt, *Army Group South*, pp. 183, 187–88; von Mackensen, *Vom Bug bis zum Kaukasus*, pp. 91–95, Ziemke and Bauer, *Moscow to Stalingrad*, pp. 362, 364–65. The 14th Panzer did not accompany von Kleist south. On 30 July, Hoth turned over XL Panzer to First Panzer.

42. Citino, *The Death of the Wehrmacht*, p. 233; Erickson, *Road to Stalingrad*, pp. 377–78; Ziemke and Bauer, *Moscow to Stalingrad*, pp. 366, 368–71, 373.

43. Citino, *The Death of the Wehrmacht*, p. 234; von Mackensen, *Vom Bug bis zum Kaukasus*, pp. 96–97; Ziemke and Bauer, *Moscow to Stalingrad*, pp. 374–75.

44. Von Mackensen, *Vom Bug bis zum Kaukasus*, pp. 100–1; Ziemke and Bauer, *Moscow to Stalingrad*, p. 379.

45. Citino, *The Death of the Wehrmacht*, pp. 242–43; Haupt, *Army Group South*, p. 201; von Mackensen, *Vom Bug bis zum Kaukasus*, pp. 103, 105–6; Ziemke and Bauer, *Moscow to Stalingrad*, pp. 453–54; Earl Ziemke, *Stalingrad to Berlin: The German Defeat in the East*, Barnes & Noble, 1996, p. 17.

46. Haupt, *Army Group South*, p. 202; von Mackensen, *Vom Bug bis zum Kaukasus*, p. 110; Ziemke and Bauer, *Moscow to Stalingrad*, p. 456. Hitler personally took command of Army Group A on 10 September.

47. Ziemke and Bauer, *Moscow to Stalingrad*, p. 493. Some portions of Fourth Panzer Army not trapped at Stalingrad would also be destroyed during Saturn, and the down-graded Little Saturn.

48. Paul Carell, *Scorched Earth*, Harrap, 1970, pp. 142, 148; Davis, *von Kleist*, p. 15; John Erickson, *Road to Berlin*, Weidenfeld & Nicolson, 1983, pp. 28, 30–32; Glantz and House, *When Titans Clashed*, p. 142; Haupt, *Army Group South*, pp. 240, 242–45; Ziemke, *Stalingrad to Berlin*, pp. 71, 85.

49. Walter Dunn, *Kursk: Hitler's Gamble, 1943*, Praeger, 1997, p. 97; David Glantz, *From the Don to the Dnepr: Soviet Offensive Operations, December 1942 to August 1943*, Frank Cass, 1991, p. 88; George Nipe, *Last Victory: The SS Panzercorps and*

Manstein's Counter Offensive, February–March 1943, Schiffer, 2000, p. 76; Ziemke, *Stalingrad to Berlin*, pp. 86, 91–93. Army Group Don was renamed South.

50. Erickson, *Road to Berlin*, pp. 51, 53; Glantz, *From the Don to the Dnepr*, pp. 99, 106, 110, 112, 118–19; Ziemke, *Stalingrad to Berlin*, p. 94. During the swirling armored battles, XXX Corps ably defended First Panzer's right, Nipe, *Last Victory*, p. 147. 'Backhand Blow' is the name preferred by English speakers for von Manstein's February–March 1943 counterattack, Germans often use Rochade, their word for the chess term 'to castle'.
51. Ziemke, *Stalingrad to Berlin*, pp. 127–28.
52. Dunn, *Kursk*, p. 146; Glantz, *From the Don to the Dnepr*, p. 245; Haupt, *Army Group South*, p. 282; Ziemke, *Stalingrad to Berlin*, pp. 137–38.
53. Erickson, *Road to Berlin*, pp. 119, 124; Haupt, *Army Group South*, p. 291; Erich von Manstein, *Lost Victories*, Presidio Press, 1984, p. 457; Ziemke, *Stalingrad to Berlin*, pp. 160–62, 164–65.
54. Erickson, *Road to Berlin*, p. 137; Glantz and House, *When Titans Clashed*, p. 171; Haupt, *Army Group South*, p. 297; Albert Seaton, *The Russo-German War*, Praeger, 1971, pp. 384–85; Ziemke, *Stalingrad to Berlin*, pp. 166, 169, 174–78. Breymayer, *Die Wiesel* , pp. 306–7. The retreating Germans used 500 tons of explosives on the dam, employed 14,000 mines and other obstacles throughout the city and bridgehead, Breymayer, *Die Wiesel*, p. 309.
55. Erickson, *Road to Berlin*, p. 138; Ziemke, *Stalingrad to Berlin*, pp. 181–84.
56. Glantz and House, *When Titans Clashed*, p. 186; Ziemke, *Stalingrad to Berlin*, pp. 221–25.
57. Haupt, *Army Group South*, p. 322; Ziemke, *Stalingrad to Berlin*, pp. 224–26.
58. Erickson, *Road to Berlin*, p. 165; Glantz and House, *When Titans Clashed*, p. 187; Haupt, *Army Group South*, p. 322; Ziemke, *Stalingrad to Berlin*, p. 226. Two perfect examples demonstrate the traps awaiting the historian: Ziemke writes that the Soviets closed the Korsun pocket on 28 January, Glantz and House say 3 February. Glantz and House name Stemmermann 'Werner' and call him commander of XLII Corps; Wolf Keilig, *Das Deutsche Heer, 1939–1945*, Podzun Verlag, 1956, names him 'Wilhelm' and says he led XI Corps!
59. Wolfgang Paul, *Brennpunkte*, Hoentges, 1977, p. 350.
60. Glantz and House, *When Titans Clashed*, pp. 187–88; Haupt, *Army Group South*, pp. 323–25, 332; Ziemke, *Stalingrad to Berlin*, pp. 232–37. Rolf Stoves, *Die 1. Panzer-Division, 1935–45*, Podzun Verlag, 1961, p. 503.
61. Glantz and House, *When Titans Clashed*, p. 189; Haupt, *Army Group South*, p. 334; Ziemke, *Stalingrad to Berlin*, pp. 275–76; Breymayer, *Die Wiesel*, p. 315.
62. Erickson, *Road to Berlin*, pp. 184, 182; Glantz and House, *When Titans Clashed*, p. 189; Ziemke, *Stalingrad to Berlin*, pp. 275–77.
63. These three divisions, under Colonel Dr Karl Mauss, commander of Panzer-grenadier Regiment 33, technically belonged to Fourth Panzer, but de facto fought in the pocket with First Panzer. Mauss was promoted to major general on 1 April.
64. Glantz and House, *When Titans Clashed*, p. 189; Paul, *Brennpunkte*, p. 367; Haupt, *Army Group South*, p. 343; Ziemke, *Stalingrad to Berlin*, pp. 279–80.
65. Paul, *Brennpunkte*, p. 369.
66. Erickson, *Road to Berlin*, p. 186; Glantz and House, *When Titans Clashed*, pp. 189–90; Paul, *Brennpunkte*, p. 368; Ziemke, *Stalingrad to Berlin*, pp. 280–81.

67. Erickson, *Road to Berlin*; Paul, *Brennpunkte*, pp. 370, 379; Haupt, *Army Group South*, pp. 344–45, 355–56; Ziemke, *Stalingrad to Berlin*, pp. 281–82. Ironically, by this point the Germans occupied very little of the Ukraine and soon lost what they did have.

68. Erickson, *Road to Berlin*, pp. 231–33; David Glantz, *Red Storm Over the Balkans*, University of Kansas, 2007, p. 6; Neidhardt, *Mit Tanne und Eichenlaub*, pp. 321–22, 324, 328; Eberhard Raus, *Panzer Operationen*, DeCapo Press, 2003, p. 279.

69. Raus, *Panzer Operationen*, p. 276.

70. Erickson, *Road to Berlin*, p. 235; Haupt, *Army Group South*, p. 379; Neidhardt, *Mit Tanne und Eichenlaub*, p. 328; Madej, *Russo-German War*, pp. 53, 56; Raus, *Panzer Operationen*, p. 280, 283, 285; Samuel Mitcham, *Crumbling Empire: The German Defeat in the East, 1944*, Praeger, 2001, p. 76; Ziemke, *Stalingrad to Berlin*, pp. 332–33.

71. Erickson, *Road to Berlin*, pp. 241–43; Raus, *Panzer Operationen*, pp. 286, 290–91; Neidhardt, *Mit Tanne und Eichenlaub*, p. 336. The 4th Mountain Division corseted the Hungarian right at the Jablonica Pass, Raus, *Panzer Operationen*, p. 293.

72. Erickson, *Road to Berlin*, p. 304; Glantz and House, *When Titans Clashed*, p. 225; Rolf Hinze, *To the Bitter End*, Helion & Co., 2006, p. 30; Mitcham, *Crumbling Empire*, pp. 95, 212; Raus, *Panzer Operationen*, pp. 291–93; Ziemke, *Stalingrad to Berlin*, pp. 359, 362; Neidhardt, *Mit Tanne und Eichenlaub*, p. 338.

73. Erickson, *Road to Berlin*, p. 394; Hinze, *To the Bitter End*, p. 60; Mitcham, *Crumbling Empire*, pp. 213, 216; Neidhardt, *Mit Tanne und Eichenlaub*, pp. 339, 359–60, 362, 364, 368. On 23 September, Army Group South Ukraine became Army Group South again.

74. Erickson, *Road to Berlin*, pp. 445, 547; Hinze, *To the Bitter End*, pp. 139, 143; Ziemke, *Stalingrad to Berlin*, p. 466.

75. Erickson, *Road to Berlin*, pp. 624–25, 627; Glantz and House, *When Titans Clashed*, pp. 272–73; Hinze, *To the Bitter End*, p. 163.

Chapter 3

1. Von Luttichau, unpublished manuscript, Chapter VI, pp. 9–10; Joachim Neumann, *Die 4. Panzer-Division*, Selbstverlag, 1985, pp. 192, 195; Günther Richter, *Geschichte der 3. Panzer-Division*, Berlin, 1967, p. 109; HP Willmott, *The Great Crusade*, Free Press, 1989, p. 149.

2. Glantz (ed.), *The Initial Period of the War on the Eastern Front*, p. 202; Richter, *Geschichte der 3*, pp. 111–13.

3. Von Luttichau, unpublished manuscript, Chapter VI, pp. 31, 37, 39, 40.

4. Ellis, *Brute Force*, p. 74; von Luttichau, unpublished manuscript, Chapter VI, p. 41; Neumann, *Die 4. Panzer-Division*, pp. 201–2; Richter, *Geschichte der 3*, pp. 116–18.

5. Clark, *Barbarossa*, p. 100; von Luttichau, unpublished manuscript, Chapter VI, pp. 52, 57.

6. Helmut Spaeter, *Die Geschichte des Panzerkorps Grossdeutschland*, Selbstverlag, 1958, p. 267. PAK, Panzerabwehrkanonen, or anti-tank gun.

7. Von Luttichau, unpublished manuscript, Chapter XIII, p. 18; Albert Seaton, *Battle for Moscow*, Stein & Day, 1971, p. 124.
8. Joachim Lemelsen, *Die 29. Division*, Podzun Verlag, 1960, pp. 117, 119, 121; von Luttichau, unpublished manuscript, Chapter XIV, pp. 20, 24; Neumann, *Die 4. Panzer-Division*, pp. 206–9; Richter, *Geschichte der 3*, pp. 125–26.
9. Von Luttichau, unpublished manuscript, Chapter XV, p. 4, Chapter XVI, p. 12. Along this stretch of river, the Dnepr's east bank represented the Stalin Line.
10. David Glantz, *The Battle for Smolensk: 7 July–10 September*, self published, 2001, p. 25; Lemelsen, *Die 29. Division*, p. 123; von Luttichau, unpublished manuscript, Chapter XVI, pp. 16–17.
11. Neumann, *Die 4. Panzer-Division*, pp. 219, 229; Richter, *Geschichte der 3*, pp. 133, 154.
12. Seaton, *The Russo-German War*, p. 162.
13. Glantz, *The Battle for Smolensk*, pp. 13–14, 21.
14. Ibid., pp. 33, 43.
15. Ibid., pp. 43, 47; von Luttichau, unpublished manuscript, Chapter XVI, pp. 47–48, 51.
16. Von Luttichau, unpublished manuscript, Chapter XVI, p. 38a.
17. Ibid., Chapter XVII, pp. 17, 20.
18. Timothy Wray, *Standing Fast: German Defensive Doctrine on the Eastern Front during World War Two, Prewar to March 1943*, US Army Command and General Staff College, 1986, pp. 40–42.
19. Spaeter, *Die Geschichte des Panzerkorps Grossdeutschland*, p. 286.
20. Von Luttichau, unpublished manuscript, Chapter XVI, p. 45 n.
21. Ibid., Chapter XVI, pp. 51, 53–55.
22. Haupt, *Army Group South*, p. 60. Ian Kershaw, *Nemesis, 1939–1945*, Norton, 2001, pp. 413–14.
23. Boog et al., *Germany and the Second World War*, Vol. IV, p. 599; Brian Fugate and Lev Dvoretsky, *Thunder on the Dnepr*, Presidio Press, 1997, p. 341; Glantz and House, *When Titans Clashed*, p. 76; Haupt, *Army Group Center*, p. 69.
24. Paul Carell, *Hitler Moves East, 1941–1943*, Ballantine Books, 1971, pp. 115–16. Three lieutenants, junior officers for such a sensitive mission, led the charge: Buchterkirch – 6th Panzer Regiment; Störck – Engineer Company, 394th Motorized Infantry Regiment; Vopel – 1st Company, 394th Motorized Infantry.
25. Bergstrom and Mikhailov, *Black Cross, Red Star*, p. 149; Erickson, *Road to Stalingrad*, pp. 206–7; James Lucas, *War on the Eastern Front: The German Soldier in Russia, 1941–1945*, Greenhill Books, 1998, pp. 187–89.
26. Bergstrom and Mikhailov, *Black Cross, Red Star*, p. 152; Erickson, *Road to Stalingrad*, pp. 207–8; Fugate and Dvoretsky, *Thunder on the Dnepr*, p. 259; Lucas, *War on the Eastern Front*, p. 190.
27. Boog et al., *Germany and the Second World War*, Vol. IV, p. 601; Clark, *Barbarossa*, p. 136; Haupt, *Army Group South*, p. 75; Haupt, *Kiev*, p. 155; Lucas, *War on the Eastern Front*, pp. 190–1. Different sources give different dates for the Lokhvitsa junction, 15 September is from Boog et al.
28. Joel Hayward, *Stopped at Stalingrad: Luftwaffe and Hitler's Defeat in the East 1942–1943*, University of Kansas, 1998, p. 136; von Luttichau, unpublished manuscript, Chapter XXX, pp. 17, 24; Klaus Reinhardt, *Moscow, The Turning Point*,

Berg, 1992, pp. 57–58; Richter, *Geschichte der 3*, p. 186. One regiment can hardly be considered an adequate reserve for an army sized formation.

29. Bergstrom and Mikhailov, *Black Cross, Red Star*, p. 195; Glantz, *Barbarossa*, pp. 144–45, 148; Haywood, *Stopped at Stalingrad*, pp. 139, 141; Reinhardt, *Moscow*, pp. 79, 82; Richter, *Geschichte der 3*, p. 186.
30. Richter, *Geschichte der 3*, pp. 305, 310.
31. Glantz, *Barbarossa*, p. 149; Haywood, *Stopped at Stalingrad*, pp. 143, 146; Reinhardt, *Moscow*, p. 87. Eremenko and an adjutant escaped and eventually made it to a 3rd Army command post several days later. On the 13th he was wounded by a Luftwaffe raid and would be out of the war for nearly a year.
32. Neumann, *Die 4. Panzer-Division*, pp. 315, 324; Richter, *Geschichte der 3*, p. 192; Willmott, *The Great Crusade*, p. 156.
33. Neumann, *Die 4. Panzer-Division*, pp. 333, 335; Richter, *Geschichte der 3*, pp. 194–95, 197–99.
34. Glantz, *Barbarossa*, pp. 162, 168; Richter, *Geschichte der 3*, pp. 199, 201–2, 208–9. When the Soviets recaptured Yasnya Polyana they claimed the Germans had done heavy damage to the place.
35. Erickson, *Road to Stalingrad*, p. 260; Glantz, *Barbarossa*, p. 172; Haywood, *Stopped at Stalingrad*, p. 167; Haupt, *Army Group Center*, p. 104; Neumann, *Die 4. Panzer-Division*, pp. 379, 383; Reinhardt, *Moscow*, pp. 224–25; Richter, *Geschichte der 3*, p. 209.
36. Haupt, *Army Group Center*, pp. 101–2; Ziemke and Bauer, *Moscow to Stalingrad*, pp. 65, 67, 73, 95. As had been the case that summer at Yelnia, final locations where panzer thrusts petered out did not always equate to the best defensive sites.
37. Haupt, *Army Group Center*, pp. 104, 106; Ziemke and Bauer, *Moscow to Stalingrad*, pp. 77, 79–81, 83, 94. 'Sick leave' was often a Nazi euphemism for 'relieved of duty', but von Bock had been suffering legitimate stomach illness much of his life. Von Brauchitsch, on the other hand, had been completely broken by Hitler.
38. Ziemke and Bauer, *Moscow to Stalingrad*, pp. 85–86, 88, 90–91, 95–97. Acknowledging the situation on the ground, von Kluge officially transferred XLIII Corps to Fourth Army on the 18th.
39. Ibid., pp. 97–100. Guderian claims to have issued the prohibited 'Order of the Day' anyhow.
40. Ibid., pp. 101, 122–23; Haupt, *Army Group Center*, p. 113.
41. Roger Edwards, *Panzer: A Revolution in Warfare*, Arms & Armor, 1989, p. 172; Erickson, *Road to Stalingrad*, pp. 316–17; Ziemke and Bauer, *Moscow to Stalingrad*, pp. 164, 169–70, 175. In mid-January, von Weichs returned from sick leave to take the helm of Second Army freeing Schmidt to command Second Panzer only.
42. Haupt, *Army Group Center*, pp. 115, 123; Ziemke and Bauer, *Moscow to Stalingrad*, pp. 178–79, 241.
43. Ziemke and Bauer, *Moscow to Stalingrad*, pp. 252, 254, 329.
44. Haupt, *Army Group Center*, p. 125; Ziemke and Bauer, *Moscow to Stalingrad*, pp. 398, 402–6.
45. Dunn, *Kursk*, p. 9.
46. Erickson, *Road to Stalingrad*, pp. 57, 59; David Glantz and Jonathan House, *The Battle of Kursk*, University of Kansas, 2004, pp. 22, 51; Glantz and House, *When*

Titans Clashed, p. 146; Haupt, *Army Group Center*, p. 142; Ziemke and Bauer, *Moscow to Stalingrad*, p. 117.

47. Erickson, *Road to Berlin*, p. 108; Glantz and House, *The Battle of Kursk*, pp. 229, 233; Ziemke, *Stalingrad to Berlin*, pp. 137, 139. With Citadel faltering, the 3rd Guards Tank Army was now available.

48. Erickson, *Road to Berlin*, pp. 113–14; Glantz and House, *The Battle of Kursk*, p. 235; Haupt, *Army Group Center*, p. 161; Ziemke, *Stalingrad to Berlin*, p. 139.

49. Erickson, *Road to Berlin*, pp. 114–15; Glantz and House, *The Battle of Kursk*, pp. 238–40; Haupt, *Stalingrad to Berlin*, p. 163; Ziemke, *Stalingrad to Berlin*, pp. 140–41.

50. Hubert Lanz et al., *German Antiguerrilla Operations in the Balkans, 1941–44*, US Army Center for Military History Publication 104–18, 1989, p. 119; Glantz and House, *The Battle of Kursk*, p. 233; Otto Kumm, *Prinz Eugen*, Fedorowicz, 1995, p. 30; Mitcham and Mueller, *Hitler's Commanders*, p. 198; Ziemke, *Stalingrad to Berlin*, p. 365.

51. Hubert Lanz et al., *German Antiguerrilla Operations*; Kumm, *Prinz Eugen*, pp. 59, 63, 69; Neidhardt, *Mit Tanne und Eichenlaub*, pp. 259, 262, 274; Alois Beck, *Bis Stalingrad*, H Abt Verlag, 1983, pp. 239, 241.

52. Kumm, *Prinz Eugen*, p. 77.

53. Ibid., pp. 73, 77, 85, 89–91; Anthony Read and David Fisher, *The Fall of Berlin*, Norton, 1992, p. 224. Volksdeutsche were Germans living outside the Reich borders.

54. Kumm, *Prinz Eugen*, p. 116.

55. Hubert Lanz et al., *German Antiguerrilla Operations*; Kumm, *Prinz Eugen*, pp. 96, 114, 116; Neidhardt, *Mit Tanne und Eichenlaub*, p. 298.

56. Kumm, *Prinz Eugen*, pp. 117–118, 141.

57. Ibid., p. 126.

58. Hubert Lanz et al., *German Antiguerrilla Operations*; Kumm, *Prinz Eugen*, pp. 120–24, 126, 130, 142, 145. Böhme committed suicide on 20 May 1947 by jumping from the fourth floor of his prison in Nuremberg.

59. Kumm, *Prinz Eugen*, pp. 159, 171; Neidhardt, *Mit Tanne und Eichenlaub*, p. 298; Mitcham and Mueller, *Hitler's Commanders*, p. 201.

60. Kumm, *Prinz Eugen*, p. 171; Mitcham and Mueller, *Hitler's Commanders*, pp. 201–2, 204–6; Ziemke, *Stalingrad to Berlin*, pp. 375–78.

61. Peter Gasztony, *Der Kampf um Budapest*, Schnell & Steiner, 1964, pp. 16, 18–19, 24; Mitcham and Mueller, *Hitler's Commanders*, pp. 228–29; Ziemke, *Stalingrad to Berlin*, p. 382. The American Standard Oil Co. built new wells at Nagykanizsa in 1939, producing 200,000 tons per year. Production increased to 600,000 tons during the war, half of which went to Germany. Perry Pierik, *Hungary, 1944–1945*, Aspekt Books, 1996.

62. Gasztony, *Der Kampf um Budapest*, pp. 59–60; Peter Gasztony, *Endkampf an der Donau, 1944–1945*, Molden Books, 1969, p. 144.

63. Erickson, *Road to Berlin*, pp. 510, 514, 516; Gasztony, *Endkampf an der Donau*, pp. 224 n. 37; Pierik, *Hungary*, p. 249.

64. Beck, *Bis Stalingrad*, p. 303.

65. Ibid., p. 292; Gasztony, *Endkampf an der Donau*, p. 271.

Chapter 4

1. Haupt, *Army Group Center*, p. 32.
2. Ibid., p. 27.
3. Ibid., pp. 27, 29; Glantz (ed.), *The Initial Period of the War on the Eastern Front*, pp. 155, 158; von Luttichau, unpublished manuscript, Chapter VI, pp. 14, 24.
4. 6th Mechanized alone possessed 960 tanks, half of them new T-34 and KV variants. The 11th Mechanized started with 305 machines. Glantz (ed.), *The Initial Period of the War on the Eastern Front*, pp. 189, 217.
5. Brian Taylor, *Barbarossa to Berlin: A Chronology of the Campaigns of the Eastern Front, 1941 to 1945*, Spellmount, 2003; Glantz, *Barbarossa*, pp. 39–40; Glantz (ed.), *The Initial Period of the War on the Eastern Front*, p. 198; Haupt, *Army Group Center*, p. 30; von Luttichau, unpublished manuscript, Chapter VI, pp. 35–36. A supporting attack by the 84th Motorized Division from Kaunas against Hoth's left flank was stillborn. Glantz (ed.), *The Initial Period of the War on the Eastern Front*, p. 162.
6. Von Luttichau, unpublished manuscript, Chapter VI, p. 31. Prior to launching Barbarossa, von Bock and Hoth agreed on the primacy of the land bridge. Barry Leach, *German Strategy Against Russia*, Clarendon Press, 1973, p. 195.
7. *Pour le merité* and Knights Cross recipient Rothenburg was wounded near Grodek on 28 June. Medics evacuated him, but in the division rear area Red Army soldiers killed him in his sedan. The Germans counterattacked to recover his corpse the next day, thereafter the 25th Panzer Regiment was often called 'Panzer Regiment Rothenburg'. Horst Scheibert, *Die Gespenster Division*, Podzun Verlag, 1981, p. 53.
8. Glantz, *Barbarossa*, p. 40; Haupt, *Army Group Center*, pp. 32–33, 37–39; von Luttichau, unpublished manuscript, Chapter VI, pp. 30–31, 37. As retold in Robert Kirchubel, *Operation Barbarossa, 1941: Army Group Center*, Osprey, 2007, p. 41, the former commanding general of 19th Panzer Division took credit for capturing Minsk, see Otto von Knobelsdorff, *Geschichte der niedersächsischen 19. Panzer Division*, Podzun Verlag, 1958, p. 78.
9. Haupt, *Army Group Center*, pp. 44, 46; Hermann Hoth, *Panzer Operationen*, Vowinkel, 1956, p. 79; von Luttichau, unpublished manuscript, Chapter VI, p. 52, Chapter XIV, p. 27. After the panzers turned south, three infantry divisions defeated twelve rifle divisions at the old fortress of Polotsk (modernized in the 1930s).
10. David Glantz, *Forgotten Battles*, Vol. I, self-published, 1999, p. 16.
11. In a rare example of panzer army cooperation, the 17th and 18th Panzer Divisions both belonged to XLVII Panzer Corps of Guderian's Second Panzer. Von Luttichau, unpublished manuscript, Chapter XVI, p. 8.
12. Glantz, *Barbarossa*, p. 78; Glantz, *The Battle for Smolensk*, p. 15; Haupt, *Army Group Center*, pp. 46–47, 49–50; Rolf Hinze, *Hitze, Frost und Pulverdampf*, Selbstverlag, 1993, p. 44; von Luttichau, unpublished manuscript, Chapter XIV, pp. 25–30, 32, 36; Seaton, *The Russo-German War*, p. 162.
13. Glantz, *Barbarossa*, pp. 81–82; Glantz, *The Battle for Smolensk*, p. 25; Haupt, *Army Group Center*, p. 54; von Luttichau, unpublished manuscript, Chapter XVI, pp. 16, 34.
14. Scheibert, *Die Gespenster Division*, p. 60.

15. Fugate and Dvoretsky, *Thunder on the Dnepr*, p. 253; Glantz, *The Battle for Smolensk*, pp. 23, 27; Haupt, *Army Group Center*, pp. 56–58. Lehr Brigade (Motorized) 900 consisted of cadre from infantry, panzer, artillery, anti-tank schools plus headquarters and support elements.
16. Glantz, *Barbarossa*, pp. 82–83; Glantz, *The Battle for Smolensk*, pp. 31, 33. For the fifth attack group of the Timoshenko Offensive see p. 69 of this volume.
17. Von Luttichau, unpublished manuscript, Chapter XV, pp. 29–32; Hinze, *Hitze, Frost und Pulverdampf*, p. 90; von Knoblesdorff, *Geschichte der niedersächsischen 19. Panzer Division*, p. 84. Also, on about 20 July, von Kluge's liaison aircraft crash landed and the field marshal was feared lost. One week later, on the 27th, he relinquished command of the panzer army.
18. Haupt, *Army Group Center*, p. 67.
19. Erickson, *Road to Berlin*, p. 214; Horst Grossmann, *Geschichte der rheinisch-westfälischen 6. Infantrie-Division*, Podzun Verlag, 1958, pp. 65–66; Paul, *Brennpunkte*, p. 139; Reinhardt, *Moscow*, pp. 58–59.
20. Paul, *Brennpunkte*, p. 142.
21. Hayward, *Stopped at Stalingrad*, p. 142; Erickson, *Road to Berlin*, p. 216; Glantz, *Barbarossa*, p. 148; Haupt, *Army Group Center*, p. 83; Reinhardt, *Moscow*, pp. 85–86. The Soviets had intelligence warnings about Typhoon but considered them a fake: they believing the Germans would never launch a (THE?) major offensive on the eve of the rasputitsa; Paul, *Brennpunkte*, p. 140. Hoth replaced ailing Seventeenth Army commander, General of Infantry Carl-Heinrich von Stülpnagel. When von Bock found out that Hoth was leaving, he wrote in his diary, 'I am loathe to lose this outstanding armor commander; he, too, would rather stay.' (5 October).
22. Glantz, *Barbarossa*, p. 148; Hayward, *Stopped at Stalingrad*, p. 142; Reinhardt, *Moscow*, pp. 86, 88.
23. Hayward, *Stopped at Stalingrad*, p. 143; Haupt, *Army Group Center*, p. 83; Reinhardt, *Moscow*, p. 88.
24. Ellis, *Brute Force*, p. 62; Glantz, *Barbarossa*, p. 149; Haupt, *Army Group Center*, p. 84; Reinhardt, *Moscow*, pp. 89, 96.
25. Erickson, *Road to Berlin*, p. 219; Glantz, *Barbarossa*, p. 154; Haupt, *Army Group Center*, pp. 84, 88–89; Paul, *Brennpunkte*, pp. 142, 144. Confused and retreating Red Army units cluttered up the road used by 1st Panzer. The division radioed headquarters that the enemy was therefore 'partly responsible for the delay in our advance to Kalinin. Please advise'. XLI Panzer Corps half-joking reply: 'Enforce march discipline!'
26. Paul, *Brennpunkte*, p. 157.
27. Glantz, *Barbarossa*, pp. 154, 162; Glantz and House, *When Titans Clashed*, p. 83; Haupt, *Army Group Center*, p. 94; Hayward, *Stopped at Stalingrad*, p. 149; Reinhardt, *Moscow*, pp. 200, 207; Ziemke and Bauer, *Moscow to Stalingrad*, p. 52.
28. Erickson, *Road to Berlin*, pp. 257–58; Glantz, *Barbarossa*, pp. 170, 172; Glantz and House, *When Titans Clashed*, p. 85; Haupt, *Army Group Center*, pp. 94–95; Hayward, *Stopped at Stalingrad*, pp. 161, 163–64; Reinhardt, *Moscow*, p. 222.
29. Scheibert, *Die Gespenster Division*, p. 83.
30. Haupt, *Army Group Center*, p. 95; Paul, *Brennpunkte*, pp. 168, 173; Reinhardt, *Moscow*, nn. 95, 96; Scheibert, *Die Gespenster Division*, p. 83.

31. Paul, *Brennpunkte*, p. 182.
32. Glantz and House, *When Titans Clashed*, p. 89; Haupt, *Army Group Center*, p. 107; Stoves, *Die 1. Panzer-Division*, pp. 291–93, 301–2, 307, 309, 312; Ziemke and Bauer, *Moscow to Stalingrad*, p. 73. The fate of wounded Germans captured in hospitals by Red Army troops was usually death by mutilation.
33. Paul, *Brennpunkte*, pp. 177, 188, 197–98, 200; Ziemke and Bauer, *Moscow to Stalingrad*, pp. 82, 92, 103.
34. Haupt, *Army Group Center*, pp. 107, 114; Ziemke and Bauer, *Moscow to Stalingrad*, pp. 124, 130–32, 134, 165. In early January Reinhardt also commanded Ninth Army in the place of the ill Strauss.
35. Scheibert, *Die Gespenster Division*, p. 87.
36. Erickson, *Road to Berlin*, pp. 309–10; Ziemke and Bauer, *Moscow to Stalingrad*, pp. 171, 174. The spring rasputitsa also meant that tens of thousands of cadavers from both sides were no longer preserved in the ice and snow, and required disposal to prevent the spread of disease.
37. Günther Nitz, *Die 292. Infantrie Division*, Bernard & Graefe, 1957, p. 113.
38. Ibid., pp. 105, 110–11, 114; Ziemke and Bauer, *Moscow to Stalingrad*, p. 404. On 19 August, the 292nd Infantry received a new division commander, Colonel Wolfgang von Kluge, the field marshal's son, Nitz, *Die 292*, p. 119.
39. Haupt, *Army Group Center*, p. 139; Ziemke, *Stalingrad to Berlin*, p. 113.
40. Ziemke, *Stalingrad to Berlin*, p. 154.
41. Ibid., pp. 115, 154.
42. Haupt, *Army Group Center*, pp. 176–77, Ziemke, *Stalingrad to Berlin*, pp. 170, 198–99.
43. Haupt, *Army Group Center*, pp. 177–78; Ziemke, *Stalingrad to Berlin*, pp. 200–4.
44. Haupt, *Army Group Center*, p. 179.
45. Ibid., pp. 178–80; Ziemke, *Stalingrad to Berlin*, p. 206.
46. Erickson, *Road to Berlin*, p. 133; Haupt, *Army Group Center*, pp. 180–83; Ziemke, *Stalingrad to Berlin*, pp. 206–7.
47. Erickson, *Road to Berlin*, p. 211; Haupt, *Army Group Center*, pp. 183–85; Mitcham and Mueller, *Hitler's Commanders*, p. 14. Ziemke, *Stalingrad to Berlin*, p. 309.
48. Steven Zaloga, *Operation Bagration: The Destruction of Army Group Center*, Osprey, 1996, pp. 10, 40.
49. Erickson, *Road to Berlin*, p. 216; Haupt, *Army Group Center*, p. 187; Zaloga, *Operation Bagration*, pp. 25, 30.
50. Erickson, *Road to Berlin*, pp. 216, 219; Haupt, *Army Group Center*, pp. 192–94; Madej, *Russo-German War*, p. 36; Mitcham and Mueller, *Hitler's Commanders*, pp. 20, 23, 26; Ziemke, *Stalingrad to Berlin*, pp. 320–21.
51. Erickson, *Road to Berlin*, p. 219; Glantz and House, *When Titans Clashed*, p. 206; Haupt, *Army Group Center*, pp. 194–96; Madej, *Russo-German War*, pp. 39–40, 42; Mitcham and Mueller, *Hitler's Commanders*, pp. 30, 33, 58.
52. Glantz and House, *When Titans Clashed*, p. 207; Haupt, *Army Group Center*, p. 197; Madej, *Russo-German War*, p. 45; Mitcham and Mueller, *Hitler's Commanders*, p. 55; Ziemke, *Stalingrad to Berlin*, p. 321.
53. Mitcham, *Crumbling Empire*, p. 58.
54. Rolf Hinze, *East Front Drama, 1944*, Fedorowicz, 1996, pp. 72, 84; Madej, *Russo-German War*, p. 47; Mitcham and Mueller, *Hitler's Commanders*, pp. 58, 64;

Ziemke, *Stalingrad to Berlin*, pp. 327–28, 333; Spaeter, *Die Geschichte des Panzer-korps Grossdeutschland*, p. 599. Evacuation of 5,000 wounded from the city's hospitals began on 2 July, Haupt, *Army Group Center*, p. 205.

55. Hinze, *East Front Drama*, p. 85; Ziemke, *Stalingrad to Berlin*, p. 338.
56. Erickson, *Road to Berlin*, pp. 324–25; Glantz and House, *When Titans Clashed*, p. 226; Haupt, *Army Group Center*, p. 216; Raus, *Panzer Operationen*, pp. 294–95.
57. Erickson, *Road to Berlin*, p. 416; Glantz and House, *When Titans Clashed*, p. 227; Haupt, *Army Group Center*, p. 217; Mitcham and Mueller, *Hitler's Commanders*, pp. 103, 105, 140; Raus, *Panzer Operationen*, pp. 296–97. The 51st Army thinned out as it went north.
58. Mitcham and Mueller, *Hitler's Commanders*, pp. 103, 105.
59. Ibid., pp. 148–49; Raus, *Panzer Operationen*, p. 297; Ziemke, *Stalingrad to Berlin*, pp. 405–6.
60. Spaeter, *Die Geschichte des Panzerkorps Grossdeutschland*, pp. 622–23.
61. Mitcham and Mueller, *Hitler's Commanders*, p. 151; Raus, *Panzer Operationen*, pp. 298–99; Ziemke, *Stalingrad to Berlin*, pp. 407–8.
62. Glantz and House, *When Titans Clashed*, p. 365, n. 32; Haupt, *Army Group Center*, pp. 223–24; Mitcham and Mueller, *Hitler's Commanders*, p. 151. Scheibert, *Die Gespenster Division*, p. 148.The Kriegsmarine evacuated Memel 23–28 January. Spaeter, *Die Geschichte des Panzerkorps Grossdeutschland*, p. 659.
63. Erickson, *Road to Berlin*, p. 421; Glantz and House, *When Titans Clashed*, pp. 228–29; Haupt, *Army Group Center*, pp. 225–29; Raus, *Panzer Operationen*, pp. 301, 309; Spaeter, *Die Geschichte des Panzerkorps Grossdeutschland*, p. 604; Ziemke, *Stalingrad to Berlin*, p. 409. Third Panzer strength does not include XXVIII Corps (95th and 58th Infantry Divisions) holed up in Memel.
64. Glantz and House, *When Titans Clashed*, p. 247; Raus, *Panzer Operationen*, pp. 307–8, 312–13, 315–16; Ziemke, *Stalingrad to Berlin*, p. 419.
65. Glantz and House, *When Titans Clashed*, p. 248; Raus, *Panzer Operationen*, pp. 316–17; Ziemke, *Stalingrad to Berlin*, pp. 430–31.
66. Erickson, *Road to Berlin*, pp. 468–69; Glantz and House, *When Titans Clashed*, pp. 247–49; Haupt, *Army Group Center*, p. 279; Ziemke, *Stalingrad to Berlin*, pp. 245, 248. Counter-intuitively, Raus is fairly complimentary of Himmler as a commander. Germans in the Samland pocket continued to fight until the last day of the war. Evidently 'to confuse students of the war', the Germans renamed most army groups in the northern theater on 26 January, Ziemke, *Stalingrad to Berlin*, p. 426.
67. Erickson, *Road to Berlin*, p. 559; Raus, *Panzer Operationen*, pp. 325, 327–29; Ziemke, *Stalingrad to Berlin*, p. 459.
68. Haupt, *Army Group Center*, p. 298–99; Raus, *Panzer Operationen*, p. 340; Seaton, *The Russo-German War*, p. 542; Ziemke, *Stalingrad to Berlin*, pp. 459–60. Less well known, during the Seven Years War, the Russians had besieged Kolberg three times, but only captured it once. Ziemke, *Stalingrad to Berlin*, p. 460.
69. Max Hastings, *Armageddon: The Battle for Germany, 1944–1945*, Vintage, 2005, p. 457; Read and Fisher, *The Fall of Berlin*, p. 284; Ziemke, *Stalingrad to Berlin*, p. 471.
70. Erickson, *Road to Berlin*, pp. 574–75; Tony Le Tissier, *The Battle for Berlin, 1945*, St Martin's Press, 1988, p. 66; Read and Fisher, *The Fall of Berlin*, pp. 331.

71. Ziemke, *Stalingrad to Berlin*, p. 477.
72. Glantz and House, *When Titans Clashed*, p. 261; Read and Fisher, *The Fall of Berlin*, pp. 339, 379; Ziemke, *Stalingrad to Berlin*, pp. 477–80.
73. Ziemke, *Stalingrad to Berlin*, p. 486.
74. Erickson, *Road to Berlin*, p. 594; Le Tissier, *The Battle for Berlin*, pp. 120, 143, 155; Ziemke, *Stalingrad to Berlin*, pp. 483–87.
75. Erickson, *Road to Berlin*, p. 621; Le Tissier, *The Battle for Berlin*, pp. 143, 174, 225; Read and Fisher, *The Fall of Berlin*, p. 431; Ziemke, *Stalingrad to Berlin*, pp. 495–96.

Chapter 5

1. Boog et al., *Germany and the Second World War*, Vol. IV, pp. 538–39; Gerhard Dieckhoff, *Die 3. Infantrie-Division*, HW Blick, 1960, p. 90; Glantz (ed.), *The Initial Period of the War on the Eastern Front*, pp. 108, 112; Friedrich-Christian Stahl, *Geschichte der ostpreussischen 121. Infantrie-Division*, Traditionsverband, 1970, p. 14; Stoves, *Die 1. Panzer-Division*, pp. 181, 185. Despite its age (causing repair part shortages), the 35(t) did have a high-velocity 37mm gun and its light weight was well suited for the weak bridges throughout much of the area.
2. Dieckhoff, *Die 3. Infantrie-Division*, p. 92; Glantz (ed.), *The Initial Period of the War on the Eastern Front*, pp. 103, 110, 113; Werner Haupt, *Army Group North: The Wehrmacht in Russia, 1941–1945*, Schiffer Military History, 1997, pp. 30, 33; Walter Hubatsch, *Die 61. Infantrie-Division*, Podzun Verlag, 1960, p. 18.
3. Erickson, *Road to Berlin*, p. 133; Glantz (ed.), *The Initial Period of the War on the Eastern Front*, p. 142; Georg Meyer (ed.), *Generalfeldmarshal Wilhelm Ritter von Leeb*, Beitrag zur Militär und Kriegsgeschichte, 1976, diary entry 23 June; von Luttichau, unpublished manuscript, Chapter VII, pp. 18, 37; Hermann Plocher, *German Air Force versus Russia*, Arno Press, 1968, p. 145; Stoves, *Die 1. Panzer-Division*, pp. 186–87, 189–90, 192. Hitler viewed his first KV 1 on 28 June, Meyer (ed.), *Generalfeldmarshal Wilhelm Ritter von Leeb*.
4. Paul, *Brennpunkte*, p. 108.
5. Boog et al., *Germany and the Second World War*, Vol. IV, p. 539; Erickson, *Road to Berlin*, p. 142; Glantz (ed.), *The Initial Period of the War on the Eastern Front*, pp. 96, 103, 116, 142; von Luttichau, unpublished manuscript, Chapter VII, p. 15; Paul, *Brennpunkte*, p. 108.
6. Von Luttichau, unpublished manuscript, Chapter VII, pp. 31–33.
7. Ibid., Chapter VII, p. 35.
8. Ibid, Chapter VII, p. 54.
9. Boog et al., *Germany and the Second World War*, Vol. IV, p. 539; Glantz, *Barbarossa*, p. 43; von Luttichau, unpublished manuscript, Chapter VII, p. 35.
10. Erickson, *Road to Berlin*, p. 145; Haupt, *Army Group North*, pp. 39, 43; Meyer (ed.), *Generalfeldmarshal Wilhelm Ritter von Leeb*, 29 June; Stoves, *Die 1. Panzer-Division*, p. 198.
11. Dieckhoff, *Die 3. Infantrie-Division*, p. 98; Erickson, *Road to Berlin*, p. 146; Glantz, *Barbarossa*, p. 45; Haupt, *Army Group North*, p. 44; Paul, *Brennpunkte*, p. 113; Albert Seaton, *Stalin*, Combined Publishing, 1998, p. 106.

12. Bergstrom and Mikhailov, *Black Cross, Red Star*, p. 78; von Luttichau, unpublished manuscript, Chapter VII, pp. 56–58, 60; Stoves, *Die 1. Panzer-Division*, pp. 203–4.

13. Boog et al., *Germany and the Second World War*, Vol. IV, p. 542; Erickson, *Road to Berlin*, p. 147; Glantz, *Barbarossa*, p. 99; Raus, *Panzer Operationen*, p. 51.

14. Stoves, *Die 1. Panzer-Division*, p. 223.

15. Bergstrom and Mikhailov, *Black Cross, Red Star*, p. 79; Boog et al., *Germany and the Second World War*, Vol. IV, p. 543; Glantz (ed.), *The Initial Period of the War on the Eastern Front*, p. 153; von Luttichau, unpublished manuscript, Chapter XXVIII, pp. 30–37; Paul, *Brennpunkte*, pp. 118, 125; Raus, *Panzer Operationen*, p. 54.

16. Dieckhoff, *Die 3. Infantrie-Division*, p. 101; Glantz, *Barbarossa*, pp. 100–1; Glantz, *Forgotten Battles*, Vol. I, p. 28; Haupt, *Army Group North*, p. 57; Meyer (ed.), *Generalfeldmarshal Wilhelm Ritter von Leeb*, 16 July.

17. Boog et al., *Germany and the Second World War*, Vol. IV, p. 633; Meyer (ed.), *Generalfeldmarshal Wilhelm Ritter von Leeb*, 21 July. The decision on XXXIX Panzer was still a month away, Boog et al., *Germany and the Second World War*, Vol. IV, p. 592.

18. Haupt, *Army Group North*, p. 75.

19. Ellis, *Brute Force*, p. 54; Haupt, *Army Group North*, p. 75; Paul, *Brennpunkte*, p. 121.

20. Raus, *Panzer Operationen*, p. 80.

21. Haupt, *Army Group North*, pp. 75, 77–78; von Luttichau, unpublished manuscript, Chapter XXIX, pp. 3–5; Raus, *Panzer Operationen*, p. 79.

22. Boog et al., *Germany and the Second World War*, Vol. IV, p. 637; Dieckhoff, *Die 3. Infantrie-Division*, p. 109; Erickson, *Road to Berlin*, p. 187; von Luttichau, unpublished manuscript, Chapter XXVIII, pp. 8–11, 13.

23. Haupt, *Army Group North*, p. 92; von Luttichau, unpublished manuscript, Chapter XXVIII, pp. 54–58.

24. Boog et al., *Germany and the Second World War*, Vol. IV, p. 641; von Luttichau, unpublished manuscript, Chapter XXVIII, pp. 59–61.

25. On the concept of the large force defending a major city as the ideal blitzkrieg objective, see Citino, *The Death of the Wehrmacht*, p. 37.

26. Boog et al., *Germany and the Second World War*, Vol. IV, p. 691; von Luttichau, unpublished manuscript, Chapter XXX, p. 24.

27. Schrodek, *Ihr Glaube galt dem Vaterland*, p. 178.

28. Glantz and House, *When Titans Clashed*, p. 79; Haupt, *Army Group Center*, pp. 81–3; Hayward, *Stopped at Stalingrad*, p. 142; Hinze, *Hitze, Frost und Pulverdampf*, p. 77; Anton von Plato, *Die Geschichte der 5. Panzerdivision*, Walhalla, 1978, pp. 143, 148; Reinhardt, *Moscow*, p. 84. The 5th Panzer was a latecomer to Barbarossa. It was uncommonly powerful for this late stage of the campaign with 55 Pz IIs, 105 Pz IIIs and 20 Pz IVs, von Plato, *Die Geschichte der 5*, pp. 139–40.

29. Boog et al., *Germany and the Second World War*, Vol. IV, p. 681; Haupt, *Army Group Center*, p. 89; Hayward, *Stopped at Stalingrad*, p. 144; Reinhardt, *Moscow*, n. 100.

30. Haupt, *Army Group Center*, p. 95.

31. Erickson, *Road to Berlin*, p. 257; Haupt, *Army Group Center*, p. 97; von Plato, *Die Geschichte der 5*, pp. 165, 169, 173; Willmott, *The Great Crusade*, p. 156. The 5th Panzer was originally intended for Africa and its vehicles were painted sand color, hence the nickname.

32. Reinhardt, *Moscow*, p. 218.

33. Von Bock, *The War Diary*, 7, 8, 14 December 1941; Erickson, *Road to Berlin*, p. 274; Glantz and House, *When Titans Clashed*, p. 89; von Plato, *Die Geschichte der 5*, p. 180; Schrodek, *Ihr Glaube galt dem Vaterland*, p. 199; Ziemke and Bauer, *Moscow to Stalingrad*, pp. 70, 73, 77, 80, 82.

34. Otto Weidinger, *Das Reich*, Fedorowicz, 1990, p. 278.

35. Ibid., pp. 262–63.

36. Von Bock, *The War Diary*, 16 December; Erickson, *Road to Berlin*, p. 285; Haupt, *Army Group Center*, p. 111; Nitz, *Die 292*, pp. 93–94; Ziemke and Bauer, *Moscow to Stalingrad*, pp. 85, 92–93, 101–2, 118.

37. Erickson, *Road to Berlin*, p. 310; Ziemke and Bauer, *Moscow to Stalingrad*, pp. 119, 127–28.

38. Erickson, *Road to Berlin*, p. 312; Ziemke and Bauer, *Moscow to Stalingrad*, pp. 133–34, 164, 166, 171.

39. Dieckhoff, *Die 3. Infantrie-Division*, pp. 162–63.

40. Ziemke and Bauer, *Moscow to Stalingrad*, p. 182.

41. Erickson, *Road to Berlin*, p. 312; Glantz and House, *When Titans Clashed*, pp. 93, 108; Haupt, *Army Group Center*, p. 116; Ziemke and Bauer, *Moscow to Stalingrad*, p. 182.

42. Von Bock, *The War Diary*, 4 June; Ziemke and Bauer, *Moscow to Stalingrad*, pp. 322–24.

43. Speater, *Panzerkorps Grossdeutschland*, pp. 439–40.

44. Citino, *The Death of the Wehrmacht*, p. 166; Erickson, *Road to Berlin*, p. 356; Haupt, *Army Group Center*, p. 147; Ziemke and Bauer, *Moscow to Stalingrad*, pp. 333–34, 336–37. The 24th Panzer was the former 1st Cavalry Division, reorganized during the winter.

45. Erickson, *Road to Berlin*, p. 358; Glantz and House, *When Titans Clashed*, p. 119; Ziemke and Bauer, *Moscow to Stalingrad*, pp. 340–44.

46. Citino, *The Death of the Wehrmacht*, p. 170; Glantz and House, *When Titans Clashed*, p. 119; Haupt, *Army Group Center*, p. 152; Ziemke and Bauer, *Moscow to Stalingrad*, pp. 344–45, 347.

47. Seaton, *The Russo-German War*, p. 276.

48. Beevor, *Stalingrad*, p. 95; Erickson, *Road to Berlin*, p. 366; Haupt, *Army Group Center*, p. 159; Ziemke and Bauer, *Moscow to Stalingrad*, p. 365.

49. Citino, *The Death of the Wehrmacht*, p. 250; Erickson, *Road to Berlin*, p. 367; Ziemke and Bauer, *Moscow to Stalingrad*, pp. 387–88, 390, 393.

50. Beck, *Bis Stalingrad*, p. 155; Beevor, *Stalingrad*, pp. 117–18; Alan Clark, *Barbarossa*, p. 243; Erickson, *Road to Berlin*, p. 391.

51. Beck, *Bis Stalingrad*, p. 162.

52. Ibid., pp. 166, 170; Beevor, *Stalingrad*, p. 249; Citino, *The Death of the Wehrmacht*, p. 300; Erickson, *Road to Berlin*, pp. 8, 12; Ziemke and Bauer, *Moscow to Stalingrad*, pp. 470–72, 478–80. The Soviets attacked 6th Panzer as it came off rail cars at Kotelnikovo, Beevor, *Stalingrad*, p. 296.

53. Raus, *Panzer Operationen*, pp. 173–74.
54. Beevor, *Stalingrad*, p. 298; Citino, *The Death of the Wehrmacht*, p. 301; Erickson, *Road to Berlin*, p. 23; Glantz, *From the Don to the Dnepr*, pp. 15, 71; Glantz and House, *When Titans Clashed*, pp. 140–41; Haupt, *Army Group Center*, pp. 215–16; Ziemke and Bauer, *Moscow to Stalingrad*, p. 496.
55. Erickson, *Road to Berlin*, pp. 32, 48; Glantz, *From the Don to the Dnepr*, p. 96; Glantz and House, *When Titans Clashed*, p. 144; Nipe, *Last Victory*, pp. 57, 89; Ziemke, *Stalingrad to Berlin*, pp. 90–91. Von Manstein's command was renamed Army Group South on 14 February 1943.
56. Glantz, *From the Don to the Dnepr*, pp. 122, 125. Glantz and House, *When Titans Clashed*, pp. 146–47; Nipe, *Last Victory*, p. 107; Ziemke, *Stalingrad to Berlin*, pp. 92–93. Hausser's organization was not known as 'II' SS Panzer Corps until later that spring.
57. Erickson, *Road to Berlin*, pp. 51–52; Glantz, *From the Don to the Dnepr*, pp. 132, 144, 209; Glantz and House, *The Battle of Kursk*, p. 13; Nipe, *Last Victory*, pp. 157, 259, 267, 328; Ziemke, *Stalingrad to Berlin*, pp. 94–97. In terms of combat-capable panzers, SS LAH had 30, DR: 26 and TK: 49, Nipe, *Last Victory*, p. 286. Hausser's disobedience cost the highly qualified Lanz his command job.
58. Beevor, *Stalingrad*, p. 298; Dunn, *Kursk*, p. 16; Glantz, *From the Don to the Dnepr*, pp. 146, 226; Nipe, *Last Victory*, p. 350.
59. All order of battle information: Dunn, *Kursk*, pp. 60–61. Panzers in workshops almost ready to rejoin their divisions: SS LAH: 25, SS DR: 16, SS TK: 47, GD: 51, 11th Panzer: 29.
60. Ibid., pp. 77, 154; Glantz and House, *The Battle of Kursk*, p. 54; Glantz and House, *When Titans Clashed*, p. 165; Ziemke, *Stalingrad to Berlin*, pp. 118, 124, 132.
61. Dunn, *Kursk*, pp. 104, 108, 121; Glantz and House, *The Battle of Kursk*, p. 94; Schrodek, *Ihr Glaube galt dem Vaterland*, pp. 268–69; Spaeter, *Die Geschichte des Panzerkorps Grossdeutschland*, p. 179; Ziemke, *Stalingrad to Berlin*, p. 135.
62. Dunn, *Kursk*, pp. 125, 127–28, 133, 135, 138; Glantz and House, *The Battle of Kursk*, pp. 112–13; Schrodek, *Ihr Glaube galt dem Vaterland*, p. 269.
63. Dunn, *Kursk*, pp. 135, 143, 147, 151, 153–54; Erickson, *Road to Berlin*, p. 106; Glantz and House, *The Battle of Kursk*, pp. 146, 164, 204, 218; Glantz and House, *When Titans Clashed*, pp. 166–67; Haupt, *Army Group Center*, p. 277.
64. Dunn, *Kursk*, p. 165; Glantz and House, *The Battle of Kursk*, pp. 246–48; Glantz and House, *When Titans Clashed*, p. 168; Ziemke, *Stalingrad to Berlin*, p. 150.
65. Spaeter, *Die Geschichte des Panzerkorps Grossdeutschland*, pp. 249–50.
66. Glantz and House, *The Battle of Kursk*, pp. 248–49, 295, 298, 304, 312, 321, 334–35, 337; Glantz and House, *When Titans Clashed*, p. 169; Schrodek, *Ihr Glaube galt dem Vaterland*, p. 275; Ziemke, *Stalingrad to Berlin*, p. 156.
67. Glantz, *From the Don to the Dnepr*, pp. 342, 361, 363, 365; Glantz and House, *The Battle of Kursk*, pp. 251, 277, 279; Schrodek *Ihr Glaube galt dem Vaterland*, pp. 277–78.
68. Erickson, *Road to Berlin*, pp. 120, 123, 126; Glantz and House, *When Titans Clashed*, p. 172; Haupt, *Army Group Center*, p. 295; Ziemke, *Stalingrad to Berlin*, pp. 169, 171.

69. Erickson, *Road to Berlin*, pp. 141–42; David Glantz, *The Soviet Airborne Experience*, Ft Leavenworth, 1984, pp. 100, 102; Glantz and House, *When Titans Clashed*, p. 173; Ziemke, *Stalingrad to Berlin*, pp. 184–85. Vatutin was to capture Kiev in time for the anniversary of the November Revolution, Erickson, ibid., p. 140.
70. Scheibert, *Die Gespenster Division*, pp. 126–27, Schultz commanded Panzer Regiment 25.
71. Erickson, *Road to Berlin*, pp. 133, 143; Glantz and House, *When Titans Clashed*, p. 174; Raus, *Panzer Operationen*, p. 258; Ziemke, *Stalingrad to Berlin*, pp. 186–87. Hoth's removal 'undermined' Army Group South, Erickson, ibid., p. 143.
72. Glantz and House, *When Titans Clashed*, pp. 174–75; Raus, *Panzer Operationen*, p. 263; Stoves, *Die 1. Panzer-Division*, pp. 442, 444, 453, 458; Ziemke, *Stalingrad to Berlin*, p. 189.
73. Erickson, *Road to Berlin*, p. 163; Raus, *Panzer Operationen*, pp. 264–65; Stoves, *Die 1. Panzer-Division*, p. 470; Ziemke, *Stalingrad to Berlin*, pp. 222–23. The XLII Corps was relieving XXIV Panzer on the panzer army right during this period.
74. Erickson, *Road to Berlin*, pp. 164–65; Ziemke, *Stalingrad to Berlin*, pp. 246–47.
75. Erickson, *Road to Berlin*, p. 183; Glantz and House, *When Titans Clashed*, p. 189; Haupt, *Army Group Center*, pp. 328, 355; Ziemke, *Stalingrad to Berlin*, pp. 274, 276, 279, 282.
76. Raus, *Panzer Operationen*, p. 269. Colonel Werner Friebe of 8th Panzer Division was the younger brother of Major General Helmut Friebe, at the time commanding 125th Infantry Division.
77. Ziemke, *Stalingrad to Berlin*, pp. 288, 330–32.
78. Erickson, *Road to Berlin*, p. 243; Hinze, *To the Bitter End*, p. 22; Mitcham, *Crumbling Empire*, p. 76; Ziemke, *Stalingrad to Berlin*, pp. 332, 337, 341.
79. Erickson, *Road to Berlin*, p. 450 (Koniev's mission included not demolishing Silesia as he captured it); Hinze, *To the Bitter End*, p. 74; Mitcham, *Crumbling Empire*, p. 168; Ziemke, *Stalingrad to Berlin*, pp. 417, 425.
80. Erickson, *Road to Berlin*, p. 457; Haupt, *Army Group Center*, p. 264; Hinze, *To the Bitter End*, pp. 90, 101, 103; Ziemke, *Stalingrad to Berlin*, pp. 421, 424.
81. Erickson, *Road to Berlin*, p. 472–73; Hastings, *Armageddon*, p. 244; Haupt, *Army Group Center*, p. 305; Hinze, *To the Bitter End*, pp. 116, 123–24; Ziemke, *Stalingrad to Berlin*, pp. 442–43.
82. Erickson, *Road to Berlin*, p. 558; Glantz and House, *When Titans Clashed*, pp. 265–67, 270; Haupt, *Army Group Center*, pp. 296, 311; Hinze, *To the Bitter End*, pp. 184, 187; Le Tissier, *The Battle for Berlin*, pp. 59, 61, 63–64, 71, 93; Ziemke, *Stalingrad to Berlin*, p. 474.

Chapter 6

1. At the same time, Rommel's much smaller Panzer Army Africa did the same with Tobruk.
2. The Fifth and Sixth SS Panzer Armies in the Ardennes and Sixth SS Panzer at Lake Balaton seized the initiative, but again, only along a 100km front and then only for one week.

Bibliography

Adair, Paul. *Hitler's Greatest Defeat: The Collapse of Army Group Center, June 1944*, Arms & Armor Press, 1996.

Barnett, Correlli (ed.). *Hitler's Generals*, Grove Weidenfeld, 1989.

Beck, Alois. *Bis Stalingrad*, H Abt Verlag, 1983.

Beevor, Anthony. *Stalingrad: The Fateful Siege, 1942–1943*, Viking, 1998.

Bekker, Cajus. *Luftwaffe War Diaries*, Ballantine Books, 1969.

Bergstrom, Christer and Mikhailov, Andrey. *Black Cross, Red Star: Volume 1, Operation Barbarossa 1941*, Pacifica Military History, 2000.

von Bock, Fedor. *The War Diary, 1939–1945*, Schiffer Military History, 1996.

Boog, Horst, Förster, Jürgen, Hoffmann, Joachim, Klink, Ernst, Müller, Rolf-Dieter and Ueberschär, Gerd. *Germany and the Second World War*, Vol. IV, *Attack on the Soviet Union*, Clarendon Press, 1998.

Breymayer, Helmut. *Das Wiesel: Geschichte der 125 Infantrie Division, 1940–44*, Vaas Verlag, 1983.

Carell, Paul, *Scorched Earth*, Harrap, 1970.

——. *Hitler Moves East, 1941–1943*, Ballantine Books, 1971.

Chales de Beaulieu, Walter Chales. *Der Vorstoss der Panzergruppe 4 auf Leningrad – 1941*, Scharnhorst, 1961.

Chamberlain, Peter and Doyle, Hilary. *Encyclopedia of German Tanks of World War Two*, Arms & Armor Press, 1978.

Citino, Robert. *The Death of the Wehrmacht: The German Campaigns of 1942*, University of Kansas, 2007.

Clark, Alan. *Barbarossa*, William Morrow, 1965.

van Creveld, Martin. *Supplying War: Logistics from Wallenstein to Patton*, Cambridge University, 1977.

Davis, CR. *von Kleist: From Hussar to Panzer Marshal*, Lancer Militaria, 1979.

Deighton, Len. *Blitzkrieg*, Triad, 1980.

Dieckhoff, Gerhard. *Die 3. Infantrie-Division*, HW Blick, 1960.

Dunn, Walter. *Kursk: Hitler's Gamble, 1943*, Praeger, 1997.

Edwards, Roger. *Panzer: A Revolution in Warfare*, Arms & Armor Press, 1989.

Ellis, John. *Brute Force*, Viking, 1990.

English, John. *On Infantry*, Praeger, 1984.

Erickson, John. *Road to Berlin: Stalin's War with Germany*, Weidenfeld & Nicolson, 1983.

——. *Road to Stalingrad: Stalin's War with Germany*, Yale University, 1999.

Evans, Martin. *The Fall of France: Act with Daring*, Osprey, 2000.

von Fretter-Pico, Maximillian. *Missbrauchte Infantrie: Deutsche Infantriedivision im osteuropäischen Grossraum, 1941 bis 1944*, Verlag für Wehrwissenschaft, 1967.

Frieser, Karl-Heinz. 'Panzer Group Kleist and the Breakthrough in France, 1940', in Michael Krause and R Cody Philips (eds), *Historical Perspectives on the Operational Art*, Center for Military History, 2005.

Fugate, Brian. *Operation Barbarossa: Strategy and Tactics on the Eastern Front, 1941*, Presidio Press, 1984.

Fugate, Brian and Dvoretsky, Lev. *Thunder on the Dnepr: Zhukov-Stalin and the Defeat of Hitler's Blitzkrieg*, Presidio Press, 1997.

Gasztony, Peter. *Der Kampf um Budapest*, Schnell & Steiner, 1964.

——. *Endkampf an der Donau, 1944–1945*, Molden Books, 1969.

Glantz, David. *The Soviet Airborne Experience*, Ft Leavenworth, 1984.

——. *From the Don to the Dnepr: Soviet Offensive Operations, December 1942 to August 1943*, Frank Cass, 1991.

—— (ed.). *The Initial Period of the War on the Eastern Front, 22 June–August 1941*, Frank Cass, 1993.

——. *Forgotten Battles*, Vol. I, self-published, 1999.

——. *Barbarossa*, Tempus, 2001.

——. *The Battle for Smolensk: 7 July–10 September, 1941*, self-published, 2001.

——. *Red Storm over the Balkans*, University of Kansas, 2007.

Glantz, David and House, Jonathan. *When Titans Clashed: How the Red Army Stopped Hitler*, University of Kansas, 1995.

——. *The Battle of Kursk*, University of Kansas, 2004.

Görlitz, Walter. *Paulus and Stalingrad: A Life of Field Marshal Friedrich Paulus with Notes, Correspondence and Documents from His Papers*, Greenwood Books, 1974.

Greiner, Helmut, Mueller-Hildebrand, Burkhardt and Greiffenberg, Hans von. *The German Campaign in the Balkans*, US Army Center for Military History Publication (104–4), 1953.

Grossmann, Horst. *Geschichte der rheinisch-westfälischen 6. Infantrie-Division*, Podzun Verlag, 1958.

Guderian, Heinz. *Panzer Leader*, Ballantine Books, 1968.

Hastings, Max. *Armageddon: The Battle for Germany, 1944–1945*, Vintage, 2005.

Haupt, Werner. *Kiev*, Podzun Verlag, 1964.

——. *Army Group Center: The Wehrmacht in Russia, 1941–1945*, Schiffer Military History, 1997.

——. *Army Group North: The Wehrmacht in Russia, 1941–1945*, Schiffer Military History, 1997.

——.*Army Group South: The Wehrmacht in Russia, 1941–1945*, Schiffer Military History, 1998.

Hayward, Joel. *Stopped at Stalingrad: Luftwaffe and Hitler's Defeat in the East 1942–1943*, University of Kansas, 1998.

Rolf Hinze, *Hitze, Frost und Pulverdampf*, Selbstverlag, 1993.

——. *East Front Drama*, 1944, Fedorowicz, 1996.

——. *To the Bitter End*, Helion & Co., 2006.

Horne, Alistair. *To Lose a Battle: France 1940*, Macmillan, 1990.

Hoth, Hermann. *Panzer Operationen*, Vowinkel, 1956.

Hubatsch, Walter. *Die 61. Infantrie-Division*, Podzun Verlag, 1960.

Hull, Isabel. *Absolute Destruction: Military Culture and the Practices of War in Imperial Germany*, Cornell University, 2006.

Jacobsen, Hans-Adolf. *Kriegstagebuch: das Oberkommando der Wehrmacht*, Bernard & Graefe, 1965.
Keilig, Wolf. *Das Deutsche Heer, 1939–1945*, Podzun Verlag, 1956.
Kershaw, Ian. *Nemesis, 1939–1945*, Norton, 2001.
Kesselring, Albert. *The Memoirs of Field Marshal Kesselring*, Presidio, 1989.
Kirchubel, Robert. *Operation Barbarossa 1941: Army Group South*, Osprey, 2003.
———. *Operation Barbarossa 1941: Army Group North*, Osprey, 2005.
———. *Operation Barbarossa 1941: Army Group Center*, Osprey, 2007.
von Knobelsdorf, Otto. *Geschichte der niedersächsischen 19. Panzer Division*, Podzun Verlag, 1958.
Kumm, Otto. *Prinz Eugen*, Fedorowicz, 1995.
Lanz, Hubert and Graisser, Karl. *German Antiguerrilla Operations in the Balkans, 1941–44*, US Army Center for Military History Publication (104–18), 1989.
Lemelsen, Joachim. *Die 29. Division*, Podzun Verlag, 1960.
Le Tissier, Tony. *The Battle for Berlin, 1945*, St Martin's Press, 1988.
Leach, Barry. *German Strategy against Russia*, Clarendon Press, 1973.
Lucas, James. *War on the Eastern Front: The German Soldier in Russia, 1941–1945*, Greenhill Books, 1998.
von Luttichau, Charles. unpublished manuscript, US Army Center for Military History, n.d.
Luttwak, Edward. 'The Operational Level of War', *International Security*, Winter 1980–81.
von Mackensen, Eberhard. *Vom Bug bis zum Kaukasus*, Vowinkel, 1967.
Macksey, Kenneth. *Panzer Division*, Ballantine Books, 1973.
Madej, Victor. *Russo-German War, Summer 1944*, Fedorowicz, 1987.
Maier, Klaus (ed.). *Germany and the Second World War*, Vol. II, *Germany's Initial Conquest of Europe*, Clarendon Press, 1991.
von Manstein, Erich. *Lost Victories*, Presidio Press, 1984.
Mehner, Kurt (ed.). *Die Geheimen Tagesberichete der deutschen Wehrmachtführung im Zweiten Weltkrieg*, 1939–1945, Vols 1 and 2, Biblio Verlag, 1993.
von Mellenthin, FW. *Panzer Battles*, Ballantine Books, 1971.
Messe, Giovanni. *Der Krieg im Osten*, Thomas Verlag, 1948.
Messenger, Charles. *Hitler's Gladiator: The Life and Wars of Panzer Army Commander Sepp Dietrich*, Brassey's, 1988.
Meyer, Georg (ed.). *Generalfeldmarschall Wilhelm Ritter von Leeb*, Beitrag zur Militär und Kriegsgeschichte, 1976.
Mitcham, Samuel. *Men of the Luftwaffe*, Presidio Press, 1988.
———. *The Panzer Legions*, Stackpole Books, 2000.
———.*Crumbling Empire: The German Defeat in the East, 1944*, Praeger, 2001.
Mitcham, Samuel and Mueller, Gene. *Hitler's Commanders: Officers of the Wehrmacht, the Luftwaffe, the Kriegsmarine, and the Waffen-SS*, Scarborough House, 1992.
Monsoor, Peter. 'The Second Battle of Sedan, May, 1940', *Military Review*, 26 January 1989.
Nehring, Walther. *Die Geschichte der deutsche Panzerwaffe*, Propyläen Verlag, 1969.
Neidhardt, Hanns. *Mit Tanne und Eichenlaub*, Stocker, 1981.
Neumann, Joachim. *Die 4. Panzer-Division*, Selbstverlag, 1985.

Nipe, George. *Last Victory: The SS Panzercorps and Manstein's Counter Offensive Febuary–March 1943*, Schiffer, 2000.

Nitz, Günther. *Die 292. Infantrie Division*, Bernard & Graefe, 1957.

Paul, Wolfgang. *Brennpunkte*, Hoentges, 1977.

Pierik, Perry. *Hungary, 1944–1945*, Aspekt Books, 1996.

von Plato, Anton. *Die Geschichte der 5. Panzerdivision*, Walhalla, 1978.

Plocher, Hermann. *German Air Force versus Russia*, Arno Press, 1968.

Raus, Eberhard. *Panzer Operationen*, DeCapo Press, 2003.

Read, Anthony and Fisher, David. *The Fall of Berlin*, Norton, 1992.

Reinhardt, Klaus. *Moscow, The Turning Point*, Berg, 1992.

Richter, Günther. *Geschichte der 3. Panzer-Division*, Berlin, 1967.

Rothbrust, Florian. *Guderian's XIX Panzer Corps and the Battle of France*, Praeger, 1990.

Scheibert, Horst. *Die Gespenster Division*, Podzun Verlag, 1981.

Schrodek, GW. *Ihr Glaube galt dem Vaterland*, Schild Verlag, 1976.

Seaton, Albert. *Battle for Moscow*, Stein & Day, 1971.

——. *The Russo-German War*, Praeger, 1971.

——. *Stalin*, Combined Publishing, 1998.

Shepperd, Alan. *France 1940: Blitzkrieg in the West*, Osprey, 1990.

Spaeter, Helmut. *Die Geschichte des Panzerkorps Grossdeutschland*, Selbstverlag, 1958.

Spick, Mike. *The Ace Factor*, Avon Books, 1989.

Stahl, Friedrich-Christian. *Geschichte der ostpreussischen 121. Infantrie-Division*, Traditionsverband, 1970.

Sterrett, James. 'Southwest Front Operations, June – September, 1941', MA dissertation, University of Calgary, 1994.

Stoves, Rolf. *Die 1. Panzer-Division, 1935–45*, Podzun Verlag, 1961.

Taylor, Brian. *Barbarossa to Berlin: A Chronology of the Campaigns of the Eastern Front, 1941 to 1945*, Spellmount, 2003.

Toland, John. *Adolf Hitler*, Vol. II, Doubleday, 1976.

Weidinger, Otto. *Das Reich*, Fedorowicz, 1990.

Werthen, Wolfgang. *Geschichte der 16. Panzer Division*, Podzun Verlag, 1958.

Williamson, Gordon. *Panzer Crewmen, 1939–45*, Osprey, 2002.

Willmott, HP. *The Great Crusade*, Free Press, 1989.

Wray, Timothy. *Standing Fast: German Defensive Doctrine on the Eastern Front during World War Two, Prewar to March 1943*, US Army Command and General Staff College, 1986.

Zaloga, Steven. *Operation Bagration: The Destruction of Army Group Center*, Osprey, 1996.

Ziemke, Earl. *Stalingrad to Berlin: The German defeat in the East*, Barnes & Noble Books, 1996.

Ziemke, Earl and Bauer, Magna. *Moscow to Stalingrad: Decision in the East*, Military Heritage Press, 1988.

Zhukov, GK. 'The War Begins: The Battle of Moscow', *Main Front*, Brassey's, 1987.

Index

Rank shown is highest attained. Units shown are brigade and larger.